Switching to a Mac®
FOR
DUMMIES®
MAC OS® X LION™ EDITION

by Arnold Reinhold

WILEY

John Wiley & Sons, Inc.

Switching to a Mac® For Dummies®, Mac OS® X Lion™ Edition

Published by
John Wiley & Sons, Inc.
111 River Street
Hoboken, NJ 07030-5774
www.wiley.com

Copyright © 2011 by John Wiley & Sons, Inc., Hoboken, New Jersey

Published by John Wiley & Sons, Inc., Hoboken, New Jersey

Published simultaneously in Canada

For general information on our other products and services, please contact our Customer Care Department within the U.S. at 877-762-2974, outside the U.S. at 317-572-3993, or fax 317-572-4002.

For technical support, please visit www.wiley.com/techsupport.

Wiley also publishes its books in a variety of electronic formats and by print-on-demand. Not all content that is available in standard print versions of this book may appear or be packaged in all book formats. If you have purchased a version of this book that did not include media that is referenced by or accompanies a standard print version, you may request this media by visiting http://booksupport.wiley.com. For more information about Wiley products, visit us www.wiley.com.

Library of Congress Control Number: 2011936932

ISBN 978-1-118-02446-1 (pbk); ISBN 978-1-118-17369-5 (ebk); ISBN 978-1-118-17370-1 (ebk); ISBN 978-1-118-17371-8 (ebk)

Manufactured in the United States of America

10 9 8 7 6 5 4 3 2

WILEY

About the Author

Arnold Reinhold has more than three decades of experience in the software industry. His first Apple product was a Mac 512. Arnold helped found Automatix, Inc., a pioneer in robotics and machine vision, and is coauthor of *The Internet For Dummies Quick Reference, E-Mail For Dummies, Green IT For Dummies,* and *Mac mini Hacks & Mods For Dummies.* He developed and maintains Diceware.com, widely regarded as the gold standard in password security, and The Math in the Movies Page (http://mathinthemovies.com).

Arnold studied mathematics at City College of New York and the Massachusetts Institute of Technology and management at Harvard Business School. You can check out his home page at http://arnoldreinhold.com.

Dedication

To Max and Grete, who put me here, and Josh, who keeps me going. B"H.

Author's Acknowledgments

Thanks to Barbara Model, Josh Reinhold, Carol Baroudi, and Barbara Lapinskas for their help and suggestions and to Rebecca, Kathy, and Dennis at Wiley for numerous corrections and suggestions that improved this book. Also, thanks to the folks at Apple and their loyal customers, who keep alive the dream that personal computers, cellphones, and music players can be not just utilitarian machines but also tools that empower and inspire us.

Publisher's Acknowledgments

We're proud of this book; please send us your comments at http://dummies.custhelp.com. For other comments, please contact our Customer Care Department within the U.S. at 877-762-2974, outside the U.S. at 317-572-3993, or fax 317-572-4002.

Some of the people who helped bring this book to market include the following:

Acquisitions, Editorial, and Vertical Websites

Sr. Project Editor: Rebecca Huehls

Executive Editor: Bob Woerner

Copy Editor: Kathy Simpson

Technical Editor: Dennis Cohen

Sr. Editorial Manager: Leah P. Cameron

Supervising Producer: Rich Graves

Vertical Websites Associate Producers: Josh Frank, Marilyn Hummel, Douglas Kuhn, Shawn Patrick

Editorial Assistant: Amanda Graham

Sr. Editorial Assistant: Cherie Case

Cover Photos: ©istockphoto.com / quavondo, ©istockphoto.com / Nico Smit

Cartoons: Rich Tennant (www.the5thwave.com)

Composition Services

Project Coordinator: Katherine Crocker

Layout and Graphics: SD Jumper

Proofreader: ConText Editorial Services, Inc.

Indexer: Sharon Shock

Publishing and Editorial for Technology Dummies

Richard Swadley, Vice President and Executive Group Publisher

Andy Cummings, Vice President and Publisher

Mary Bednarek, Executive Acquisitions Director

Mary C. Corder, Editorial Director

Publishing for Consumer Dummies

Kathy Nebenhaus, Vice President and Executive Publisher

Composition Services

Debbie Stailey, Director of Composition Services

Contents at a Glance

Table of Contents

Introduction

Maybe you love your iPad, iPhone, or iPod and are curious about Apple's Macintosh computers. Maybe you've had one virus scare too many and are fed up with Windows. Maybe the daunting prospect of upgrading to Windows 7 has made you open to other possibilities. Maybe you're a Mac fan who wants to help a friend discover how easy and productive Macs can be. Wherever you're coming from, I hope you find that this book meets your needs.

Apple, Inc., of Cupertino, California, is more than 35 years old, and few brands in the history of business generate such fierce customer loyalty as Apple and its Macintosh line of personal computers. That loyalty runs both ways. Apple knows that the people who decide to buy its products are, for the most part, the ones who have to use them. Offering products that satisfy and even delight its users is a matter of survival for Apple.

Many virtues of the Macintosh are a matter of taste: its easy-to-use graphical interface, its elegant industrial design, and its integrated suite of software. But one virtue is a simple matter of fact: In recent years, when Windows users endured wave after wave of computer viruses, worms, spyware, botnets, and other types of evil software, Mac users were essentially immune. 'Nuff said.

About This Book

Macintosh computers and the OS X operating system have more in common with Windows than all the hoopla would suggest. Still, differences exist, big and little, that can cause problems for newcomers to the Mac.

In this book, you find helpful guides for every aspect of your switch, from deciding that you do in fact want to switch to a Mac, to making buying decisions, to setting up everything. You also find help getting started with all the cool software that comes with your Mac, including iPhoto for organizing your snapshots and iMovie and GarageBand for making your own media extravaganzas. I tell you how to use your Mac with other Apple products you may own, such as the iPad, iPhone, iPod, and Apple TV. You even find suggestions, responsible and irresponsible, for what to do with your old PC.

This book looks at switching to a Mac from a Windows user's perspective. You find out the best way to transfer your information from Windows to a Mac, as well as tips on how to do common Windows tasks the Mac way. But most any new Mac user can find help here. I also address the needs of both home and business users who are making or considering a switch. And if you have an older Mac and want to move stuff on it to OS X, check out the bonus chapter available on this book's web page: `www.dummies.com/go/switchingtoamac`.

OS X often provides more than one way to accomplish a task. I try to describe one straightforward method for each task, perhaps with a keyboard shortcut, rather than confuse you with lots of options.

If you've already decided to buy a Mac, you can skip the first chapter. If you've already bought a Mac, start with the second part of the book.

You can read this book from cover to cover if you're that kind of person, of course, but I try to keep chapters self-contained so that you can go straight to the topics that interest you most. Wherever you start, I wish you and your new Mac well.

Foolish Assumptions

Try as I may to be all things to all people, when it comes to writing a book, I had to pick who I thought would be most interested in *Switching to a Mac For Dummies*. Here's who I think you are:

- **You're smart.** You're no dummy. Yet the prospect of switching to a new computer platform gives you an uneasy feeling (which *proves* that you're smart).

- **You own a personal computer based on an operating system different from Apple OS X.** This book is aimed mostly at Windows XP users, but I think it will be helpful to users of Windows 7, Windows Vista, and even older Windows editions.

- **You're considering buying or have bought an Apple Macintosh computer.** You want to transition to your new computer expeditiously. I suggest straightforward methods and don't attempt to cover every possible solution.

    ✔ **Alternatively, you're a Mac user who knows OS X well but wants a resource to give (okay, even lend) to friends who are considering abandoning the dark side.** What a good friend you are.

    ✔ **You've used the Internet and know about browsers (such as Internet Explorer) and search engines (such as Google).** I briefly cover getting your own Internet connection in case you're not hooked up at the moment or it's time to update your service.

    ✔ **You're looking to buy a new machine.** This book addresses only the Intel Macs (ones based on microprocessors from Intel Corp.), which are all Apple has sold since 2006. It also focuses on the Lion version of the Macintosh operating system, OS X, which comes with new Macs and the iLife '11 application suite.

Whoever you are, welcome aboard. I think this book can help you.

How This Book Is Organized

I divide this book into the following highly logical (to me) parts. Each is self-contained, for the most part. Feel free to skip around.

In **Part I, "Informed Switching Starts Here,"** I explain why the Apple Macintosh is a big deal and why you should consider buying one. I also introduce you to the Apple product line and present a few different approaches to conversion (no dunking in water involved).

Part II, "Making the Switch," helps you decide what to buy and find what you can reuse from your old setup. Then I hold your hand as you make the big leap, moving your computing life to a Mac. OS X is a little different from Windows. I tell you what you most need to know to get started.

Part III, "Connecting Hither and Yon," tells you that Macs are to networking what ducks are to swimming: It comes naturally, but a few tricks are involved. I describe what you need to do to get your Mac online and talking to any other computers you have, including that old PC, as well as your iPad, iPhone, iPod, and Apple TV.

In **Part IV, "More Software, More Choices,"** you find out that your Mac is supplied with a ton (0.907 metric ton) of preloaded software, and you can buy — or even download for free — a lot more, especially from Apple's Mac App Store. Windows advocates complain that little software is available for the Mac, but so much is out there that I could write several books about Mac software. And yes, lots of cool games are available, too.

Kids, people with special needs, and businesses all have a lot to gain from the Mac way of doing things. In **Part V, "Specialty Switching Scenarios,"** I dive a bit deeper into OS X.

If you've read other *For Dummies* books, you're no doubt familiar with **Part VI, "The Part of Tens,"** which consists of entertaining lists containing ten (more or fewer) elucidating elements. They're fun to write; I hope they're fun to read.

There's more! In addition to providing all these elements, I've included a glossary in the back. The Mac world uses a vocabulary all its own, and you may encounter other technical terms on your switching journey. (Everything is a journey these days.) I think you'll be happy to have this guide to Mac jargon on your bookshelf. There's also a Cheat Sheet listing common commands and shortcuts (found at `www.dummies.com/cheatsheet/switchingtoamac`) and a bonus chapter that's aimed at helping people still using old, pre-OS X versions of the Mac operating system (found at `www.dummies.com/go/switchingtoamac`).

Typographic Conventions

For the most part, stuff that you need to do on a Mac is graphical, but from time to time, I may ask you to type something. If it's short, it appears in boldface, like this: Type **elm**. When I want you to type something longer, it appears like this:

```
terribly important text command
```

Be sure to type the line just as it appears; then press the Enter or Return key. Capitalization usually doesn't matter on a Mac. But OS X is based on Unix (as I discuss in Chapter 19), and Unix considers the uppercase and lowercase versions of the same letter to be totally different beasts.

In the text, web addresses are shown in this typeface: `www.ditchmypc.com`. I leave out the geeky `http://` part, which Mac browsers don't need you to type, anyway.

Apple keyboards have a special key with a fan-shaped squiggle that looks like this: ⌘. It has various nicknames — fan key, propeller key, Apple key — but in the text I use its formal name, the *Command key*.

You also see the Apple logo () in menu commands. It refers to the Apple menu, headed by that symbol, in the top-left corner of your screen.

Icons Used in This Book

A tip is a little tidbit that can save you time or money or make life a little easier. ("Avoid jackrabbit starts to save gas.")

Pay attention. Trouble lurks here. ("Never open the radiator cap on a hot engine.")

Keep these words of wisdom in mind, and save your derriere in the future. ("Have your car battery checked before each winter.")

Macs keep the gears and pulleys pretty well hidden. This icon marks under-the-hood stuff for the technically inclined; if that's not you, you can skip it. ("Regenerative braking converts your hybrid's kinetic energy back to electricity.")

Where to Go from Here

Hey, it's a Mac. You're set. If you have problems not covered in this book, lots of resources are available online to help you. You can visit my website: www.ditchmypc.com. I'd be happy to hear from you directly at switch tomac@ditchmypc.com. I'd love to know what you think of this book and how it can be improved, but I can't promise individual advice.

Meanwhile, use your new Mac to build a Facebook page, create a business, solve the world hunger problem, write the great novel of the 21st century, produce your first feature film, meet some cool people, or just have fun. After all, the rest of your computing life has just begun.

Occasionally, technology books require updates due to changes in hardware or software. If this book does have any technical updates, you can find them at dummies.com/go/switchingtoamacfdupdates.

Part I

Informed Switching Starts Here

In this part . . .

Perhaps you're fed up with Windows and are ready to try something different or maybe you're a happy Microsoft user who's curious to read what silly justifications I come up with for switching to a Mac. In this part, I suggest some reasons for switching that I find compelling and address common objections. Then I introduce you to the Mac family and help you figure out what to buy when you're ready to take the plunge.

Chapter 1

Why Switch? Demystifying the Mac Mantra

A pple Macintosh computers aren't perfect. They can't cure bad breath, save your marriage, or fix a bad hair day. Talk to enough Mac owners, and you'll find one who thinks he got a lemon and wasn't satisfied with Apple's service. You can probably find a cheaper computer that will do what you really need. The majority of computer users get by using Microsoft Windows, and you can, too.

So why even think about switching? Macs offer a far better experience, that's why. Value matters in tight economic times. In big ways, such as security and industrial design, and in countless little details, Apple makes the extra effort to get things right — right for the user, not for some corporate purchasing department. For those of us who spend a good part of our lives in front of a video display, those easier-to-use controls, well-thought-out software choices, and better hardware fit and finish all add up to create a tool that lets us do what we want and doesn't get in our way. For more casual users, the simpler Mac design means less head-scratching while you figure out how to perform that task.

Life is too short for Windows aggravation. Computers are now integral parts of our lives: We use them for work, for play, and for communication; we use them to find mates, to shop, to express ourselves, to educate our children, and to manage our money. They help us fix our homes, cure our diseases, and make new friends. No one has time to fuss over them, fix crashes, fight viruses, clean out hard drives, figure out why the printer won't work, reload the software, or press Ctrl+Alt+Delete. We need computers to be there when we want them. For the most part, Macs *are* there when we need them. Macs just work.

Steve Jobs' other company

Steve Jobs helped found Apple and is widely credited with creating the company culture of excellence. For ten years, Jobs moonlighted in another job: running Pixar Animation, now part of Disney. There have been many movie studios in the history of film, but few have produced ten smash hits in a row: *Toy Story; Toy Story 2; Toy Story 3; A Bug's Life; Monsters, Inc.; Finding Nemo; The Incredibles; Cars; Ratatouille;* and *Wall-E.* All were critically acclaimed box-office successes that made extensive use of the very latest in computer animation technology. But the key to their popularity was subordinating the gee-whiz special effects to the telling of a compelling story. Want to know what makes Macs different? Rent one of these movies.

Microsoft isn't run by a bunch of idiots. The company is managed by some very smart people, and it hires top-notch engineers. Just getting a product as complex as Windows out the door takes extraordinary talent. But Windows is designed for corporations. A Microsoft engineer revealed in his blog that one of the company's corporate users had 9,000 programs for Windows. The user simply couldn't afford to update them for new releases. Microsoft Windows has to support all the old software that's out there. Apple is better able to let go of the past and therefore is more nimble in developing new ways to make your life easier.

Apple sees its mission as harnessing the rapid advances in computing hardware to create revolutionary new products that improve our lives. The Macintosh, the iPad, and the iPhone are all filled with groundbreaking innovations. They're cool to look at and to own. Why buy boring?

Taking Your Best Shot

The question of which is a better personal computer — a Macintosh or a Windows PC — provokes passion matched by few other controversies. Were the world less civilized, Apple fans would long since have been burned at the stake by the more numerous Windows users who are fed up with hearing how great Macs are. Instead, the debate rages over claims that Macs aren't suitable choices because they're too this or can't do that. The following sections outline the principal objections.

"Macs are too expensive"

These days, every dollar counts. At this writing, you can buy a new Windows computer for as little as $300. Netbooks sell for even less. But a cheap product that causes you daily aggravation — and has to be replaced in a couple of years — is no bargain. When you price configurations from quality manufacturers that match the standard features on a Mac, the difference in price drops and often disappears. In the United States, you can buy a complete and very usable Mac desktop setup for less than $600 (assuming that you already own a suitable display, keyboard, and mouse), and you can buy an ultralight MacBook Air laptop for less than $1,000. If those prices are too much for your budget, see the tips in Chapter 3 for getting a Mac for less.

The arguments for buying a Mac are based on quality and total cost of ownership, not on initial purchase price. PCs have hidden costs, such as virus-protection software and periodic disk rebuilding, and they generally are replaced more often than Macs are. Few people boast about how cheap their car is or how little they spent for their home entertainment center. Quality matters, and when cash is scarce, quality matters even more.

"Switching is too hard"

I'm not saying that switching from a Windows PC to a Mac is painless. If you've been using Windows for a while, you're used to its idiosyncrasies. You made a big investment in learning how to use all that Windows software, not to mention the amount you paid for it. You may find some aspects of the Mac hard to get used to, though I guide you through them all in Chapter 4. But on the whole, switching isn't that bad. Macs and Windows PCs have more commonalities than they have differences. And Apple has new tools to make switching even easier, including a Windows Migration Assistant, described in Chapter 6, and an optional One-to-One program at the Apple store that does the file transfer work for you. All in all, I think that you'll find a switch easy enough and worth the effort.

"I'll be left with no software"

Many Windows advocates claim that less software is available for the Macintosh. The standard smart-aleck Mac-user answer is "Yeah, we really miss all those viruses and spyware programs." But some truth to this objection exists. Certain highly specialized programs run only in Windows. Where equivalents exist for the Mac, you may have fewer choices.

On the other hand, thousands of software titles are available for the Mac, and they cover the needs of most users quite well. In fact, some great software is available only for the Mac. Every new Mac comes with the following:

- ✔ **Apple applications:** These applications handle your e-mail, instant messaging, address book, calendar, and (of course) iTunes.

- ✔ **The Apple iLife suite:** This collection of programs lets you manage photos, make movies, authoring DVDs, create websites, and compose your own music. It even teaches you how to play an instrument.

- ✔ **The Mac App Store:** An easier way to buy quality, inexpensive software. Pioneered for the iPhone. It attracts an army of developers, big and small.

- ✔ **A built-in camera and powerful FaceTime videoconferencing software:** All new Macs (laptops and iMac desktops) that have a built-in display have the camera, and the software works with industry standards.

Some longtime Windows-only software is now available for the Mac, as developers have realized that they were missing an important market. One example is AutoCAD, widely used by architects and mechanical designers. Another is the popular QuickBooks accounting system for small business, though it lacks some features of the Windows version. Moreover, the Mac OS X operating system is built on top of Unix, and Apple follows the Single Unix Specification (SUS). Therefore, a large amount of software developed for Unix and Linux operating systems can run on your Mac, including many popular, free open-source packages. Much of that software *doesn't* run in Windows.

Finally, Macs can also run Windows, so you can still run the odd program for which an equivalent isn't available on the Mac. All new Macs run on Intel microprocessors — the same ones that power most Windows machines. In fact, any Mac sold since mid-2005 is also a full-fledged, strictly kosher PC, one that can run the Windows 7 operating systems as well as any PC on the market. So if you must run software that's available only for Windows, you can use it on a Mac, too. Yeah, you have to buy and install Windows separately, but I walk you through that task in Chapter 16.

"Macs are dying out"

Macs *were* close to dying out in the 1990s. Their share of the personal computer market was less than 3 percent. That share has been climbing steadily, however, and at last report was 15 percent in the United States. Market share doesn't tell the whole story, however. Apple commands some 35 percent of all profits made from selling personal computers. Its competitors are locked in a death spiral, competing on price and doing everything they can to shave costs at the expense of quality. The success of the iPad, the iPhone, the iPod, and the iTunes Store makes more PC users consider Apple. More than half of all new Macs are purchased by people who were using Windows, and 40 percent of college students buy Macs.

"Macs are not expandable"

Since the earliest days of the IBM Personal Computer, PCs have come in big boxes that a user could open to install expansion cards or to add memory and hard drives. Steve Jobs horrified the techie end of the PC world when he built the original Macintosh as a self-contained unit that users weren't supposed to open. Although Apple offers a model with expansion slots (the top-of-the-line Mac Pro), and although memory slots on current Macs are easy to access, Apple encourages expansion by hooking up accessories with easier-to-use high-speed cabling. Apple invented FireWire, a blazingly fast expansion port that lets users attach high-performance devices without opening the box. The PC world responded by developing its own fast expansion port, USB 2.0, which Apple then adopted.

Now Apple and Intel have jointly developed an even faster way to hook up accessories: Thunderbolt. (It's not easy to top a name like FireWire.) Thunderbolt packages on a wire the same PCI Express technology used in modern PC expansion slots. It's a game changer, with speeds up to 20 times faster than USB 2.0 and 12 times faster than FireWire 800. You can connect more than one device to a Thunderbolt port, and it even doubles as a Mini DisplayPort so that you can hook a large video display to the end of that Thunderbolt daisy chain.

All new Macs offer Thunderbolt and USB 2.0 ports, and many include a FireWire port, allowing a wide range of accessories to be attached just by plugging them in.

See Chapter 2 for an introduction to the Mac models now available.

"Macs don't comply with industry standards"

Early in Apple's history, Steve Wozniak, a co-founder of Apple and its engineering genius, came up with a clever way to squeeze more bits onto a floppy disk (an early form of portable data storage). Unfortunately, this design made floppy disks written on early Macs unreadable on IBM PCs. That gave Apple a reputation of being an odd duck from a standards standpoint. Apple has never been able to shake that reputation completely, even though it later added PC-compatible floppy drives and is now exemplary in sticking to industry standards. Indeed, Apple was the first to popularize now-ubiquitous computer industry standards such as Wi-Fi wireless networking and the Universal Serial Bus (USB). Other standards gobbledygook that Macs support include Gigabit Ethernet, Bluetooth, IEEE-1394 FireWire, PCI Express, Thunderbolt (see Chapter 3 for more details), and the Intel microprocessor architecture. The Apple web browser, Safari (also available for Windows), carefully follows the latest HTML5 Internet standards — more so than Microsoft's Internet Explorer does.

Will Apple license OS X for other PCs?

A perennial question in the Apple-watching community is whether Apple will license its OS X operating system to run on other PCs. After the Apple switch to Intel processors, there remains no technical reason why this can't be done. Indeed, Apple has to go to some lengths to discourage clever programmers from modifying *(hacking)* OS X to run on personal computers sold by other manufacturers. One scenario has Apple mimicking the Microsoft strategy and selling OS X to anyone to run on any computer that meets minimal standards. Every indication says that Apple will continue to try to keep OS X to itself and follow its high-end branding strategy, but Apple is known for creating surprises.

"I need Windows for work"

So run Windows on your Mac. You have to buy a copy, which is an added expense. But both operating systems run fine on a Mac, and you can still use Mac OS X when you're not working. Using third-party virtualization software, you can run both operating systems at the same time, with Windows applications appearing on the Mac OS X desktop alongside native Mac applications. I tell you more about how all this works in Chapter 16.

"Macs are a poor game platform"

True, more games exist for the PC, but plenty are available for Macs, including top titles like *World of Warcraft, Call of Duty, StarCraft II,* and *Spore.* Many more are coming. Large game companies like Blizzard have committed to the Mac platform, though many independents have not. The Apple iPad, iPhone, and iPod touch have proved to be successful portable game platforms, attracting new game developers to the Apple universe. All low-end Macs include integrated graphics processors; the high-end Mac mini, all iMacs and the 15- and 17-inch MacBook Pro laptops add a second high-performance AMD Radeon HD graphics chip; and the Mac Pro can be ordered with two top-of-the-line graphics processors. Multicore main processors add more graphics performance, and Lion's OpenGL unlocks the power of these graphics devices for more computing tasks. If you're a serious gamer, you probably know all about the latest graphics processors, but I tell you more about them in Chapter 2.

"Windows 8 will kill Apple"

Microsoft spent five years and billions of dollars developing the Vista operating system, in part to end the scourge of computer viruses and spyware that have plagued the PC world for more than a decade. After Vista proved to be an embarrassment, Microsoft spent more years and more billions to rework it into Windows 7. During the same period, Apple has been devoting its energy to improving its OS X operating system from the user's perspective. While Windows 7 and Windows Vista were gestating, Apple released six improved versions of OS X, code-named Jaguar, Panther, Tiger, Leopard, Snow Leopard, and now Lion. (Someone at Apple likes big cats.) Perhaps Windows 8 will close the gap. We'll see.

Considering All Aspects — Advantage Apple

Apple has adopted strategies that give it important advantages over the competition provided by Microsoft. The following sections explore what you need to know about each one.

One neck to wring

Microsoft sells its Windows operating system to dozens of companies that make personal computers. This practice has benefits in that competition among these PC vendors keeps prices down, but it also means that Microsoft has to support a bewildering variety of hardware designs and components. This support includes not just all the variations now being sold, but also products that are no longer being sold but are still in use, including PCs made by companies that have left the business. Outside a brief flirtation with licensing in the mid-1990s, Apple has maintained complete control of the design and manufacture of products that use its software. This *vertical integration* greatly simplifies Apple's development efforts, allowing it to bring out new versions of its operating system much more often than Microsoft has been able to.

Vertical integration also has benefits for customers in terms of reliability and service. If you have a problem with hardware or software, Apple has a strong incentive to fix it. With the computer, operating system, and much of the software supplied by a single vendor, Mac users don't have to worry about being shuttled from company to company ("I'm sorry, but you'll have to contact Fly-by-Night Software to solve your movie-editing bug; it makes that application"). Any problems with the extensive suite of software that comes with a Mac are Apple's problems. There's only one neck to wring.

Are Mac users too smug about viruses?

Computer-industry pundits are continually warning Mac users that the pandemic of viruses, worms, Trojans, and other malware that plagues the PC world will soon be coming to Macintosh users. They've been issuing these warnings for more than a decade, as I remember, but that doesn't mean they won't be right someday. The Mac market is no longer too small for virus writers to bother with. On the other hand, Apple has the resources, skills, and commitment to try to keep ahead of the malware threat. OS X Lion introduces important security improvements, and Apple issues regular security fixes through its Software Update program. Good security practices still make sense in the Mac world, and I tell you ways to keep your Mac secure in Chapter 10.

Apple is the industry thought leader

Anyone who follows the high-tech industry is used to reading articles about amazing new technologies that are going to revolutionize our lives — and then never hearing about them again. One of Apple's roles in the computer industry is picking and choosing among those new ideas. For the most part, technologies that Apple picks are adopted by the rest of the industry, particularly by Microsoft. Apple may not have invented the graphical user interface, Wi-Fi wireless networking, USB, the smartphone, or tablets but Apple's adoption and careful implementation of these technologies made them industry standards. Apple users get the good new stuff first.

Appearances matter

Sometimes, you *can* judge a book by its cover. Sometimes, function follows form. Early in Apple's history, Steve Jobs recognized that aesthetics matter. The design team that created the first Macintosh computer included a fine artist who was involved in everything from the design of the graphical interface to the artwork on the cardboard box that the Mac came in. When Jobs returned to Apple, he restored artistic quality to prominence at Apple. From the original lollipop-colored iMacs to the latest iPad, Apple products have won awards for excellence in industrial design. Figure 1-1 shows the elegant current iMac all-in-one computer.

Quality industrial design means more than arranging all the buttons and jacks in a pleasing way. It also means questioning each feature and eliminating unnecessary doodads. The result is something that isn't just easy to look at, but also easy to understand and simple to work with.

Figure 1-1:
The iMac
offers
everything
you need in
one smart
package.
The Magic
Trackpad
shown here
is a handy
option.

Photo courtesy of Apple, Inc.

A case in point is the optional Apple Remote. Remotes for most consumer products rival an airplane cockpit in complexity; the Apple version has just six buttons.

Looking forward, not backward

Apple leadership in technology extends beyond picking winners. Apple is also the company that decides when to tell a once-popular technology, "You're fired." It was the first to introduce 3½-inch floppy disks on personal computers and the first to drop their use as a standard feature. Other technologies that Apple was the first to drop include the RS-232 serial port and the dialup modem. You can still find these features as external add-ons if you really need them, but Apple realized that most of us no longer do. Letting go of old technology wards off the feature bloat that plagues the computer industry. Unneeded features increase complexity and make machines harder to use and more prone to problems.

Getting top-notch products

Apple makes money on the products it sells. Unit for unit, Apple is the most profitable company in the industry. How does the company do that with such a small share of the market? The same way that Mercedes-Benz or BMW or Armani does: by branding. Apple doesn't sell products that are interchangeable with products sold by half a dozen other companies. It sells unique products — products that are sufficiently superior that customers willingly pay a bit more for them. The benefit to you, as a Mac buyer, is the simple reality that no company can keep such an enviable position in the long run without delivering top-notch goods. You do get what you pay for.

iPad, iPod, and iPhone

Apple's runaway success with the iPod personal music player, introduced in 2001, has given the company the kind of market dominance in mobile computing that Microsoft has enjoyed in the PC market.

The iPhone has been hailed as a revolution in personal communications. It comes in two versions: a four-band phone that uses the worldwide GSM standard, allowing its use anywhere, and a version compatible with the Qualcomm standard used by Verizon in the U.S. Both versions include iPod music, a pair of cameras, and video technology and direct Internet access via Wi-Fi or cellular phone links. Apple includes a version of its operating system called iOS in the iPhone, iPad, and iPod touch, with a well-integrated and easy-to-use interface, all in spectacularly elegant packages.

Apple gives away a version of its iTunes music software that runs in Windows. The company is betting that iPod, iPad, and iPhone customers who use Windows will be impressed by iTunes' ease of use and will give the Macintosh a closer look when they're ready to upgrade their computers. You find out more about iTunes in Chapter 11.

Switching Sides Can Sting

The Mac-versus-PC debate ranks as one of the great divides in the modern world. Just because these feelings are whipped up by marketing departments doesn't mean that they lack emotional impact. Your computer choice forms part of your personal identity. Mac users have a reputation for a certain smugness. ("You just got a virus? You mean, like a cold?") Much of that attitude is defensive, of course. It's no fun being a minority in a PC-dominated world. ("You bought a what? Are they still making those?") Few other choices we make in life can be as self-defining — perhaps religion, political party, and sports team to cheer for. People who move from New York City to Boston, for example, invariably suffer mental scars inflicted by changing their baseball allegiance from the New York Yankees to the Boston Red Sox. (Some of them never recover and have to live the rest of their lives eking out a living writing books for technology novices.)

This kind of psychological trauma doesn't have to happen to you just because you switch computer platforms. Think of it this way: The PC won the great war. Apple was forced to abandon the Motorola processor family and convert to Intel. Macs are now just PCs in more stylish packages with better software. You're not abandoning your mother's cooking — just sampling a different cuisine.

No matter what I say, you probably won't completely escape the emotional side of switching to a Mac. When you feel the shame of betrayal and the pangs of guilt coming on, repeat this mantra: "It's just a computer. It's just a computer. It's just a computer."

An optional brief history of Apple

You don't need to read this sidebar to make your decisions, but no book on switching to the Mac would be complete without a little history of how Apple got where it is today. None of the science-fiction magazines that warped our formative minds dared to predict the level of computing power that we have beneath our fingertips or in our shirt pockets today. Further, no high-tech story is as compelling as the legend of Steve and Bill, two kids from the West Coast of the United States who revolutionized the world.

Apple Computer was founded on April Fools' Day, 1976, by three young men: Steve Jobs, Steve Wozniak, and Ronald Wayne. Their original mission: Sell low-cost circuit boards on which hobbyists would build their own computers, based on the newly invented microprocessor. That mission quickly changed when Jobs found that a local electronics shop wanted

more fully assembled systems and gave him an order for several dozen of them. The price of the first Apple product, the Apple I, was $666.66, more than the price of today's far more capable Mac mini. Adjusted for inflation, the Apple I would cost about $2,600 in 2011 dollars — more than enough for a Mac Pro, or a top-of-the-line 27-inch iMac plus an iPad.

The Apple I used a 6502 microprocessor, which was considered to be easier to program than the early groundbreaking devices from Intel and Zilog, and featured a BASIC interpreter. *BASIC* is a particularly simple computer language invented by Dartmouth professor John Kemeny to help teach programming. A young programmer named Bill Gates dropped out of Harvard — horrifying his parents — to start a business selling software to the fledgling microcomputer industry. He chose the imaginative name *Microsoft* for his venture. A BASIC

(continued)

(continued)

interpreter for microcomputers was the company's first product, and Apple was among its earliest customers. The choice of corporate names was prophetic: a utilitarian contraction versus a friendly fruit icon.

The Apple II quickly supplanted the primitive Apple I and propelled Apple Computer to early leadership in personal computing. Dan Bricklin wrote VisiCalc, the world's first spreadsheet program, for the Apple II. If you crunch numbers for a living, imagine what the world was like when a spreadsheet was just a wide piece of ruled paper on which calculations were recorded one at a time by hand, and you can appreciate the impact of VisiCalc.

Microsoft got its big break when International Business Machines (IBM) decided to try its hand at making a personal computer and chose Gates' company to supply the all-important operating system. Although IBM is now a well-respected name in computing, back in the 1970s, it pretty much owned commercial computing. Almost every major corporation in the world used IBM computers. Young computer professionals were told by older hands that no one was ever fired for buying IBM. Some Apple IIs had made their way into the corporate world because of VisiCalc, but they were soon replaced by beige boxes sporting IBM logos, the Microsoft operating system named DOS, and an even better spreadsheet program: Lotus 1-2-3.

The Apple II was a hard act for Apple to follow. Apple made two disastrous attempts: the Apple III (a souped-up Apple II) and the Lisa. The Lisa was a machine ahead of its time, pioneering the use of a mouse to move a pointer on the screen and letting users initiate actions by manipulating icons representing programs, data files, and hard drives, for example. But this *graphical user interface* couldn't overcome a $10,000 starting price, and few Lisas were sold.

Jobs, fed up with the increasingly corporatized development environment at Apple, led a renegade team to develop a more affordable computer, based on much of the same technology as Lisa. The new Macintosh was announced during the 1984 Super Bowl in what is perhaps the best television commercial ever made. You can view it at `www.uriahcarpenter.info/1984.html`.

Besides its mouse and graphical user interface, the Macintosh was packaged as a single unit with a built-in, high-resolution (for its time) black-on-white screen that crisply displayed the information that would eventually print on paper. IBM PCs offered green letters on a black background in just one font. The higher-quality Mac display enabled a "what you see is what you get" document-creation process and started the desktop publishing revolution. The Mac also introduced 3½-inch floppy disks, and its Motorola 68000 microprocessor could address more memory than the Intel 8088 in the IBM PC, allowing the use of more sophisticated programs.

Microsoft hedged its bets by developing software applications for the new Mac, including the word processing program named Word and the spreadsheet named Multiplan. Jobs and Gates personally negotiated a contract that let Microsoft sell a simplified version of the graphical interface named Microsoft Windows 1.0. When Microsoft later released a full-blown graphical user interface in Windows 3.0, Apple sued, but the courts ruled that it was covered by that one-page contract. Word became the flagship word processor for Windows, and Excel, with a graphical interface like Multiplan's, drove out Lotus 1-2-3.

Jobs left Apple in 1985 after some disagreements with the board of directors and started a new computer company, NeXT. It built a graphical interface on top of an operating system named Unix that was developed by the American Telephone & Telegraph Company (AT&T). Unix was popular with computer researchers because of its flexible design and because a version with source code was available.

Apple continued to introduce more powerful versions of the Macintosh, adding hard drives, laser printers, and high-resolution color displays. Its share of the personal computer market continued to decline relative to IBM PCs and their clones. In 1994, Apple switched from the Motorola 68000 series microprocessor to the PowerPC chip, jointly developed by Motorola, IBM, and Apple. The PowerPC was designed to allow programs to run faster than those run by the Intel chips, but the theoretical advantage never materialized as Intel chip engineers used innovative techniques to keep up.

In 1997, Apple acquired NeXT, and Steve Jobs rejoined the company, soon taking the helm. A year later, he reinvigorated Apple sales with the iMac, an all-in-one computer that echoed the original Macintosh. A flat-panel version appeared in 2002. Apple soon replaced its OS 9 operating system (the lineage of which goes back to the first Macintosh) with a new system: Mac OS X, based on the NeXT operating system. The iPod was launched in 2001.

In 2005, Jobs ended the personal computer microprocessor wars when he announced that Apple would switch to x86 Intel microprocessors, the same microprocessors used in Windows PCs. All Macs manufactured since 2006 employ Intel microprocessors. In 2007, Jobs introduced the Apple TV (TV), extending the Apple brand to the living room, as well as the spiffy iPhone, setting a new standard in mobile communication. The companion iPod touch shares many iPhone features except the phone and has become a popular game platform. In 2010, Apple introduced another revolutionary product, the iPad, replacing it a year later with the iPad 2. More than 425,000 inexpensive or free applications for the iPhone, iPod touch, and iPad are available online at the iTunes Store.

In 2010, Jobs announced that he was taking a leave of absence from day-to-day Apple management for health reasons, though he was on hand at Apple's 2011 developer conference to introduce OS X Lion. Sadly, Steve succumbed to his illness on October 5, 2011. The world mourned his passing. The amazing team he assembled continues to lead Apple, with Tim Cook as president.

Chapter 2

Meet the Mac Family

· ·

· ·

Switching to a Macintosh means getting a computer manufactured by Apple, Inc. No one else currently makes Macs. If you found shopping for Windows PCs to be a bit bewildering, you're in for a pleasant surprise. Apple has only a few models in each category, and each model has a name, not a number. If you love having many vendors to choose from and lots of catalogs to look through, with the prospect that *something* is always on sale, the Apple experience may require some adjustment.

In this chapter, I touch on the various available Mac models and related products. In Chapter 3, I point out your options, including memory size and disk capacity, and help you figure out which model is best for you overall.

From time to time, Apple upgrades its products, drops old models, and introduces new ones. Check www.apple.com for the latest specifications.

Checking Out Common Features

Apple typically offers three or so versions of each model: a lowest-price basic version, an intermediate version, and a loaded version. Certain features, including the following, are common to all current Mac models:

> ✔ **Processors:** The processor in a computer carries out the instruction steps and is sometimes called a CPU (for central processing unit) or a microprocessor (because such things once filled large rooms but now are about the size of a postage stamp). All Mac models made in the past five years use fast Intel microprocessors, similar to those used in most

PCs. Apple uses CPUs that feature two or more processor cores, allowing them to work faster. They all support 64-bit operation, allowing main memory greater than 4GB, though not all Mac models let you install so much memory. Unlike in Windows, you don't need a special 64-bit version of the operating system to take advantage of this capability. Mac OS X is 64-bit ready and also supports older, more common 32-bit applications. Apple typically offers a couple of faster processor options for each Mac model.

✔ **Memory:** As with PCs, Macs come with two types of memory:

- *Random Access Memory (RAM):* Stores programs and data while the computer is actively processing them. All Macs come with at least 2GB (2 gigabytes) of RAM. Having more RAM lets you do more things at a time and is especially important if you work with very large files, such as movies.

- *Hard drive mass storage:* For long-term data storage. A bigger hard drive means more space for music, photos, and video files. Some models include solid state drives instead of, or in addition to, traditional hard drives. These offer faster performance but are more expensive for the same amount of storage.

- *Graphics:* All Macs include a graphics processor unit (GPU) to speed the display of pictures and video. The low-end version of Mac mini and 11- and 13-inch Mac laptops use an Intel HD 3000 graphics processor integrated into the CPU chip set. Higher-end models add more powerful GPUs in addition to the integrated unit. The integrated graphics are fine for web browsing, watching high definition (HD) video, and light-duty gaming. Serious gamers (you know who you are) need the higher-performance GPUs.

- *High performance video output and data I/O:* All new Macs include a Thunderbolt input/output port, which is compatible with Mini DisplayPort for output to high definition video displays and allows very high-speed peripherals to be connected as well.

- *LED displays:* All Mac displays feature a screen that lights up using light-emitting diodes (LEDs) rather than the fluorescent lamps used in many other flat-panel displays, which contain trace amounts of mercury, a hazardous material.

- *Headset jack:* All Macs have a minijack that works with regular headphones and also supports Apple iPhone compatible headsets, so you can use such a headset to make FaceTime and iChat calls. High-end Macs have a separate audio line-in jack as well.

- *Software:* All new Macs come with OS X Lion software, and all Macs except the Apple mini server include the integrated iLife suite of digital lifestyle applications. I introduce you to OS X in Chapter 5. I describe in Part IV the iLife suite and other software goodies you can get for Macs.

✔ **Wireless networking support:** All new Macs have built-in wireless networking using the latest Wi-Fi and Bluetooth standards. Apple was the first computer company to embrace Wi-Fi, using Apple's own brand name, AirPort.

This wireless support is especially handy in Mac laptops because lots of places offer Wi-Fi hotspots where you can jump online. Look for hotspots in coffee shops and public libraries, train stations, airline terminals, hotels, shopping centers, and even doctors' waiting rooms. With an Apple laptop under your arm, you're never out of touch.

The Bluetooth networking is a short-range wireless personal networking scheme that connects to nearby electronic devices. Cellphones use it to connect to headsets without a wire. Bluetooth connects your Mac to wireless keyboards and mice. If your cellphone has Bluetooth, you can use it to connect to the Internet if your phone and cellular carrier support such use.

✔ **Wired networking support:** All new Macs, except the minimalist, ultra-thin MacBook Airs, have Gigabit Ethernet jacks for wired networking and connecting to high-speed cable and DSL modems. See Chapter 9 for more on networking the Macintosh way.

✔ **No built-in dialup modems or floppy drives:** You can buy an Apple Modem (a small external modem) as an accessory, and external USB floppy drives are available from third parties.

✔ **SuperDrive:** All models except the mini and MacBook Air can read, play, and write (burn) CDs and multilayer DVDs, incorporating what Apple calls a SuperDrive. The SuperDrive is slot-loading (except on the Mac Pro), so you have no slide-out tray to break, but they only work with full size discs. Apple offers an optional external SuperDrive for the mini and Air and software that allows these models to use a CD/DVD reader on another Mac or even a PC.

✔ **HD support:** Apple displays are normally set up with a 16:10 aspect ratio (width versus height), which is ideal for HD video.

Other discriminators among models are screen sizes for laptops and iMacs, memory, and hard drive space. The more expensive models also have bigger hard drives and faster processors, though the speed difference generally isn't dramatic — 20 percent or so.

In the sections that follow, you take a closer look at how the various Mac models are suited for different tasks and uses.

Connecting on the Go with Your Apple Laptop

Laptops are the most popular Mac models. Compact and elegantly designed, they show up more and more at meetings where clunky Windows laptops used to predominate. Quality construction matters more in mobile devices like laptops, and Macs are among the best-built machines out there. Even if you run only Windows on it (yes, you can), an Apple laptop is a first-class choice.

One unique feature of Apple laptops is the large *Multi-Touch* glass trackpad, which understands gestures you make using more than one finger at a time. You can pinch an image to shrink it, for example, or swipe with two fingers to scroll or with four fingers to move windows out of the way so that you can see your desktop. The Multi-Touch trackpad registers a click if you push down a little harder on it, which eliminates the need for a separate button. If you're wondering how to work without a second button, a click while you have two fingers on the trackpad of any laptop model is understood to be a right-click.

Apple builds their laptops into sturdy unibody aluminum cases and back-lights the keyboards, so you can work during airplane movies, in a darkened presentation room, or in bed at night when someone else is trying to sleep.

All new Apple laptops include a built-in FaceTime video camera. It's located on the lid, above the display, along with an omnidirectional microphone. Stereo speakers and a headphone jack are also provided. Coupled with easy, high-speed Internet connectivity and OS X iChat and FaceTime communication software, these cameras let you videoconference from just about anywhere. You can turn off the camera for ordinary audio phone calls, if you prefer. No one needs to know what you look like first thing in the morning.

Speaking of the lid, it's kept closed by a magnet; you find no mechanical catch to break. That's not the only magnetic feature of Mac laptops: The power cord is magnetically attached, too. Apple named it *MagSafe* because it's designed not to pull your laptop off the table if you trip over the cord. MagSafe is a fine example of Apple's attention to detail.

Apple laptops come with a separate power supply that runs on 100–240 volts AC, 50 to 60 Hz, so they can be used anywhere in the world with an adapter or power cord for the wall outlets in the country you're visiting. Apple power supplies meet U.S. EPA Energy Star requirements, reducing energy waste. An airplane MagSafe power cord is available as an option.

All Apple laptops come with built-in AirPort Extreme Wi-Fi wireless, supporting the 802.11a, b, g, and n standards. They also support Bluetooth 2.0 with Enhanced Data Rate (EDR). So you can use your Apple laptop with any Wi-Fi hotspot and any Bluetooth device.

Apple divides its laptops into three product lines: MacBook, MacBook Air, and MacBook Pro. I summarize the different laptop models in Table 2-1. Figure 2-1 shows the Apple aluminum laptop lineup from left to right: the MacBook Air and the 13-inch, 15-inch, and 17-inch MacBook Pro models.

Figure 2-1:
The
MacBook
Pro laptop
family.

Photo courtesy of Apple, Inc.

Table 2-1	Mac Laptop Comparison				
	MacBook Air (11-inch)	**MacBook Air (13-inch)**	**MacBook Pro (13-inch)**	**MacBook Pro (15-inch)**	**MacBook Pro (17-inch)**
Screen size (inches diagonal)	11.6	13.3	13.3	15.4	17
Resolution (pixels)	1336 x 768	1440 x 900	1440 x 900	1440 x 900	1920 x 1200
Backlight	LED	LED	LED	LED	LED
Finish	Glossy	Glossy	Glossy	Antiglare option	Antiglare option
Weight	2.38 lbs. 1.08 kg	2.96 lbs. 1.35 kg	4.5 lbs. 2.04 kg	5.6 lbs. 2.54 kg	6.6 lbs. 3 kg
Thickness	0.68 in. 1.7 cm	0.68 in. 1.7 cm	0.95 in. 2.41 cm	0.95 in. 2.41 cm	0.98 in. 2.5 cm
CPU	Dual-core i5	Dual-core i5	Dual-core i5	Quad-core i7	Quad-core i7
Speed (GHz)	1.4– 1.6	1.86–2.13	2.3–2.7	2.0–2.2	2.2–2.3

(continued)

Table 2-1 *(continued)*

	MacBook Air (11-inch)	MacBook Air (13-inch)	MacBook Pro (13-inch)	MacBook Pro (15-inch)	MacBook Pro (17-inch)
Maximum RAM	4GB	4GB	8GB	8GB	8GB
Graphics	Integrated	Integrated	Integrated	Integrated+ AMD Radeon HD 6490M (opt. 6750M)	Integrated + AMD Radeon HD 6750M
Optical SuperDrive	External option	External option	Yes	Yes	Yes
Video Port	Thunder-bolt	Thunder-bolt	Thunder-bolt	Thunder-bolt	Thunder-bolt
USB 2.0 ports	2	2	2	2	3
Ethernet port	External option	External option	Gigabit	Gigabit	Gigabit
FireWire port	None	None	800 Mbps	800 Mbps	800 Mbps
Card slot	None	SD Card	SDXC Card	SDXC Card	Express Card/34
Wi-Fi	802.11n	802.11n	802.11n	802.11n	802.11n
Bluetooth	2.1+EDR	2.1+EDR	2.1+EDR	2.1+EDR	2.1+EDR
FaceTime camera	Yes	Yes	Yes	Yes	Yes
Microphone	Yes	Yes	Yes	Yes	Yes
Headset jack in/out	Yes	Yes	Yes	Yes	Yes
Audio line in jack	No	No	No	Yes	Yes
Trackpad	Multi-Touch	Multi-Touch	Multi-Touch	Multi-Touch	Multi-Touch
Keyboard backlight	Yes	Yes	Yes	Yes	Yes
MagSafe power adapter	45 watts	45 watts	60 watts	85 watts	85 watts

Traveling light with MacBook Air

The two MacBook Air models, 11-inch and 13-inch, are ultraportable laptops, ideal for students and road warriors. Apple has stripped out components that aren't generally needed on the road in an effort to keep size and weight to a minimum. Both Airs are shown in Figure 2-2. Figure 2-3 gives you an idea how thin the Air is. (The second USB port and Thunderbolt port are on the other side.)

Figure 2-2: The 11- and 13-inch MacBook Airs.

Photo courtesy of Apple, Inc.

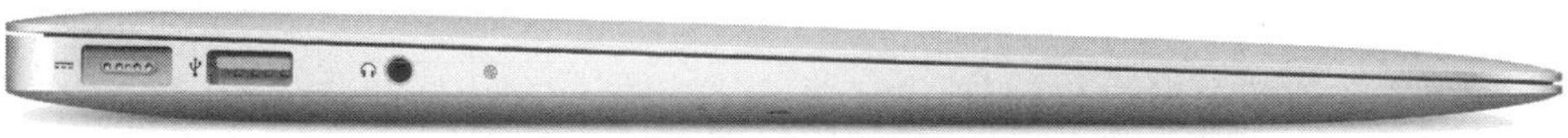

Figure 2-3: It's not a printing smudge but a side view of a MacBook Air.

Photo courtesy of Apple, Inc.

The Air employs solid-state flash memory (64GB, 128GB, or 256GB) for mass storage instead of a hard drive, reducing size, weight, and power consumption while allowing an Air to wake from sleep almost instantly. Other MacBook Air features include

- An Intel dual core Core i5 processor. The processor runs at a slower speed maximize battery life.

- Two models, both with LED-backlit, glossy widescreen displays. The smaller Air's screen has 1366 x 768 resolution and measures 11.6 inches diagonally (294mm); the larger screen, measuring 13.3 inches (338mm) diagonally, has 1440 x 900 resolution.

✔ A very thin but strong aluminum case.

✔ An integrated Intel HD 3000 graphics processor with full 3D support.

✔ Two USB 2.0 ports.

✔ An SD Card slot on the 13-inch model, useful for downloading photos from many digital cameras.

✔ A 45-watt AC power module.

✔ A full-size keyboard, including 12 function keys and 4 arrow keys (inverted *T* arrangement).

✔ A Multi-Touch trackpad for cursor control.

✔ An optional external dual-layer-burning, slot-loading SuperDrive.

✔ An optional wired Ethernet-to-USB adapter.

✔ A lithium-polymer battery that provides up to 5 hours of wireless web access on the 11-inch model and 7 hours on the 13-inch model.

The MacBook Air cable connections include

✔ Analog headset 3.5 mm minijack, with support for Apple earphones with remote and microphone

✔ MagSafe power connector

✔ Two USB 2.0 ports

✔ Thunderbolt/Mini DisplayPort external video

Taking the high ground with MacBook Pro

The MacBook Pro is Apple's full-featured laptop line, with a number of features that set it apart from the MacBook Airs:

✔ A wider choice of display sizes (13.3, 15.4, or 17 inches)

✔ Faster processors with more memory

✔ Two graphics processors on the 15- and 17-inch models for faster gaming and 3D support

✔ Built-in SuperDrive for reading and writing CDs and DVDs

✔ Gigabit Ethernet port

✔ FireWire 800 Mbps port

✔ SDXC Card slot (13-inch and 15-inch models) or ExpressCard/34 slot (17-inch model)

✔ Separate audio line in jack (15-inch and 17-inch models)

✔ Kensington cable lock slot for physical security

✔ Heftier, 85-watt AC power module on some models (which can also power a MacBook Air, but the 45-watt power module that comes with the MacBook Air isn't powerful enough to supply the bigger MacBook Pros)

Details, details, details. Each MacBook Pro includes these items:

✔ **A glossy widescreen display:** The 17-inch model can be ordered with a higher resolution of 1920 x 1200. (Table 2-1 lists standard resolutions.) You can order the 15- and 17-inch models with a reduced-glare screen rather than the standard glossy model. Many graphics designers find that glare interferes with precision color editing.

✔ **Intel Sandy Bridge processor:** The 13-inch model has two processor cores; the 15- and 17-inch models have four cores. All models come with at least 4GB of RAM. Two SO-DIMM slots support up to 8GB of RAM.

✔ **An Intel HD 3000 graphics processor:** The more-expensive models add an AMD Radeon HD and graphics memory; see "Getting the Right Graphics Processor," later in this chapter, for details.

✔ **A 320GB hard drive on the 13-inch model, 500GB on the 15-inch model, and 750GB on the 17-inch model:** You can order your MacBook Pro with larger disk drives or solid-state disk drives, if you prefer.

✔ **Full-size backlit keyboard:** The keyboard includes 12 function keys and 4 arrow keys (inverted *T* arrangement).

✔ **Scrolling Multi-Touch trackpad for cursor control:** Senses one, two, three, or four fingers, allowing for a wide variety of gestures.

✔ **Thunderbolt port with Mini DisplayPort support**

✔ **Two USB 2.0 ports** (three on the 17-inch model)

✔ **An aluminum case**

✔ **Lithium-polymer battery:** The battery supports up to 7 hours of wireless web use.

The MacBook Pro cable connections, shown in Figure 2-4, include

✔ MagSafe power connector

✔ Gigabit Ethernet

✔ FireWire 800 Mbps port

✔ Thunderbolt port with Mini DisplayPort external video

✔ Two USB 2.0 ports (three on the 17-inch model)

✔ SDXC card slot (13-inch and 15-inch models) or ExpressCard/34 slot (17-inch models)

✔ Combined digital audio input/audio line in — 3.5mm minijack (13- and 17-inch models)

✔ Combined digital audio output/headphone out — 3.5mm minijack

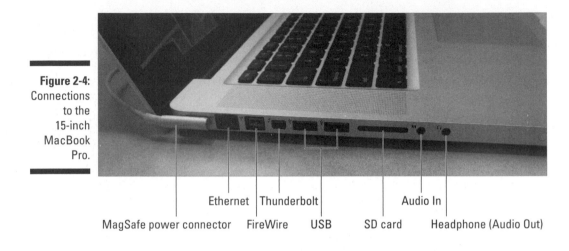

Figure 2-4: Connections to the 15-inch MacBook Pro.

Ethernet   Thunderbolt   Audio In

MagSafe power connector   FireWire   USB   SD card   Headphone (Audio Out)

Furnishing Your Lair with Mac Desktops

Laptops are great, but sometimes you want more permanence in your setup, whether it's your workplace, home office, or entertainment center. Apple offers a range of desktop models — from the petite but well-equipped mini to the graceful all-in-one iMac to the industrial-strength Mac Pro — that you can use to build just the computing environment you want. In the sections that follow, I describe the different models. Their features are summarized in Table 2-2.

Table 2-2	Comparing Mac Desktops			
	Mac mini	*iMac (21-inch)*	*iMac (27-inch)*	*Mac Pro*
Screen size (inches diagonal)	None	21.5	27	None
Resolution built-in (pixels)	N/A	1920 x 1080	2560 x 1440	N/A
Resolution external (pixels)	2560 x 1600	2560 x 1600	2560 x 1600	2560 x 1600

	Mac mini	*iMac (21-inch)*	*iMac (27-inch)*	*Mac Pro*
Screen finish	N/A	Glossy	Glossy	N/A
Weight	2.7 lbs.	20.5 lbs.	30.5 lbs.	41 lbs.
	1.22 kg	9.3 kg	13.8 kg	18.7 kg
CPU	Quad-core i5 or i7	Quad-core i5 or i7	Quad-core i5 or i7	Xeon 4, 6, 8, or 12 cores
Speed (GHz)	2.3–2.5	2.5–2.8	2.7–3.4	2.4–3.3
Maximum RAM	8GB	16GB	16GB	32–64GB
Graphics	Integrated	Radeon HD6750M	Radeon HD6770M	Radeon HD5770
Optional graphics	Radeon HD 6630M	Radeon 6770M	Radeon HD6970M	Radeon HD5870 or two 5770s
PCI Express slots	None	None	None	3
Optical SuperDrive	None	1	1	1 or 2
Thunderbolt port	Yes	Yes	2	2 Mini DisplayPorts
HDMI port	1920 x 1200	No	No	Dual-link DVI
USB 2.0 ports	4	4	4	5
Gigabit Ethernet ports	1	1	1	2
FireWire ports (800 MHz)	1	1	1	4
SDXC Card slot	Yes	Yes	Yes	No
Wi-Fi	802.11n	802.11n	802.11n	802.11n
Bluetooth	Yes	Yes	Yes	Yes
FaceTime HD Camera	No	Yes	Yes	No
Microphone	No	Yes	Yes	Yes
Headset jack	Yes	Yes	Yes	Yes, plus Toslink jack
Audio in jack	Yes	Yes	Yes	Yes, plus Toslink jack

Starting small: The Mac mini

The mini is Apple's least-expensive Macintosh model. As its name implies, it's quite small — about the size of an external DVD drive. Aimed in part at PC users who are considering switching to a Mac, it doesn't come with a keyboard, mouse, or video display. It can work with almost any video monitor. You can also use your USB keyboard and mouse, if you like, or order new ones from Apple.

The mini's small size (7.7 inches square by 1.4 inches high) and unobtrusive package fit almost anywhere and make it ideal for living-room home entertainment centers. It makes almost no noise and uses very little power when it's idle. Apple has adopted the mini's quiet styling for other products, including the AirPort Extreme base station and Apple TV. In Figure 2-5, you can see the mini's simple appearance from the front.

Figure 2-5:
The petite
Mac mini.

Photo courtesy of Apple, Inc.

The mini has an Intel Core 2 Duo processor with up to 8GB of memory and an integrated graphics processor with the ability to drive two high-resolution displays. The low-price version has a 500GB hard drive. You can special-order one with a 256GB solid-state drive or a 256GB solid-state drive and a 750GB hard drive. Both models include AirPort Wi-Fi networking, Bluetooth, and an SD Card slot.

The mini's power button and all cable connections are on the back, as shown in Figure 2-6. These connections include

- Power connector for cable from separate power adapter
- Gigabit Ethernet
- FireWire 800 Mbps port
- HDMI external video
- Mini DisplayPort external video
- Four USB 2.0 ports

✔ Combined optical digital audio input/audio line in — 3.5mm minijack

✔ Combined optical digital audio output/headphone out — 3.5mm minijack

✔ Kensington cable lock slot for physical security

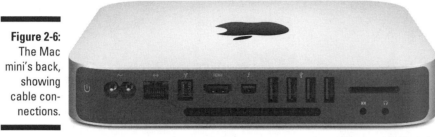

Figure 2-6:
The Mac
mini's back,
showing
cable con-
nections.

Photo courtesy of Apple, Inc.

The lowest-priced mini comes with 2GB of RAM. You'll probably want more. You can order it with more memory, have a computer store add memory for you, or install more memory yourself — there's a pop-up cover on the bottom with the memory modules readily accessible.

Apple also offers the mini configured as a computer server, with the internal CD-DVD drive replaced by a second hard drive. The mini server is aimed more at small offices than at the large server farms that run the Internet. It includes a license for Mac OS X Server software, with no limit on the number of clients. Several companies, including Macessity and Sonnet, offer rack mount kits for the mini.

Getting it all in one box: The iMac

The Apple iMac continues a tradition that goes back to the first, revolutionary Macintosh: packaging the computer and display as a single unit. Having it all in one box means a single power cord, fewer connecting cables, nothing to tuck under the desk, and less clutter all around. And who couldn't do with less clutter?

The current iMacs take this idea one step further. All you have on your desk, besides your keyboard and mouse or trackpad, is what looks like an ordinary flat-panel display. Well, not quite ordinary: With an aluminum case and sculpted stand, it's well turned out. But that's all there is. The computer is tucked inside the display. All connections are in the back. Figure 2-7 shows the two iMac model sizes: 21.5 inches and 27 inches.

Figure 2-7:
The iMac
family with
Magic Mice.

Although the computer is out of sight, it has plenty of mind. The iMac can keep up with most desktop machines on the market.

Each iMac sports a built-in FaceTime HD camera for videoconferencing and chat. Each has an Intel i5 or i7 quad-core microprocessor, AirPort Wi-Fi, Gigabit Ethernet, built-in microphone, and audio in and out. The built-in stereo speakers are powered by a 24-watt digital amplifier, with ample volume for watching videos or listening to music. Both models come with a wireless keyboard and Apple's Magic Mouse or Magic Trackpad.

Both have four USB 2.0 ports and one 800 MHz FireWire port. The 21.5-inch model has one Thunderbolt port; the 27-inch model has two. All ports are neatly lined up along the bottom-left corner of the iMac as you face the rear, so there's no more groping under the desk to get at cable connections.

The lower-cost model is good enough for most ordinary uses. The next model up offers a lush 27-inch display, more RAM, and a larger hard drive for not that much more money. If you have more to spend, you can order up to 16GB of RAM, a terabyte of hard drive space, faster CPU chips, and more capable graphics processors. (See "Getting the Right Graphics Processor," later in this chapter, for the advantages of more powerful graphics.) The larger screen of the 27-inch model lets you have more open windows onscreen when you're doing complex tasks like editing a video or researching a paper. And with dual Thunderbolt ports, you can add two more widescreen monitors and surround yourself with so much information that your head might explode. Or you could win a Nobel Prize, like Al Gore, who owns such a setup.

Computer displays aren't as bright as flat-screen television sets, but if you don't mind dimming the lights in your living room, you can build a complete home entertainment center with an iMac and an HDTV tuner, such as the eyeTV from www.elgato.com. It's a helpful solution for a small apartment.

An optional VESA mounting kit, available from the Apple Store, meets the Video Electronics Standards Association (VESA) Flat Display Mounting Interface (FDMI) standard, allowing you to attach a 27-inch iMac to a third-party VESA mounting device.

Maxing out with a Mac

If you have a big budget and need lots of computing power, Apple has the answer. In the following section, you find out about the stand-alone Mac Pro.

Mac Pro

As its name suggests, the Mac Pro is Apple's most capable Macintosh. The base model comes with a quad-core Intel Xeon processor. Maxed out, it can hold dual Intel Xeon six-core processors, 8TB (8 terabytes) of hard drive space, and 64GB of RAM in eight DIMM slots that incorporate error-correcting codes (ECC) for greater reliability. That's 12 very fast computers in one box.

Although most Macs are designed with the expectation that their cases will never be opened, the Mac Pro is a major exception. It's built into a full tower–size case that opens easily to give you access to most Mac Pro components. Figure 2-8 shows a Mac Pro with the cabinet splayed open to reveal its insides.

Also unlike with other Macs, you have room inside for expansion. The units contain four hard drive bays, and you can install dual SuperDrive optical drives. Apple typically offers several configurations for the Pro with different graphics cards for high, very high, and extreme performance. Check www.apple.com/macpro for their latest offerings.

Three additional full-length PCI Express (PCIe) slots are available for plug-in cards, which allow expansion of your Mac's capabilities. These are the same types of expansion cards used in newer PCs. They aren't compatible with the older PCI, PCI-X, or ISA cards, however. The PCI Express slots can hold high-speed communications cards, such as Fibre Channel, or as many as three more graphics cards for a maximum of four. A total 300 watts of power are available just to power these cards. The whole Mac Pro can draw 12 amps at 120 volts — half that at 240 volts. If your office is a bit chilly, convince your boss that you need one of these puppies under your desk to keep you toasty warm.

The Mac Pro has two connector panels: a main one in back, shown in Figure 2-9, and a smaller one in front.

Figure 2-8:
The Mac
Pro, opened
up.

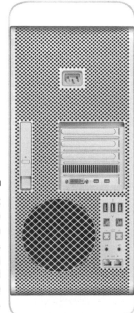

Figure 2-9:
Mac Pro
from
the back,
showing
slots and
cable
connections.

The rear panel includes

- ✔ Three USB 2.0 ports
- ✔ Two FireWire 800 Mbps ports
- ✔ Optical digital audio input and output Toslink ports
- ✔ Analog stereo line-level input and output minijacks
- ✔ Two independent Gigabit Ethernet ports

The front panel conveniently supplies

- ✔ Two more FireWire 800 Mbps ports
- ✔ Two more USB 2.0 ports
- ✔ Stereo headphone minijack

Bluetooth and Wi-Fi are standard on the Mac Pro.

You can also order the Mac Pro as a server with Lion Server edition installed.

Xsan and RAID

Xsan is Apple's storage-area network (SAN) software. A *storage-area network* aggregates all disk drives in the local-area network into a single entity, allowing all servers to access that data at the same time. It can support up to 2 petabytes of data. (That's 2 million gigabytes.) It can be used with commercial RAID (Redundant Array of Inexpensive Disks) systems such as the VTrak from `www.promise.com/apple`.

Getting the Right Graphics Processor

In modern personal computers, a graphics processor (GPU) takes over from the central processing unit much of the work of generating visual displays. All current Apple models come with GPUs designed to perform the intricate mathematical calculations needed to render 3D objects realistically at speeds fast enough to keep up with real-time game play and capable of driving two high-definition displays simultaneously at full resolution. Virtual reality becomes more real than life.

Apple supports a variety of models in its Macintosh line:

- ✔ **Integrated GPU:** Lower-end Apple models use an Intel HD 3000 graphics processor that's integrated with the processor chipset. The integrated graphics processors are fast and quite respectable for watching and editing videos, engaging in moderate 3D game play, or visiting 3D virtual-reality worlds such as Second Life. The integrated GPUs are a compromise, however. They share memory and the CPU, and they can't use too much power, which further limits their performance. High-end videogames have to be set to lower resolution to work properly with integrated GPUs.

✔ **Graphics cards:** Separate graphics card**s** have their own memory, offer significantly better graphics performance, and can keep up with more games. The iMacs and the 15- and 17-inch MacBook Pros add a second ATI Radeon graphics processor, and you can order them with even better graphics cards. You can also order a Mac mini with fast Radeon graphics.

If you're into serious game play or professional video work and need the highest performance, the Mac Pro blasts out graphics with top-end PCI Express graphics cards. ATI, now owned by AMD, and NVIDIA vigorously compete to be king of the graphics hill. Each has loyal fans. You likely have used one or both of these companies' products in your PC experience, and you may have your own opinion.

Adding On and Filling In

Apple is judicious in its choice of the peripherals and other accessories it provides. Although it was among the first company to sell laser printers, for example, it no longer brands its own printers but supports most models made by others. For the most part, printers just work on a Mac as long as they have a USB, Ethernet, or Wi-Fi connection.

Apple does offer displays and other hardware, software, and support packages, which may come with your Mac or which you can purchase as add-ons. The following sections explain the most popular options to help you decide what you may want — or want to ignore.

Apple 27-inch Thunderbolt display

Apple sells an attractively styled but pricy ($999) flat-panel display: the 27-inch Apple LED Thunderbolt HD Display, with 2560 x 1600 resolution.

The 27-inch display is designed to serve as a docking station for Apple laptops. It includes a FaceTime HD camera; a microphone; 2.1 speakers with a 49 watt amp; a built-in 85 watt power supply that can charge any Apple MagSafe laptop; and a complete set of peripheral ports that includes Thunderbolt, Gigabit Ethernet, 800 MHz FireWire, and three powered USB 2.0 ports. The display's cable to your computer has just two plugs: MagSafe power, and

Thunderbolt, so it's easy to dock your Mac laptop. You can use the 27-inch display with a Mac mini or Pro or as a second display for your iMac (it looks just like an iMac) and still use the MagSafe as a charger for your laptop. There's also a Kensington security slot to keep your Thunderbolt Display on your desk while you're on the road.

An optional VESA mounting kit is available from the Apple Store, allowing you to attach your Apple display to a third-party VESA mounting device, including a variety of fancy mounting brackets and arms that use the VESA system.

Time Capsule Wi-Fi base station and backup disk

The Apple Time Capsule combines a Wi-Fi base station and a 1TB or 2TB backup hard drive. Wi-Fi connects computers and other devices in your home or office without running wires. Those computers, PCs and Macs, can access the Time Capsule hard drive over your wireless network. Macs can also use Time Capsule to make automatic backups with the Apple Time Machine backup software, as described in Chapter 5.

In a normal installation, you run an Ethernet cable from the back of the Time Capsule, shown in Figure 2-10, to your high-speed Internet-connected modem: cable, DSL, or satellite. If you're in a school or an office that has a direct Internet connection, plug your Ethernet cable into that connection.

Figure 2-10: Time Capsule, shown from the back.

Photo courtesy of Apple, Inc.

Time Capsule comes with these features:

✔ **Support for all Wi-Fi standards:** Time Capsule supports all current Wi-Fi standards, including 802.11a, b, g, and n. Therefore, it should work with just about any Wi-Fi–equipped computer and other Wi-Fi devices, such as the iPhone and Apple TV.

✔ **Two frequency bands:** Time Capsule operates on both Wi-Fi frequency bands, 2.4 and 5 GHz, simultaneously for maximum range and performance.

✔ **Broad support for security standards:** The security standards basically keep anyone parked on the street or your next-door neighbor from hopping onto your network to use your Internet access. Time Capsule supports all the Wi-Fi security standards — WEP, WPA, WPA2, 802.11X, Radius, and so on — and includes a firewall. I tell you how to turn on Wi-Fi security in Chapter 10.

✔ **Parental controls:** You can set permissible times for access for each authorized computer, which is great for limiting kids' access.

✔ **Even more ports:** Time Capsule does more than just supply high-speed Internet to any Wi-Fi device within range — which, by the way, is about 150 feet (50 meters), though your footage may vary. In the rear (refer to Figure 2-10), it has three local Ethernet ports so that you can hook up computers that lack Wi-Fi capability, or if you prefer the greater speed and security of a wired connection. It also has a USB 2.0 port that lets you attach a printer that can be shared by your network. Alternatively, you can attach a second USB hard drive and then share it over the network.

What's that? You want *both* a printer *and* a hard drive? Don't be so greedy. Okay, okay. But you need to get a USB 2.0 hub. It's inexpensive, and then you can have multiple printers and multiple hard drives. Go wild.

Time Capsule is styled like the Mac mini. It's 7.7 inches (197mm) square (same as the mini), weighs 3.5 pounds (0.753 kg), and runs on 100–240V AC — no separate power brick required.

AirPort Extreme Wi-Fi base station

AirPort Extreme is basically a Time Capsule without the built-in hard drive. As supplied, AirPort Extreme provides the same Wi-Fi base-station services as Time Capsule and has the same set of connectors on its back, including a USB port for a printer or hard drive. Add a big hard drive, and you get the Time Capsule backup functions, but with more boxes and wires.

The AirPort Extreme is also styled like the Mac mini. Its footprint is 6.5 inches (165mm) square, and it weighs 1.66 pounds (0.753 kg). It comes with an AC power adapter but runs on 12 VDC, so you can put one in your car to run a Wi-Fi network at your next geek picnic.

AirPort Express, a Wi-Fi relay

The AirPort Express is smaller and simpler than the AirPort Extreme. The AirPort Express looks like the Apple laptop power supply (see Figure 2-11). It even has the same "duck's head" snap-off power connector.

Figure 2-11:
The AirPort Express, plugged in.

Photo courtesy of Apple, Inc.

Although AirPort Express can function as a Wi-Fi base station to share an Internet connection, it's intended more to serve as a relay and an audio interface so that you can pipe music from iTunes to your home entertainment system. It supports the 802.11b and g signaling speeds.

AirPort Express has just four connections:

- ✔ An AC wall plug (just stick it in any outlet)
- ✔ An Ethernet port
- ✔ A USB 2.0 port
- ✔ A combined optical digital audio output/headphone out — 3.5mm minijack

The USB port supports a shared printer. The audio port can connect to your stereo. You just need a 3.5mm stereo phone plug–to–RCA phone plug adapter cable. You can get one from the Apple Store or your local Radio Shack. If you have more than one sound system, you can install multiple AirPort Express units.

You can pack the AirPort Express in your suitcase and use it to create a Wi-Fi network in your hotel if the hotel has only wired Internet.

iPhone, iPad, and iPod

If you haven't yet heard of the Apple iPad tablet, the iPod portable music player, or the revolutionary iPhone, please return this book for a full refund. These devices are everywhere and have changed the way we surf the 'Net, listen to music, and use our cellphones.

Although iPhones, iPads, and iPods work fine with PCs, they're particularly well integrated with Macs and their digital-lifestyle applications, including Mail, Address Book, iChat, and iPhoto. I talk more about the iPad, iPod, iPhone, and the mothership — the iTunes Store — in Chapter 11.

Apple TV (TV)

Apple TV is a small box that bridges the Internet, your Macintosh or Windows PC, and your big-screen home entertainment center. It can stream video from the Internet, including popular sources like YouTube and Netflix. Apple TV also plays videos that you stored or rented on iTunes from your computer or even from your iPhone, iPad, or iPod touch. You can play music from your iTunes library and display your photos at high definition in your living room. Apple TV connects your home computer network (Mac or PC) to your living-room electronics suite in several ways:

- AirPort/Wi-Fi 802.11n for fast access to your wireless network
- High-Definition Multimedia Interface (HDMI) for high-definition video and audio
- Optical audio for the latest sound systems
- 10/100 Base-T Ethernet if you prefer a wired connection to your computer
- Micro USB for service and support
- Infrared receiver for use with the Apple Remote (one comes with the Apple TV)

The Apple TV is tiny, as you can see in Figure 2-12: 3.9 inches (98mm) square and less than an inch high (just 23 mm). It weighs 0.6 pounds (272 grams). Its power cord connects directly to a wall outlet or a power strip, with no space-hogging power adapter. We don't need *their kind* in our living rooms.

Figure 2-12:
Apple TV and Remote, hooked up to your high-definition television.

Support

Apple doesn't just sell hardware; it also *supports* that hardware (and software). Most Apple products come with 90-day free telephone support and a one-year warranty on the hardware, subject to the usual fine print that says it's limited and doesn't cover products hurled into active volcanoes, used to stop stampeding elephants, and subjected to other forms of abuse. In my experience, Apple gives customers the benefit of the doubt.

Each Apple retail store includes a Genius Bar — a section at or near the back of the shop where Apple-trained experts are available to answer your questions and provide technical support for Apple products. The service is free, but it's best to make an appointment, which you can do online at `www.apple.com/retail/geniusbar`.

The following sections introduce you to the three big support programs that Apple offers as add-ons.

AppleCare

AppleCare extends the phone service and warranty that come with your Mac, usually to three years, but always check the terms before you buy.

Service policies are a form of insurance. If they're priced properly, you pay a bit more for the policy than your losses are likely to be on average. But the term *on average* is the kicker. If something goes wrong with your computer after the warranty expires, repairs can be very expensive — often, a good fraction of the cost of a new machine. Portable devices, like laptops and iPads, take a lot of abuse. For a new Mac user, I think that the free phone support and peace of mind justify the added cost.

One to One

If you'd like additional support while you're switching to a Mac, consider a $99 one-year membership in Apple's One to One support program. Apple will even set up your Mac and transfer the files from your PC.

OS X upgrades

OS X is included with new Macs. The version you get has a number, such as 10.7.2. Here's what that number means:

- ✔ The *10* refers to OS X. *X* is the Roman numeral 10.

- ✔ The *.7* is a major release; 10.7 is also known by its not-so-secret Apple code name, Lion.

- ✔ The *.2* is a minor upgrade, known as a *point release* that typically includes bug fixes, security improvements, minor feature enhancements, and support for new hardware.

Apple traditionally provides point releases and other minor changes, such as security patches, for free via its Software Update service. You're notified about the availability of such changes once a week unless you change the settings.

Expect major releases every 18 months to 2 years. Apple charges for these releases, but the last two releases, Snow Leopard and Lion, cost only $30 for an upgrade. When a major new operating system release comes out, it's usually a good idea to wait a bit to see whether it receives negative reviews or whether the upgrade breaks programs that you use. (Lion eliminated support of older PowerPC applications, for example.) But Apple upgrades have been relatively painless, and the added features are usually worth the expense, so expect to buy an upgrade at least once in the lifetime of your Mac.

Application software offerings

Although Macs come with an impressive array of easy-to-use applications that are ready to go, Apple sells several additional software tools. They break down into three groups, roughly by price and power.

Small, extra-cost upgrades

Apple has a few of these upgrades, including Jam Packs that add music and tools to GarageBand.

Advanced applications

These applications typically sell in the $80-to-$300 price range and are suitable for quality commercial work. They include the following:

- **Aperture:** Aperture is the top-of-the-line Apple solution for professional photographers.

- **Bento:** This simple-to-use, inexpensive but powerful personal database syncs with versions for the iPad, iPhone, and iPod touch.

- **FileMaker Pro:** This full-featured database application is also available in a fully compatible version for Windows.

- **iWork:** This Apple office suite includes the Pages word processor and page-layout program; Numbers spreadsheet program; and Keynote, Apple's answer to Microsoft PowerPoint presentation software.

- **Logic Express:** Logic Express is a powerful music-creation package.

Pro applications

These applications are world-class solutions that hold their own against any solutions on the market and are generally less expensive than their top competitors:

- **Final Cut Pro X:** Final Cut Pro X gives you everything you need to edit and post-produce a full-length feature motion picture or a TV series. Movies edited in earlier versions have won an Emmy and received one Oscar nomination.

- **Logic Pro:** This application is a powerful music-composition tool that I don't begin to understand.

Server software solutions

Mac makes a mean server version of OS X, and the full version is licensed without the per-seat head tax that brand-M imposes. Server products include

- Apple Remote Desktop
- FileMaker Server, which doesn't require OS X Server
- Mac OS X Server
- WebObjects for Java server applications
- Xsan Storage Area Network (SAN) for Mac OS X

Green Apples

Many people insist that the corporations they buy from address the impact of the corporation on global warming and other environmental problems. Apple takes these concerns seriously and has moved aggressively to make its products green. Some of the steps Apple has taken include

- **Improving the energy efficiency of its products, especially when they're in idle or standby mode:** Idle computers consume substantial amounts of electricity, which releases carbon dioxide — a major cause of global warming. All Macs meet stringent Energy Star 4.0 requirements. See www.energystar.gov.

- **Designing its products to be easy to recycle:** Apple fabricates the chassis of new Macs from aluminum, which is particularly easy to recycle and commands high scrap value.

- **Using LED backlighting in displays:** LED backlighting is more energy-efficient than the fluorescent lamps that Apple and other companies previously used. LEDs are also mercury-free.

- **Eliminating the use of hazardous chemicals in making circuit boards, cables, and other components for its computers:** These components are now free of BFR and PVC, and comply with European Union hazardous-material reduction regulations (RoHS).

- **Reducing size of its packaging:** Less packaging means less waste.

- **Providing a carbon life-cycle analysis of its products:** This is something that few companies do. You can find these reports at www.apple.com/environment/.

- **Taking back old computers and displays (even PCs) when you buy a new Mac:** Apple recycles computers collected in North America at carefully vetted facilities; it doesn't ship equipment overseas for disposal. To find out about its recycling programs, see www.apple.com/environment/recycling.

Also, Apple computers tend to last longer than PCs do, and much of the energy consumption and other environmental damage during a computer's lifetime happens during its manufacturing. For more information on green Apples, visit www.apple.com/environment. I suggest other beneficial ways to use your computer in Chapter 21.

Chapter 3

Deciding What to Buy

- -

In This Chapter

▶ Selecting a conversion strategy

▶ Figuring out where all those wires go

▶ Using what you already have

▶ Picking the right options for your Mac

▶ Deciding where to buy

- -

*B*uying a computer can be a bewildering experience. Stores are stuffed with oodles of models in different shapes and sizes, and those models are offered in a wide range of prices. Many of the options you're asked to select involve options that only a geek could love, like the number of bytes of RAM to buy (what if I don't like lamb?) and the hard drive capacity (what if I prefer a soft drive?).

Computer-store salespeople can be helpful, but all too often, they give questionable advice. Many aren't knowledgeable about the latest features and software. Sometimes, they receive financial incentives to sell in-stock models that aren't moving.

Buying a Macintosh simplifies things quite a bit. Apple has only half a dozen or so models and relatively few options for each one. It doesn't sell cheap, lowball models that require expensive upgrades to do anything useful. The lowest-price Apple models can more than meet the needs of most users.

Still, you need to make choices, and you generally should make your decision (or at least narrow it to a couple of possibilities) before you go off to the store or log on to Apple.com.

In this chapter, you find tips that can help you decide which type of Mac suits your needs. (If you skipped the two preceding chapters, I give a detailed introduction to the different models in Chapter 2.) Switching to a Mac may also affect how you connect your computer accessories and access the features you need, because your new Mac is likely an upgrade to better technology and because some ports and options on new Macs are different from those on older Windows computers. In this chapter, you find the most important concepts you need to know, and I provide a section at the end that helps you decide where to buy.

Selecting a Conversion Strategy

Time to take a deep breath. Before I dig into which model and which options to buy, I want you to think about what you're trying to accomplish and then consider the best way to get exactly what you want. (I'm just talking about computers here — don't get too excited.) There's more than one way to peel an Apple.

To begin, answer the following questions honestly (the mind-reading chip in the spine of this book is automatically disabled when you're on this page, so no one will know your answers):

- **How often do you use your computer?** Is it less than once a week, several times a week, every day, or hours each day?
- **What do you use your computer for?** Do you crunch numbers in a spreadsheet, write *For Dummies* books, check social-networking sites such as Facebook.com and Google+, surf the Internet, text friends, look for soulmates, download music, or play games?
- **Which new tasks do you want to use it for?** Do you want to organize photos, develop a website or podcast, or edit movies?
- **Where do you use your computer?** Do you use it in a den or office, anywhere in the house you feel like, at work only, at work and at home, or on the road?
- **What's your budget?** Are you limited to spending less than $1,000, less than $2,000, or will you spend whatever it takes the get the very best performance? Remember, even a top-of-the-line Mac Pro costs less than the first Macs and IBM PCs did.

Depending on your answers, you have several switching approaches to consider. I try to group them sensibly and give the categories cute, easy-to-remember names.

I'm not a big fan of computers for small children. They spend, and will spend, too much of their lives in front of video screens as it is. But if you're buying a computer for your kid or kids, make sure that you understand how to set limits. OS X has some useful features, called Parental Controls, to help you enforce them. Before buying anything, be sure to look carefully at the section in Chapter 17 that discusses Macs for kids.

Taking it slow

No need to rush things. The Mac mini is perfect if you're the cautious type who wants to convert gradually and not spend a lot of money. Start out with worry-free Internet surfing and switch over additional applications as you become more comfortable with OS X. You can use the spiffy iLife applications that come with the Mac mini as soon as you set it up, of course.

Taking it slowly, which can be the lowest-cost conversion strategy, assumes that you already have a fairly up-to-date PC set up, with a good-quality flat-panel or CRT display. All you really need to buy is a Mac mini. The tiny mini doesn't take up much room; it's not much bigger than an external hard drive. Just find a spare outlet for it on your power strip.

If you don't have a compatible USB keyboard and mouse, you can add those items to your shopping list — literally. Many supermarkets now carry these accessories. (But I recommend getting a keyboard designed for Macs — from Apple or a third-party vendor such as McAlly— if you're replacing the keyboard you have now.)

For extra convenience, purchase a USB *KVM switch,* which lets you share a keyboard, mouse, and display between two computers. (More-expensive KVM models can support more than two computers.) In a KVM setup, you can work on the PC, press a special key combination on your keyboard, quickly switch to the Mac to check a website, and then return to the PC with another key press. Be sure to buy a USB KVM switch, not the more common PS/2 type. (I'm assuming that your PC is new enough to have a USB port. If it isn't, you need a separate keyboard and mouse for your Mac.) I tell you more about which items to buy later in this chapter, in the section KVM switch, and I describe how to hook up a KVM switch in Chapter 4.

If your PC is already part of a Wi-Fi wireless network, you can easily incorporate the mini into the network. If you don't have one, you may need an Ethernet or Wi-Fi router and a cable — inexpensive items. See Chapter 9 for details.

Macs tend to keep their resale value longer than PCs do, so you aren't taking much of a financial risk with this approach. If you aren't happy with the Mac mini, you probably won't have any trouble unloading it on eBay or Craigslist.

Living on the go

If you travel a lot, or simply like to work or be online in different parts of your house, a MacBook Air or MacBook Pro laptop may be just right for you. If you need to bring your computer to work and also have it at home, you probably already have a laptop, but maybe you want something more up to date.

Mac laptops are complete, powerful computer systems. They're elegant-looking and priced competitively with all but the cheapest PC laptops. You can buy one and still keep your PC setup intact. These laptops can network with your PC, just like the mini, and share your printer.

Giving your PC the heave-ho

Maybe you're the type who just dives into the pool without dipping your toe in first. You may as well plan on just replacing your PC with a new Mac. I tell you how to transfer all your files in Chapter 6. Either the iMac or MacBook Pro model can take your old PC's place in the home:

✔ **A desktop iMac can fit on your desk where the PC display now sits.**

If you have a good-quality video display and enough room, you can keep your display on your desk and plug it into the iMac for two-screen computing. You need a video adapter cable. Then all you have to do is tell the iMac where the other display sits relative to the iMac, in System Preferences —> Display, so that OS X knows how to match them up to allow you to drag windows from one screen to the other, across the adjacent screen edges.

✔ **If your only computer is a laptop, switching to a MacBook Air or MacBook Pro is simple.** If the PC laptop has Wi-Fi networking, the two laptops should talk to each other without much ado, allowing you to transfer files. (See Chapter 9.) Otherwise, a simple Ethernet cable should do the trick. Mac OS X Lion includes a utility program called Windows Migration Assistant that simplifies the process — or buy the Apple One to One plan, discussed later in this chapter, and let Apple transfer the files. If the laptop is so old that it has no network port, or the network port isn't working you have to get a bit more creative, and I cover those details in Chapter 6.

Spending lots of dough

If you have the money, I recommend a Mac Pro with the large Apple Thunderbolt Display — or, even better, two Thunderbolt displays. (Al Gore has three.) It'll knock your socks off. And while you're at it, grab a thin, light MacBook Air laptop to take with you on trips, and some MacBooks and iPads that other family members can use. (You weren't going to stick your kids or spouse with that old PC, were you?)

Why not Linux?

You have another way to escape the clutches of Microsoft that's cheaper than buying a new Mac. No doubt you've heard of Linux, an operating system developed by volunteer computer programmers. Linux is closely related to the Unix operating system that underlies Mac OS X, but differences exist. Linux was once a toy for übergeeks, but it has come a long way. Some people now use it as their only personal computer operating system. You probably can use it with your existing PC hardware. Linux still lacks the polish and ease of use of a Mac or even a Windows PC, however. If you're technically inclined and want to find out how operating systems work, by all means give Linux a try. Readers of this book are probably better off with a commercially supported operating system. The good news is that much of the software that runs on Linux also runs on Macs.

Gaming glow

Does playing computer games, particularly those with detailed three-dimensional visuals, dominate your computer use? Your life? If so, you may not be happy with the lower end of the Mac line (the cheapest mini, the MacBook, and the 13-inch MacBook Pro). All use a built-in Intel 3000 graphics processor that's quite powerful but not able to keep pace with the most demanding games. But for higher performance, the one-notch-up mini, the 15- and 17-inch MacBook Pros, the iMacs, and the Mac Pro blast out 3D imagery with more powerful graphics engines. The Mac Pro accepts graphics cards from either ATI or NVIDIA.

Relaxing as a couch potat-oh

Computers are invading our living rooms. The home entertainment center is going online. Channel surfing is merging with Internet surfing. If nothing on the tube is worth watching, try YouTube. If you want to integrate your Mac with your TV watching, you have these options:

- ✔ **Set up a few cables and then relax:** All Macs have video outputs designed to display stunning images on large-format, high-definition TVs and displays — though you probably need adapter cables. See the section "Ports that require an adapter for Macs," later in this chapter.

- ✔ **Integrate your computer and TV:** The simple-to-use, $99 Apple TV (TV) coupled with a Mac mini can let you effortlessly switch among broadcast content, an Internet feed, home movies and slide shows, and other video material. You can also download free home theater applications such as XBMC, Boxee, or Plex and use your Mac mini's HDMI output to directly drive your monster TV.

✔ **Never get off the sofa:** Alternatively, you can buy just the Apple TV, which connects with any Macs and Windows PCs, as well as iPads, iPhones, and late model iPod Touches, around your house by way of wireless (or wired) Ethernet. You can play downloaded digital content — movies, TV shows, music videos, songs — as well as home videos and photos right on your large-screen HDTV or projection system. It's all controlled by the tiny Apple Remote.

Getting a Mac for less

Bargain hunting is harder in the Mac world than it is in the PC world. Generally, price reductions happen most often when the inventory of a product is too high or when a new product is about to be introduced. Because so many PC manufacturers exist, these supply problems happen often for PCs. Apple, however, has better control of its distribution chain and tries very hard to keep Macintosh clearance sales from happening. They still do appear, but nowhere nearly as often as with PCs, and even when they do, the price cuts are rarely as dramatic. If you're ready to buy a Mac, it's not worth waiting months for one of these sales. Peripheral devices such as printers, scanners, and hard drives are another matter; they're often discounted. Also, Apple sometimes offers refurbished Macs at its online store. They typically come with the standard Apple warranty. You can search the Apple Store with the keyword *refurbished* to find what's on sale.

Apple often offers an education discount, so if you have an affiliation with an educational institution (student, teacher, staff member), bring ID with you when you visit the Apple Store. In my experience, the store staff is liberal in which types of ID it accepts.

I don't recommend buying a used Mac in most cases. There's something about unpacking a brand-new machine and setting it up that builds confidence. You know that the stuff was recently tested at the factory and should work. You have Apple tech support and, possibly, the people at the retail store to call on if you have trouble. In the worst case, you can return the Mac for a refund. Switching from one computer system to another is a complex-enough task without having to worry about possible hardware problems. Also you may not find much of a bargain; Macs tend to command higher prices on the used market than PCs of comparable vintage. But if you want to try your luck on the used market, here are some tips:

✔ Buy locally, such as from www.craigslist.org or someone you know, and pick up your Mac in person. That way, you can check it out before you hand over money. You also avoid the risk of product damage during shipping.

✔ Buy only a used Mac that has an Intel processor. Choose the About This Mac option from the Apple (🍎) menu to see the processor type. Macs sold before 2006 use a different microprocessor, the PowerPC (or, if they're really old, a Motorola 68k series). These models are significantly slower, and Apple support for PowerPC machines is winding down. (The 68k models are for antique computer collectors only — a fun hobby but not what this book is about.)

✔ If possible, find a machine that has time remaining on an AppleCare contract.

✔ Don't pay more than the price of a new, low-end Mac. A new basic machine will likely approach or exceed the performance of a more advanced but older model, for example, and you receive all the benefits of a new unit.

Following the KISS principle

KISS stands for "Keep it simple, stupid." Whichever way you go, I recommend that you start with your Mac configured pretty much the way it is when it comes out of the box. You can customize lots of settings, and you can download software add-ons. But the fewer of these things you do, the less likely you are to get into trouble and the easier it is to obtain support. Later in this book, I mention a few customizations that I think are worthwhile.

Figuring Out What's on Your Windows Computer

Before deciding what to buy, figure out what's on your existing computer. You want your new Mac to have at least the capabilities of your present computer, plus lots of room to grow. You may know some of this information, and much of it may be on the sales receipt or the original box your computer came in. If you've added options and peripherals, however, that info may be out of date.

If you're having trouble with your PC, skip this section for now, and see the section on recovering data from a damaged PC in Chapter 6.

The easiest way to find the information on your current configuration is to ask Windows to give it to you. Follow these steps:

1. **Choose Start⇨My Computer (or just "Computer" on Windows 7).**

   The My Computer window should appear, and you should see a section labeled Hard Disk Drives. If more than one drive is shown, start with the drive labeled C:.

2. **Select your C drive and then choose File⇨Properties (or right-click the drive and choose Properties from the contextual menu).**

   Figure 3-1 shows the Local Disk C: Properties dialog box, which tells you how much disk space is used and how much is available.

3. **Make a note of the drive's total capacity and how much of it is used space.**

   The numbers to the right, shown in gigabytes (GB), are all you need. You can organize your notes in the following form:

Drive letter	C:_____	_____	_____
Total capacity	_____	_____	_____
Used space	_____	_____	_____

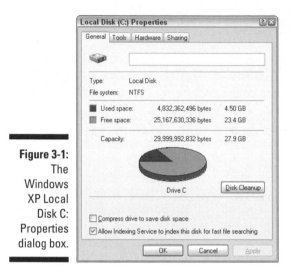

Figure 3-1:
The
Windows
XP Local
Disk C:
Properties
dialog box.

4. **When you're done, click the Cancel button to close the drive's Properties dialog box.**

5. **Repeat this procedure for any other hard drives shown in the My Computer window.**

6. **You should see, at the bottom of the My Computer window, the Control Panel icon; click it.**

   Alternatively, you can select the Control Panel directly from the Start menu. When the Control Panel window appears, double-click the System icon.

7. **On the General tab of the System Properties dialog box that appears (see Figure 3-2), make a note of the following information:**

   • Operating system (for example, Microsoft Windows XP or Windows 7)

   • Edition (for example, Home)

   • Last installed Service Pack (for example, SP2)

   • Manufacturer and model number

   • Speed (for example, 1.8 GHz)

   • Amount of main memory (for example, 500MB RAM)

Figure 3-2:
Windows
XP system
information.

Navigating from PC to Mac Ports

When you're deciding which Mac model to buy (and what you can afford), you need to figure out which of the devices you already own will work with your selected model. Unfortunately, few things about computers are as confusing and annoying as the bowl of spaghetti wiring underneath the desk. That's why you find in this section a quick guide to what goes where in the Mac world. Much of it is the same as on a modern PC, but some old favorites are no longer with us. In many cases, you can buy adapters to make the necessary connections; in other cases . . . well, it's time to move on.

Finding your way around the back of a Mac

When you're trying to figure out where to plug in things, the good news is that Apple keeps things simple by limiting the number of ports it uses, and it has a good track record of picking the most useful ones. In the sections that follow, I summarize the ports available in new Macs now on the market. Except as noted, the ports in this section are common to all current Macs. They're also common on late-model PCs.

If a plug doesn't fit into a jack with a firm but modest push, don't try to force it in. Triple-check to make sure that the shapes and icons match; then look for dirt or other obstacles in both the plug and jack.

Audio input and output

All Macs come with one or two little round jacks that look like the earphone jacks on a portable radio or an iPod. One of them is marked with a tiny pair of earphones. The other, if present, is a *line-in* jack, which accepts audio from other devices. Both accept ⅛-inch (3.5mm) stereo plugs, and you can buy a wide variety of cables, adapters, and other accessories that work with them at your local Radio Shack. But on many models these diminutive jacks are much cleverer than that. They also can work with newer optical digital audio devices that use the *Toslink* standard, which is becoming more popular in the world of consumer electronics. If you shine a light down the little hole, you can see the tiny optical port in the center shining back at you. You'll need a Toslink cable and an adaptor for the 3.5mm jack, both of which are available from the Apple Store or www.xtrememac.com. Finally, on most models, the headphone jack works with the headsets that includes a microphone, which Apple sells for the iPhone.

Ethernet

Ethernet is the most popular technology for enabling computers to talk to each other over a wire. Ethernet came from the same Xerox lab that developed the graphical interface first popularized by the Mac. Ethernet is available in 10, 100, and 1,000 Mbps versions (the last is sometimes called Gigabit Ethernet). Most Macs support all three; the exception is the MacBook Air, which requires an optional separate adapter for wired Ethernet.

Ethernet connectors (<...>) look like fatter versions of the connectors used on most telephones in North America. Just like with the telephone connectors, you find a little, easy-to-break plastic tab that you have to squeeze to pull the connector out. Be gentle.

Don't plug your telephone line into this port — it could damage your computer. Current Macs don't have built-in telephone modems. Apple sells an external modem that plugs into a USB port.

Universal Serial Bus (USB)

Intel invented USB technology to let a wide variety of low- and medium-speed devices connect to a computer using only one type of port. Apple was the first to popularize it for use with keyboards and mice. USB is a *bus* because more than one device can share the same port. *Serial* means that all the data marches down a single pair of wires.

All new Macs have one or more USB 2.0 ports, which you identify by the pitchfork logo. USB 2.0 can support high-speed devices such as disk drives. Older USB 1.0 and 1.1 devices should plug in and work fine in a USB 2.0 port, though they can slow its performance. Apple has chosen not to add the newer, faster USB 3.0 ports to its products, instead opting for the even faster Thunderbolt standard, which I tell you about in a moment.

FireWire

Apple created a different serial bus, *FireWire,* to support connecting high-speed devices. Also known as IEEE-1394, FireWire comes in two speeds: 400 megabits per second (Mbps) and 800 Mbps. Several camcorder manufacturers adopted FireWire 400 (Sony calls it *i.Link),* but USB 2.0 is almost as fast, and most nontape video recorders now use USB 2.0. High-end Macs sport FireWire 800 ports, which use a different connector, although 800-to-400 cables are available and inexpensive. The FireWire logo looks like a bumpy *Y.*

Thunderbolt and Mini DisplayPort

All new Macs include a Thunderbolt port for video and ultra-high-speed data. Thunderbolt, developed in collaboration with Intel, combines two high-performance standards, Mini DisplayPort and PCI Express, into one unassuming cable connector. A Mini DisplayPort cable sends images to a display in digital form, preserving the images' full fidelity for viewing on flat-panel computer screens and high-definition televisions (HDTVs). Older (analog) methods of sending signals to displays, such as VGA, limit the quality of pictures that can be shown.

PCI Express is the same protocol that the newest PC motherboard expansion cards use — the classic open-the-cover-and-plug-a-card-in-the-motherboard model. Thunderbolt includes two PCI Express data channels, each operating at up to 10 Gigabits per second. That's twice as fast as USB 3.0 and 20 times as fast as USB 2.0. With Thunderbolt, you can enjoy the speed and flexibility of PCI Express for expansion devices without ever touching a screwdriver.

Thunderbolt uses the same connector as the Mini DisplayPort. You tell the difference by the logo. A Mini DisplayPort is tagged with a widescreen rectangle between two vertical bars, whereas Thunderbolt sports — surprise! — a lightning bolt. What happens if you plug a display with a Mini DisplayPort cable into a Thunderbolt port? It works just fine. In fact, things are even better than that. You can hook up more than one Thunderbolt device — say, hard drives or high-speed scanners — to a single port on your Mac. Each Thunderbolt device is supposed to have two jacks, so you can connect one device to your Mac using one of the jacks. The next device plugs into the second jack on the first device, and so on. At the very end of this *daisy chain* of high-speed devices, you can plug in a display with a Mini DisplayPort cable, and everything should work. Apple's Thunderbolt Display has an extra Thunderbolt jack, so it can sit in the middle of such a chain, as well as at the end.

Apple and other vendors sell converter cables that let you hook up Mini DisplayPort and Thunderbolt ports to most digital and analog video displays, including most large-screen television sets. Thunderbolt adapters for many other high-speed data cables, including perhaps USB 3, are expected to be available.

PCI Express cards (Mac Pro only)

If you really need actual PCI Express cards themselves, buy a Mac Pro. Of all Apple computers, only the Pro has these slots — four of them, one of which is typically occupied by the graphics card. You can use the slots for more graphics cards or for ultra-high-speed communications cards, and they're also handy for other specialized applications. These capabilities excite video producers and serious gamers, but if you don't know why you need an expansion card, you probably don't need one.

PCI Express isn't compatible with the older PCI or PCI-X cards.

Wi-Fi and Bluetooth

Strictly speaking, Wi-Fi and Bluetooth aren't ports, in that there's no place to connect a wire. That's because they support *wireless* communications. Wi-Fi is mostly used for networking computers within a home or office; it's essentially Ethernet without wires. Bluetooth has a shorter range and is mainly for connecting small devices (such as printers, wireless keyboards, and mice) and for wireless headsets of the type used with cellphones. Macs support both Wi-Fi and Bluetooth.

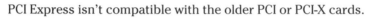

Infrared

Infrared (IR) is a form of invisible light that's used in most remote controls supplied with televisions, stereos, and other devices. When you press a button on the remote, it projects a beam of invisible light out the front that's coded with a signal that tells the TV or other device which button you pushed. A magic spot on your TV or device receives these IR signals, and if you point the remote in its general direction, the device should do what you want. An iMac can work with its own, optional Apple Remote, so it has a magic spot too. (Apple seems to be phasing out IR support on its Macs, so check with Apple before buying a remote for your new iMac.)

ExpressCard/34 (17-inch MacBook Pro only)

The ExpressCard/34 is an older standard for expansion modules, which are basically cards that you can slide into personal computers, though they're mostly used with laptops.

Only the 17-inch MacBook Pro has an ExpressCard/34 slot. Figure 3-3 shows a MacBook Pro with an ExpressCard/34 card installed to access Verizon Wireless Internet service. Accessing such a wide-area network is probably the most common use for the ExpressCard/34 slot, though USB has largely replaced even this application.

Figure 3-3:
Express-
Card/34
for wide-
area
networking
installed
in a
MacBook
Pro.

Camera memory cards

The Mac mini, the 13-inch MacBook Air, and the 13- and 15-inch MacBook Pros come with an SD Card slot, where you can plug in the SD Cards used in many digital cameras and camcorders. All but the Air can read the higher-capacity SDXC cards as well. Many other card types are out there, but Apple apparently chose not to clutter its spiffy boxes with half a dozen camera-card slots. USB adapters that accept most card types are inexpensive and readily available. Macally.com sells an ExpressCard Media Reader that works with a 17-inch MacBook Pro, and you can hook up most cameras directly by using a USB cable.

Ports that require an adapter for Macs

If you have a device with a connection type that a Mac doesn't support directly, you may still be able to connect your device by using an adapter. This section covers the types of connections that Macs no longer support but that you can still use with an adapter. By adding the adapters you need to your list of items to buy, you can set up your new Mac faster, with less hassle.

Before you buy any adapter, make sure that the manufacturer supports the latest version of Mac OS X. Many manufacturers don't support Macs, and some support only old versions of Mac OS. Also realize that when an adapter maker says that it supports OS X, that doesn't guarantee that your printer, scanner, or digital breadmaker will work perfectly. If you're buying new stuff, avoid peripherals that require an adapter.

Fiber Distributed Data Interface (FDDI): This high-performance data network sends information over optical fibers rather than wires. You need a Mac Pro and a PCI Express FDDI card, which Apple sells and supports. FDDI adapters are expected to become available for Thunderbolt.

High-Definition Multimedia Interface (HDMI): HDMI input is standard on most flat-panel and high-definition televisions. Although many HDTVs also allow analog input, HDMI is the input to use if you want the video quality you're paying those big bucks for. The Mac mini has an HDMI port, and vendors such as Monoprice.com sell adapters that let you connect a Mac with a Mini DisplayPort or Thunderbolt to that HDMI port. You may also need a separate connection for audio. You'll be amazed when your Mac's display fills your living-room wall. The mini's HDMI port also supports multichannel audio.

Musical Instrument Digital Interface (MIDI): This music-industry standard was introduced in 1983 for connecting musical keyboards (the ones with black-and-white ivories, not the kind you use to write e-mails). The Apple Core Audio framework offers strong MIDI support in software. Many new MIDI devices use USB or FireWire interfaces and work directly with Macs that have the appropriate interface. Older instruments may have a five-pin DIN connector — and yup, you need an adapter.

Modem: Macs no longer come with dialup modem ports (the type you can plug a phone line into). For about $50, Apple sells a modem built into a short cable that plugs into a USB port. Other USB modems are on the market, and some are cheaper, but make sure that they support Mac OS X.

Parallel printer (IEEE-1284): This printer interface is also known as a *Centronics* port, named after a long-defunct company that made printers for minicomputers back when Richard Nixon was president. If you have a printer you love that speaks only parallel port, Keyspan.com makes a USB–to–parallel port adapter that supports OS X.

RCA audio: This simple connector (which dates back to the early 1940s) is common on home audio systems. Belkin, Monoprice.com, and Radio Shack sell a cheap cable that plugs into your Mac's 3.5mm stereo audio output and has a pair of RCA plugs at the other end that can be inserted into your stereo. For RCA video, see "S-Video," near the end of this list.

Small computer system interface (SCSI): Apple popularized this interface for hard drives with the Mac Plus, and SCSI (pronounced "scuzzy") is still used in high-end applications. Apple has long since adopted the Serial ATA standard used by most PC manufacturers, however. USB-SCSI adapters are available, but they generally don't work with OS X. Ratoc Systems, Inc. (`www.ratoc systems.com`), sells a FireWire-to-SCSI adapter that it claims does work with OS X. It's a tad pricey, and it uses the latest UltraSCSI connector, so you need special cables for first-generation SCSI devices. That old SCSI scanner had better be worth it.

Serial port (RS-232, RS-422): Apple dropped serial ports in favor of USB ports when it introduced the first iMac. Several companies sell USB–to–serial port adapters. Try Keyspan.com and Serialio.com. You can also buy Bluetooth-to-serial adapters that let you control serial devices without running wires.

S-Video: Apple sells an inexpensive adapter that converts your Mac's video output to S-Video and composite video (an RCA jack), the two most common analog television standards. With one of these adapters, you can show your photo collection on any TV with a video input jack.

Video Graphics Array (VGA) and Super VGA: VGA and SVGA are by far the most popular ports for connecting older analog computer monitors. Apple offers adapters that connect VGA/SVGA displays and other devices to the Mac's video output port. This adapter is free with some Mac models and costs extra (about $20) with others.

Stuff that won't work

You may have some plug-in cards that do specialized tasks in your PC. Sorry, but unless they're PCI Express (PCIe), they don't work on any current Mac. Much of the functionality that these cards were used for, such as Ethernet networking, is built into Macs, and Thunderbolt, USB, and FireWire devices replace other uses.

Using Your Old Equipment with a Mac

If you've been a PC user for a while, you've probably purchased some accessories. Some of them may be usable with your new Mac, saving you the expense of buying new stuff. Whether a particular device is Mac-compatible depends on its port interface — the type of cable you use to hook it to the computer — and on whether Mac software that works with the device is available.

You might also consider the device's age and whether your new Mac will offer a different and improved way of accomplishing what your old, familiar accessories do. Older devices may not have much life left in them, and worse, they may simply be obsolete. Maybe you have a SCSI Zip drive, for example. The storage capacity of a Zip drive was impressive in its day, but now it's dwarfed by the capacity of a cheap thumb drive that's usable in any Mac, so it may not be worth finding an adapter that lets you hook it up to your new Mac unless you have a large collection of Zip disks — and even then, you're probably better off copying them all to your PC and then transferring them to the Mac. Or you could look for a Zip drive with a USB connection. It should work on a Mac with no fuss.

I can't possibly discuss every combination of Mac model, non-Apple device, and software version, so check with the device manufacturer where possible.

Displays and projectors

If you're buying a mini or Mac Pro, using the display you have can save you money. A big, high-end display often costs more than a computer. Even if you're buying a Mac with a built-in display, an extra display is handy. A Mac can use it as an extension to the desktop area, letting you drag an icon or window from one screen to the other. Or you can set up the second display to mirror what you're seeing on your main display — handy for letting others see what you're doing. (To set it all up, choose Apple⇨System Preferences, and click the Displays icon.)

The following sections help you assess what you need to connect your Mac to commonly used displays.

CRT displays

CRT (cathode-ray tube) displays are rapidly going the way of the dinosaur, perhaps for the same reason: They're too big and consume too much energy. Still, if you have a good-quality CRT display and a tight budget, or if you need the richer color fidelity that CRTs offer for high-end graphics work, using that old display may make sense. The good news is that almost all computer-grade CRTs produced since the 1990s use a VGA cable that should work fine with the Apple VGA adapter.

Otherwise, you should replace that CRT with an iMac, which saves you acres of space on and under your desk — and you'll have no display cables to worry about. Just be careful when the time comes to get rid of that CRT because it can be dangerous. In Chapter 22, I tell how to recycle your old CRT safely.

Flat-screen displays and HDTVs

Flat screens work fine with Macs, including those with built-in displays. The same goes for flat-panel or high-definition television sets. The only question is whether to connect your Mac to your flat-screen display or HDTV via a digital or an analog interface (that is, the available port where you connect the cable from your Mac to your display). In either case, make sure that you have the right adapter cables. Digital and analog interfaces are described in this list:

- ✔ **Digital:** Digital connections generally produce better results. For a digital interface, see which video output connector your Mac has (see Chapter 2) and which connector or cable your display has. If your Mac comes with only a Mini DisplayPort (most do), for example, and your HDTV has an HDMI connector on the back, you need to get a Mini DisplayPort–to—HDMI adapter. Check the booklet that came with your display and the booklet that came with your Mac for details about your specific equipment. Also see the list of connector types in the section "Navigating from PC to Mac Ports," earlier in this chapter.

- ✔ **Analog:** You need a VGA adapter that you plug into the DVI port on your Mac. Some Macs come with these adapters; otherwise, order one from Apple.

Projectors

Big-screen projectors and Microsoft PowerPoint presentations dominate business communication these days and are rapidly taking over our schools. I hate to contribute to this cultural disaster, but the truth is that these projectors generally work with a Mac. Most projectors take VGA, so you need that VGA adapter.

Keyboard and mouse

To help you decide whether you can use a keyboard or mouse that you already have, here's the short version of the story:

- ✔ **If you have a two-button scroll wheel mouse with a wire coming out of it that has a USB connector:** If you have this flat, rectangular metal plug (which is about the size of a fingernail) at the other end, the mouse is something worth keeping.

- ✔ **If you have a Windows keyboard with a USB connector:** It works fine, but a couple of keys are labeled differently from those on Mac keyboards, which may make it more trouble than it's worth.

- ✔ **If you have a cool keyboard, mouse, or other pointing device that you like:** You may have a wireless device, for example. Read on for the longer story.

- ✔ **If you have some old piece of junk:** Skip this section and buy something new.

Connections, connections

Check how your keyboard and mouse connect to your PC. The three most common methods are USB cable, PS/2 cable, and wireless:

- **A USB cable** should work just fine with your Mac.
- **A PS/2 connector** is round and has a pastel-colored shell. PS/2 doesn't work with your Mac.

    These days, many manufacturers make only USB keyboards and mice, and include an adapter that converts them to PS/2. Take a closer look at what you think is a PS/2 plug to see whether it's just one of these adapters, in which case you're in luck; just pull the USB plug from the adapter and plug it into your Mac.

- **Wireless devices** have a built-in radio transmitter rather than a wire. The receiver is often in a finger-size pod that plugs into the computer, or it can be built in. Some devices transmit by using technology that's proprietary to the maker; others use Bluetooth. All Macs come with Bluetooth inside, and Bluetooth devices generally work with Bluetooth-equipped Macs, but you may need special software to take full advantage of this feature on a Mac. A wireless device that uses a USB receiver module and a proprietary transmission scheme may need special software as well. Check with the manufacturer in either case.

Keyboard layout

Mac keyboards have two special keys in the bottom row, to the left of the spacebar. One is labeled *Option,* and to its right is a key with a fan symbol (⌘), known as the *Command key* in Apple-ese. (Some Apple keyboards also show an Apple logo () on this key.) On PC keyboards, these two keys are the Windows key and the Alt key, respectively. If you just plug a PC keyboard into a Mac, the Windows key works as the Command key, and the Alt key works as the Option key. Unfortunately, their positions are reversed from where they are on Mac keyboards. Because you're new to the Mac way of doing things, you don't need this tactile confusion. You can buy DoubleCommand software (`http://doublecommand.sourceforge.net`), which lets you reverse these keys. Also, some of the keyboard shortcuts I describe in this book are specific to newer Apple keyboards. You can see and change the shortcuts for your keyboard by selecting ⟳System Preferences⟳Keyboard⟳Keyboard Shortcuts.

If all this seems more trouble than it's worth (I think so), buy a Mac keyboard. Figure 3-4 shows an Apple wireless keyboard, with its special keys. This model comes with iMacs and the Mac Pro. You can also choose an Apple wired (USB) keyboard that includes a numeric keypad.

Figure 3-4:
Apple
wireless
keyboard.
Note the
row of
smaller
function
keys along
the top.

Courtesy of Apple, Inc.

The Magic Trackpad alternative

Apple's OS X Lion is designed to let you use the Magic Trackpad to interact
with your computer more directly than you can with an old-fashioned mouse.
The laptops all have big trackpads that understand gestures you make with
one or more fingers. You can enjoy the same smooth interface with a desktop
Mac by purchasing Apple's wireless Magic Trackpad, shown in Figure 3-5. It's
designed to sit comfortably next to the Apple wireless keyboard, as shown in
Chapter 1 (Figure 1-1). You can use the Magic Trackpad and a mouse at the
same time; the trackpad won't mind. I tell you more about how these input
options work in Chapter 5.

Figure 3-5:
Apple's
Magic
Trackpad
awaits your
finger
gestures.

Courtesy of Apple, Inc.

KVM switch

A KVM switch lets you share your keyboard, video display, and mouse between two computers — or more than two, with fancier KVM models. Some KVMs also let you share a set of audio speakers or headphones.

Two types of KVM switches are available, based on the type of connection they use for the keyboard and mouse: USB and PS/2. *Buy only a USB KVM switch.* Most recent PCs accept a USB input connection for the mouse and keyboard.

Many USB keyboards and mice come with USB-to-PS/2 adapters. The adapters aren't general-purpose converters, however. The USB keyboards and mice are smart enough to also talk PS/2, and the adapters just take the wires from the USB connector and jigger them into a PS/2 plug. Don't expect one of these adapters to convert the USB output of your KVM switch to PS/2.

Relics of days gone by

The mice and keyboards supplied with computers in the 1980s used RS-232 serial-port connections. They're useless. Old Apple USB keyboards work fine on current Macs. If you have an older Apple keyboard or mouse with a round plug (Apple Desktop Bus), you can get an ADB-to-USB converter, but it's not worth the bother.

Printers, scanners, and fax machines

If you want to use your current printer, scanner, or fax machine with your new Mac, you may not have to buy anything extra — or you may need an adapter. The following tips can help you figure out what you need to do:

- ✔ If your PC printer is of reasonably recent vintage and connects with USB, Ethernet, Bluetooth, or Wi-Fi, it probably works with your Mac with little fuss. Macs come with oodles of drivers installed for current devices. If none works, check for updated Mac drivers at the printer manufacturer's website.

- ✔ Older printers with parallel ports require USB–to–parallel port adapters, and the chance of them working is a bit more iffy (though I've had good luck using them with old HP laser printers).

- ✔ All-in-one units generally work, but some features — such as receiving faxes on your hard drive — may not work with the Mac. (Get an Apple USB modem if your all-in-one's fax feature doesn't play Mac.)

The mantra, again, is "Check with the manufacturer." Ask if it supports Apple's OS X Lion edition.

The scanner story is much the same. Recent USB and FireWire scanners should be fine, the latter assuming that your Mac has a FireWire port. Older SCSI devices need a pricey SCSI-to-FireWire adapter and still may not work. I wouldn't bother.

In Chapter 5, I talk about how to set up printers and scanners in OS X.

External hard drives and flash drives

External hard drives and *flash drives* are storage devices that you can plug into your computer by using USB or FireWire connections. If you have one of these drives, you know how handy it is for storing backups or transferring files. USB and FireWire external hard drives should work fine, even if they were formatted for your PC. Just plug them into the appropriate Mac port, and a drive icon appears on the Desktop; then you can double-click this icon to access your files. The same goes for USB flash drives.

All Macs except the mini and MacBook Airs come with a CD and DVD burner: the *SuperDrive.* Apple sells an external SuperDrive for the Air and mini, but if you have an external CD/DVD drive you can probably use it (see "Getting Ready to Buy," later in this chapter).

An external USB or FireWire DVD reader or burner can also come in handy if you want to watch DVDs from countries outside your zone. (The movie industry has obnoxiously chopped up the world into six zones, and it insists Macs play DVDs from only one zone.) An external DVD reader that has a pop-out tray instead of a slot can come in handy if you have small-size, or "business card," CDs and DVDs to read, such as those used in some video cameras or supplied with some video games.

Internal drives

Because new drives have so much more capacity than those from even a couple of years ago, reusing an internal hard drive (the one inside your PC) may not be worth the bother. But if you have an internal drive that you want to use with your new Mac and have some screwdriver skills, buy hard drive enclosures that let you install your PC's internal hard drive and then plug it into your Mac via USB 2. You need to know which type of connection your hard drive uses (ATA and Serial ATA are the most likely choices) and what size your hard drive is. Alternatively, a computer store or fix-it shop can do this for you.

Keeping your drive to connect to your Mac solves more than one problem: It gives you a direct backup for your PC files, and it keeps the data on your PC from getting into the wrong hands. But follow the steps in Chapter 6 to transfer your files before messing with the internal drive so that you have copies on your Mac before you risk losing the drive and its contents altogether.

Networking devices

Most of the hardware you use to create a home network (technically, a *local-area network,* or *LAN*) for sharing broadband Internet access should work with a Mac, including the items described in this list:

- ✔ **Ethernet switches and routers and Ethernet cabling:** Create a network with wires.

  If you decide to buy a new Ethernet router or hub, be sure to get a model that supports at least 100Base-T speeds. (1000Base-T is blazingly fast but expensive and probably more than you need.) If you own older 10Base-T equipment, you can use it if you like.

- ✔ **Cable modems and DSL modems:** These modems come with high-speed Internet connections from your cable or digital subscriber line (DSL) provider, respectively. In all likelihood, you don't need any different hardware to use your existing Internet connection with your Mac.

- ✔ **Wireless routers and access points:** Set up the popular Wi-Fi wireless networking. The 802.11a, b, g, and n standards all work with a Mac. The *n* version is the fastest, and *b* is the slowest.

  Wi-Fi networks work at the speed of the slowest device on the network, so an older laptop that supports only 802.11b is best left off the network (turned off) when it isn't needed.

  The Wi-Fi standard 802.11a operates in a different frequency band (5 GHz) from *b* and *g* modes (2.4 GHz). The radios in Wi-Fi-equipped Macs can operate on the 802.11a band as well and can even work both bands simultaneously.

Digital cameras and camcorders

Macs and OS X provide extensive support for digital photography. Macs work with most digital cameras and support the *RAW mode* that high-end cameras produce when you want the best-quality images from them. The most common way to connect a camera to your Mac is to use a USB cable. Many Mac models come with a slot for reading SD and SDXC cards — the most popular high-end camera memory cards. See "Camera memory cards" earlier in this chapter.

Digital video recorders are also well supported. Some use USB 2.0, and others use FireWire, though manufacturers may call it IEEE-1394 or i.Link (the Sony brand name). USB works fine on all Macs; for FireWire, you need a FireWire-equipped Mac and, likely, a FireWire 400–to–FireWire 800 cable. The movie-editing software that comes with new Macs also supports the new high-definition (HD) camcorders, so you're ready for the latest in videography.

Cellphones and portable music players

Needless to say, iPhones, iPads, and iPods work hand in glove with Macs. After all, Apple makes all these items.

Android cellphones work fine with Macs, too, as do BlackBerry devices and most other smartphones. Most dumb phones have some way to sync Address Book and other info via a USB cable. Even Windows Phone 7, recently adopted by Nokia, has some Mac support. Search for *Mac* or *OS X support* on your cellphone company's web page.

Most non-Mac music players can connect to your Mac by way of USB so that you can at least transfer music files in an open format (such as MP3) to the player. Non-Apple players don't play songs purchased from the iTunes Store directly under OS X, but you can burn a playlist to CD and then read it back in and transfer the files to your player.

The Microsoft Zune music player doesn't even have this USB option. Some third party may create a way to transfer files between Macs and Zunes, and of course, you can run Windows on the Mac and transfer files that way. But if you're seriously considering purchasing both a Mac and a Zune, you may be reading the wrong self-help book.

CardBus cards

CardBus cards, also known as PCMCIA cards or PC cards, are about the size of credit cards, though a bit thicker, and they're designed to plug into special slots on PCs — primarily laptops. The good news is that many of the capabilities that PC cards were typically used for, such as adding Ethernet, are built into Macs or can be added in other ways, such as with the Apple USB modem. Another common use of CardBus and ExpressBus cards — wireless modems — has largely been supplanted by equivalent USB devices that work with any Mac.

If you need to add functionality to your Mac by using a CardBus card, you have a few options:

REMEMBER

✔ **Get a 17-inch MacBook Pro with ExpressCard/34.** ExpressCard/34 slots are basically the latest version of the PC card technology. With the introduction of Intel-based laptops, Apple switched to this newer standard. The ExpressCard, which is a little smaller than a PCMCIA card but has a much faster connection to a computer's innards, is available for many other uses because newer PC laptops come with ExpressCard slots, too. CardBus-to-ExpressBus adapters are available.

ExpressCard/34 is available only on the 17-inch MacBook Pro.

✔ **Get a USB PC card CardBus reader that works with your card.** If you depend on a PC card for what you do, this may be your only choice. You insert your PC card into the reader and then plug the reader into your Mac by using the USB port. One vendor is Litronic (`http://store.litronic.com/DMS_FORTEZZA_Readers_s/21.htm`).

✔ **Get a Mac Pro and install a PCIe CardBus reader expansion card.** This provides the most flexibility, but make sure the card manufacturer supports Macs.

Miscellany

You probably have accumulated a pile of computer-related items. Some of them are still useful, and others can be given away or recycled. This list gives you the rundown:

Blank discs: Keep full-size blank CD-Rs and DVD-Rs. Miniature discs and discs the size of credit cards don't work in the Mac's slot-loading drive (don't even try), though they work in external tray-loading optical drives or in the tray-loading drives in the Mac Pro. Blank floppy and Zip disks can go away unless you work with folks who still use them and can get hold of an external drive that supports them. (Save one floppy disk to show your grandchildren.)

Cables: Ethernet, USB, and FireWire cables are worth hanging on to. Serial, SCSI, and proprietary cables can go. The ubiquitous three-pin power cords used with most desktop PCs (IEC–C13) don't fit most Macs. One or two are always handy to keep around, however, for peripherals.

Computer furniture: A desk is a desk, and switching to a Mac can free some space on one, but if yours doesn't have good ergonomic design (see `www.apple.com/about/ergonomics`) or just looks terrible, it may be time for an upgrade.

Floppy-disk holders: Holders for the ancient 5¼-inch floppy disks are handy for CDs and DVDs. Holders for 3½-inch disks are good for organizing tchotchkes such as flash drives, the Apple Remote, camera memory cards, and small cable adapters.

Power strips, surge protectors, spider cables, and the like: You always need more of these.

Printing supplies: You can use your printer paper, address labels, and the like. Give away or recycle ink or toner cartridges for your printer if you aren't keeping it.

Uninterruptible power supply (UPS): Some of these devices connect to your computer to tell it to shut down when the power goes out. Check with the UPS manufacturer to see whether it has Mac software to support this feature. If not, you can still use the UPS to supply backup power.

USB hubs: These hubs connect more than one device to a single port. If they're USB2 hubs, they're keepers. Don't forget to save the matching power supply if you have one.

Getting Ready to Buy

After you review the different approaches to switching and consider which items you can use from your PC, you're most likely ready to decide what to buy. I tell you about the different Apple models in Chapter 2. It's time to take out a sheet of paper and work up a couple of configurations that meet your needs, compare them with your budget, and pick one. The rest of your computing life begins today.

Choosing options for your new Mac

All the Macs that Apple sells have enough processing power, memory, and disk space to be fully usable systems, but some options and accessories are worth considering. Apple typically stocks three or four configurations for each model, and you can custom-order additional options. The following sections walk you through the key decisions you need to make when you order.

Hard drive size

The hard drive is where your computer retains information that you want to keep. If you plan to manage your photos, movies, and music on your Mac, or if you plan to run Windows, you want lots of hard drive space. You can buy an external drive (and you want one for the Apple Time Machine backup feature), but it's handy to have your main files in one place. On the Mac Pro, adding a bigger drive is easy, but most models require a technician to install one.

Bottom line: Spend a little more for a bigger hard drive, but save some money in your budget for an external unit too.

Processor speed

Apple charges a little extra for the fastest versions of the Intel processors it uses. Computer reviews tend to dote on 10 percent differences in speed, even though most users hardly notice the difference. All Macs have more than one central processing unit (CPU) — the part of the chip that carries out program instructions. Most have two, but the highest-performance models have four or more. If you don't know why you would need that much processing power, you probably don't.

Random access memory

Random access memory (RAM) is where your computer temporarily stores information so that the CPU can quickly (in billionths of a second) access the data while it's working on that data. Other terms used include DRAM and SDRAM. When your computer runs out of RAM, it writes the data that it hasn't used in a while to the much slower hard drive.

Adding memory reduces the need for these memory swaps and typically improves performance more than getting a faster chip does. The 2GB of RAM (two billion or so characters of information) that low-end Mac minis and Airs are supplied with is barely adequate. It's fairly easy to upgrade memory on a Mac mini, but getting at least 4GB to begin with is usually worth the money.

Selecting other accessories

Configure your computer the way you want it when you buy it. You can buy other accessories with your purchase or later, when you need them.

AppleCare

A Mac typically comes with a 1-year warranty and 90-day free phone support. You can extend the warranty and phone support by signing up for AppleCare. Although you can do this at any time before the warranty expires, extending the warranty when you buy is best; otherwise, you may forget. Alternatively, mark your iCal calendar about a month before the warranty expires. Also see "One to One," later in this chapter.

Apple could change its terms, so verify the warranty info in this section before you buy. Don't take my word for it.

External floppy drive

If you have a collection of 3½-inch floppies, your best bet is to read them all onto your PC's hard drive and then back them up, either directly to a CD or DVD or to your Mac when you transfer the rest of your files (see Chapter 6). But if you own too many of them and don't want to spend the time, get an external USB floppy drive for your Mac.

External hard drive

If you don't already own a high-capacity external hard drive, get one — at least 1TB worth. It's pretty much a must-have item if you want to get decent use from the Apple Time Machine backup software. The external drive is also handy for transferring files from your PC. External hard drives offer capacities in the terabyte (1000GB) range for less than $100. You can buy a 3TB (3,000GB) drive for less than $150. If your Mac supports FireWire, buy a hard drive with both FireWire and USB 2.0 interfaces, giving you maximum flexibility. This type of drive typically costs a bit more, but that way, you can use USB 2.0 with your PC and use the faster FireWire with your Mac.

External optical drive

An external CD/DVD optical drive is worth considering if you buy a MacBook Air or a Mac mini, as these don't have a built in optical drive. Apple is supplying all its software and updates on line, but many software vendors still sell their wares on CDs or DVDs.

Some inexpensive CD/DVD drives have two USB plugs because they require more power than one USB port supplies. That gets awkward with a MacBook Air because its two USB ports are on opposite sides of the laptop. Make sure you get a model, like Apple's, that only requires a single USB connection.

Singing the Blu-ray blues

Apple doesn't offer a drive that can read Blu-ray discs. These discs are the same size as CDs and DVDs but hold much more data — up to 50GB — and are used to distribute high-definition (HD) movies. You can buy Blu-ray drives from MCEtech.com that you can install in a Mac Pro. MCE also sells external Blu-ray drives that work with other Macs, and it even has one that can replace your Mac's internal SuperDrive. (It reads and writes CDs and DVDs, too.) You can use the Blu-ray drive to back up files and, if you buy the extra software, create HD movies that you can play on standard Blu-ray players.

The one thing you *can't* do (as of this writing) is play commercial Blu-ray movies directly on your Mac under OS X. (You can do it if you boot under Windows.) Apple isn't happy with the Blu-ray license terms; Steve Jobs called them "a bag of hurt." Apple distributes HD movies via the iTunes Store, so adding Blu-ray may not be at the top of Apple's priority list.

Flash drive

If you don't already have at least one of these tiny, inexpensive USB mass-storage units, it's time you got one. It's also known as a *thumb drive* or *keychain drive.* A typical unit is shown in Figure 3-6, with a peanut for comparison. There's nothing like knowing that you have the files you need in your pocket. Get at least an 8GB unit.

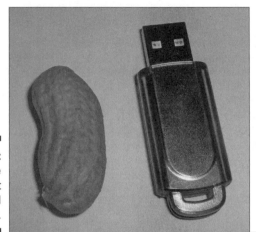

Figure 3-6:
A flash drive
(USB plug at
the top) and
a peanut.

Microsoft Office

Microsoft Office is still the most widely accepted tool for creating text documents and spreadsheets. You can safely send documents back and forth between the Macintosh version of Office and the Windows version. If you feel that you need Microsoft Office for work or school, check on whether special deals are available with the purchase of a new Mac. Unfortunately, you can't transfer your Windows Office license to OS X.

Modem

Current Mac models don't include a modem. If you need dialup Internet access at home or on the road, or if you need to send fax documents from your computer, get the tiny Apple USB modem, which sells for about $50.

Networking equipment

If you already have high-speed Internet access and maybe even a home network, your Mac plugs right in. If not, see Chapter 9, where I tell you about the various options:

✔ **Wireless:** If you're buying a laptop or just don't want wires strung all over your den, consider getting a Wi-Fi router. The Apple offerings are the AirPort Extreme Base Station (AirPort Extreme is Apple's name for the 802.11n Wi-Fi standard) and Time Capsule, which combines Wi-Fi with a large hard drive for automated backup. Just about any 802.11n router will do, however. See Chapter 10 for tips on setting up your wireless router securely.

✔ **Ethernet (wired):** If you plan to use wired networking, check to see whether you have an extra Ethernet port available on your router or cable modem. If not, you may need an Ethernet router. Getting one that also includes Wi-Fi doesn't cost much more, however.

Another handy accessory is a USB hub, a small box that multiplies the number of USB devices you can plug in at the same time. You may already have one, but make sure that it supports the faster USB 2.0 standard. If not, get a new one, preferably the type with a separate power supply so that it can power additional devices.

Printer deals

When you buy a new Mac, you're typically offered a reduced price or rebate on a new inkjet printer. Sometimes, the rebate covers the purchase price of the printer, so even if you already own a printer, it may be worth getting a new one as a spare or as a gift for someone else.

Internet Recovery mode versus OS X on a thumb drive

Apple used to include a copy of OS X on a DVD with every new Mac. One use for that DVD was fixing your Mac if your hard drive became corrupted — you'd boot from the DVD and run Disk Utility to make repairs. No more. Macs now come with a recovery partition on the hard drive. You run repair software by pressing ⌘+R or holding down the Option key when you reboot your Mac. What if you hard drive isn't working well enough for the recovery software to load? The newest Macs, the Air and the mini as of this writing, offer Internet Recovery. If you're connected to a broadband Internet connection and your hard drive can't load the recovery partition, your Mac will load the same recovery software over the Internet. It will even let you reinstall OS X via the Internet.

However, if you aren't comfortable relying on a fast Internet connection being available when your hard drive's a-major-presentation-is-due sensor kicks in, Apple sells a copy of OS X on a thumb drive for about $70.

There's no such thing as a free lunch, however. Printer manufacturers sell their printers cheap and force you to buy ink or toner from them at prices that work out to a few cents per page for a text document to a half-dollar or more for a color photograph — in effect, a tax on every page. New printers often come with starter cartridges that print fewer pages than a purchased cartridge, so you may as well buy a cartridge with that new printer and save yourself a trip to the store.

Most inkjet printers use ink that runs when wet, but some inks are more smearproof than others. Ask to have a sample page printed, and apply a drop of water or saliva to the printout to see what happens. If you need a relatively waterproof print, go with a laser printer.

If you have a printer that you like, and it's supported by OS X, you may want to forgo the printer deal and shop for a new one when you need it.

One to One

For about $100, Apple sells the one-year personal setup and training plan One to One, which offers several services that aren't included in the standard warranty or in AppleCare. You can buy One to One only when you buy a new Mac and only from an Apple store (retail or online).

For setup service, you must bring your new Mac and your old PC to an Apple retail store, where the staff will set up your Mac for you, installing additional software you purchased, such as Microsoft Office. If you bring your old PC as well, they will also transfer your files from the PC to the Mac. The PC has to be working and must have an Ethernet port and at least Windows 98 — and of course, you have to schlep it in.

I tell you how to transfer files from your PC to your new Mac in Chapter 6, but letting Apple do it for you is a lot less of a hassle. Be sure to request One to One service when you purchase your Mac.

Travel accessories

If you're planning to travel with a Mac laptop, here are some other accessories worth considering:

How big is a gigabyte?

The international metric system prefix *giga* means 1,000,000,000 — a billion, in North American English — so a gigabyte is a billion bytes, right? Well, in the computer world, it's not so simple. A gigabyte (or GB) sometimes refers to that amount, and sometimes it's 1,073,741,824 bytes. (You can make any geek's day by asking him why.) The latter version is always used for RAM. Hard drive manufacturers use *gigabyte* to mean 1,000,000,000 (1 billion) bytes. It's kind of the opposite of a baker's dozen, putting one fewer doughnut in the bag. Pretty much every manufacturer does this the same way, so you aren't being cheated. Also, you should buy at least twice as much hard drive space as you think you need, so none of this really matters.

✔ **Airplane power adapter:** If you take long plane trips, you may want to get the Apple airplane power adapter. Many airlines provide laptop power outlets, though less often in economy seating. You can find out which seats on your flight have power adapters at www.seatguru.com. *Note:* The Apple adapter powers your laptop but doesn't charge its batteries.

If you're traveling to other countries, the good news is that the power adapter that comes with Mac laptops runs on any AC power source in the world — 100–240 volts, 50 Hz, or 60 Hz — but you may need to buy a travel adapter to plug it in. You can buy one at Radio Shack and many travel stores. You don't need the transformer type.

✔ **Three-way extension cord:** I'm talking about the inexpensive two-prong type that you buy in any supermarket, not a bulky three-prong power strip. Those of us who travel spend untold hours in airports, and most of those airports have only a few power outlets, usually located for the benefit of the cleaning crews. When you do find a pair of outlets, another road warrior has probably already claimed them for his laptop and cellphone. But most people are willing to share the outlet if you ask nicely and produce your three-way cord.

✔ **Security cable:** If you plan to use your Mac laptop at work or school, consider buying a security cable that lets you lock it up when you have to leave it unattended. You can find a variety of such locks at www.kensington.com.

Look for the Mac logo

Macs work with most USB, FireWire, and networking devices — such as printers, scanners, and wireless base stations — so don't be afraid to try what you already own. But if you're buying new equipment, make sure that the package says it's designed for Mac and OS X. If you do, you're more likely to own a product that works with little or no fuss. If you run into problems and don't find the solution in this book, you're more likely to find useful help from that vendor's customer service department if the box specifies that it supports Macs.

Shopping for Your New Mac

You may be fed up with choices by now, if you've read the entire chapter, but you have one more decision to make: where to buy your Mac. Here's the gist of it: You can buy online or in a traditional bricks-and-mortar store, and you can buy directly from Apple or from an independent retailer. All these options have pros and cons, and the sections that follow can help you decide.

Wherever you go to buy your Mac and its accessories, make sure that you take a list of all the specs and accessories that you know you need, based on the information you gathered earlier in this chapter. Your list should include not only which Mac model you want but also how much RAM you need, what size hard drive you want, and which options to choose (such as a higher-end graphics card). By having all these notes at the ready, you're much more likely to stay within your budget (if you have one) and to get no more or no less than you need.

Shopping at your local computer store

The nice thing about going to a computer store is that you can see the various models before you make your final decision. You can also ask the friendly salesperson questions and maybe even get useful answers. Assuming that what you want is in stock, you get to take your new toy home with you. Also, if you have a problem, most stores have a place where you can talk to someone face to face. (Ask your salesperson to show you the service department before you buy.)

Not all computer stores carry Macs. Apple is choosy about which establishments it does business with. It doesn't want Macs stacked along the wall with all the Windows models in a department staffed with salespeople pushing the PC that happens to be on sale that week. You can find a list of authorized Apple resellers near you at www.apple.com/buy. Call ahead to see whether what you want is in stock.

Visiting the Apple Store

Frustrated with the way that its computers were being sold, Apple defied conventional business wisdom and built its own chain of computer stores. Designed with the usual Apple panache and propelled by the success of the iPod, this venture has made its customers and stockholders very happy. If you choose to buy your Mac at an Apple Store, you'll find that the stores are well stocked with most Apple models and attractively displayed. The stores carry lots of accessories, both from Apple and third parties — printers; external hard drives; carrying cases; software; games; and (of course) iPads, iPhones, iPods, Apple TVs, and other items in the growing list of Apple consumer electronics.

The coolest thing about the Apple Store is its *Genius Bar,* a section staffed by people who know their Macs and can answer your questions. After you buy your Mac, the Genius Bar can take your hardware for repair, if necessary. If the store is busy — and it usually is — you have to sign in and wait a bit. Most stores give you a pager so that you can shop elsewhere or visit the food court if the Apple Store is in a mall, as many are. You can visit the Genius Bar and bring in your Mac to the Apple Store for service regardless of where you purchased it originally. You have to pay for service, of course, if your Mac is no longer under warranty or isn't covered by AppleCare.

Apple claims that a large chunk of the population of North America is within a 45-minute drive of an Apple Store. You can also find Apple Stores in many other parts of the world. Discover how close the nearest stores are to you by visiting www.apple.com/buy.

Buying your Mac online

Buying online can be very convenient. Pick out the model you want, and enter your shipping address and credit-card number. In a day or so, depending on how cheap you were about shipping, your computer arrives. If you don't have an Internet connection, or if your PC is so riddled with viruses that you don't trust it with your credit card, most online stores also have toll-free phone numbers and even printed catalogs that you can request.

Surfing to the Apple online store

You can buy all the products Apple makes from its electronic Apple Store at www.apple.com (or by calling 1-800-MY-APPLE).

The online Apple Store is your best bet if you want to buy a build-to-order configuration. Select the Buy Now option for the model you want, and you're presented with all possible options for that model. You aren't committed to buy anything until you enter your credit-card information and confirm your order.

Buying from other online retailers

A few other online stores sell Macs, including Amazon.com, MacConnection.com, and MacZone.com. Again, you can find a full list at www.apple.com/buy. These stores sometimes offer discounts or deals on extra memory. They may stock only the most popular configurations, however.

If you live in the United States, you may be able to avoid paying sales tax by purchasing from one of the independent online stores. The independent store has to collect sales tax only if it has a business presence in the state where you live. (Apple has a presence in most states, so it has to collect sales tax.)

Did you buy the wrong book?

In past editions of this book, I tell all readers to get a Macintosh computer. Now there's an alternative that may make more sense for some people. It's still from Apple, but it's not a Mac — it's the iPad. In the last edition, I said, "Many in the industry believe that Apple is developing an innovative product to compete with netbooks, perhaps a media tablet that can connect to the Internet by way of the cellular telephone network and Wi-Fi — something like a large iPhone." Well, for once, the industry rumor mill got it right. That's exactly what Apple did. And users love it.

If you use your computer mainly for surfing the web, watching videos, keeping up with Facebook, and answering a few e-mails each day, the iPad may meet all your needs. It costs less than a Mac and is easier to use. But if you use your computer for more demanding tasks, such as writing, keeping track of your finances, or managing large photo or video libraries, or if you've accumulated lots of data on your PC that you'd like to be able to access, a Mac — a real computer — is still your best bet. You can still have the best of both worlds, of course, by buying a Mac *and* an iPad.

Part II
Making the Switch

The 5th Wave   By Rich Tennant

"It's been two days, Larry. It's time to stop enjoying the new computer smell and take the iMac out of the box."

In this part . . .

You did it. You got a Mac. Now what? This section guides you through setting up your new Mac and introduces you to the latest Apple OS X operating system, code named *Lion.* I suggest ways to move over your files and help you deal with the most important application programs you need in order to get started.

Chapter 4

The Big Day: Setting Up Your Mac

Congratulations! You've done it. You bought a Mac. A new world is about to unfold. Apple does an excellent job of making the task of setting up a new Mac simple and painless, and it usually is. But computers are by far the most complex consumer products ever sold, and things can go wrong. Also, some simple preparations can make the setup process smoother and much less stressful. So resist the temptation to start hooking things up, and read on.

Plan B: Let Apple do it

If you buy your Mac at an Apple Store, you can sign up for Apple's One to One program. If you buy online, select One to One on the Configure Your Mac page. The friendly clerk at an Apple retail store will likely offer you the option, but if not, ask. Membership costs $99 for one year and gives you access to a special website, in-store workshops, and even face-to-face sessions with a personal Mac trainer (gym clothes not required). Best of all, Apple will set up your new Mac for you and transfer files from your PC. You have to bring in the PC and leave the new Mac at the store. When it's all done, you and Apple schedule a Meet Your New Mac session, where the proper introductions are made. In theory, you must sign up for One to One when you buy your new Mac, but Apple often extends a few days' grace period from the time of purchase. Give your local Apple Store a call, and ask if it will extend this courtesy. Feel free to use my name.

Unpacking and Setting Up

You're ready to unpack your new Mac. (If you did this as soon as you got it home, please just gather all the pieces in one place and pretend that you didn't.) I hope you notice the attractive presentation. Apple has elevated packaging to an art form, with everything snugly in its place and waste cut to a minimum. I also hope that you notice the tiny manuals that come with the Mac. They explain the basics but leave plenty of demand for aftermarket books such as this one. Thanks, Apple.

Getting organized

The first thing to do is to make room for the new machine and clear away the clutter on your desk or work table so that you can keep track of everything. Next, find a shoebox or plastic storage container so that you have a place to store the software, manuals, and other bits of stuff that come with the Mac. A friend of mine services computers in his apartment complex and is forever telling people to put the software and papers in a safe place when he sets up a new computer. When he has to go back sometime later, his clients can never find the stuff. So think of a place you'll remember, and write down the location here, in the margin of this book.

Like most computer companies, Apple used to ship software on DVD discs. But some Apple models, like the MacBook Air, don't come with a built-in DVD reader, so Apple sometimes ships the software for restoring your Mac on an even-easier-to-misplace thumb drive, making it even more important to find a cozy, memorable home for all these tchotchkes.

Hooking up your computer

It's time to put your computer together. Looking through the manual that comes with your Mac for the latest info is always a good idea, but the following sections provide a quick guide on what to do, depending on your computer model.

If you have a good surge protector left over from your PC setup, grab it. If not, get one. A surge protector is cheap insurance for any electronic product.

iMac

The iMac is an easy setup. Apple once ran an ad showing a 7-year-old putting together an earlier model. If anything, the task has become easier since then. I don't recommend letting a 7-year-old lift an iMac out of its box, however, particularly if you buy one of the models with a large screen. The largest iMac weighs almost 31 pounds (14 kg), and you really don't want anyone to drop it. (Don't be ashamed to ask another adult for help.) After it's unpacked, here's what you need to do:

1. **Unpack the wireless keyboard and mouse or trackpad that came with your iMac, and turn them on**.

   There are switches on the bottom of the mouse and on the right side of the keyboard.

   Alternatively, if you have a USB keyboard or mouse that you prefer, plug it in to the USB port on the back of your iMac.

2. **Pass the power cord through the hole in the support stand and plug it into the power socket on the back of the iMac; then plug its other end into an AC wall outlet, power strip, or surge protector.**

3. **If your power strip or surge protector has a switch, make sure that it's set to On.**

   You're done.

Wireless mice and keyboards

Your iMac comes with a Bluetooth wireless keyboard and mouse or trackpad with batteries installed and all ready to go. If you buy a different wireless input device, you have to install batteries and then introduce the keyboard and mouse to the computer. No, I'm not making a joke here; the process is called *pairing*. (The devices that come with your iMac are paired at the factory.)

The details are in the little booklets that come with the wireless devices, so hang on to them or visit www.apple.com/support/bluetooth.

Always check and double-check which way the batteries are inserted in any electronic device. Look for the + and – marks inside the case, and don't assume that you know. Inserting batteries improperly is the most common cause of small electronics not working.

MacBook, MacBook Air, and MacBook Pro

Apple laptops require little setup. Here's what you do:

1. **Plug the power adapter into an AC outlet or power strip.**

   At the other end of the power adapter, you find the MagSafe power connector.

2. **Remove the power connector's little plastic protective cover; then just hold it horizontally and bring it near the power receptacle (located on the left side of your laptop near the display hinge).**

   When it's close, the connector snaps into the laptop as though it were magnetic — because it is. It doesn't matter which side of the MagSafe connector is up; it works properly either way.

The MagSafe connector has a tiny light, and when you first apply power to your new laptop, the light should be green and then promptly switch to orange, indicating that it's charging the batteries. When the battery is fully charged, the light turns green again.

A good friend of mine trashed a nice Apple PowerBook, the predecessor of the MacBook Pro, by tripping over the power cord and sending her laptop crashing to the floor. It never booted up again. The MagSafe connector is designed to prevent such tragedies by popping out if you tug on it, without imparting a big-enough jerk to pull the laptop off a work surface. Still, pulling on the cord isn't the best way to unplug the MagSafe connector from your machine. Apple recommends that you grasp the connector itself and pull, but that sucker sticks on tight. The easy way to remove it is to gently lift it from the bottom — it tilts up pretty easily — and then pull it out.

3. **While you're waiting for me to tell you to press the On button, take a moment to examine the power adapter.**

    After you take off all the clear plastic wrapping, you see two little tabs on either side of the power cord, which swing out to form a cradle on which you can wind up the power cord. Also (at least in North America), two power blades swing out and plug directly into a power outlet. They're mounted in a small module that Apple calls a *duck's head,* which you can pull free and replace with the longer power cord that comes with the Mac (see Figure 4-1). The U.S. power cord has a grounding plug, so if you're working in a place with older wiring, the duck's head may be more convenient because it fits into just about any outlet, as well as into inexpensive two-wire extension cords.

4. **Okay, press On now.**

Mac mini, Mac Pro

The top and bottom of the Mac line are both a little more complicated to set up because neither has a built-in display; you have to supply your own and hook it up to the computer. That brings up the ugly question of adapters:

✔ The ultra-light Mac mini has both a Mini DisplayPort and an HDMI port video output connector, and comes with an HDMI-to-DVI adapter. Apple sells a Mini DisplayPort–to–VGA adapter, along with other Mini DisplayPort adapters.

✔ The Mac Pro is heavy — 42 pounds (19 kg) — but it has conveniently placed carrying handles on top that make it easier to lug. The standard Mac Pro has two Mini DisplayPorts and a dual-link DVI port. It comes with no adapters.

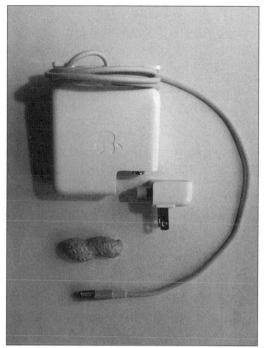

Figure 4-1:
The
MacBook
power
supply with
duck's head
detached.

Selecting the right adapters can be confusing. You may even need more than one. Check these tips:

- ✔ **If you're hooking up to your PC's monitor:** You probably want a VGA adapter, but first check your display's service manual to see whether your monitor has digital input and, if so, what type (such as DVI). It's better to use digital if it's available.

- ✔ **If you're hooking up to a high-definition TV (HDTV):** Unless you bought a Mac mini, you need a Mini DisplayPort–to–HDMI cable. The online Apple Store sells some, but you might use Google to search for a less pricey vendor. One example is the Mini DisplayPort–to—HDMI adapter sold by www.monoprice.com.

  DVI, HDMI, and VGA cover most displays on the market, but you may have something different. Also, older TVs with only analog input are not supported by the latest Apple computers, but you can stack a VGA-to-video converter on a Mini DisplayPort–to–VGA adapter. You can buy the VGA-to-video converter from www.svideo.com/vga2videosmall.html.

- ✔ **If you plan to use two displays with a Mac mini:** You need two video cables or adapters — of different types, one adapter that plugs into the Mini DisplayPort and one that plugs into the HDMI port.

Network

If your PC is connected to the Internet via a Wi-Fi wireless network, you're all set. Your Mac should see your Wi-Fi signal, and all you have to do is select your network and enter the right password when the time comes.

If you have a wired Ethernet network at home, plug your Mac into it. (MacBook Airs require an Apple USB-to-Ethernet adapter for wired connections.) You likely already have a wired network. If you have high-speed Internet (via cable TV, DSL, or satellite), and your PC is connected by a wire with a plug that looks like a telephone plug but is fatter, a wired Ethernet network is what you have. You need an Ethernet router or switch to share this connection. If you don't have one, don't worry. You can unplug the connection from your PC, plug it into your Mac for now, and pick up a router the next time you're near a computer store, or you can order one online. See Chapter 9 for more on networking your Mac.

KVM

A KVM box lets you share a keyboard, video monitor, mouse, and speakers between your Mac and your PC, as shown in Figure 4-2. You don't need one, but it's handy if you plan to continue using your PC and want to share the same display. Hooking up the box involves a lot of wires, but the idea is simple enough. With luck, you got a USB KVM. It should say so on the package. If it doesn't, or if it says PS/2, return it and get a USB unit.

The following steps walk you through the setup process:

1. **Plug your monitor, keyboard, mouse, and speakers into the KVM box.**

   Normally, the monitor and speakers have only one possible connection apiece. You should find two USB jacks — one for the keyboard and one for the mouse — but it shouldn't matter which goes where.

   You also have two sets of cables — more if you bought a multiport KVM.

2. **Plug one end of each cable into the KVM box.**

   The other end of each cable has a set of plugs.

3. **Plug the other end of one cable into your PC and the other end of the second cable into your Mac.**

4. **Plug the speaker cables into the speaker outputs of each computer, and plug the USB plug (you should see only one per cable) into an available USB socket on the computer.**

   Finally, you have a VGA video plug to contend with.

5. **Connect the VGA plug on the PC cable to a matching jack on the PC.**

6. **To connect to KVM box to the Mac , use a Mini DisplayPort–to–VGA adapter (available from the Apple Store).**

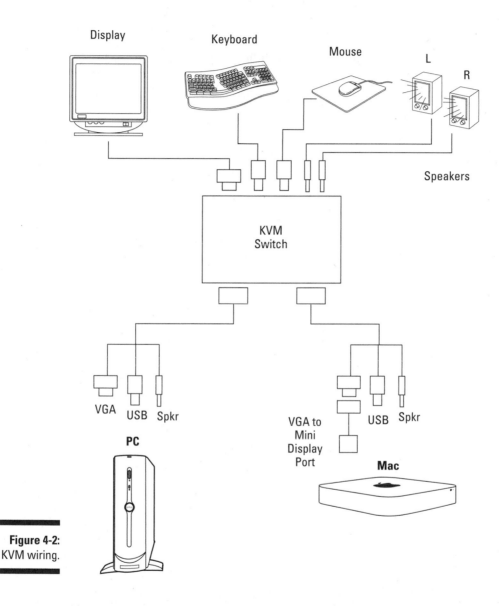

Display

Keyboard

Mouse

L   R

Speakers

KVM
Switch

VGA USB Spkr

PC

VGA to
Mini
Display
Port

USB Spkr

Mac

Figure 4-2:
KVM wiring.

After you set everything up, switching between the Mac and PC should be easy. Check the manual that came with your KVM box for the details on which method it uses to control the switching.

Turning your Mac on and off

The power switch on most Macs is a round, white, or silver button marked with the *discus interruptus*, a circle broken at the top by a short vertical line. This circle is actually the international symbol for a *soft power switch* — one that tells the equipment to go on or off but doesn't control the power directly. The power button is at the upper right on Apple laptops, just above the keyboard, and is near the lower-left corner in back of the display on iMacs. Press the power button briefly to turn your Mac on.

To turn your Mac off, use the Shut Down command. The Shut Down command is in the Apple menu (the one headed by the Apple logo:). After you choose Shut Down, you're asked whether you really want to shut down your computer. If you choose ⇨Restart, you see a similar message.

OS X is quite a stable operating system, but if it doesn't seem to do anything after you tell it to shut down, you can try a couple of things. First, be patient. Some programs, particularly the Apple Safari web browser, can take a while to close. Also, look at your screen to see whether an application is asking whether you want to save a file you're editing. Then hold down the command () and option keys and then press esc. Force quit for any applications that are listed as not responding.

If that fails, hold down the power button for at least 10 seconds, until the screen goes black and all fan noise stops. Wait a few seconds, then briefly press the power button again and your Mac should restart. See Chapter 20 for additional troubleshooting tips.

Configuring Your New Mac

You're almost ready to turn on your Mac. When you do, it asks a bunch of questions. First, I recommend that you gather some information so that you have the answers ready during the initial setup. Then you're ready to step through the setup process with the Startup Assistant. The following sections explain just what you need to know.

Collecting information you need

After you get your Mac plugged in and turned on, your Mac starts asking you a bunch of questions. Things go more smoothly if you collect the answers ahead of time, so the following sections discuss the information you need. With a few exceptions, you can change the information later, but you may as well get it right the first time if you can. Make notes of your choices in the margins of this book (assuming that you're not still browsing in the bookstore).

Name

This information seems straightforward enough, but give some thought to how you want your name presented: Mary Smith, Mary Ann Smith, M. Smith,

M. A. Smith, or just Mary. If you're setting up the computer for a youngster, you may not want to include his last name, but don't use a too-cute nickname that the child will outgrow in a couple of years.

If the family is sharing the computer, you can easily set up individual accounts for each member. I recommend doing this rather than having several people share one account. The first account should be the person who will be in charge (the *administrator*) of the computer, though this account can be changed later and you can have more than one administrator. Some tasks, such as installing new software or setting parental controls, can be done only by an administrator.

Short name

This entry is the name of your home directory, and it can't be changed easily. Your Mac proposes the full name you gave, in all lowercase letters and with no spaces. I suggest that you pick something shorter, however, such as msmith or mas. Each account must have a different name.

Password

This is the password you use to log on to your Mac. You're asked for it at other times, too, such as when you install new software or change security settings. Don't use the password you've used for everything else in your life. I suggest that you pick something different and stronger. The security of your computer begins with a well-chosen password. When you see the screen that asks for the password, look for a little key icon next to the password entry box. Click it, and OS X suggests a password. Pick one of its suggestions, write down the password, and keep it in a safe place. I explain why, and give some tips on other easy ways to make up a password and not forget it in Chapter 10.

Wi-Fi network name and password

If you already have a Wi-Fi network, your Mac will probably pick up yours. If you live in a built-up area, you may see several networks listed — perhaps dozens. It helps to know your network's name. If you have WEP or WPA security enabled, you need your Wi-Fi password, passphrase, or key. If you've long forgotten them, see Chapter 9 for information on how to reset your access point and set up new security.

If you're setting up a new Wi-Fi network, look over Chapter 9 to decide whether you need to enable security. If so, see Chapter 10 for info on how to generate a strong passphrase to protect your network. You may as well have the passphrase ready before you begin setting up your Mac's software.

Apple ID

If you've purchased music or other items from the iTunes Store, you already have an Apple ID and password that let you sign in to make your purchases. Take a moment to look them up.

Internet account information

If all goes well, you may not need all the following information, but it's handy to have if problems occur:

- ✔ The name of your Internet service provider (ISP)
- ✔ Service type: cable, DSL, satellite, dialup, or other
- ✔ Account name
- ✔ Password
- ✔ The ISP's customer service telephone number
- ✔ If you're using a dialup Internet connection, the phone number that your computer dials to connect

E-mail service information

If you check your mail online using your browser — say, if you have an account with Yahoo! or Gmail — you needn't do anything special. Otherwise, check the website of your e-mail service to see whether it has any special instructions for Mac users. Keep handy the following info for every e-mail service you plan to use:

- ✔ Service provider's name
- ✔ Customer service phone number
- ✔ E-mail address
- ✔ E-mail password
- ✔ Type of account: POP (the most common), IMAP, or Microsoft Exchange
- ✔ Mail server address
- ✔ SMTP server address

Getting through the Startup Assistant

Finally, it's time to press that power button. As your Mac powers on, you hear the soft "boing" that has long been part of the Mac experience. Next, follow these steps:

1. **When the Select Main Language screen appears, choose the language you prefer.**

   You see the message Starting Mac OS and then a "welcome" video. Then you're asked to select the country or region you're in. If you chose English as your main language, the Mac presents English-speaking countries. (If you're somewhere else, select the Show All check box to view the complete list, including Heard & McDonald Island and the Holy See.)

If you wait a few seconds, you hear an announcement offering to tell you more about VoiceOver, a technology that Apple provides for people who have difficulty seeing.

Either way, make your choice and then click the Continue button.

2. Select the country or region you're in.

Assuming that you chose English in step 1, you see the choices U.S., Canada, UK, AZ, NZ, and IRE. You can ask for more choices.

3. Select your keyboard layout.

If you chose English in step 1, select U.S. or Canada (you can add other keyboard versions later) and then click the Continue button.

4. Specify whether you want to transfer information from another computer or backup device.

You're asked whether you want to do this because you can transfer information from another Mac, a PC, a disc, or a Time Machine backup (see Chapter 5). If you're not ready to do so, click the Don't Transfer Now button and then click the Continue button.

5. Select a wireless service.

Things start to get exciting now. If you have Wi-Fi at your location, and you aren't using exotic security tricks to make your network invisible, your Wi-Fi base station should show up on the screen, along with any others your Mac has found.

If you have security enabled, you need to know the WEP or WPA password or key to connect. If all goes well, at this point, you're online. If you're not, don't worry; just move on for now. I go over networking your Mac in more detail in Chapter 9.

6. Enter your Apple ID and its password if you have an iTunes Store (or MobileMe) account; then click the Continue button.

You can skip this step and enter this info later, using iTunes or the MobileMe pane in System Preferences.

7. Supply the requested registration information (or as much as you're willing to tell Apple) and then click the Continue button.

You should see a notice that says, "The warranty for your Apple product does not require you to register the product."

8. Continue answering some optional questions from the assistant and click the Continue button when you finish.

You can decide whether Apple is being too nosy. The questions include where you will use the computer and what best describes what you do.

Deselect the Stay in Touch check box if you don't want e-mail announcements.

9. **In the Set Up This Account screen of the assistant, verify the account name, enter your password, and then click the Continue button.**

   Make sure that the account name is the one you want. This name is one thing that you can't easily change later. Enter the password you prepared (twice). If you didn't have a password ready, click the key icon next to the password entry field; Password Assistant suggests some passwords. Pick one and write it down on a slip of paper that you'll keep in a safe place. (See Chapter 10 for more on how Password Assistant works and picking passwords.)

10. **Select a picture, if you want, for this account.**

    If you have a Mac with a built-in camera (the iMac, MacBook, MacBook Air, and MacBook Pro all have one, as do new Apple displays), the Startup Wizard offers to take your picture to use as an icon for this account. You can retake the photo if you don't like the results, and you can change it later by choosing System Preferences⇨ Users & Groups. Alternatively, you can choose an image from a picture library.

11. **Select a time zone, click the Continue button, and then set your date and time if necessary.**

    Macs are supplied already set to Pacific Standard Time (PST) and Cupertino-USA — Apple's hometown. Click the map or select the closest city in the list. After your time zone is set, the date and time displayed are likely to be close to correct. If you're connected to the Internet, your Mac sets itself by using a time server that's aligned to the U.S. government's atomic clock.

Are we there yet?

If all went according to plan, you should see an OS X Desktop waiting for you to work or play with. If you have a modern Internet hookup, you should be online as well. I give you an introduction to OS X in the next chapter. Later chapters tell you more about getting online, setting up e-mail, moving files over, increasing your computer's security level, and solving any problems you may encounter. You also find out more about the various neat things you can do with your Mac. Chapter 22 suggests some creative (as well as some mundane) things you can do with your old PC.

Dive on in!

Maintaining parental control

As I say in Chapter 3, I'm not a big fan of computers for small children, but even teenagers need limits on computer use because games and networking sites are highly addictive. Before you hand over a computer account to your child, be sure to read Chapter 17, which tells you how to use OS X Parental Controls. It's very hard to introduce those controls later, when you realize that a child is spending *way* too much time in front of the screen.

Chapter 5

Mac OS X for Windows Users

• •

• •

*A*s a PC user, you're already familiar with the operating system known as Windows. It's a complex piece of software developed by Microsoft, and some version of it comes with most personal computers now sold, with one big exception: Apple doesn't sell its Macs with Windows software. Instead, Apple equips its Macintosh computers with Apple's own operating system, Mac OS X. Apple pronounces it "oh ess ten," as in the Roman numeral *ten*. (The previous Apple operating system was OS 9.) Apple computers are stylish and well made, but OS X is the main reason to buy a Mac. (You can have Windows on your Mac in addition to OS X, but you have to buy it and install it yourself, as I explain in Chapter 16.)

Apple and Microsoft are locked in a battle over which company can produce an operating system that offers a better experience for the user. Both companies are forced to keep improving their offerings. Most Mac users believe that Apple keeps coming out ahead.

PC and Mac: We Have a Lot in Common

Microsoft adopted many Mac OS features when it created Windows, so you find much that's familiar when you try OS X. The fundamental idea is much the same: The operating system

✔ Stores data as files that have names

✔ Organizes files in a hierarchy of folders

✔ Runs applications

✓ Talks to external devices such as printers, scanners, music players, and cameras

✓ Connects to other computers by way of local area networks, the Internet, and the World Wide Web

You interact with the computer by using a *graphical user interface (GUI),* which presents a simulated Desktop on the screen, with icons you can move around and click. Information appears in rectangular windows, and you can choose options from pull-down menus. You use a pointing device, such as a mouse or trackpad, to move a cursor around the screen. The cursor normally is an arrow, but it sometimes changes its shape to reflect what's going on.

Over the years, the computer industry has adopted numerous standards to ensure that different products can work well together. Nowadays, Apple is at the forefront of this process, adopting most standards and frequently contributing some new ones that other companies adopt. Here's a quick rundown of the alphabet soup of standards that Mac OS X shares with Windows and other operating systems:

✓ **Data formats:** ASCII, H.264, JPEG, MP3, MPEG, PDF, RTF, TIFF, and Unicode

✓ **File systems:** Apple HFS+, ISO 9660 CDs, Microsoft FAT, Microsoft NTFS (read-only), NFS, UDF 1.5 DVDs, and 3½-inch HD floppy (with external drive)

✓ **Input/output:** Bluetooth, FireWire/IEEE-1394, PCIe (Pro), Toslink audio, USB, Thunderbolt

✓ **Networking:** Bonjour, Ethernet, HTTP, LDAP, POP mail, RSS, S/MIME, TCP/IP, and Wi-Fi

✓ **Security:** AES, HTTPS, RADIUS, SSH, SSL/TLS, WEP, WPA, and WPA2

✓ **Software standards:** BootP, BSD, CalDAV calendaring, DHCP, EFI, Java, JavaScript, LP64 64-bit, Microsoft Exchange, OpenGL graphics, POSIX, PPPoE, Ruby on Rails, SOAP, UNIX 03, X11, and x86

This list isn't complete, and I don't expect you to know what all these geeky acronyms mean. I explain the most important ones in Chapter 3 and other ones as I go, and you can check the glossary for the rest. But I'm about to dive into all the differences, and I want to emphasize how much overlap exists between the two operating systems. After you get used to a few new concepts and some different terminology, you'll feel right at home using OS X.

Adjusting to the Differences

You do, of course, encounter differences between Windows and Mac OS X. Some differences are merely a matter of terminology. Others just take getting used to, and a few you may find annoying. For most of those annoying issues, I point out, in a reasonably familiar way, ways to accomplish what you want to do.

Comparing Windows- and Mac-speak

Computers seem to run on jargon. Many of the buzzwords used on Macs are exactly the same as those used in Windows: *files, users, log in, log out, open, close, shut down, help,* and most networking and Internet terms. Terms used to describe the graphical interface are mostly the same, too: *menu, check box, dialog* or *dialog box, radio button, drag, click,* and *double-click.* Table 5-1 provides the equivalent terms or types of programs for each platform.

Table 5-1	Windows Terms versus Mac Terms
Windows	*Mac OS X*
Control Panel	System Preferences
Ctrl+Alt+Delete	Option+⌘+Esc
Exit or Close (Alt+FX)	Quit (⌘+Q)
Hourglass cursor (busy signal)	Spinning beach ball or gear (busy signal)
Internet Explorer	Safari
My Computer	Finder
My Documents	Documents folder
My Music	Music folder
My Pictures	Pictures folder
Notepad	TextEdit
Outlook Express	Mail
Recycle Bin	Trash
Right click	Secondary click
Settings	Preferences
Shortcut icon	Alias
Taskbar and tray	Dock
Windows Explorer	Finder window
Windows Update	Software Update
Wizard	Assistant

Some things, fortunately, have no equivalent in the Mac world. No activation is required to use OS X, for example; you can skip registration if you like. You find no Windows Genuine Advantage checking and deciding (sometimes inaccurately) whether your copy of Mac OS X is authentic, and no animated paper clip offers inane help. Also, you don't run into DLL files or any equivalent of the Windows Registry — both notorious sources of problems.

Seeing the big picture: The desktop and menus

After you answer all the startup assistant's questions, you see the Mac Desktop, shown in Figure 5-1.

The basic idea is the same as on the Windows desktop: Most of the screen is filled with a pattern or an image that resembles a tablecloth on which you see various icons that represent files, storage media, and applications. You also find an arrow cursor that you can move around by using the mouse or trackpad. You can move icons by placing the arrow cursor over them, clicking the mouse or trackpad, and continuing to press down as you move the cursor.

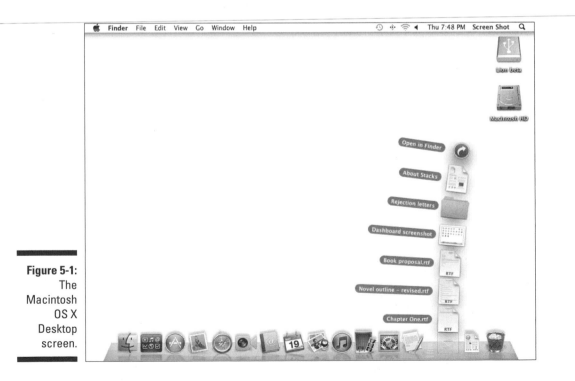

Figure 5-1:
The Macintosh OS X Desktop screen.

The big differences between the Mac and PC desktops are at the top and bottom. At the top of the Mac Desktop, you find all OS X menus. Each application has a different menu set. The menu set shown is for the application whose window is in front. That application is said to *have focus* or to be the *current application.* Open an application, say TextEdit, and look at the menu at the top of your screen.

- ✔ The first menu on the left is always headed by an Apple logo (🍎) and is called the Apple menu, naturally. It contains system-related stuff, such as System Preferences and Shut Down.

- ✔ The next menu over to the right is headed by the name of the current application. That menu is where you find entries that change preferences and Quit (exit) the application.

- ✔ Continuing from the left, you typically see File and Edit menus that work much like the corresponding Windows menus. The Help menu is always at the right end.

At the bottom of the screen, you see a bunch of largish icons (you can make them smaller, move them or hide them, as I explain later in this chapter). This area, the *Dock,* roughly corresponds to the Windows taskbar and tray. Here's what you see:

- ✔ Each icon on the Dock represents an application, a file, or a folder; you click an icon once to start or open it. Click a folder or *stack* on the Dock, and its contents spring out as a graceful arc (refer to Figure 5-1) or as a grid if there are too many items for the arc.

- ✔ If you don't know what an icon represents, move your cursor over it, and a label appears.

- ✔ You add applications and folders to the Dock by dragging them there.

Dragging something to the Dock doesn't move it from the folder it's in, but if you miss hitting the Dock, the item will be moved to the Desktop. You can put it back by choosing Edit⇨Undo.

I say more about menus and the Dock in the following sections.

Pointing the way: The mouse and trackpad

One of the great divides between Apple and Microsoft concerned whether computer mice should have one or two buttons. You may think it bizarre that adults would fret about such a thing, but the debate invoked great passions. Apple touted the simplicity of having a single button, avoiding the need to explain what each button did. Microsoft eventually found a good use for the second button — the one on the right. That button displayed menus of possible actions appropriate to the window in which the right click occurred. Later, scroll wheels appeared, allowing users to move up and down in a window by using intuitive finger actions. Apple added similar functions to laptops by using multi-finger gestures. Clicking on the trackpad with two fingers was the same as right-clicking, for example. Then Apple incorporated the multi-finger idea into a mouse that it named Magic Mouse and released a large trackpad that can be used with desktop Macs called the Magic Trackpad.

A wireless Bluetooth Magic Mouse comes with the iMac and Mac Pro. You can buy a Magic Mouse to use with other Macs (including laptops) if you like. At first glance, this mouse looks like a single-button mouse. Here are a few pointers on using the Magic Mouse:

- ✔ Move the mouse around as you would any other mouse to move the pointer or cursor displayed on your screen.

- ✔ The top of the Magic Mouse is a single shell. To perform a right click, you press the top-right corner. To perform a regular (left) click — the most common action — press anywhere else.

- ✔ Sliding one finger on the top surface is like turning a scroll wheel, but depending on which way you move your finger, you can scroll horizontally as well as vertically.

- ✔ Sliding two fingers left or right on the top surface switches items, such as pictures in an iPhoto album or pages open in your browser.

- ✔ Hold down the Control key and slide up or down with one finger to zoom in or out.

- ✔ If you want to customize these gestures (to make the top-left corner the secondary click, for example), choose ⌘➪System Preferences➪Mouse. You see many choices for each gesture, for the speed of your mouse, and for other settings.

So Apple has gone from the simplicity of one button to a very handy multi-function input device that in a way still looks like one button.

If your Mac came with a Magic Mouse or Magic Trackpad, by all means give them a try; I think they're slick. But if yours didn't, or if you find all of that multi-gesture stuff too confusing, I suggest that you start off with a standard two-button, USB, scroll-wheel mouse. If you already have one that you like, great; if not, go buy one. Wired (as opposed to wireless) optical mice are inexpensive, and almost any will do fine. Just plug it in to a free USB port or your USB hub. You don't even have to turn off the computer; and no setup is necessary. Apple software uses the left button for primary clicks, the scroll wheel to scroll up and down, and the right button to bring up context-sensitive menus, just as Windows does. If you're a left-handed user, you may want to switch the buttons by using the Mouse pane in System Preferences. If you have a different USB pointing device that you love, such as a track ball, give that a try as well.

Gesturing with Multi-Touch

Apple laptops feature a large glass trackpad that can tell whether one, two, three, or four fingers are touching it. The entire trackpad surface also functions as the click button. PC laptops generally have two buttons. You can signal a right click on a Mac laptop by holding down the Control key and clicking the trackpad surface. Another way is available, however: if you place two fingers on the trackpad when you click, your Mac understands that as a right click.

Apple has taken the trackpad gesture idea several steps further. Here are some gestures you can express with your fingers:

- ✔ *Two fingers:*

  Swipe to scroll up, down, left, or right.

  Rotate pictures by twisting your thumb and forefinger.

  Pinch or spread two fingers to zoom out or in.

- ✔ *Three fingers:*

  Swipe left or right to change pages, if you have more than one page open in the Safari web browser.

- ✔ *Four fingers:*

  Swipe up to move all windows off the Desktop; swipe down to bring them back.

  Swipe down to show all windows; swipe up to restore their previous positions.

  Swipe left or right to see all active applications.

You can use keyboard shortcuts for many of these features. You can use your two-button USB mouse with your laptop, too. Just plug it in.

If you don't have a laptop but want to use the Multi-Touch gesture feature, Apple sells a wireless Magic Trackpad that works just like the laptop trackpads but sits cozily next to your keyboard.

The key to keyboards

The wireless Apple keyboard layouts look much like standard Windows keyboard layouts, but without the numeric keypad and the special keys above the arrow keys. (Apple sells a wired keyboard with a numeric keypad if you need all those keys.) The other big difference is the two keys on either side of the spacebar. On a PC, the keys closest to the spacebar are labeled Alt; the next ones over sport a Windows logo. On a Mac, the keys closest to the spacebar have an icon (⌘) that looks like a four-bladed propeller or electric fan. The Mac world calls them the Command keys; they have the same function.

The Command key (⌘) is used in almost all keyboard shortcuts. It's one of the most important things to know about the Mac.

The next one over is the Option key (⌥). It's often used as a modifier along with the Command key. It's analogous to the Alt key on PC keyboards.

Another key that may not be familiar to PC users is in the top-right section of Apple keyboards. It's the Eject key (⏏) for the optical drive (the drive that reads and writes CDs and DVDs). The eject button on home audio devices sports the same symbol. To the left of the ⏏ key, you find two keys that raise and lower the volume, as well as a key with only a speaker symbol; this key turns the system sound on and off. It's a mute button, in effect. Next to the Escape key (esc) at the far-left end, you find brightness controls and two keys with funny symbols: one a box of boxes that shows all windows that are open, and the other (which looks like a fuel gauge) that brings up the Dashboard, which I describe later in this chapter. The sound-control, screen-brightness, and other controls are also the function keys. To make these keys work as function keys, you hold down the Fn key while pressing the function key you want. Older Apple keyboards may have different arrangements.

Backspace versus Del versus Delete

Fasten your seat belts for this one. The large key on the right end of the numeral row on PC keyboards is generally labeled Backspace. It doesn't really backspace, however; the left-arrow key does that. Instead, the PC Backspace key deletes the character to the left of the insertion point, which is the blinking vertical line that tells you where in a block of text you're editing. Long ago, Apple decided to label this key Delete because that's truly what it does. The problem is that PC keyboards have another, regular-size delete or del key in the group of keys above, or sometimes next to, the arrow keys. If you never use this key on your PC, skip the rest of this paragraph, but if you depend on it, here's the deal: This second delete key deletes the character to the *right* of the insertion point. Apple laptops and standard keyboards omit this key. The optional Apple keyboard with numeric keypad includes the second delete key, also labeled Delete. It bears a standard delete symbol that looks like a boxy arrow pointing to the right with an *x* in it. (The big Delete key doesn't have a symbol on it, though one exists, and it has the same boxy arrow pointing to the *left*.) On keyboards that don't have the second delete key, you request the right delete function by holding down the function key (Fn) when you press delete.

Scrolling up, scrolling down: A touching story

When you're using a mouse to scroll through a document, you're used to moving the scroll bar down to see the end of a page, but Apple thinks that finger gestures on a trackpad should feel like physically moving the page itself, so you should slide two fingers *up* on the trackpad to scroll down a page. That's also how the iPad and iPhone work. I think you'll get used to it,

but if the new way to think about scrolling is too confusing, you can change it by choosing ♦⇨System Preferences⇨Trackpad. Just clear the check box that says Move Content in the Direction of Finger Movement When Scrolling or Navigating. You'll find many other ways to customize the meanings of your multi-finger computer caresses in the Trackpad pane.

Keyboard shortcuts using the Command key versus the Ctrl key

Keyboard shortcuts are little incantations combining a couple of key presses that carry out a task without your having to plow through the menus. PCs have two kinds of keyboard shortcuts. For some, you hold down the Ctrl key and a letter key; for others, you press the Alt key and type one letter from each menu item's name — often, but not always, the first letter. Mac keyboard shortcuts are similar to the first type, but you use the Command key (⌘) rather than the Ctrl key. The following examples show some Mac keyboard shortcuts:

Keyboard Shortcut	*Action*
⌘+C	Copy
⌘+X	Cut
⌘+V	Paste
⌘+F	Find
⌘+G	Find Again
⌘+A	Select All
⌘+S	Save
⌘+Z	Undo

Replacing the PC Ctrl key press with the Command key (⌘) also applies to most Ctrl+key shortcuts in programs such as Microsoft Office.

The letters in keyboard shortcut combinations are always shown capitalized in this book and onscreen, but don't hold down the Shift key unless it's explicitly called for. Thus, ⌘+Q quits the current application, and ⌘+Shift+Q is the Log Out shortcut.

Although the Mac OS X menu layout appears to be intuitive and easy to follow, it's fair to say that Apple gets a little carried away with shortcuts. It has dozens of them. Don't try to remember them all. The most important shortcuts are the ones I've already mentioned, many of which you probably already know from Windows (remembering to use ⌘ instead of Control). Pick up others as you need them, and take advantage of this book's online Cheat Sheet.

OS X displays the available shortcuts for menu items directly on the pull-down menu itself. Some combinations use different and even multiple modifier keys. Apple uses other symbols in addition to the ⌘ symbol and symbol to indicate these keys. Here's a quick guide (also see the Cheat Sheet):

- **Option (⌥):** This key often modifies a shortcut or menu item by telling it to do more. Pressing ⌘+W closes the front window, for example, and pressing ⌥+⌘+W closes *all* windows for the front application. Shortcuts can be complex, too. The shortcut in TextEdit for Edit⇨Paste and Match Style is ⌥+Shift+⌘+V.

- **Control (∧):** This key's symbol looks like a hat. You press the key in combination with a mouse click to create a right click.

- **Shift (⇧):** You can press either the right or left Shift key. Pressing the Caps Lock key has no effect on shortcuts that include a Shift key.

- **Escape (⎋):** This key's symbol looks a lot like the power-button icon, but the line is at an angle and has a little arrow pointing out. Escape is a shortcut for Cancel in dialogs.

Many other Mac keyboard shortcuts exist. Choose ⇨System Preferences⇨ Keyboard and then choose Keyboard Shortcuts to see a list. The Keyboard pane has many other options for customizing your input experience. Explore, but don't get carried away.

If you have difficulty holding down combinations of keys, you can activate the Sticky Keys feature by choosing System Preferences⇨Universal Access. See Chapter 17 for other accessibility tips if you have difficulty using computers.

Special characters and other languages

Macs let you enter text in a wide variety of languages. Choose ⇨System Preferences⇨Language & Text⇨Input Sources, and select the check box labeled Keyboard & Character Viewer. While you're there, check the boxes for another language you know or would like to learn. On the menu bar, in the top-right corner, you should see a little national flag that corresponds to the language of the keyboard you selected during the startup process. The Stars and Stripes appears for the U.S. keyboard, for example. If you click this flag, a menu of options appears. Choose Show Character Viewer from this menu, and you can browse a variety of symbols. Click the gear symbol in the top-left corner of the Characters pane and choose Customize list to select more of the available character sets in OS X to display; dozens of them are available.

Choose Flag➪Show Keyboard Viewer, and a small onscreen keyboard corresponding to the language you chose appears. You can enter characters with this keyboard by clicking its buttons.

Mac windows versus Windows windows

This section refers to windows spelled with a lowercase *w* — those rectangular boxes on your computer's screen where all the action happens. Again, the basic idea in OS X is similar to what you're used to in the Microsoft operating system. You see a title bar at the top of each window, with colored buttons you can click. From left to right:

- ✔ **Red:** Closes the window
- ✔ **Yellow:** Minimizes the window (it slurps down to the Dock)
- ✔ **Green:** Resizes the window to make better use of the screen

You move a window by clicking the title bar and dragging with the mouse. A scroll bar and slider appear on the right side. You can also adjust the window size by dragging any edge or corner.

Keep it simple

You have oodles of ways to customize Mac OS X by using system and application preferences, and you can download software that gives you even more possibilities. I recommend restraint. Don't customize OS X more than necessary, particularly when you're getting used to working with it. The closer your Mac software is to its out-of-the-box configuration, the easier it is to get help when you have a problem, whether that help is from this book, from websites, or from Apple customer service.

May I See the Menu, Please?

As I mention earlier in this chapter, the menu bar in OS X is at the top of the screen, not in each window. The menu you see changes depending on which application's window is at the front. You change which application window is in front by either clicking a window that's behind the one in front or clicking the application's icon on the Dock.

You can see a summary of all open applications by holding down the Command key (⌘) and pressing the Tab key. As shown in Figure 5-2, you see a translucent bar with icons for each running application. Release the Command key, and the selected application comes to the front. Keep holding down the Command key and press the Tab key repeatedly to cycle through all applications. This feature is similar to the one performed by pressing Alt+Tab in Windows. If Shift+⌘+Tab cycles through the application icons, too, but in the other direction (from right to left).

Figure 5-2:
The ⌘+Tab display.

Apple menu

The leftmost menu is always the Apple menu (), and it always offers the same set of choices, regardless of which applications are in use. Those choices are described in this list:

- **About This Mac:** Provides a quick summary of your computer's configuration, including memory, processor, and operating-system release. Choose More Info for an excruciatingly complete rundown of everything in, on, or attached to your computer.

- **Software Update:** Updates your Mac to the latest versions of the software that came with it. Your Mac checks for updates every week automatically unless you change the System Preferences setting, which is labeled (unsurprisingly) Software Update.

- **App Store:** Opens the App Store application, where you can download neat stuff — some free, some not.

- **System Preferences:** Lets you see and change the numerous settings associated with OS X system software. It's the equivalent of Control Panel in Windows. Figure 5-3 shows the main window that you see when you choose System Preferences, with all the icons you click to complete specific settings chores.

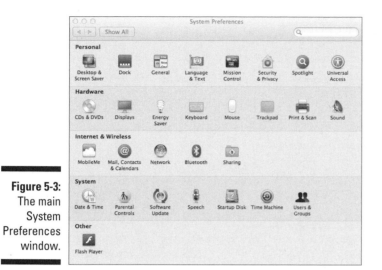

Figure 5-3:
The main
System
Preferences
window.

TIP

 ✔ **Dock:** Lets you control the size, location, and behavior of the Dock. Depending on your choices, the Dock can be your best friend or be truly annoying.

 The option I like best is Turn Hiding On, which moves the Dock off the screen until you steer your cursor all the way to the bottom edge, at which time the Dock pops up, ready to do your bidding. Move the cursor away from the bottom of the screen, and the Dock hides itself again.

 ✔ **Recent Items:** Offers a quick way to return to the application, document, or server that you were just using. You can tell OS X how far back the Recent Items lists should go in the Appearance pane under System Preferences. The default is ten items.

 ✔ **Force Quit:** Lets you kill any application that isn't responding to commands (see Figure 5-4). Yes, Mac applications freeze, just as Windows applications do, though they rarely affect other running applications. Commit to memory the Force Quit keyboard shortcut: Option+⌘+Esc. You may need it if you can't open the menu for some reason. It's the Mac equivalent of the Windows "three-finger salute": Ctrl+Alt+Delete.

 ✔ **Sleep, Restart, Shut Down, and Log Out:** Perform the same tasks as they do in Windows. Apple provides only one sleep option; there's no separate hibernate nonsense. You control the sleep settings in the Energy Saver pane of System Preferences.

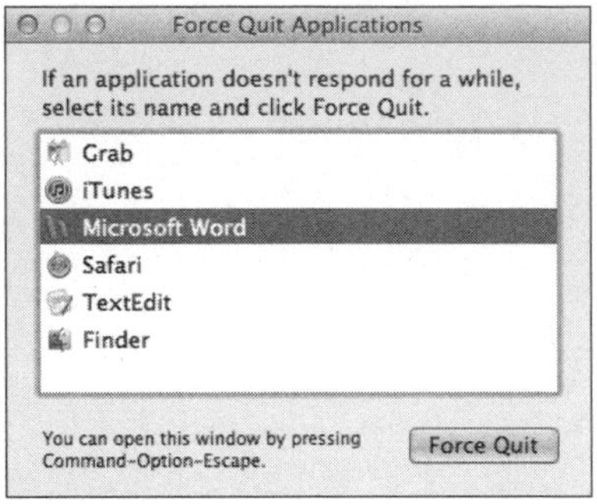

Figure 5-4:
The Force
Quit
window.

> **Force Quit Applications**
>
> If an application doesn't respond for a while, select its name and click Force Quit.
>
> 🎨 Grab
> 🎵 iTunes
> 📄 **Microsoft Word**
> 🧭 Safari
> 📝 TextEdit
> 🖥 Finder
>
> You can open this window by pressing Command-Option-Escape. [Force Quit]

Application menu

The menu to the right of the Apple menu has the same name as whichever application is in front, and looking at that menu is the easiest way to find out just which application is active, if more than one is open. As with the Apple menu, this menu's contents are essentially the same from application to application. The top item displays the About screen for the application, which gives the application's version number, copyright notice, and any other information that the application's developers want to tell you.

Other menu choices to expect are described in this list:

- ✔ **Services:** Links to other Mac programs that may aid in what you are doing — for example, e-mailing a document you are editing or a high-lighted portion of the document.

- ✔ **Hide and Hide Others:** These items (and their keyboard shortcuts) are handy to keep in mind when your screen becomes cluttered. Keep pressing ⌘+H until the application you want is in front; press Option+⌘+H to hide the rest.

- ✔ **Show All:** Unhides any applications you've hidden while leaving the current application in front.

- ✔ **Preferences:** Choose this menu item to change the application's settings. It's one of the most important menu items for PC-to-Mac switchers to know about.

- ✔ **Quit (and its shortcut, ⌘+Q):** This menu item tells the program to terminate; it's equivalent to Exit in Windows.

The Finder's application menu is where you empty the Trash. (That's the same as emptying the Recycle Bin in Windows.) When you choose Finder⇨ Empty Trash, any files you've deleted are removed from the file system so the space they occupy can be written over, but note that they are not necessarily erased. Choose Finder⇨Secure Empty Trash if you want the data truly gone from your Mac, but if the files are large, this operation can take a while. See Chapter 6 for more on purging data.

File and Edit menus

In most applications, the two menus just to the right of the Apple menu are the File and Edit menus. These two closely resemble their Windows counterparts.

One big difference is that the Quit command isn't on the File menu; instead, it's on the application menu, to the left. This is one of the more annoying differences between Windows and OS X. Just remember the ⌘+Q shortcut for Quit and avoid the aggravation. Also, Preferences — the OS X equivalent of Settings in Windows — isn't on the Edit menu. It's on the application menu. It has a shortcut, too: ⌘+, (press command and then the comma key).

When you save a new document for the first time or choose File⇨Open or File⇨Save As, you see a dialog much like the one you'd see when you do the same things in Windows XP or Windows 7 . Figure 5-5 shows many of the navigation features of this dialog, including the sidebar with your favorite destinations and the option to choose among Icon, List, Column, and Cover Flow views. Note also the disclosure triangle in the top-right corner.

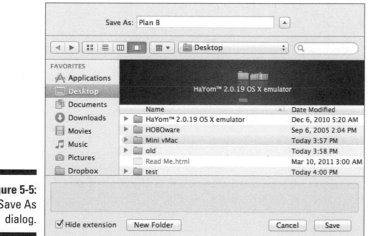

Figure 5-5:
The Save As
dialog.

If you see the shortened version of the Save As dialog, shown in Figure 5-6, rather than the full version (refer to Figure 5-5), click the little disclosure triangle to the right of the filename text field toward the top of the dialog to bring back the full dialog.

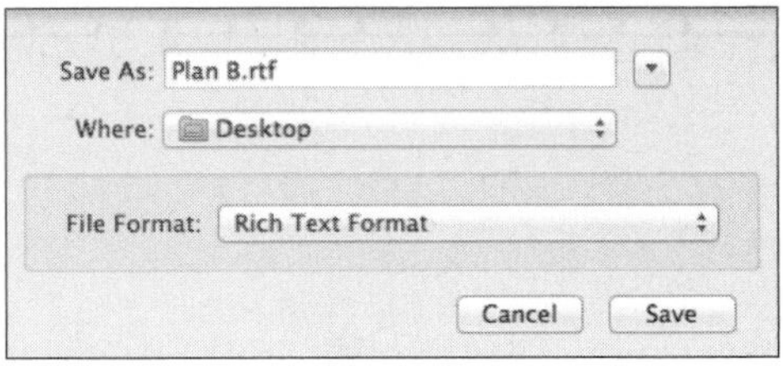

Figure 5-6:
The stunted
Save As
dialog.

Save As: Plan B.rtf

Where: 📁 Desktop

File Format: Rich Text Format

Cancel   Save

Help and Window menus

The Help menu is located to the right of the menus associated with the application, just as in Windows. To the Help menu's left, you usually find a Window menu, similar to the one in many Microsoft Windows applications. The Window menu lists which windows the application has open and lets you bring the one you want to the front. You can also press ⌘+~ (command tilde) to cycle through an application's open windows.

Applications typically have several other menus between the Edit and Window menus; these other menus are usually organized in ways that should be familiar to Windows users.

Filing Away in OS X

Files in OS X are similar to files in Windows or any other operating system, with one exception that you probably don't need to know about, so skip the next paragraph unless you're curious. The rest of this section explains what you *do* need to know about file types, filenames, your disks and volumes, and aliases (which work like shortcuts in Windows).

In most operating systems, a *file* is just a bucket of bits — 1s and 0s that programs can interpret as a text document, photograph, music, or whatever. The operating system is responsible for storing the file accurately and copying or deleting it if asked to, but that's it. Macs may add the resource fork to this notion of what a file is supposed to be. (*Fork* is used here in the sense of a fork in the road, not a fork in the steak.) The resource fork contains additional information about what's in the file that the application can use. OS X also has packages, which are files that bundle other files and even directories into a single unit; all the files an application program needs are typically bundled with the application into a package, for example. The good news is that you probably don't have to worry about these features. Resource forks are less common in newer applications, and OS X handles the forks and packages automatically. The files you bring over from Windows don't have resource forks, anyway.

File types

Many of the file types you're used to on the PC are supported directly by OS X: documents in Microsoft Word format, photographs in JPEG format, and music MP3s, for example. Others require additional software. Still others — particularly music files purchased under one of the proprietary Microsoft formats, such as for the Zune music player — may not be usable except (of course) when you're running Windows on your Mac. I give you the gory details about moving files from your PC to your Mac in Chapter 6.

Filenames

Filenames in Mac OS X can be as long as 255 characters, and you can use any characters you like except the colon (:). Windows doesn't allow any of the following special characters in filenames:

> : \ / | * ? " < >

If you're planning to move files back and forth between your PC and Mac, follow the more restrictive Windows naming rules so that filenames don't get mangled.

Extensions

In the Windows world, filenames have *extensions:* a period (.) and a few cryptic letters that are added to the end of a filename, as in `Chapter5.doc`. The file extension tells the operating system which type of file it is so that the OS knows which program should open it. OS X uses file extensions in the same way, but it also has a separate way to know the file's creator, using a special four-character code that is assigned to each application and is stored with the file's directory entry.

Pathnames

A file is stored in a folder, which may be in another folder, which may be in another folder, and so on. Operating systems keep track of all that hierarchy by using a *pathname,* which lists all the folders you have to visit in turn to find your file. The names are separated by a special character. In Windows, this character is the backslash (\). For Macs — and in Unix, in Linux, and on the Internet — the forward slash (/), sometimes called the front slash, is used. You can make nice patterns by stringing them together, like so — \/\/\/\/\/\/\/\/\/\/\/ — but this has nothing to do with what I'm talking about.

In Finder you can see the path for a folder by command-clicking on its name in the title bar or by choosing View➪Show Path Bar, which displays the path at the bottom of the folder window.

Disks and volumes

Select what types of disks you want to see on your Desktop by choosing Finder➪Preferences. You can choose to see any or all of these items: hard disks, external disks (including flash drives), CDs, DVDs, iPods, and connected servers. The selected items appear on the Desktop just as files do, but with distinctive icons (see Figure 5-7). The internal hard drive icon looks like the real hard drive in your computer. Unfortunately, most people have never taken apart a computer and don't have a clue what a hard drive looks like. External hard drive icons resemble an external drive, with either a FireWire or USB logo on it, indicating the manner of connection. Optical disc icons look like . . . well, optical discs. Flash drive icons usually look like old external floppy drives, as do the virtual volumes that appear whenever you open a disk-image file (which has a .dmg extension).

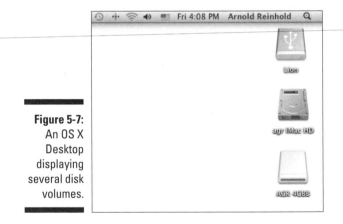

Figure 5-7: An OS X Desktop displaying several disk volumes.

The Mac way to eject or dismount one of these disk volumes is to drag the volume to the Trash. This peculiar idiom goes back to the earliest Macs. You aren't deleting any information when you do this, and the Trash icon changes to an Eject icon (⏏) when you're dragging a disk or volume to emphasize that nothing is being trashed. If dragging disks to the Trash seems too weird — you've become a true Mac person when it makes sense — right-click the disk or volume icon and choose Eject from the menu that appears. Ejectable volumes also appear in Finder windows' sidebars and have Eject symbols (⏏) next to them that you can click.

Aliases

Maybe you used shortcuts in Windows. A *shortcut* is an icon that points to another file, program, or disk drive. Macs have a similar feature — the *alias* — which is quite handy. You can create an alias by clicking the name or icon of the file, program, or disk volume you want to alias and then choosing File⇨Make Alias. (It's worth remembering the keyboard incantation for making aliases: ⌘+L.) Just as in Windows, the alias icon appears with a little arrow in its bottom-left corner, and you can move the alias anywhere you want. You can even move it to the Trash if you no longer need it; the original file doesn't go away. Mac OS X has one big improvement over this Windows feature, however: In Windows, if you move the original file to another folder or change its name, Windows becomes unhappy and doesn't know where to find the file anymore. OS X keeps track of where the file went, and the alias still works as long as the file stays on the same drive. If you delete the original file or eject the drive it's on, OS X can't do much about that.

Watch out for aliases when you want to copy files to another medium, such as an external hard drive, CD-R, or flash drive. If you drag an alias, only the alias is copied, not the file. To copy the file or folder that the alias points to, click the alias and choose File⇨Show Original, or just press ⌘+R.

The Finder Is Your Friend

When you first start your computer, you find yourself in a special program that Apple calls the Finder. The Finder is somewhat like Windows Explorer, but it's an even more basic tool on the Mac than Explorer is in Windows. You use it all the time.

You can reach the Finder by clicking anywhere on the Desktop or selecting its icon on the Dock. Pressing ⌘+F3 makes all windows go away, and you see only the Desktop and the Finder. Press ⌘+F3 again to bring everything back.

Moving around with Finder windows

You use Finder windows to move around among folders. You see a window when you double-click a folder or choose File⇨New Finder Window.

As shown in Figure 5-8, the name of the folder is at the top of the Finder window. The icon to its left is live; you can drag it wherever you want, just as you would drag the folder's icon in its parent folder or on the Desktop.

Figure 5-8:
A Finder
window in
Cover Flow
view.

Finder windows have a sidebar on the left with a list of favorite folders at the top and available storage volumes at the bottom. You can customize them by dragging folders into or out of the list area. Each Finder window has a toolbar at the top. You can choose any of four ways to view files: icon, list, column, or Cover Flow view:

- **Icon view** shows icons for each file or subfolder. You can neaten the display and sort the icons by choosing View ➪ Clean Up By and selecting in what order they should appear (Name, Date Modified, and so on).

- **List view** includes details such as when the file was last modified, its size, and its kind (Word document or picture, for example). Folders have small triangles next to them. If you click one, the folder expands to show its contents. You can expand and manipulate more than one folder this way.

- **Column view** shows you the contents of the current folder and the folder that contains it, along with (optionally) a preview of any file you select, along with info about the file. Widen columns by dragging the lines separating them. You can customize the contents of the file view by choosing Finder➪View➪Customize View Options.

- Cool **Cover Flow view** is based on the way that iTunes and iPods display album covers to help you find the music you want, but in the Finder, Cover Flow view shows a preview of file contents. Click the Quick Look "eye" icon at the top of the window (or press the spacebar), and you see a readable, scrollable preview of the center file. Click the double-arrow icon at the bottom of that view, and you see a full-screen version. Quick Look supports most image file formats, along with text files, PDFs, movies, Keynote presentations, and Microsoft Word and Excel files. There's no need to open files in an application just to see what's inside.

Let's look at All My Files

Apple sees the world moving to a "post-PC era," where the nasty complexities of a personal computer will be hidden from us mortals. One of those complexities that Steve Jobs feels is too confusing for users is the file system and its mind-numbing hierarchy of folders inside folders inside folders and on and on. The iPad and iPhone try to hide all that from the user, organizing user files by applications and only allowing one level of folders for storing the applications themselves. Mac OS X Finder gives you a peek at what the brave new world will look like. Click on All My Files in the Finder sidebar and you see all the documents, images, and so on that you've created or downloaded, organized by file type and date (most recent first), and without all the ugly internal system files. It works great if you don't store a lot of stuff. But for those of us who've been using computers for many years and tend to keep our old projects on our hard drive, I'm not sure it's the wave of the future.

A Finder window's toolbar also has back- and forward-arrow buttons that are initially grayed out. As you open and close folders, these buttons let you return to a previous view, much like the Back and Forward buttons in a web browser. The toolbar also has an action menu with a gear icon that lets you choose options that are also available in the Finder menu. You can even customize the toolbar from the View menu and add icons. I find the Path icon particularly useful because it shows all the folders that include the current one and lets you pop back to any one of them. You can also drag files and folders to a Finder window's toolbar, and the item then appears in all Finder windows. Command-drag the icon to remove it from the toolbar. A temporary (Temp) folder can be handy when you're rearranging files, for example.

Getting info about files and disks

Click an icon on the desktop or in a Finder window, and press ⌘+I. A window appears, displaying everything you always wanted to know about that file but were afraid to ask, including what kind of file it is, how big it is, where it's located, and when it was created and last modified. You can find much more if you click the little triangles next to other items in the Get Info window, such as Name & Extension, Open With (which lets you pick the application to open this file or all files of this type), Preview, and Ownership & Permissions. This last section lets you control who can read and who can change the file or folder. See the section about understanding file-permission basics in Chapter 19 for more info on permissions.

Click a disk or storage volume icon on the desktop and press ⌘+I to find out how much space remains on that disk drive or storage volume. This technique is the easiest way to find out how much disk space you have available.

Providing accessibility

Mac OS X has a range of features designed to improve accessibility for users with disabilities. These features include ways to make the mouse easier to use (including making the cursor bigger) and to operate the computer by using only the keyboard; the speech-recognition technology, which lets OS X respond to spoken commands; and the ability to attach some assistive-technology devices. You find the settings for most of these features by choosing ⬤⇨System Preferences and then selecting either Universal Access or Speech. See Chapter 17 for more on accessibility.

Installing software

When you try to install software on your Mac, OS X asks you for a password. If more than one user has an account on the computer, only those with *administrative privileges* can install software. Chapter 10 has more on setting up accounts; also, see the section "Setting Up Additional Accounts," later in this chapter. If you give your kids an account, don't give them admin status. That way, you can control what software they load.

In most cases, installing software on your Mac is simple. For applications you get from the Mac App Store, the process is automatic. For software that comes on a CD or DVD disc, follow these steps:

1. **Insert the software disc.**

   The downloaded file or installation disc opens as a window, such as the one shown in Figure 5-9. If the disc does not open automatically, double-click the disc's icon in the Finder.

2. **Drag the icon or folder that contains the application into the Applications folder, which normally is in the sidebar of all Finder windows.**

   Some applications come with install scripts. For those, you just double-click the install icon and follow the instructions. You may be given an option to customize your installation. Unless you're absolutely sure that you know what you want, installing the default configuration recommended by the software's publisher is best.

 If you're new to the Mac and are buying only new software, you aren't likely to run into software written for the older PowerPC processors that Apple used to use. Once upon a time, an Intel Mac could run software written for older PowerPC Macs by using a program called Rosetta. OS X Lion doesn't allow this function, and it can't run software for OS 9 and earlier Mac operating systems, either. Ways exist to work around this limitation, but they aren't easy or aren't fully functional. I describe some of these methods in the bonus chapter at www.dummies.com/go/switchingtoamac.

Printing and Scanning on the Mac

Printers are the Bermuda Triangle of personal computing: Setting them up strikes fear in the hearts of most geeks. Apple has done a lot to simplify the process. It has introduced the Bonjour technology, which many printer manufacturers have adopted. Bonjour automates all the messy stuff. Also, OS X comes with drivers for dozens of printer models. So if you have a fairly new printer, everything should go smoothly.

To set up your printer and do a test print, follow these steps:

1. **Make sure that the printer has power and is connected to your Mac.**

   If it's a USB printer, plug it into one of your USB ports. If it's an Ethernet printer, make sure that it's connected to the same network as your Mac. If it's a Wi-Fi printer, make sure that AirPort is on. Bluetooth printers may take some extra steps; check the printer's manual for instructions.

2. **Turn on the printer.**

3. **Open a short document or create one with TextEdit.**

4. **Choose File⇨Print.**

   Your printer's name should appear in the Print dialog.

5. **Select your printer, and click Print.**

   Off you go.

If your printer doesn't appear, try these steps:

1. **Choose System Preferences⇨Print & Scan and click the plus (+) icon.**

2. **Wait half a minute.**

   You see a drop-down menu with all the printers that your Mac can find. The first item in the menu is Add Printer or Scanner.

3. **If your printer still doesn't appear in the list, select** Add Printer or Scanner **from the drop-down list, and select the printer you're using.**

4. **If nothing seems to work, go to the printer manufacturer's support website for the printer you're using, and see whether you can find software for Mac OS X to download.**

   See Chapter 20 for more printer troubleshooting tips.

Your Mac knows about most scanners, too. Before you download any special scanner software from your scanner manufacturer's website, check whether the following steps work with your scanner:

1. **Open the Image Capture app.**

   Its icon — a camera — should be in Launchpad. This application is the OS X tool for scanning. You should see your scanner listed.

2. **You can also scan documents from the Preview Application, which you find in the Dock and Launchpad. Choose File⇨Import from Scanner.**

3. **If you don't see your scanner listed, select Include Networked Devices and give it a few seconds to show up.**

Setting Up Additional Accounts

If more than one person will be using the computer, you should give each person her own account. To do so, follow these steps:

1. **Choose ➔System Preferences and click Users & Groups in the System Preferences window.**

2. **In the Users & Groups pane, click the plus sign (+) below the list of accounts.**

   If the list is grayed out, click the lock icon below it to unlock it. You have to enter an administrator password to complete this step.

3. **For each new account you create, when prompted, enter the account holder's name, a short name that's the name of the account holder's home directory, and the password for the account.**

   The account holder can change her password later, if she wants.

4. **(Optional) Select a picture for the account holder.**

5. **(Optional) Specify which programs will start up automatically for that account.** You have to log in to the account to set login items.

6. **(Optional, but important) Set up Parental Controls if this account is for a child.**

   Read Chapter 17 *before* setting up the account; I have lots of tips about the best way to set up an account for a child.

Backing Up

The most important thing to remember about backing up is to swivel your head to look in all directions before putting the car in gear; don't rely on the rearview mirror. Wait — that's not the right advice for this book. The most important thing to remember about backing up your computer is that you have to *do it.* Regularly. Most people don't back up their data even once a month, and that isn't often enough.

National Public Radio once ran a story about a woman who worked for a company that recovers data from defunct hard drives. The company charges lots of money for this service, but it isn't successful for all customers. The woman was trained as a grief counselor, and the company hired her to break the bad news to those unfortunate customers that their precious data was gone forever.

Time Machine and Time Capsule

Fortunately, the OS X feature Time Machine makes backing up your computer easier than backing up your car. Plug an external drive into your Mac, and Time Machine asks whether you want to use it as your backup device. Agree, and Time Machine takes over, backing everything up. It works in the background so that you can carry on with whatever you're doing with your Mac. You want a big external drive — 1 TB (1000GB) or more. The Apple Time Capsule includes a large hard drive and a Wi-Fi router that lets all Macs running at least OS X version 10.5 to back up by using Time Machine.

Time Machine awakens every hour and backs up everything that has changed since the last backup. Every night at midnight it consolidates the hourly backups into one backup for the day, and then once a week and once a month it consolidates them further. You can change the time, of course, and your Mac must be on or sleeping, not shut down. Time Machine organizes the backup files by date and presents the data as a series of Finder windows stacked up behind one another, stretching into the past. You can easily cycle back to the time you want and restore the version of the file you want. If you have stuff that you'd rather not back up — and I won't speculate on what those items might be — you can tell Time Machine to skip them. You can also tell Time Machine to back up to a server on your network, if you prefer: Just click the Time Machine icon in System Preferences to make all these choices. Finally, if you're planning to back up out of your driveway, make sure that no toys, kids, or pets are behind your car before you get in.

Optical discs

Time Machine is truly cool, but I still like to burn important files to CD-ROMs or DVD-ROMs every now and then, and keep them in a location that's separate from where I keep the computer. I like having data on something I can touch and know won't be reused for something else.

Portable media

For short-term backup, you can't beat USB flash drives. They're tiny and inexpensive, and many can hold many gigabytes of data. Having all the projects you're working on in your pocket feels good and lets you work on other computers when you need to.

Backing up into the cloud

Several services on the Internet offer large amounts of storage that you can use to back up files. Free services include Google Gmail and Adrive.com. Dropbox.com makes it easy to back up your files and share them with other people as you collaborate on your next great project. These plans offer the following advantages and disadvantages:

- ✔ They provide off-site backup, so your files are safe even if your house burns down.

- ✔ The companies that provide these plans generally back up their servers, so you have an additional layer of protection.

- ✔ Large Internet services have experienced data breaches and reliability problems. We hope that they learn from their mistakes and will improve.

- ✔ If you're concerned about what's left of our privacy in the Information Age, you should be aware that — in the United States, at least — your data enjoys far fewer legal protections when it's stored outside your premises.

Uninstalling software

Some applications come with an uninstaller, which you should use if available. Otherwise, you uninstall software in OS X by moving the folder or icon you originally installed to the Trash. If you don't know where the program icon is, right-click any of its aliases, including the one on the Dock; then choose Show in Finder from the menu you see. If the program icon looks like a package, drag it to the Trash. If the icon is contained in a folder associated with the software, drag the folder to the Trash. In either case, don't empty the Trash until you're sure that everything else is working properly.

You can also use Launchpad to remove an application from your Mac by dragging its icon from the Launchpad into the Trash on the Dock. You're asked if you really want to do this, if you agree, the application is completely removed, not placed in the Trash.

If you uninstall an application that you purchased from the Mac App Store, you can generally reinstall it at no charge. Select ⌘⇨App Store and click on the Purchased tab. The Install button will be active for apps you can reinstall.

Enjoying the Difference

So far in this chapter, I've concentrated on what you need to get comfortable with Mac OS X, but there's much more to know. The following sections offer a quick rundown on some of the cooler features. I cover others in later chapters.

Launching apps with Launchpad

Take a peek at the left side of the Dock. You see a smiley face; that's the Finder icon. Next to it is an icon that looks like a blackboard with other icons sketched on it. That's the Launchpad icon. If you own an iPad, iPod touch, or iPhone, Launchpad may look familiar. With Lion, Apple is trying to bring the simplicity and ease of use of its iPad family to the Mac. Here's what Launchpad can do for you:

- **Launch applications:** Click the Launchpad icon and you see icons of selected applications. Just click one of the icons to launch that application. Click the Launchpad icon again or press the Esc key, and the icons go away.

- **Organize pages of icons:** Launchpad can have more than one page. Swipe to the right or left to see other pages, or click the tiny dots centered below the icons. The right- and left-arrow keys work, too. You can rearrange icons on the Launchpad by moving them around and even create icon folders by dragging one icon on top of another. Utilities come set up in such a folder.

  To add applications to the Launchpad, drag the application icon from the Finder to the Launchpad icon in the Dock.

Again, if you own an iOS device, all this should be familiar. If not, you're being trained for the one in your future.

Showing applications full screen

Having a mess of windows open on your screen can distract you from the task at hand. Mac OS X Lion lets you switch applications to full-screen mode. Apps that allow this feature have two little arrows in their top-right corner. Click there, and the app takes over the entire screen. You get back to the desktop by swiping right with four fingers. You can even navigate between different apps in full-screen mode using the trackpad by swiping left and right with four fingers or holding the control key down and using the left and right arrow keys. You guessed it — this feels like the way the iPad switches screens. To get an application out of full-screen mode, you may have to move the mouse pointer to the top-right corner of the screen and wait for the two arrows to appear.

Adding widgets to the Dashboard

Press F4 (the key with the meter symbol) or swipe to the right on the track-pad with four fingers, and a whole new window of small applications appears. Welcome to the Dashboard. You see only a few programs (Apple calls them *widgets*): a calculator, an analog clock, a desk calendar, and a weather fore-cast. Move the cursor over the bottom-right corner of the analog clock. A little *i* appears. Click it. The clock flips over so that you can change its set-tings. Try the same trick on other widgets. Press F4 a second time, and the Dashboard goes away, letting you resume your other work.

You can download thousands more Dashboard widgets, many for free. Just go to www.apple.com/downloads/dashboard. Some of my favorites include

- ✔ **iStat Pro:** System monitor
- ✔ **Kennedy Space Center:** Video feed
- ✔ **PEMDAS:** Scientific calculator
- ✔ **Translator:** Language translator (as in French and German, not C++ and Python)

You can even make your own widgets. For more info, see the section in Chapter 15 about adding handy widgets to the Dashboard.

Triggering Exposé and Mission Control

Exposé is a handy set of functions that Apple assigned to these function keys:

- ✔ **F3 or three-finger swipe up:** Organizes all open windows on your dis-play in neat little piles by application so that you can pick the one you want. Apple calls this mode Mission Control. Click a pile, and the associ-ated application comes to the front, with all its windows. The particu-lar window you clicked becomes the front window. You also see the Dashboard and any full-screen apps along the top.
- ✔ **Control+F3 or three-finger swipe down:** Presents all the windows, sepa-rated, for the application in front.
- ✔ **⌘+F3:** Makes all open windows move offscreen so you can see the desk-top. Click in the empty desktop space to see the Finder. The trackpad gesture of this mode is a bit hard to explain but fun to do. Put all five fingers on the trackpad, and spread them apart. All application windows scurry away to the edges of the screen as though your fingers had scat-tered them.

Pressing any of these keys a second time restores your original view of the screen.

If you have a laptop with the Apple Multi-Touch trackpad, you can access Exposé with four-finger swipes. You can set up a Magic Mouse, if you have one, to do this as well. Refer to "Pointing the way: The mouse and trackpad" and "Gesturing with Multi-Touch," earlier in this chapter.

Searching with Spotlight

Spotlight is the Apple search tool for Mac OS X. Its icon, a magnifying glass, is located on the menu bar in the top-right corner of your screen. Its keyboard shortcut is ⌘+spacebar. Mac OS X maintains an indexed database of key-words and updates it as new files are added, so searches are fast. Spotlight starts displaying stuff as you type, so you often don't even have to finish typing the word you're searching for. Here are some tips on using Spotlight:

- **If you type more than one word,** Spotlight searches for items that match both words.
- **If you want searches to match either item,** place a vertical bar (|) between them.
- **If you want Spotlight to exclude a word,** precede the word with a hyphen. You might search for *dogs|cats –lions –pitbulls,* for example.

You also find a Spotlight search box in the top-right corner of each Finder window. If you click the Save button below the search box, OS X saves the results of a search in a *Smart Folder,* which updates automatically as you add, change, and delete files. You can also tell Spotlight to ignore certain files by choosing ⌘⇨System Preferences⇨Spotlight.

Sometimes, you just want to search for an old-fashioned filename. In that case, choose File⇨Find (or press ⌘+F), and select your options.

Displaying photos as your screen saver and desktop background

Leave it to Apple to turn the boring screen saver into a killer app. The following steps explain how to set up your Desktop picture and screen saver by using your own photos:

1. **Choose System Preferences⇨Desktop & Screen Saver.**
2. **On the Desktop tab that appears, select a background pattern or photo for your desktop screen.**

3. **Click the Screen Saver tab, and choose Pictures Folder if you want your screen saver to display all the photos in your Pictures folder.**

   The screen saver kicks in after your computer has been idle for a few minutes. (You can tell it how many minutes with the slider you see.)

   Apple provides several artistic displays to choose from (I like Cosmos), but the choice I like best is the Pictures folder. The screen saver randomly selects and animates pictures from your collection. You can also limit its choices to a folder or slide show. If you enjoy taking pictures but rarely get to look at your collection, using this screen saver will bring tears to your eyes.

   Apple has gone one step further, however. You can set things up so that you can send pictures to *someone else's* Mac over the Internet. It's a helpful way to let grandparents keep up with what's happening with their grandkids. See Chapter 17 for more details.

Chapter 6

Moving Files from Your PC to the Mac

*Y*ou have your Mac up and running, and you played around with OS X a bit, so you at least know how to start programs and make folders. You're ready to take the plunge and begin using your Mac for the bulk of your work. It's time to move those files off that PC and onto your Mac.

Backing Up and Movin' On

I hate to be a nag, but when was the last time you backed up your PC? If you're like most users, it's been a while. Even if you're planning to keep using your PC, it's worth moving your files to the Mac just to have another backup. The next PC virus could be your last.

I subscribe to the belt-and-suspenders approach to backing up. You should back up everything to your Mac *and* make copies of your most important files on a removable hard drive; flash drive; or (best of all) permanent, write-once CD or DVD. For extra credit, store your complete backup at a different location — perhaps in a safe deposit box or a friend or relative's basement.

If you made an inventory of your PC's files, as I suggest in Chapter 3, look over the inventory, and add anything you may have missed. If not, now would be a good time to make an inventory. One important question your inventory should answer is how much data you need to back up. If you save mostly word processing documents and e-mail, you may well have less than the 700MB that a single CD-R optical disc can hold. If you take some digital pictures and occasionally download music, all your files may fit on a 4.7GB DVD-R, an 8.5GB dual layer DVD+R, or a 16 or 32GB flash drive. If you're an avid photographer, videographer, or music collector, you're better off using an external hard drive.

The good news is that you have many methods by which to accomplish this moving job. I describe a bunch of ways, but you don't need to read them all. Pick one that sounds as though it might work for you, and give it a try.

Windows Migration Assistant

Mac OS X Lion comes with a tool called Migration Assistant to help you move files from your PC to your Mac. Migration Assistant has some requirements and limitations, however:

- Your PC must run Windows XP or later and be reasonably up-to-date
- Your Mac and PC must be on the same network, wired or wireless
- You must download an Apple setup program to run on your PC
- Migration Assistant cannot transfer some data from your PC, including passwords, event attachments and Windows Live calendars and contacts
- Migration Assistant will transfer accounts on your PC to new accounts on your Mac
- Data for Microsoft Outlook (2003, 2007, or 2010 32-bit versions), Outlook Express, Windows Mail, and Windows Live Mail can only be transferred for the PC account currently logged in. To transfer data for these programs from other accounts on your PC you must log in to those accounts on at a time and re-run Migration Assistant.

To use Migration Assistant, follow these steps:

1. **On you PC, go to** `support.apple.com/downloads` **and download** `WindowsMigrationAssitantSetup.exe.`

   Review any instructions that come with the setup.

2. **Make sure your Mac can see your PC on the network by choosing Go⇨Network from the finder menu.**

   If the PC doesn't not appear on the Network list, see "Ethernet or Wi-Fi at your service" later in this chapter for help in connecting the two machines.

3. **Run** `WindowsMigrationAssitantSetup.exe` **on your PC by double-clicking its icon or using the Start⇨Run command.**

4. **Run Migration Assistant on your Mac — it's in the Utilities folder — then follow the onscreen instructions.**

   The two programs work together to transfer your PC's files. The files for each account end up in the Documents folder in the corresponding new account on your Mac. You can manually move pictures to the Pictures folder, music to the Music folder, and so on, if you wish. You assign passwords to each new account when you first log in.

External hard drive

High-capacity external hard drives are quite affordable these days. You can buy a 1-terabyte (TB) drive for less than $100. A *terabyte* equals a trillion bytes, or 1,000 gigabytes, or the equivalent of 700,000 floppy disks — a stack more than a mile high. You probably don't need that much space, so if money is tight, consider a drive half that size (500GB). It sells for less than $60.

Be sure to buy an external drive labeled "for Mac and PC." These drives are usually formatted in the Microsoft FAT32 format, which both Macs and PCs handle well. If your drive is formatted in the newer Microsoft NTFS format, your Mac should be able to read it, but not write to it. You can reformat the drive to the HFS+ format Macs prefer with the OS X Disk Utility after you finish transferring your data to the Mac.

Here's how transferring files with an external drive works:

1. **Plug the external drive's USB cable into your PC and copy your files to the drive.**

2. **After everything is copied, shut down Windows and unplug the hard drive's data cable from the PC.**

3. **Plug the cable into your Mac.**

   The drive's name should appear on your Mac's desktop.

4. **Double-click the drive icon.**

5. **Copy your files from the external drive to your Mac.**

   Either copy everything to the Mac (make a folder for all the files), or just copy the files you need and keep the rest on the external drive. Remember that you can use the Finder to navigate to your Documents folder, Pictures folder, and others.

Flash memory

USB flash drives are handy for moving modest amounts of data. Smaller-capacity models are very inexpensive. Follow the procedure for an external hard drive, as outlined in the preceding section.

Optical media: Burn, baby, burn

If your PC has a CD burner or (even better) a DVD burner, you can move files by burning discs on your PC and reading them on the Mac. Use ISO format, and avoid "sessions" or "packet write." This approach has an added advantage: Your files will be stored on separate media that you can put away for safekeeping. I like read-only media, such as CD-Rs and DVD-Rs, better than read-write (R/W) media because I'm not tempted to reuse it for something else. Read-only media tends to last longer, too. One source of free CD- and DVD-writing software for Windows is cdburnerxp.se.

Ethernet or Wi-Fi at your service

If your PC has an Ethernet port or a Wi-Fi wireless connection, you can network your PC to the Mac, set up your PC as a file server, and then copy over everything you need. This process has five steps:

1. **Connect the Mac and PC to the same network.**
2. **Enable file sharing on the PC.**
3. **Make sharable the files and folders you want to transfer.**
4. **Access the shared folders from your Mac.**
5. **Move the files.**

When it works, networking is the easiest way to transfer your files. But some settings can easily be messed up along the way, and you may find it hard to figure out what the obstacle is when networking becomes *not*working. You also need enough free disk space on the Mac to hold all your files. When you're all done transferring the files, you still should make a backup copy of everything. These are the reasons why I recommend using an external hard drive in most cases.

I talk more about networking in Chapter 9, but here's a quick approach to setting up your PC for file sharing:

1. **If your home network doesn't have Wi-Fi, you need an Ethernet cable. Plug the Mac into your Ethernet router or (even better) just run an Ethernet cable between the Mac and the PC.**

   You can borrow the cable that connects your PC to your high-speed Internet modem, if you have one. Don't forget to put it back when you're done.

2. **Determine whether your Mac has already detected your PC on the network. In the Finder, choose Go⇨Network. Then click the various icons in the Network browser that appears to see whether your PC's icon is among them.**

3. **If you don't see your PC from the Mac, choose Start⇨Control Panel on the PC, double-click the Network Setup Wizard icon, and follow the wizard's instructions.**

   In the margin of this page, make a note of the name you give your computer and the workgroup name you assign.

4. **After you set up file sharing, drag the folders on the PC that you want to access on your Mac to the Shared Folder on the PC desktop.**

   Alternatively, in Windows, you can right-click any folder you want to share and choose Properties from the menu that appears. Click the Sharing tab, and select the Share This Folder on the Network check box (see Figure 6-1).

5. **On the Mac side, choose Go⇨Network; look for icons with the names you just assigned; and double-click those icons.**

   You should see your PC folders on the Mac Desktop.

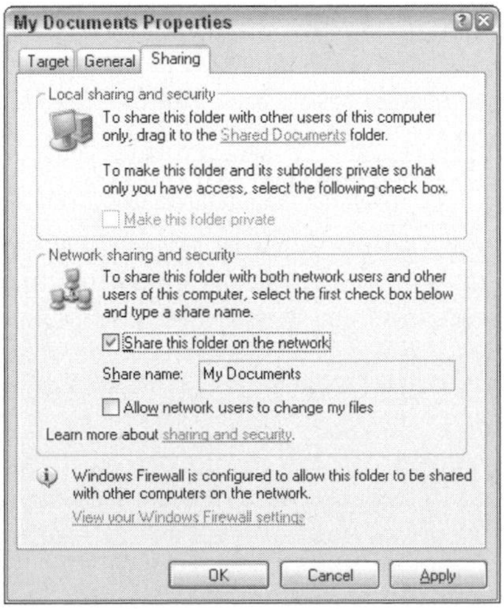

Figure 6-1:
The
Windows
XP folder
Properties
Sharing tab.

My Documents Properties

Target | General | Sharing

Local sharing and security

To share this folder with other users of this computer only, drag it to the Shared Documents folder.

To make this folder and its subfolders private so that only you have access, select the following check box.

☐ Make this folder private

Network sharing and security

To share this folder with both network users and other users of this computer, select the first check box below and type a share name.

☑ Share this folder on the network

Share name: My Documents

☐ Allow network users to change my files

Learn more about sharing and security.

Windows Firewall is configured to allow this folder to be shared with other computers on the network.

View your Windows Firewall settings

OK | Cancel | Apply

6. **Choose Finder⇨New Folder, and name the folder My PC Files or whatever you want.**

7. **Drag all the files you want to this folder.**

   For extra neatness points, make separate folders for each folder you bring over from the PC, such as My Documents, My Pictures, and My Movies, matching the names you used on your PC. After your files and folders are safely on the Mac, you won't regret spending some quality time organizing them. When you're done, move them all to your Mac's Documents folder.

Commercial solutions

Moving files isn't hard, but if you'd rather leave this task to someone else, some folks would be happy to help for a modest fee.

Apple One to One

Perhaps the easiest way to move your files is to sign up for the $99 Apple One to One personal support plan when you buy your Mac at the Apple Store (retail or online). As part of the plan, the folks at the Apple Store move your files for you. You have to take in your PC within a limited time after you buy the Mac. Ask at the store for current details.

Apple offers additional suggestions on moving files at www.apple.com/lae/switch/howto.

Move2Mac

Move2Mac is a commercial file-transfer product from www.detto.com that costs about $40. You have to install Move2Mac software on both machines, so the PC must be in good-enough shape to do this. Just in case it isn't, I explain other approaches later in this chapter. (See the section "Recovering Data from a Damaged PC").

A big advantage of using commercial solutions is that the providers of these services have worked through many more moving scenarios than I have space to tell you about. Move2Mac claims to move documents, spreadsheets, e-mail, photos, music, files, folders, Internet Explorer (IE) favorites, an IE home page, graphics; databases, an address book, and backgrounds.

Move2Mac doesn't try to convert application data files from PC format to Mac format; I discuss those issues in "Dealing with Common File Types," later in this chapter. If your life is on the PC, a commercial solution may be worth the money.

Clone your PC on your Mac, virtually speaking

If you're thinking about running Windows on your Mac, consider using one of the third-party virtual hosting solutions — Parallels or VMWare — described in Chapter 16. Both applications allow you to copy your entire PC, operating system, applications, files, and settings to your Macintosh. You need to have enough hard drive space on your Mac to hold everything that's now on the PC, of course, and still leave plenty of room for all the Mac stuff you want to add. Also, you have to determine what the licenses you have for Windows and your application packages permit. In all likelihood, you need to remove all purchased software from the PC after you make the transition success-fully. Make sure that you have a complete backup of everything before you erase the PC's hard drive. (See Chapter 22 for suggestions on what you might do with the erased PC.)

In some ways, the Windows-on-a-Mac approach is ideal. You have your com-plete PC environment on the Mac — files, applications, and all your settings. On the other hand, you haven't yet transitioned to OS X; you merely have a new PC. Still, this approach allows you to take things gradually, moving one set of applications and files at a time as you're ready. Meanwhile, you can surf the Internet in safety from the OS X side of your computer.

Files on floppies, Zip disks, magnetic tape, and other media

If you have a collection of files on floppy disks, Zip disks, magnetic tape, or other obsolescent removable media, the simplest solution is to read them all onto your PC's hard drive and then move them to the Mac with your other files. If you have too many disks or tapes for this strategy to be practi-cal, or if you have only a few disks that you really need, but you're not sure which ones, a few possibilities exist. You can look for a Zip drive with a USB interface on eBay.com or Amazon.com. For 3½-inch floppy disks, several companies (for example, www.tigerdirect.com) sell a USB floppy drive that can read PC floppies. For other media, such as 5¼-inch floppies or mag-netic tapes, some companies can transfer your files for a fee, but you may be better off hanging on to your old PC until you're sure that you no longer need any of the older files.

Before sending out removable media for conversion or working on it yourself, open the write-protect tab on the media to reduce the likelihood of accidental erasure.

Do you have an old Mac in the closet?

Many current Windows users were once Mac users but switched to Windows for work or other reasons. If you have an old Mac with files on it that you want to transfer to your new Mac,

I have some tips for you in the bonus chapter, "Converting from OS 9 and Other Operating Systems," available at www.dummies.com/go/switchingtoamac.

Recovering Data from a Damaged PC

We all know the safe-computing rules by heart: Use a good antivirus program, never open e-mail attachments you weren't expecting, and back up your files regularly. Most of us aren't so careful, or maybe the kids figured out how to get around whatever security system you set up. Anyway, your PC is barely working, if it even boots. What do you do?

This problem has several solutions; in fact, a whole industry is devoted to it. The following sections cover a couple of solutions that you can do yourself.

Try accessing your PC from the Mac

If your PC boots, try accessing it from your Mac by using an Ethernet cable, as described in "Ethernet or Wi-Fi at your service," earlier in this chapter. Even if the PC is barely responding, the server software may still be fully functional.

 If your PC is so trashed that the mouse no longer works, you may still be able to control it by using the Windows accessibility tools. To do so, follow these steps:

1. **Press the Windows key on your PC's keyboard to open the Start menu.**

2. **Use the arrow keys to highlight the Control Panel option; then press Enter.**

3. **Use the arrow keys to highlight the Accessibility Options option; then press Enter.**

4. **Press Shift+Tab and then the right-arrow key to select the Mouse tab.**

5. **Press Alt+M to select the Use Mouse Keys check box; then press Enter.**

6. **Press Num Lock to turn on the numeric keypad.**

   Now you should be able to use the numeric keypad to move the cursor around without using the mouse. The 5 key is the mouse button. Press – (the minus key) for right-clicking, and press / (the division sign) to get back to left-clicking. Press Insert to hold down the mouse button for dragging, and press Delete to stop dragging.

If you mess up at some point, pressing Esc activates the Cancel button in dialog boxes in Windows — and in OS X.

Use the Windows System Restore program

The *System Restore* tool in Windows lets you roll the operating system back to a kinder, gentler time, before all the nasties got into it. To use it, follow these steps:

1. **Save any open files.**

2. **Choose Start➪All Programs.**

3. **Choose Accessories➪System Tools➪System Restore.**

4. **Select the Restore My Computer to an Earlier Time option and then click the Next button.**

5. **Select a date far enough back when you dimly remember that your computer was working well; then click the Next button.**

If this restore date works, transfer your files and perform a backup as described in "Backing Up and Movin' On" at the start of this chapter. If the date you chose doesn't work, you can try other dates, earlier or later.

Knoppix to the rescue

The complete PC operating system Knoppix fits on a single CD-R or DVD-R optical disc and can boot up most PCs automatically. The DVD version has more software, but you probably don't need it. Knoppix isn't Windows or OS X, however; it's a version of the Linux operating system. That's the bad news and the good news:

✔ **The bad news:** You have enough of a challenge on your hands getting used to OS X without being introduced to a third system.

✔ **The good news:** Linux isn't affected by whatever cooties your computer has. Also, you need to deal with only a few Linux commands.

You can make a Knoppix disc on your Mac that should boot in your PC, assuming that the PC hardware isn't broken and its peripheral devices are fairly standard. Knoppix can detect and use most common peripherals. If your PC's hard drive is encrypted, however, Knoppix can't read it.

To make the Knoppix disc, you need a blank CD-R disc. Here's the recipe:

1. **Go to `www.knoppix.org`, and click the English flag in the top-left corner.**

2. **Scroll down to Getting Knoppix, click the Via Postal Mail button, and find a company in your country that sells Knoppix on CD for a nominal fee.**

   or

   Click the Download button, and select a download server located on your continent.

   You're asked to concur with a "use at your own risk" agreement. (You expect a warranty with free software?)

   If you accept the agreement, you see a list of available downloads. You normally want the latest English version, which will have a filename that looks something like `KNOPPIX_V6.4.4CD-2011-02-08-EN.iso`, where `6.4.4` is the version number, EN means English version, and `.iso` means disk image. You also can download files with similar names but with the extensions `.md5` and `.sha1`. These cryptographic signatures enable you to verify that the files are authentic. For extra credit, download them as well. They're very short, and you may as well act as though you're interested. The `.iso` file, on the other hand, is big — about 730MB. It just fits on a CD-R. The size isn't a big deal if you have a broadband connection, but plan on an overnight download if you use a dialup connection.

3. **Download the files you selected by dragging them to the Desktop; do the short ones first.**

   When you have the `.iso` file on your Mac's Desktop, you're ready to burn it to the blank CD-R disc.

4. **Open the Application folder and then the Utilities folder.**

5. **Double-click the Disk Utility icon, and when the Disk Utility window opens, click the Burn button in the top-left corner.**

6. **In the Select Image to Burn dialog, find the `.iso` file, click it, and click the Burn button.**

7. **Pop in a blank CD-R, and let 'er rip.**

   Chill.

   When the CD-R is all cooked, you see a message saying whether the burn was successful; if it wasn't, try again on a fresh CD-R. After you complete a successful burn, eject the CD by right-clicking its icon and choosing Eject from the contextual menu. Label the CD with a soft marking pen.

Now you can put your new Knoppix disc into the PC's CD reader and restart your PC. Knoppix takes a couple of minutes to boot, and lots of text flashes by as it does its thing, but when it's done, you should see a nice welcome screen. On the left side of the screen, you see icons for all the drives that Knoppix found as it booted up, and you should see an icon for your PC's hard drive (if it's working) labeled something like hda1. Double-click that icon. You should see the contents of your PC's hard drive. With your PC contents on display, you can gather your files in one of the following ways:

- ✔ **If you have one, connect a portable hard drive or a flash drive to the PC.** Its icon should appear on the Knoppix desktop. Now you can drag files from the PC to the device you plugged in.

  When you're done transferring files, right-click the removable drive's icon, and choose Unmount. Alternatively, shut down Knoppix by choosing Log Out from the K menu in the bottom-left portion of the Knoppix taskbar.

- ✔ **If you have an Internet e-mail account, such as Yahoo! or Gmail, you can e-mail the files to yourself.** Log in to your account by using Konqueror (the Knoppix web browser and file manager), and mail yourself files as attachments.

- ✔ **If your PC hardware has a second optical drive that can burn optical discs, you can also write your files to a CD or DVD by using Knoppix.** Right-click in an open directory window, choose Action⇨Create Data CD with K3b, and follow the instructions.

Knoppix can do a lot more, including repair a damaged Windows file system and network directly with your Mac, but these topics are too complex to cover here. Take a look at *Knoppix For Dummies,* by Paul G. Sery, if you want to do more with this powerful tool.

More-extreme measures

If none of the preceding measures works to recover data from your damaged PC, consider removing the drive and putting it in an external drive enclosure to mount on your Mac. It's a bit tricky — you have to determine what type of hard drive you have to get the right enclosure — and more often than not, in a bad PC it's the disk that's shot. If you're not experienced in doing work on your computer's insides, get a technician or repair shop to do this job.

Get an enclosure that's designed to work with Macs as well as with PCs. (Most enclosures are.) Putting your PC hard drive in a portable enclosure gives you another usable backup of your old files.

Should you run antivirus software before transferring your files?

PC viruses don't hurt OS X, but they could cause problems if you plan to run Windows on your Mac or exchange files with Windows users. So updating and running your antivirus program before transferring your files is probably a wise move. If your PC is truly on the edge, however, you probably should move your important files off before running any programs. In that case, I suggest doing the file transfer twice: before and after an antivirus run. If the latter transfer goes smoothly, the first set of files can be erased.

Note that disks formatted in Windows NTFS open in OS X as read-only. Unless your PC's hard drive is 250GB or larger, it makes no sense to try to use the old drive as an accessory to your Mac because new drives are so cheap. Just put the old drive somewhere safe when you're done, and keep it as a backup. If you do want to reuse the old drive, and you're satisfied that all data is safely transferred and backed up, use the OS X Disk Utility to reformat the drive (which *deletes* all your files but doesn't *erase* them fully) and use it as you want. Disk Utility can also erase the drive after you format it. Click the Erase tab and then click the Erase Free Space button. Later in this chapter, I tell you how to dispose of the old hard drive safely, if that's your preference.

If truly valuable (worth more than $1,000) files are on your hard drive, and you can't read the disk, look for a hard drive data recovery firm. Visit www. myharddrivedied.com for interesting presentations on the process. This site suggests some things you can do yourself if you're willing to risk doing more damage.

Dealing with Common File Types

Most PC file types can be used with appropriate programs on the Mac. The following sections describe some of these file types.

Portable Document Format (.pdf)

The popular Portable Document Format, originally developed by Adobe. com, is the standard display mode in OS X. The Preview program that comes with the Mac conveniently displays PDF documents. OS X can also create

PDF files; it's an option you find by choosing File➪Print in most programs. You don't need to download or buy software to work with PDF files, although Adobe Acrobat offers capabilities beyond what OS X's Preview application provides.

JPEG photos (.jpg)

JPEG stands for Joint Photographic Experts Group, the name of the committee that pulled together the format. Macs love JPEGs. The OS X Preview application displays them; and the iPhoto program stores them, organizes them, slices them, dices them, and spits out slide shows and coffee-table books. Both programs come with every Mac sold. I discuss iPhoto more in Chapter 12, but the quick way to get your photos into iPhoto is to move the files to your Pictures folder, open iPhoto, and choose File➪Import to Library.

MPEG movies (.mpg)

The Motion Picture Experts Group came up with this family of standards for moving images. Apple QuickTime, which comes with each new Mac and is available free for Windows, is happy to screen MPEG-1 and MPEG-4 files for your viewing pleasure. Apple offers an MPEG-2 Playback Component that you can download for about $20 from www.apple.com/quicktime/mpeg2.

A free open source alternative media player, VLC, handles all MPEG formats and a whole lot more. It's available from www.videolan.org.

If you're into video editing, see the discussion of iMovie in Chapter 13.

Music (.mp3, .aiff, .wma, and others)

The iTunes program in Windows is compatible with iTunes on the Mac, so if you're using iTunes on your PC, you can transfer all the music, videos, audiobooks, and podcasts you've accumulated. One exception is .wma files; Macs don't play them without additional software. You can download the free, open source multimedia player VLC from www.videolan.org/vlc. Inexpensive solutions that you can download are available from www.flip4mac.com and www.easywma.com. You can also import any music or other sound files that are in .mp3 format (MP3), as well as files in .aiff or .wav format. Your Mac can't play files in Microsoft PlaysForSure (.pfs) format or protected Zune files, however. These files use a digital rights management technique that isn't compatible with the Apple FairPlay system.

You have several ways to transfer your iTunes music library from a PC to a Mac. You can simply copy all the files from the Music\iTunes folder on your PC to the Music folder on the Mac and then choose File⇨Import within iTunes. However, Apple recommends that you use the Backup to Disc feature in iTunes. You need a CD burner or (better yet) a DVD burner on your PC to use this method. See http://support.apple.com/kb/HT1382 for details.

ASCII text (.txt) and Rich Text Format (.rtf) files

Text files are supposed to be as simple as anything gets in computers. They're just a bunch of characters in American Standard Code for Information Interchange (ASCII) encoding. Unfortunately, even these files aren't so simple. The three operating-system families — Windows, Unix, and Mac — use different conventions for ending a line or paragraph of text. Unix uses a line-feed (LF) character, Mac OS 9 used a carriage return (CR), and Windows uses both (CR+LF).

The TextEdit program that comes with OS X reads text files created by Windows, Unix, and Mac OS. By default, however, it saves files in Rich Text Format (.rtf), which (among other things) preserves basic formatting of text. You can change the default settings to text format in the TextEdit preferences.

Transferring your e-mail address book

If you're using an online e-mail service such as Yahoo! or Gmail, you don't need to do anything; your address book is stored on the mail service's servers, and you can access it just as well from your Mac.

If you're using Microsoft Outlook Express, you can transfer the addresses by using vCard records. To do this, prepare a new folder on your external hard drive or flash drive. (You can call it Outlook Addresses.) Start Outlook Express and choose Tools⇨Address Book. Choose Edit⇨Select All. Drag all addresses to the folder you created. Then you can import them into the Apple Mail program (see Chapter 8). I discuss moving your AOL address book in Chapter 8.

Digital rights management — curse or blessing?

A popular form of entertainment on the Internet is *trolling,* or mentioning a hot-button topic in a discussion group and watching the heated controversy erupt. Few topics are more effective as troll bait than digital rights management (DRM), which is seen as being an enabling technology that allows music and movies to be enjoyed by way of the Internet or an evil, dangerous technology that allows all information to be centrally controlled by powerful interests. Both viewpoints have merit.

The rights that DRM manages are the rights that copyright law gives content owners. When it works, DRM encrypts content and then allows decryption only on the computer or player that the copyright holder authorizes. DRM can also restrict the number and quality of copies made and the number of times content can be viewed. Providers of Blu-ray high-definition video are insisting that all computers that will show such content implement strict DRM.

Anti-DRM activists are concerned that the technology gives content creators too much power. Apple has switched from its own DRM system, FairPlay, which was relatively benign, to selling DRM-free music in its iTunes Store. (Apple calls DRM-free music iTunes *Plus.*) You can even unlock past purchases for a small fee. But movies and iOS applications still use DRM.

Apple president Steve Jobs called for an end to DRM music in 2007, saying, "Imagine a world where every online store sells DRM-free music encoded in open licensable formats. In such a world, any player can play music purchased from any store, and any store can sell music which is playable on all players. This is clearly the best alternative for consumers, and Apple would embrace it in a heartbeat."

Purging Your Files Before Disposing of the Disk

When you're satisfied that you have all your files safely moved to your Mac and backed up, it's time to remove from your PC hard drive any data that you may not want others to see. That data can include e-mail, personal correspondence, proprietary work documents, and financial information. Sensitive information, including credit-card numbers and passwords, may be stored in your computer without your knowing about it, in the form of temporary cache files and cookies. *Cookies* are blocks of information that your Internet browser often stores so that websites you revisit know about your past use.

The simplest solution is to erase (not just delete) everything on the PC's hard drive. Doing so makes your computer much less usable if you decide to sell or donate it, however. If you still have the original discs that came with the computer, you can restore the operating system after you erase. You can also restore any applications you own.

Alternatively, you can just erase the data files you're concerned about. The My Documents folder is an obvious candidate, but you must also check to see where other files may be stored. This approach is more risky, and I recommend it only if you're planning to give the computer to another family member or someone else you trust.

Removing the hard drive

A third approach, and perhaps the safest one, is to simply remove the hard drive before you dispose of your PC. This approach is relatively easy for a tower PC, but more tricky for a laptop. You can pay a technician at a computer store to do the job for you. The computer will be much less usable without a hard drive, of course, although it can still be used with a Knoppix CD, as I describe earlier in this chapter. If the machine is reasonably current, it may be worth it for the next owner to install a new (and perhaps larger) hard drive. Hard drives are relatively inexpensive.

You can simply keep the old hard drive in a safe place, or you can ask the technician who removes it from your PC to install it in a portable hard drive enclosure. Refer to "More-extreme measures," earlier in this chapter.

Wiping data off your hard drive

Safely removing files from your PC isn't just a simple matter of deleting them. When Microsoft Windows deletes files, it only removes information about those files from its file directory and makes the space on the hard drive available for reuse; it doesn't erase the data itself. Programs are available that can often recover deleted files if they haven't been erased. Even if a file has been erased once on older hard drives of less than 15GB capacity, it's sometimes possible to recover data by using highly specialized equipment. According to the U.S. National Institute of Science and Technology, however, "most of today's media can be effectively cleared by one overwrite."

You can use the following programs to overwrite your data one or more times:

- ✔ **SDelete:** Microsoft suggests using this free command-line program. You can see instructions and a download link at `www.microsoft.com/technet/sysinternals/utilities/SDelete.mspx`.

- ✔ **Eraser:** This program is also free, although a donation is suggested to help support the author. You can download it at `www.heidi.ie/eraser`.

- ✔ **Darik's Boot And Nuke:** You burn this free program to a self-contained boot disk. It also works with Macs. You can download it at `ww.dban.org`.

Mac OS X has a built-in file-wiping utility. When you drag files to the Trash, you can choose Finder⇨Secure Empty Trash. In addition, the OS X Disk Utility can erase all your free space, so you can get rid of any files that you didn't erase securely.

Safely destroying your PC hard drive

Perhaps you don't want to (or can't) reuse your PC's hard drive but simply want to destroy it. Maybe the drive is so far gone that you can't access it with any program, but you know that it contains sensitive data, which someone with the right tool and a big budget could still get at. You have a bit of a problem. It's hard to dispose of a hard drive in a truly safe and environmentally friendly way. The most widely recommended ways include melting, incineration, crushing, or shredding — yes, shredding. Several companies offer this service.

Perhaps the simplest solution is to erase it as best you can, remove it from the PC, and take it apart. You need some small screwdrivers; often, a screw or two is hidden under a label. The process is instructive, though, and you find some neat, powerful magnets inside. Simply bending the disks renders them essentially unreadable. (Some newer disks — generally more than 50GB — are made of glass and may shatter, so pick a safe location and wear eye protection.) Figure 6-2 shows a disassembled hard drive with an ordinary claw hammer used to bend the platters. The supermagnets are in the top-left corner of the hard drive's case. Be careful with them; they're strong enough to pinch.

Figure 6-2: Dis-assembled hard drive with bent disks.

Chapter 7

Switching Applications

*T*he Apple Macintosh comes with an amazing collection of software programs to help you create and enjoy what Apple refers to as your *digital life:* music, photos, home movies, and web content. They're so useful that I devote Chapters 11 through 14 to telling you more about them. I also cover the quite capable word processor TextEdit that comes with OS X later in this chapter. The programs in the iLife suite and the chapters that cover them are described in the following list in the order in which they appear in this book:

✔ **iTunes:** Manages your music and videos; syncs with your iPad, iPhone, or iPod; and talks to the online iTunes Store. Versions are available for your PC as well as the Mac, and both are free downloads from Apple. (See Chapter 11.)

✔ **iPhoto:** Takes care of everything associated with digital photography, including retrieving images from your digital camera, performing basic editing, organizing images into slide shows and albums, and printing albums. (See Chapter 12.)

✔ **iMovie:** Lets you import and edit all those home movies you took of your vacations and kids (but never watch), and turn them into professional-looking mini-biopics that won't bore your guests. They might even garner 15 minutes of fame on YouTube. In your work life, you can produce video clips that present your ideas compellingly. (See Chapter 13.)

✔ **iDVD:** Burns those edited iMovie shorts and epics (along with iPhoto slide shows) to DVDs that you can play on almost any DVD player or computer with a DVD reader. Make the grandparents very happy. (See Chapter 13.)

✔ **GarageBand:** Helps you put together the original score for the home video epic or just fan your long-suppressed creative musical talents. Also use it to record podcasts and teach yourself how to play guitar or piano. (See Chapter 13.)

✔ **iWeb:** Builds all this creative output into spectacular web pages. (See Chapter 14.)

Because all these programs are built by Apple, they work well together. You can use an iTunes playlist as a background for your iPhoto slide show, for example, or integrate iPhoto images into your iMovie, animating the images by using cinematographic techniques popularized by Ken Burns. Your creations can also extend beyond your Mac. You can carry your digital works on your iPod and iPhone, or show them on your home entertainment center by using Apple TV.

Although Apple emphasizes the personal use of these products, they have obvious business uses as well, such as organizing slide shows for presentations, presenting sales and training videos, and creating less-boring websites.

You don't need to worry about installing iLife. It's on your Mac already, in your Applications folder, with shortcuts on the Dock. There's nothing extra to do. Sorry.

Although iLife covers many needs, you may have applications on your PC that you use regularly or need occasionally that don't have direct equivalents among the programs included with OS X. In the rest of this chapter, I guide you through the more common situations and point you to additional resources for others.

Keeping Your Appointments with iCal

OS X comes with the sophisticated calendar program iCal. You find it on the Dock, represented by an icon that looks like a desk calendar open to today's date. (Does anyone even remember what a desk calendar looked like?) It supports multiple calendars (for work, personal, and rule-the-world conspiracy, for example) and offers daily, weekly, and monthly views of your schedule. Apple iCal is fully compliant with the iCalendar standard, which is supported by many other calendaring systems, including Microsoft Outlook.

You can move your Outlook calendar to your Mac by following these steps:

1. **Export your Outlook calendar in iCalendar format, using the free tool available at `http://outlook2ical.sourceforge.net`.**

2. **Move the resulting `.ics` file to your Mac.**

   Chapter 6 explains all sorts of ways to move files from your PC to your Mac.

3. **Import your Outlook calendar into iCal by choosing File⇨Import.**

Using iCloud, you can keep your calendars in sync with your desktop, laptop, iPad, iPhone, iPod touch, and even your PC.

iCal works with other calendaring systems that support the CalDAV standard to let you check your colleagues' availability, arrange meetings with them, and book a conference room with a projector and party hats. You send everyone meeting material simply by dragging the document icon or icons to the event in the iCal window.

Processing Words and Numbers

Once upon a time, in the dim ages of the past century (before *Mad Men*), people who wanted to produce a written document for other people to read sat down in front of a mechanical contraption called a *typewriter,* which was filled with levers connected to keys arranged in much the same way as the keys on a computer keyboard. Writers checked their spelling by looking up unfamiliar words in a paper book.

Today, it would be considered a form of abuse to make someone write without the aid of a good word processor. If you're working with other people in most organizations, you're pretty much expected to read and produce documents in a format compatible with Microsoft Office — particularly Microsoft Word.

The need for Microsoft Office compatibility complicates what would otherwise be a clean, bare-knuckle-competitive relationship between Apple and Microsoft. Apple needs Office, and Microsoft makes good money selling it to Mac users. Bill Gates once half-joked that he made more money when Apple sold a Mac than when a Windows PC was sold because Mac users were more likely to buy Office.

Many word processing solutions work with a Macintosh, ranging from the software that comes free with OS X to the full Microsoft Office for Mac suite to several other possibilities.

TextEdit

The humble word processor included with OS X, TextEdit, is quite powerful, with many more features than its Windows equivalent, Notepad. You find TextEdit in the Applications folder. In particular, TextEdit can read and save documents produced by Microsoft Word. Although TextEdit reads ASCII text files generated in Windows, Unix, Linux, and Mac OS, unless you change its preferences it doesn't save files in ASCII text format, for reasons discussed in Chapter 6. Instead, TextEdit normally saves files in Rich Text Format (`.rtf`), a relatively simple format for styled documents that Microsoft introduced in 1987. TextEdit can also read and save documents in Hypertext Markup Language (HTML), Microsoft Word (`.doc`), Microsoft Extensible Markup Language (XML), Open Office XML, and OpenDocument formats. Further, it can produce PDF documents when you choose its Print command.

TextEdit supports character formatting and the inclusion of graphics and multimedia images. Some of its most powerful features can be a little hard to find. To make and edit tables, for example, you choose Format⇨Text⇨Table. Choose Format⇨Text to find more list management features. TextEdit allows sophisticated control of letter spacing and even speaks text aloud, but it doesn't support multicolumn documents. Its simple editing screen, shown in Figure 7-1, understates its capabilities.

Figure 7-1:
The simple
TextEdit
editing
screen.

> ◯◯◯　　　　　　　　　Untitled
>
> ¶▾ [Helvetica ▾] [Oblique ▾] [12 ▾] ■ [a²] B I U ▤ ▤ ▤ ▤ [1.0 ▾] ▤▾
>
> ▼₀ ▶₁ ▶₂ ▶₃ ▶₄ ▶₅ ▶₆ ▶₇ ▼
>
> This is the OS X TextEdit window.
>
> *TextEdit is simple but powerful.*

TextEdit has full support for *Unicode,* a computer-industry-standard character set that includes the written characters of most of the languages now used in the world — and a few ancient ones, such as Linear B. (See Chapter 5 for more information on keying in special characters and other languages.) A committee is studying the addition of Egyptian hieroglyphs to Unicode. In the meantime, you can purchase the glyph processor MacScribe 2.1 at www. macscribe.com. The site is in French, but if you understand Egyptian hieroglyphics, you probably speak French, too.

If you want to edit HTML files in TextEdit, choose TextEdit⇨Preferences, and select the Ignore Rich Text Commands in HTML Files check box. You also see this option for a particular file when you choose File⇨Open.

Word and Office from Microsoft

Microsoft Word and the other Microsoft Office applications (Excel for spreadsheets and PowerPoint for presentations) are the most widely used standards in most workplaces and schools. Microsoft sells versions of these programs for the Mac (in fact, they were first developed for the Mac). If you frequently need to use files created by these programs, buying Word or the entire Office suite may be a wise investment. Microsoft Office 2011 is file-compatible with Office for Windows.

You can buy Microsoft Word (shown in Figure 7-2) by itself, or you can buy the entire Office suite, which includes Word, Excel, PowerPoint, and Outlook. Outlook isn't included in the Home and Student edition of Office, however. I discuss Outlook a bit more in Chapter 8.

Microsoft Office is pricey, especially if you aren't upgrading from a previous version and don't qualify for the Home and Student version. As I mention in the preceding section, TextEdit, which comes with OS X, can open files in Microsoft Word (.doc) format. You have other alternatives if you want full independence from the Redmond empire.

If you're planning to install Microsoft Windows on your Mac and need to work with Office documents only occasionally, one approach is to install the Windows version of Office in Windows, and use it there. If you use the virtual technologies for installing Windows, you can use the Office applications alongside Mac applications. (See Chapter 16 for more on this option.) But if you're planning heavy use of Office, you'll be happier installing the Mac version.

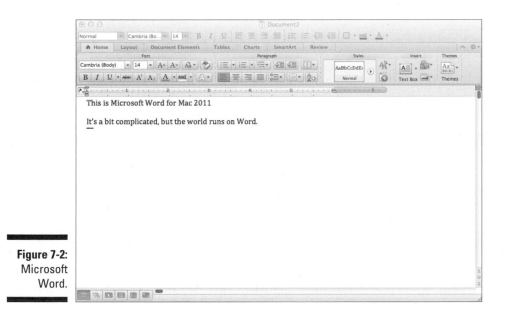

Figure 7-2:
Microsoft
Word.

Note that Microsoft Office 2008 dropped support for Visual Basic, but it's part of Office 2011, so if your life depends on Visual Basic and you've heard that it's not supported on the Mac, relax. It's back.

OpenOffice.org

OpenOffice.org is a suite of office applications, developed by the open-source community, that largely parallels the capabilities of Microsoft Office. The program can generally read and write files in the various Microsoft formats but is most comfortable with OpenDocument format. Oh, and it's free.

OpenOffice.org says that it appends the .org suffix to its name because someone else owns the OpenOffice trademark.

The program can be used on a variety of computing platforms besides the Macintosh, including Windows, Linux, and most other forms of Unix. OpenOffice.org consists of these components:

✔ **Base:** A relational database management system

✔ **Calc:** A spreadsheet

✔ **Draw:** A vector-graphics drawing program

✔ **Impress:** A presentation program, similar to PowerPoint

✔ **Write:** A word processor

OpenOffice.org 3.4 runs on the Mac via the normal OS X user interface. (Earlier versions employed X11, a windowing system developed years ago at MIT.) To install it, follow these steps:

1. **Point your web browser to `http://download.openoffice.org`, and click the Download OpenOffice.org link.**

   While the installation image is being downloaded, OpenOffice asks you for a voluntary donation. Be nice and give up some money; the software is quite a good deal. You can also look at the large library of available extensions and try versions of OpenOffice that are still under development, though I suggest that you avoid doing the latter. Downloading experimental software voids the warranty on this book — or would if we were offering a warranty.

2. **After the installation image has downloaded, double-click it (it's in your Downloads folder) and drag the OpenOffice.org icon into the Applications folder.**

   OpenOffice uses the Java programming language. If Java is not already installed on your Mac, OS X will offer to install it the first time you try to run OpenOffice. (See "Adding Functionality as You Need It" toward the end of this chapter for more on Java.)

Figure 7-3 shows a screen shot of OpenOffice.org displaying a draft of this chapter stored as a Microsoft Word document.

The OpenOffice.org also links to extensions to the program that add more capabilities. All in all, OpenOffice.org is a powerful program.

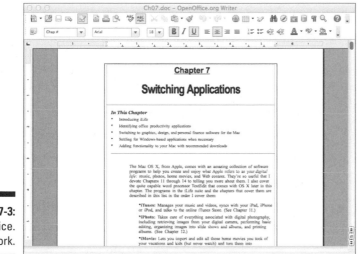

Figure 7-3:
OpenOffice.
org at work.

iWork

The extra-cost Apple package iWork includes Pages, a word processing program; Numbers, a spreadsheet program; and Keynote, a presentation program. All are quite impressive.

Pages

Pages is a word processor that incorporates many of the features of a page-layout program. You don't just type and format text with Pages; you create finished documents ready for printing or display on the World Wide Web or as PDF files. Check out these features:

- ✔ **Charts:** Pages has three-dimensional charting capabilities, so you can rotate a chart image in 3D mode to create exactly the effect you want.

- ✔ **Image editing and page layout:** You can edit images in Pages; you don't need to jump back and forth to an image editor for image adjustments. You can also crop images to arbitrary shapes that you create in Pages and flow text around them. What's more, Pages comes with a set of templates that Apple designed to give your documents a professional look. Nearly everything can be edited in real time.

✔ **Mailings:** Pages can do mail merges, even using your Address Book or a spreadsheet table in Numbers to create personalized mailings and newsletters.

✔ **Organizational tools:** Outline mode lets you create a multilevel outline that you can reorganize quickly by dragging and dropping. To help with long documents, Pages shows detailed color thumbnail images for every page in the left sidebar.

✔ **Tables and calculations:** Pages can create tables that perform simple calculations, such as addition, multiplication, and averaging.

Pages can read and export Microsoft Word, HTML, RTF, and text-only files from the Mac or PC. It even supports Apple's older AppleWorks format. Pages does a good job of retaining the formatting of the documents it imports, including Word revision tracking. It also works with the popular MathType and EndNote programs for adding math equations and bibliographic references, though you need to buy the latest Mac versions of these programs.

Numbers

The world runs on spreadsheets, but they're kind of boring. Apple adds pizzazz with a flexible canvas on which you can place intelligent tables, 3D charts and graphs, text, pictures, and whatever. Canned templates and lots of small touches, such as one-click formulas and Formula List view, make Numbers easy for non-bean-counters to use. Don't worry: It can read and write most Microsoft Excel files.

Keynote

Keynote is Apple's attempt to one-up PowerPoint, which has become the primary means of business communications in the 21st century. In a joke about two kidnapped businesspeople about to be executed but offered a last request, the first person asks whether he can finally give the talk he was working on before his capture. The second person asks to be killed first so that he doesn't have to sit through one more PowerPoint presentation.

Keynote is designed to make it easy to create killer presentations that don't bore the audience to death. Apple president Steve Jobs claims that he's Keynote's prime customer and that he demands ever-improved features for his numerous presentations. Keynote has a dizzying array of special effects, transitions, slide builds, animation tools, and templates. It also calls on tools from Pages and the iLife suite to simplify slide creation so that you can have tables that update when you change the numbers and 3D charts that you can rotate. You can also export Keynote presentations in PowerPoint format (`.ppt`), but some of the cooler effects may not translate fully.

Always be sure to preview your presentation by using the computer, program, projector, and (if possible) room you'll be using when your audience shows up. Put your presentation on automatic play, and sit in the back of the room to see how legible those slides are from that vantage point.

Web-based office applications

In a major new trend in computing, websites are offering software applications, either free or for a subscription fee. All you need to use them are a computer with an Internet connection and a reasonably modern web browser. You don't have to download any software. You sign up for the service and use the Internet to access your documents and the programs you need to create and edit them. The process works a lot like web-based e-mail, so it's no surprise that one of the foremost vendors of this type of service is Google, but other companies have gotten in on the act as well. Here's a quick look at the pros and cons of web-based apps:

- ✔ **The upside:** A special advantage is that you can access documents stored on the website from any computer, anywhere you find an Internet connection. Your documents are password-protected, of course, but most sites have a way for you to share documents with colleagues and work on them collaboratively.

- ✔ **The downside:** Obviously, you can't work when you're out of range of an Internet connection — say, when you're traveling with your laptop. Also, you need to have a fast Internet connection, and even then, response times can be slow compared with desktop programs.

Google Docs

Google offerings include a word processor and a spreadsheet program. If you have a Google account and a password for Gmail, Groups, or another Google service, you simply log on to use Docs & Spreadsheets. Otherwise, you can register for a new account with little effort. All Google requires is your e-mail address. Even your full name is optional. Docs & Spreadsheets lets you

- ✔ **Create or upload documents.** They're stored on Google's servers. You can also upload documents in Microsoft Office .doc and .xls formats, as well as .rtf, OpenDocument, and plain-text formats.

- ✔ **Share a document with other people.** Enter someone's e-mail address, and that person receives an e-mail invitation to see and edit your document as soon as sign-in is complete. Multiple people can view and edit a document at the same time. The spreadsheet program even has a chat window, allowing all the editors to discuss what they're up to.

- ✔ **Track changes to a document.** You can see who made changes, when the changes were made, and what was changed.

✔ **Store, download, or post the final document.** When you're done, you can leave the document on the Google server. You can also download the document to your Mac in a variety of formats (including `.csv`, `.doc`, `.html`, `.ods`, `.odt`, `.pdf`, `.rtf`, and `.xls`) or publish your document on the web in `.html` format.

Figure 7-4 shows Google Docs displaying a draft of this chapter, which was uploaded to Google in Microsoft Word `.doc` format. Figure 7-5 shows a simple Google spreadsheet.

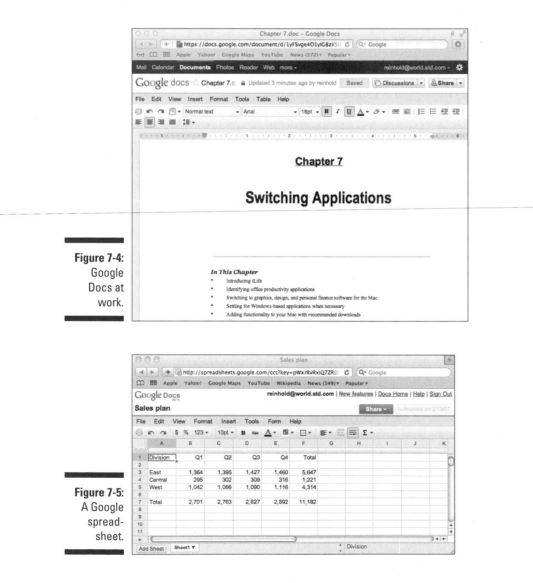

Figure 7-4:
Google Docs at work.

Figure 7-5:
A Google spread-sheet.

Other online office applications

Several other websites are offering online office applications. This list describes a few:

- ✔ **EditGrid:** This online spreadsheet program has strong collaboration features. It's free for personal use and requires a monthly fee for businesses. See whether you can guess its web address.

- ✔ **ThinkFree:** ThinkFree (`www.thinkfree.com`) offers Write for word processing; Calc, a spreadsheet program; and Show for presentations. It supports iPhone and Android smartphones.

- ✔ **Zoho:** Zoho Virtual Office includes word processing, spreadsheet, and presentation programs. It's available free for individuals at `www.zoho.com`. Business users pay a small monthly fee and get a few additional features.

Personal finance

If you use Quicken or QuickBooks in Windows, you'll be glad to know that versions of these programs are available for the Mac from Intuit.com. It's possible to transfer records between the Windows and Mac versions of these programs, but the process isn't perfect, and some types of data don't get converted. You can find full information at `www.intuit.com/support`. Select the product that interests you, and enter **"converting to Mac"** in the search box. I'd advise waiting until the end of your accounting year to change to the Mac version from the PC version of a program you depend on, or just keep running the PC version you already use under Windows on your Mac. (See Chapter 16.)

AccountEdge (`www.accountedge.com`) sells another popular line of accounting packages that work on both platforms. You'll find other business and finance applications for your Mac at `www.apple.com/downloads/macosx/business_finance`.

Accessing Databases

The only major application missing from Microsoft Office for the Macintosh is Access, the Office database component. Not only is Access not supported on the Mac, but Microsoft also doesn't make it easy to transfer Access databases to other systems. Your simplest option is to export Access tables as Excel files on your PC and then import those data tables into whichever database solution you choose on the Mac. You have to reconstruct any relations, forms, or queries on the Mac side. The following sections describe the main database alternatives available on the Mac, from simple to more complex and esoteric.

Bento

Bento is an inexpensive ($49) consumer- and small business–oriented database program from FileMaker, Inc., a wholly owned subsidiary of Apple. Its name alludes to the tidy, compartmented bento boxes used to serve assortments of Japanese delicacies (yum!). Bento is well integrated with standard OS X applications such as Address Book, iCal, and Mail, as well as Numbers and Microsoft Excel. Also, a $5 version of Bento for the iPhone, iPad, and iPod touch syncs with the Mac version. Although you can easily configure Bento to your own database needs (if they're not too complex), the program comes with a wide variety of preformatted and themed database templates, from Animal Stats to Wine Collection. Small-office templates include Customers, Inventory, Issue Tracking, and Time Billing. No programming or configuring are necessary; just enter your data.

FileMaker Pro

FileMaker Pro is a full-featured commercial database program, also (duh!) from FileMaker, Inc. Considered to be one of the better database programs out there, it has a loyal following. It's easy to use (for a database) and has many powerful features. FileMaker Pro is also available in a Windows version, and the two versions can be networked, allowing databases to be shared between users employing both platforms. The .fp7 database format is the same on both platforms, but differing fonts sometimes cause problems if you don't stick to OpenType fonts or the Windows TrueType fonts on both platforms. A FileMaker Go version for the iPhone, iPad, and iPod touch allows interaction with FileMaker databases created on the Mac or in Windows.

FileMaker is suitable for a range of applications, from small and simple to large and complex, with web-based access. If you add ODBC-compliant drivers, it can interact with Microsoft Access data. A strong community of FileMaker developers exists. FileMaker Pro costs about $300, and numerous add-ons are available, including FileMaker Server, FileMaker Advanced, and FileMaker Server Advanced. FileMaker provides the following white paper, which compares its database with Access: www.filemaker.com/products/file maker-pro/docs/11/comparison_fm_access.pdf

MySQL and PostgreSQL

Both the MySQL and PostgreSQL open source, multiuser, web-oriented database programs are available for the Mac. SQL stands for Structured Query Language, and most industrial strength databases are built around SQL. MySQL, for example, powers some of the most famous sites on the Internet, such as Craigslist.org classified ads, Flickr.com photo sharing, and the Wikipedia.org free online encyclopedia. PostgreSQL is another alternative, and the Mac OS X server edition comes with it built in. Using either MySQL or PostgreSQL requires programming skills and is significantly beyond the level of Microsoft Access. For more info MySQL, see *PHP & MySQL For Dummies,* 4rd Edition, by Janet Valade.

OpenOffice Base

The Base component of OpenOffice.org is a relational database written in the Java programming language. Its look and feel mimic Access, but it has limited ability to import and export database files, and then only in the Windows version. See the following web page for details: `http://wiki.services.` `openoffice.org/wiki/Connecting_to_Microsoft_Access`.

Base, a relatively new open-source project, is still being improved. It's free with the rest of the OpenOffice.org suite. It's worth playing with or trying out on small projects. Future releases may be more suitable for mission-critical stuff, though I said the same thing in the last edition of this book.

Finding Graphics and Design Programs

Many people use graphics and design programs for personal and professional uses, and the market leaders in each category have versions for both Windows and the Mac, with good compatibility between them. For the most part, all that's involved in switching is getting hold of a Mac version of the program in question. Check with each vendor to see whether switching to the Mac version entitles you to the upgrade price or other discounts.

Graphics editing

Basic graphics-editing features are built into the Apple iLife suite (see Chapter 12), including the ability to crop images, adjust brightness and contrast, and remove the red-eye effect that sometimes appears when you use flash illumination to take pictures of people. Apple's Aperture, a professional photographer's program, provides still more features. Still, these programs don't match the capabilities of top-of-the-line graphics editors.

The **Adobe Photoshop** graphics editor has altered the meaning of photography from being a way to capture reality to a way to make an image of anything imaginable. My favorite example of the sophistication of this program is a wrinkle-removal feature that includes a slider so that you can adjust how many wrinkles to remove. It lets you make a portrait subject look just a bit younger — but not so much younger as to strain credibility. Photoshop is available in Mac and Windows editions that share underlying .psd file types. The CS3, CS4, and CS5 versions of Photoshop have native support of Intel.

Photoshop Elements, Photoshop's less-expensive sibling, also has file-compatible versions for both platforms, as do most of the members of the Adobe family. Although it's not quite as capable as Photoshop, Elements can meet the needs of many amateur photographers at a much lower cost. It's occasionally included free with products such as scanners.

The GNU Image Manipulation Program (GIMP), `www.gimp.org,` is a free, open-source graphics-editing program with many, but not all, of the capabilities of Photoshop. The latest release of GIMP, version 2.6, requires the X11 window manager, which comes with OS X. Because it runs under X11, the GIMP 2.6 user interface (shown in Figure 7-6) is more Windows-like than Mac-like. In particular, menus are associated with each window, and keyboard shortcuts use the Control key rather than the ⌘ key that you expect with OS X–native programs. So in Gimp, Control-X means *cut* and Control-V means *paste.*

Figure 7-6:
A photo of the family dog, touched up using GIMP 4's powerful image-editing tools.

GIMP is one of the most mature open-source programs, with a wide following and much Internet support. (Visit `www.ghuj.com`, for example, for a large collection of GIMP tutorials.) GIMP handles a wide variety of image formats and allows editing by layers and individual color channels. If your budget is limited, and you need more image-manipulation capabilities than the iLife suite provides, GIMP is worth a try before you spend lots of money on Brand P (Photoshop).

You can find more info at `www.gimp.org`. If you want to give it a try, download the Mac application bundle for GIMP, available at `http://gimp-app.sourceforge.net`. Open the disk image for the application bundle and drag GIMP to your Applications folder. When you start GIMP, it automatically starts the X11 window system. When you quit Gimp, you still must quit the X11 system separately. You can also download the experimental 2.6–native version from the same site, if you want to give it a try.

GraphicConverter, available at `www.lemkesoft.com`, is an extremely handy shareware program that has long been part of the Macintosh universe. It includes several image-editing tools and even accepts many Photoshop-compatible plug-ins, allowing a variety of special effects. Its best attribute, however, is its ability to import some 200 file formats and to save in 80 formats. It's well worth the $35 shareware fee.

Page-layout programs

Desktop publishing was born on the Macintosh, taking advantage of Apple's introduction to the industry of a high-resolution, what-you-see-is-what-you-get (WYSIWYG) display, a graphical interface, and laser printing. Even in corporations that have standardized on the Windows operating system, Macs are plentiful in the graphics or design department. As I mention earlier in this chapter, Apple's Pages program provides many tools for high-quality page layout and may be all you need if you're not a professional designer. But Pages is no threat to the top two programs the industry uses: Adobe InDesign and QuarkXPress. Both programs have a long and strong association with the Mac platform. QuarkXPress started on the Mac, and InDesign traces its lineage to PageMaker, also a Mac-first program. Both are strongly supported on the Mac, and file transfer is generally straightforward. In fact, Quark uses the same application on both platforms.

Adobe also sells the document-processing program FrameMaker, often used for high-end technical documentation. The current version isn't available for OS X, however, so if you need it, run it in Windows on your Mac.

Discovering Other Specialized Programs

It used to be that many specialized programs critical to certain industries weren't available for the Macintosh. That's less true now, as the availability of programs in this section for the Mac demonstrates. Still, in some software categories, the market leader doesn't yet offer an equivalent program that runs on Macs. Also, some companies expect their employees to use programs developed by that company's information technology (IT) department that run only in Microsoft Windows. The simple answer to these problems is to install Windows on your Mac — a process that I discuss in detail in Chapter 16. In some of these software categories, you find quality Mac programs that are worth switching to. Also, more IT departments are replacing their internal applications with software that you can access from any web browser.

Computer-aided design

In the early 1970s, when industry first began to use computer-aided design (CAD) systems to replace old-fashioned drafting boards, the software ran on 16-bit minicomputers with $\frac{1}{1000}$ the speed and $\frac{1}{10}$,000 the memory of a low-end Mac. Those systems cost a couple hundred thousand dollars per seat, back when a single-family home cost less than $50,000. Modern CAD programs run on standard personal computers but are still pricey, often costing more than the computers they run on. The most popular CAD program now on the market probably is AutoCAD, from Autodesk. After a long absence, Autodesk now sells a Mac version of AutoCAD for $3,995 (no, I didn't leave out a decimal point), along with a free drawing viewer for the iPad/Phone/Pod.

Several less-expensive CAD programs for the Mac are well reviewed and can exchange `.dwg` files with AutoCAD. Some players in this field include ArchiCAD, BOA, CADintosh, CADtools, DenebaCAD, MacDraft, PowerCADD, TurboCAD, VectorWorks, and Vellum Draft.

In addition, Google offers Google SketchUp (`http://sketchup.google.com`), which can meet many design needs. Check out *Google SketchUp 8 For Dummies,* by Aidan Chopra, for help getting started with this program. Another option is OmniGraffle from `www.omnigroup.com`; it's a really nice alternative to Visio. The website `www.architosh.com` has reviews and other information for people, especially architects, who want to work with CAD on the Mac.

GPS navigation

The Global Positioning System (GPS) has revolutionized navigation. Adding GPS to a laptop can enable any number of innovative applications, from providing navigation info to vehicles (cars, boats, planes, and even balloons) to collecting survey data. For a long time, GPS receiver manufacturers supported only the PC. Garmin, a leading brand, fully supports Mac users with some applications, such as BaseCamp, available through the AMac App Store. Mac GPS software is also available at `www.gpsy.com` and `www.macgpspro.com`.

Share the wealth

Many of the most creative ideas in personal computers come from individual developers who distribute their products as shareware. Most developers let you try their program for free, simply asking for a modest payment if you choose to keep using the program. Others distribute programs as freeware, asking for a donation from those who are motivated to make one. Do the right thing and pay up when these programs provide a useful service or feature that you don't get from the big software companies!

You also need a GPS receiver. Many GPS units communicate by using a serial protocol, which you can often accommodate with a serial-to-USB adapter, but this solution typically means keeping track of two cables. Newer GPS receivers use USB or even Bluetooth. Both are better for Mac use, and Bluetooth is ideal because no cable is required.

Voice dictation

"Take a letter." In days of old, an executive would utter those words, and a secretary would enter the office with a notepad in hand, ready to take down the boss's words in shorthand for later transcription on the newfangled typewriter.

These days, good software is available for personal computers that converts your speech to text and that you can edit and use with a word processor. The current top-rated product, Dragon NaturallySpeaking from Nuance.com, is available in a Mac version.

OS X has built-in speech recognition that allows you to verbally order the operating system around. It also has the ability to go the other way by turning text into speech. I talk more about these features in Chapter 17.

Adding Functionality as You Need It

You can download oodles of shareware and freeware programs to add functionality to your Mac. I recommend that you take it easy at first and work with your Mac pretty much as it comes out of its box. Explore this rich world of add-ons when you've grown more used to your Mac and have an easier time detecting when something isn't quite right after a program is installed. Still, I recommend making a few downloads sooner rather than later, because they have particular relevance to easing the switching experience. I mention GraphicConverter, the excellent Swiss Army knife for image formats by Lemkesoft, earlier in this chapter. The following sections describe a few more programs that you might keep in mind.

Adobe Flash Player

Adobe's Flash is widely used on the web to display multimedia files, particularly video. Apple used to include Flash with OS X but decided to drop it. Steve Jobs posted a letter explaining his concerns about Flash at www. apple.com/hotnews/thoughts-on-flash, citing its lack of an open standard, security, and performance. He believes that the new, open HTML5 standard will ultimately replace Flash on the web. Users of iPads and iPhones have no choice but to live without Flash, but as a Mac user, you can add Flash to your web-browsing experience if you want. Adobe offers a free player for OS X, which you can download from www.adobe.com. In my experience, Flash does cause Safari to crash regularly, but restarting Safari when this happens is easy. I suggest trying Safari without Flash and see whether you're missing a lot before you download Flash Player, or try the Chrome or Firefox browser when Flash is an issue on Safari.

Java

The Java programming language is very popular for business applications. It was once expected to be used extensively for personal computer applications as well, but few such programs materialized. Unlike other computer languages, Java requires that you install special software, called the Java Virtual Machine (JVM), on your computer before you can run any Java programs. Apple once maintained its own version of Java but has since decided to let Oracle, which acquired Java when it acquired Sun Microsystems, do the heavy lifting. This arrangement should ensure that Apple users get the latest version of Java instead of being a revision behind. Oracle releases new versions on its own schedule, however, not Apple's. As a result, OS X no longer includes Java, but you can download it from Apple. Also, when you try to run a program that requires Java, Lion offers to download it then.

Don't confuse Java with JavaScript, a different programming language that's used on many websites. JavaScript is built into Apple's Safari web browser and all other modern browsers, so you don't have to worry about it. See Chapter 8 for more on web browsers.

Flip4Mac

Quite a bit of content on the Internet is available only as Windows Media files (`.wma` and `.wmv`). With Windows Media Components for QuickTime, by Flip4Mac, you can play these files directly in QuickTime Player as long as they don't have digital rights management (DRM) restrictions. Flip4Mac also lets you view Windows Media content on the Internet from your web browser. A free version is available from the Microsoft Mac site: `http://windows.microsoft.com/en-US/windows/products/windows-media-player/wmcomponents`.

Alternatively, you can look for the link to the free version at `http://flip4mac.com`, where you can buy other, more capable versions if you like.

StuffIt Expander

OS X can open a variety of compressed files and archives, and can do Zip compression (select the file or files you want to compress and choose File⇨Compres from the Finder menu). StuffIt Expander (`www.stuffit.com`), from Smith Micro Software, can open many more formats, including some older Mac formats such as `.sit` and `.hqx`. It comes free from the website, but you have to navigate past offers for more-capable programs that aren't free. StuffIt Expander was once a must-have download for Mac users, but now I suggest that you wait until you encounter a file that needs StuffIt.

Part III
Connecting Hither and Yon

The 5th Wave   By Rich Tennant

"Wow, I didn't know OS X could redirect an e-mail message like _that_."

In this part . . .

*L*ikely the first things you want to do after your Mac is
set up are get online and check your e-mail. Apple
software makes it easy to accomplish these tasks — most
of the time. But connection scenarios vary and hiccups
happen. In this part I help you get online quickly. Then I
take a closer look at the various ways you can network a
Mac. In Chapter 10, I deal with security. Hassle-free safe
surfing is one of the great benefits of switching to a Mac,
but you can do some simple things to make Mac use even
safer. In Chapter 11, I tell you how your Mac can work
with Apple's popular mobile devices, such as the iPhone,
iPad, and iPod.

If you're browsing in the bookstore and have no intention
of buying a Mac or this book, at least read what I have to
say about security in Chapter 10. The advice there can
reduce security problems with your Windows and Internet
use, and that's in everyone's interest.

Chapter 8

Getting Your Mac Online

In This Chapter

▶ Using your current Internet service or maybe something better

▶ Choosing among Mac browsers

▶ Setting up your e-mail

▶ Using other forms of online communication: Chat, voice, and video

Getting a Mac online is like teaching a duck to swim: It usually comes naturally. If you answered all the questions during the setup process outlined in Chapter 4, you're probably already online and working away. But if you have a problem, the solution may not be obvious. In this chapter, you discover tips for connecting to the Internet; surfing with the Safari browser; setting up e-mail on your Mac; and staying in touch with other popular online tools like instant messaging, online telephone services, and (of course) social networking.

Using Your Current Internet Account

If you have Internet service that you like, you can probably stick with it. Most Internet service providers (ISPs) support Macintosh users, and Macs generally can connect anyway with the few ISPs that say they don't. The first thing is to see what kind of Internet connection you currently have. If you have a high-speed modem — cable, DSL, or satellite Internet — you should be all set.

If you run into a glitch, the fixes depend on whether you're using an Ethernet or a wireless connection for high-speed service. Also, if you're using dialup Internet or Internet service at work or school, you have different items to check. The following sections have the details.

If you're looking to upgrade to cable, DSL, or satellite high-speed service, see the section "Upgrading Your Internet Service," later in this chapter.

Checking wires on an Ethernet connection

A wired Ethernet connection uses an Ethernet networking cable that plugs into your computer. Ethernet cables have plastic plugs that look like the plugs used on telephones in North America, only fatter. (But don't try to use a phone cable.) The following tips can help if you have this type of connection:

✔ **If your high-speed modem is connected to an Ethernet router,** see whether the router has an extra Ethernet port and run an Ethernet cable from it to the Ethernet port on your Mac.

   If you don't have a router or switch, you should get one; it's cheap enough. In the meantime, you can unplug the Ethernet cable from your PC and plug it into your Mac to get started.

✔ **If your PC is connected to your high-speed modem by a USB cable —** a rectangular metal plug — you may not be able to use that cable with your Mac, even though the Mac has USB ports. Check with the modem manufacturer to see whether it supports USB connections to OS X. If not, you must use an Ethernet cable.

   Most modems that support USB connections also have Ethernet jacks, but with many, you can use only one or the other, not both together. If you want to use the PC and your Mac, but your PC doesn't have an Ethernet port, you need a combined USB-and-Ethernet router.

Picking up Wi-Fi signals at home

If you'll be using wireless Internet with your computer, life is even easier. All new Macs include built-in AirPort — the name Apple uses for Wi-Fi. Another common name is 802.11, Wi-Fi's very own IEEE standard number. The number 802.11 is followed by a letter that indicates the speed and frequency band supported: a, b, g, or n. Macs handle them all.

All you need to use an existing Wi-Fi service is the Wi-Fi password — and not even that if security isn't enabled. See Chapter 9 for more about Wi-Fi security, including what to do if you forget the password you initially set up.

If you don't already have Wi-Fi, and you have or plan to get an Apple laptop, consider buying a Wi-Fi router. It offers these benefits:

✔ Having one lets you use your laptop anywhere you choose to work, as long as it's within range of the router's signal.

✔ If your desktop installation isn't near a phone or cable TV jack, the wireless capability means that you don't need to run cables everywhere. (Your MacBook's MagSafe power connector protects your laptop from damage if you trip over the power cord, but not if you trip on the Ethernet cable.)

Apple sells a Wi-Fi router combined with a backup hard drive named Time Capsule. It has many cool features that make it worth considering as your first Wi-Fi base station. You can find out more about Time Capsule in Chapter 9, too.

Setting up dialup service

If you're connecting to the Internet by using an old-fashioned dialup connection — the kind that makes "beep-boop-beep-wah-wahhh" noises (often called *whale songs*) every time you connect — you need a USB dialup modem to continue using that connection with your Mac. New Macs don't have built-in modems. Apple sells a tiny USB + dialup modem for about $50. Other USB dialup modems generally work. Again, check with the manufacturer.

To get your dialup service to work on your new Mac, you need certain information, such as your account name, password, and the phone number your computer must dial to get connected. If you don't have this information handy, and you've been using your PC to access your dialup account, follow these steps on your PC to find the information you need:

1. **Choose Start⇨Control Panel and double-click the Network Connections icon.**

2. **Right-click your ISP's icon in the dialup area, and choose Properties from the context menu.**

3. **Write down the settings info you see.**

Alternatively, just give your ISP a call and ask the folks which settings you need. In either case, save the paper with the dialup-settings info along with your Mac's manuals, or write the settings in the margin here.

When you have the needed information, follow these steps to set up your modem on your Mac:

1. **Plug your modem into a USB port and then plug the phone cable into the modem.** Almost all new modems take their power from the USB port, but if you have an old modem that needs AC power, plug that in as well.

2. **Choose ⌘⇨System Preferences.**

3. **Click the Network icon.**

4. **Click the modem line in the list box.**

5. **Fill in the requested information.**

Surfing the Wi-Fi cloud

Many people who operate a Wi-Fi access point or router don't turn on *any* security. Because the usable range of a Wi-Fi signal can be a couple of hundred feet, someone outside the premises of the router owner can see the access point in his list of available connections and may be able to connect by using it. Your computer may connect to another available access point without much warning if the access point you normally use isn't available. In densely populated urban areas, several open signals can be available from many locations.

A Wi-Fi connection is open because its owner didn't take the extra steps necessary to turn on one of the encryption features included in all Wi-Fi access points. That can happen because the owner didn't know how to turn on encryption; didn't want to be bothered; or deliberately chose to leave it off, thereby inviting others to use it. I go over the steps necessary to secure your Wi-Fi connection in Chapter 9.

Open Wi-Fi access points raise questions of security, ethics, and legality:

✔ **Security:** If your computer is well locked down, and you use secure sites for activities like online banking, you have relatively little risk that an intruder will access your

files through an open Wi-Fi signal — yours or someone else's.

✔ **Ethics:** Advocates of open access argue that turning on encryption is simple enough that any open access point is an implicit invitation for use.

✔ **Legality:** Someone could use your connection for a nefarious purpose, and you might have some explaining to do to the authorities. Sharing your Wi-Fi connection with others may violate your ISP's terms of service, and many jurisdictions have laws against unauthorized access to someone else's computer.

Quite a few locales offer free Wi-Fi hotspots, and some municipalities have free Wi-Fi in certain neighborhoods. OS X conveniently shows you which access points are open in the list that drops down when you click the Wi-Fi icon in the menu bar; they're the ones without lock icons. Being able to check your e-mail quickly or find directions to a restaurant from any street corner or coffeehouse is certainly handy, and it's neighborly to allow that capability. If you have an iPhone or iPad, download the Wi-Fi Finder app that helps you locate Wi-Fi hotspots, open and paid, in your area.

Connecting at school, work, or elsewhere

If you plan to use your Mac at work or school, you'll likely connect by using that organization's Internet service, as follows:

✔ **If Wi-Fi is available,** try selecting the school's or company's signal under the Wi-Fi icon on your Mac's menu bar and then open your web browser. A page will likely open, with instructions for logging in. You typically need a login ID and password, though some organizations have guest accounts.

✔ **If you'll be using wired Internet,** look for instructions on your organization's web page or intranet on another computer, or visit your system administrator. Fresh-baked cookies are always welcome.

Upgrading Your Internet Service

When you buy your new Mac, you may find that it's a good time to upgrade your Internet service. If you're still using dialup, check out DSL, cable, or satellite service. Or maybe you just got a MacBook and want to be able to go online wherever you go. Whatever your reasons, the following sections help you get started with common Internet service upgrades.

Speeding up with DSL or cable service

If you're using dialup, or you aren't satisfied with the service you're using, now may be a good time to upgrade. If you live in an urban area, you probably have a choice of getting high-speed Internet service from your telephone company or from your cable television provider. The telephone company service is usually DSL (digital subscriber line), but you may encounter the older term *asymmetric DSL* (ADSL). Both cable and DSL can work quite well, so it's worth checking what pricing plans and special features each one offers. Here are some things to remember:

- High-speed service can be more expensive than dialup, but you can share it with several computers, and it doesn't tie up your landline voice service.

- The speeds quoted by service providers are best-case speeds. Things can run slower at peak times of the day or when a news event draws many people to the Net. Also, speeds for downloading data may be much faster than those for uploading, such as when you send messages with large attachments.

- Top cable speeds are generally higher than those for DSL, but cable prices are usually higher as well.

- You may not be able to get DSL service if you're too far from the telephone company's switching equipment.

- Some phone companies are installing fiber-optic lines to homes and businesses. One example is Verizon's FiOS. Fiber optic lines support very high-speed connections, as well as cable TV and phone service.

- You may have a choice of buying the high-speed modem you need or renting it from the service provider. Find out the difference in price, and figure out how long it will take to pay for the modem in higher fees. Also consider that rented modems usually include free service if the unit dies, which isn't uncommon.

- Check for package deals that bundle Internet access, television, and even phone service. These can be significantly cheaper than buying the services individually, but watch out for promotional prices that are good for only six months or a year. Ask what the rates will be after the promotion expires.

✔ Ask whether your service provider has a phone number you can call for dialup access when you're traveling.

✔ Ask your neighbors which Internet provider they're using, whether they like it, and what their customer service experiences have been like.

✔ Back up your data before your installation appointment and then disconnect the backup device. The service provider's personnel aren't necessarily computer experts and can cause unexpected problems.

Mobile Internet: Taking your connection with you

If you use your Mac when traveling, you can choose among several ways to access the Internet, some of which involve little expense. When you're making travel reservations, look for hotels that offer free Internet access. (Make sure that it's available in the room you reserve.) Coffeehouses and public libraries often offer free Wi-Fi connections. You can also take advantage of the Wi-Fi cloud, described in the sidebar "Surfing the Wi-Fi cloud," earlier in this chapter. If you need something more dependable, you can try using a wide area network (WAN) or using your cellphone as a modem.

In this section, you just skim the surface of connecting to the mobile Internet with your Mac. If you're curious about all that the mobile Internet has to offer businesspeople or the whole family, check out *Mobile Internet For Dummies,* by Michael J. O'Farrell, John R. Levine, Jostein Algroy, James Pearce, and Daniel Appelquist. Also, check out free articles and videos at Dummies.com that can help you get started.

Going first class

Many cellphone service providers offer wireless wide area networking (WWAN) that communicates via radio signals using a special device that you plug in to your laptop. Wide area service is most often used by businesspeople. Although this service can be pricey, you typically get connect-anywhere service within the provider's coverage area. If you're considering this service, keep these points in mind:

✔ Most WWAN radios plug into a USB port; you should be able to use them on any new Mac.

✔ Don't get a WWAN card in PC card, PCMCIA, or ExpressCard/54 format. None of these cards plugs into any Mac now sold — though you may be able to find a clumsy adapter that works. WWAN radios in ExpressCard/34 format work only with the 17-inch MacBook Pro because it's the only model that accepts these cards.

✔ Make sure that the WWAN coverage area covers the areas you need covered.

The Mac road-warrior kit

If you're on the road a lot with your Mac laptop, consider creating a travel kit that's always ready to go. Here are some items you should include:

✔ A short (3-foot) Ethernet cable.

✔ A cheap two-wire, three-way extension cord — to share power outlets at airports and lamp power outlets in hotel rooms.

✔ An airplane MagSafe power adapter (available at the Apple Store).

✔ International power adapters (use Radio Shack Model 273-1405 or visit the Apple Store).

✔ USB flash drive loaded with backup copies of files you need.

✔ Apple Ethernet adapter if you use a MacBook Air.

✔ A couple of blank CD-Rs or DVD-Rs, and a spare flash drive or two.

✔ A checklist for other items you want to take, including your laptop and cellphone chargers and the serial number of your laptop. (You can also review the checklist before you leave your hotel room to make sure you didn't leave anything behind.)

Putting your cellphone to work as a Bluetooth modem

Some cellphones, including the iPhone, can connect your Mac to the Internet via a feature called *tethering*. You don't even need a special cable; the cellphone talks to your Mac by using Bluetooth wireless networking. You need a cellphone that has this capability and a cellular service provider that allows such use. (Some providers don't, and those that do generally require additional monthly fees.)

Internet from space: Satellite service

If you live far from a cable or DSL Internet service and want something better than dialup, consider getting Internet service via satellite. Compared with other high-speed services, satellite Internet service can have performance problems, particularly with online games and Voice over IP (VoIP) telephony, because the signals take a relatively long time to reach a satellite in a geo-synchronous orbit and bounce back down to Earth. Also, upload speeds are slower than download speeds. Despite the drawbacks, high-speed Internet service can make rural living feel a lot less isolated, and satellite service may well be worth the money if no other high-speed services are available.

The following tips can help you get started:

✔ A couple of variations exist, but you should look for two-way satellite service. It's relatively expensive, with a high initial cost for equipment and high monthly usage fees.

Where am I on the Internet?

The Internet has two ways of referring to a computer hooked up to it: A *domain name* has several snippets of text separated by dots, as in www.dummies.com. The last snippet (.com, in this case) is the *top-level domain (TLD).* Other common TLDs include .edu for schools; .gov, reserved for the U.S. government because it invented the Internet; and .org, usually for not-for-profit organizations. Two-letter TLDs are country codes: .us for the United States, .uk for the United Kingdom, .bk for Burkina Faso, and so on. You can find a complete list of TLDs at www.iana.org/root-whois.

To find a computer, the inner guts of the Internet use a bunch of numbers known as the *IP address.* When you type a domain name in your browser's address bar, the name is sent to special computers on the Internet, *domain name servers,* that look up the corresponding IP address in their databases. The common form of IP address (IPv4) consists of four numbers separated by dots, such as 123.4.56.78. Each number is between 0 and 255. A computer with full status on the Internet has a permanently assigned IP address. Most people who connect through an Internet service provider are assigned one "leased" IP address for their entire home network. That number may change from time to time. Special blocks of IP addresses are reserved for private networks and are never transmitted on the public Internet; your router uses them for local computers. A newer form of IP addressing, known as IPv6, has lots more numbers, so every computer, cellphone, and refrigerator can have its own IP address. Macs can handle IPv6, but the system has yet to be widely adopted.

✔ Professional installation is generally required at an added cost. A small dish antenna is mounted outside your home.

✔ The installer needs to place the dish in a spot with an unobstructed view of the southern sky — assuming that you live in the Northern Hemisphere.

✔ One satellite ISP that explicitly supports Macintosh customers is Skycasters.com. A Google search can find others.

Starting Up Your Web Browser

To surf the Internet, you need a browser. Most people use Internet Explorer as their PC browser, but you may have switched to an alternative browser, such as Mozilla Firefox or Safari. In this section, you find out what your browser options are and find a quick introduction to Safari, the browser included in Mac OS X.

Picking a browser

In addition to Apple's own browser, Safari, you can use Mac versions of several other popular browsers, including Firefox. You can download the following browsers for free and use them with your Mac:

- **Camino:** http://caminobrowser.org
- **Chrome:** www.google.com/chrome
- **Firefox:** www.mozilla.com
- **OmniWeb:** www.omnigroup.com/applications/omniweb
- **Opera:** www.opera.com
- **Shiira:** http://shiira.jp (Japanese)

For the most part, the choice of browser is a matter of taste. Various Mac browsers interpret Internet standards in different ways (though standards compliance is better than in the Windows world). As a result, some websites don't work with Safari but work with Firefox, for example. Opera has strong support of accessibility; you can use it without a mouse. Camino boasts speed and elegance. Shiira has excellent Japanese support.

I suggest that you start off using Safari unless you already use and like the PC version of one of the other browsers previously listed. Consider downloading and installing Firefox, too. It's a chance to practice installing a Mac program, and you'll have it handy if you run into a website that doesn't work with Safari. The Firefox screen is shown in Figure 8-1.

Some websites and corporate intranets require Internet Explorer for Windows. The most common reason is that they use *ActiveX controls,* which are available only in Windows. If you need to access a website that depends on ActiveX controls, you can run Windows on your Mac or use your old Windows machine.

Introducing Safari

Safari is a full-featured web browser with good support for numerous web standards. It includes these features:

- Tabbed browsing
- Bookmarks set up to match the popular iTunes interface
- Built-in Google search box
- Full screen browsing

Figure 8-1:
The Firefox
web
browser.

✔ Reading List, for marking stuff to view later

✔ Password management using Keychain, a well-respected security system built into OS X

✔ Automatic form filler

✔ Pop-up ad blocker and anti-phishing feature

Safari, shown in Figure 8-2 displaying the Alliance for the Prudent Use of Antibiotics page, is built on WebKit, an open source web-rendering engine. This computer program knows how to display the various multimedia formats that the web is built on. Apple has added much functionality to WebKit, and it's being used by several other open-source projects. Safari is built into the iPhone, iPad, and iPod touch, and a free version is available for Windows.

Setting up Safari

Safari is ready to go out of the box. You might want to adjust these settings to suit your needs:

1. **Choose Safari⇨Preferences.**

2. **If you don't see the General preferences pane, shown in Figure 8-3, click the General icon in the top-left corner.**

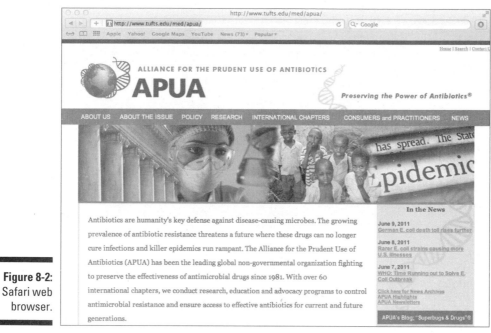

Figure 8-2:
Safari web
browser.

3. **Select the options you prefer.**

   The General pane lets you specify your home page, and control where downloaded files are stored and how long they're kept. You can also change your default browser here.

   Note that tabbed browsing is off by default. Click the Tabs icon and select the Enable Tabbed Browsing check box if you want to try this feature.

   The Open Safe Files After Downloading check box is worth remembering. It's normally selected, allowing many types of multimedia to start up automatically after you download them. If you hear about viruses affecting these types of files on a Mac, deselect this check box for the duration of the security scare. (Our tech editor suggests deselecting the box, regardless.)

   Reach other Safari preferences panes by clicking the icons at the top of the window.

4. **When you're done, close the preferences pane.**

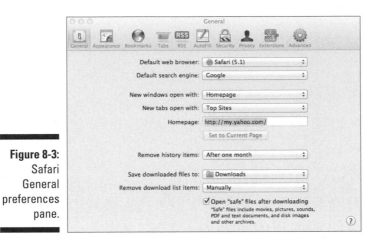

Figure 8-3:
Safari
General
preferences
pane.

The Firefox Preferences settings are similar to Safari's.

Safari, Firefox, and most other browsers keep a history of the sites you've visited in the past few days. This can be handy when you want to go back to something interesting you saw, but it can compromise your privacy if others have access to your computer. The following items describe how to clear your history:

- ✔ In Safari, choose History⇨Clear History.
- ✔ In Firefox, choose Firefox⇨Preferences and click the Privacy icon. Then click the Clear button on the History line.

Switching Your E-Mail to Your Mac

These days, just about everyone has an e-mail address. A large part of getting your Mac online is transferring all your e-mail accounts and addresses.

Moving to Apple Mail

OS X comes with the good e-mail program: *Mail.* Although other mail readers are available for OS X, Apple Mail has a couple of big advantages:

- ✔ It's free and already installed.
- ✔ Apple supports it, so no finger-pointing takes place if you have a problem and call AppleCare.

✔ It's well integrated with OS X and the applications that come with it, including Address Book, iChat, and iPhoto. You can search individual mail messages by using Spotlight, the OS X search tool, and you can easily include photos, resizing and cropping them as needed without leaving Mail.

I've long been a fan of plain-text e-mail. It's what nature intended e-mail to be. But the world has gone for a more multimedia e-mail experience. Apple Mail leads the way with stationery templates that let you include photos, artwork, and fancy backgrounds in every message. You can (and should) have separate stationery for different purposes: personal messages, business correspondence, love letters, party invitations, marriage proposals, press releases, breakups, birth announcements, subpoenas, sympathy cards, classified documents, extortion notes, book proposals — the list is endless. Apple supplies a set of professionally designed templates to get you started. Figure 8-4 shows Apple Mail composing a templated message. But be aware that recipients using some older e-mail programs will not be able to properly view templated messages — they'll get a long list of attachments, instead.

Another cute Mail feature lets you send messages to yourself. Called *notes,* these reminders are integrated with the Apple calendar program, iCal, so you can tack a note or to-do list to an appointment or another type of event.

Figure 8-4:
Apple Mail
with a
template.

I discuss how to get the information you need to set up an e-mail account in Chapter 4. If you entered that information when you first turned on your Mac, you may already be good to go. Otherwise, Mail guides you through the process when you first start it up. And if that doesn't work, choose Mail⇨ Preferences and click the Accounts icon; then enter the information there. See Figure 8-5.

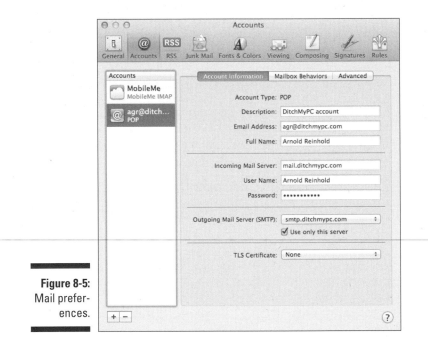

Figure 8-5:
Mail prefer-
ences.

You can move your collection of e-mail messages from your PC. Mail can import mailboxes created by several other mail systems, including Outlook Express. You find instructions for moving messages from online mail services later in this section.

Exchanging data with Microsoft Exchange

If you work for an organization that uses the Microsoft Exchange e-mail and calendaring system, you should be all set. Support for Microsoft Exchange is built into OS X Mail, Address Book, and iCal. OS X accesses your e-mail, contacts, and calendar on your organization's Exchange Server, using the Microsoft Exchange Web Services protocol. Simply select Exchange in the Account type list when setting up your work mail account.

Choosing Outlook (from Microsoft)

Several other mail readers work well in OS X, but if you're new to the Mac, you should stick with Apple's Mail. You might also consider Outlook, the Microsoft e-mail and personal organizer for the Mac. Outlook is included in Microsoft Office for Mac 2011. If you really like Outlook for Windows or have to work with a Microsoft Exchange mail server at work, Outlook may be a better choice. The Mail program can work with Exchange Server and is certainly worth a try, but the one-neck-to-wring philosophy works against Mail here. Using a Microsoft product to connect to a Microsoft server may get you better support from Microsoft and your company's IT department.

Using Address Book

In OS X, Address Book is a separate application. Mail and other OS X applications, including iChat, make use of the Address Book database of contacts. You can search it with Spotlight. Apple's Address Book supports industry standards for contact information, including vCard and IMAP.

Some mobile devices require additional third-party software to sync with your Mac. Pocketmac.com, for example, sells software that adds support for the BlackBerry and Windows Pocket PC devices. It can also link Outlook on your Mac with a wide variety of mobile devices. Markspace.com sells MissingSync synchronization software for Android, BlackBerry, PalmPre, Palm OS, Windows Mobile, Symbian OS, and other mobile devices.

Transferring addresses from other mail services

You'll want to use the large collection of contact information you have accumulated over the years on your Mac. Different mail services often use proprietary formats for storing this information. Many tools are available on the web that can assist you in moving your contacts.

Transferring your Outlook Express addresses

Fortunately, Outlook Express addresses are relatively easy to transfer. You start by grabbing your contacts from your PC, as follows:

1. **Plug a flash drive or external hard drive into your PC.**

2. **Create a new folder on that drive and name it.**

   You might name it **addresses to transfer**, for example.

3. **From your PC's Start menu, open Outlook Express.**

4. **Choose Tools⇨Address Book and then choose Edit⇨Select All.**

5. **Drag the selected addresses to the addresses to transfer folder.**

6. **Click the Remove Hardware icon in the Windows system tray.**

7. **Click the Safely Remove Mass Storage Device line that matches your flash drive in the window that appears, count to ten, and then unplug the drive.**

Then, on your Mac, follow these steps:

1. **Open the OS X Address Book application.**

   The Address Book should be in the Dock; if not, it's in the Applications folder.

2. **Plug the drive into your Mac.**

3. **Double-click the drive icon and then the** `addresses to transfer` **folder.**

4. **From the Finder menu, choose Edit➪Select All.**

5. **Drag the selected contacts to the Address Book window.**

6. **Right-click the drive icon and choose Eject from the contextual menu.**

Transferring your AOL address book

You can use your AOL address book if you continue to use the AOL mail service, of course. You may want to switch to Apple's Mail or another service, however, or consolidate all your contacts in the Apple Address Book. In either case, you have a couple of options:

- ✔ AOL Sync (`http://aolsync.aol.com`) synchronizes your AOL address book with Outlook Express, and you can transfer from there to the Mac, as described in the preceding section. You can also use AOL Sync to synchronize your AOL address book with an iPhone or iPod touch, if you have one. From there, you can sync to the OS X Address Book.

- ✔ Another option is the Windows program ePreserver, from `www.connectedsw.com`. It can also transfer your AOL address book to Outlook Express.

- ✔ Other possible approaches don't require a PC, but they typically involve transferring data through several e-mail programs.

Opting for online mail services

If you use your PC web browser to access one of the online mail services, such as Google's Gmail, MSN's Hotmail, or Yahoo! Mail, you can continue to do so by using any of the Mac browsers. Just enter the URL you normally use in the Mac browser's address bar.

Gmail and Yahoo! Mail also allow you to download and read your mail on your computer, using a mail program such as Apple Mail. Both support the Post Office Protocol (POP). This feature is free in Gmail, but you must pay $20 per year to use it in Yahoo! Mail or Hotmail.

- ✔ For Gmail instructions, go to the Gmail website's Help page, and click the POP Access link.

- ✔ To sign up for the Yahoo! Mail POP service, click the Mail Upgrades link in your Yahoo! Mail window and then click the Upgrade to Yahoo! Mail Plus button.

- ✔ Hotmail users should sign up for Hotmail Plus.

Hushmail.com, a secure e-mail service, supports OS X and is worth considering if mail confidentiality is a concern. Read the section in Chapter 10 on picking a strong passphrase before signing up.

Handling common e-mail problems

The utility of e-mail has diminished in recent years because of the rise of a variety of antisocial uses. The first was junk e-mail advertising, known as *spam.* The name comes from a skit on *Monty Python's Flying Circus,* the BBC television comedy series. A Google search for *Monty Python spam video* is likely to turn up a clip of the original sketch. Watch it.

Unsolicited commercial e-mail or spam

One big problem with spam is that it can drown out your real messages, wasting your time and possibly causing you to miss something important. Most of the better e-mail services use special software intended to filter out spam. They aren't completely effective, however. The Mail program has its own spam filter that you train by indicating the messages that you think should have been caught as spam. It learns some of your criteria as you do this. It may realize, for example, that you're happy with the size of your body parts and suppress messages offering to enlarge them.

You can reduce the amount of spam you receive by selecting an unusual e-mail address — either random letters or some initials that your friends might remember but spammers wouldn't come up with, such as `agrfrom nyc`. Avoid e-mail addresses that end in numbers, such as `sampark456` because spammers try all the numbers after common names. And don't post your e-mail address on websites and mailing lists without a disguise, such as `reinhold{you know what to type here}theworld.com`, or use a separate, free online address that you change when the spam gets excessive.

The mail-order virus

Another concern is the use of e-mail for distributing viruses, worms, and other malware. This issue is less prominent on Macs because few OS X viruses have been found in the wild.

Still, it's worth remembering the advice you followed as a PC user: Don't open file attachments that you weren't expecting. The Mac has an added twist because it asks for permission and a password when installing new software. If you get this type of request after opening an e-mail or its attachment, just say no. And if other people have accounts on your Mac, particularly kids, don't give them administrative privileges and don't let them know your password. That way, they have to ask you before this type of installation takes place.

See Chapter 10 for more security tips.

419s and phishing

Most of us have been deluged with mail requesting assistance in handling a large sum of money, in return for which you receive a nice cut of the proceeds. If you reply, you're eventually asked to advance a modest sum of money for necessary fees — a trivial amount compared with your eventual cut. After the criminals have you on the hook, you see more requests for fees and perhaps an invitation to travel to a Third World country, where all sorts of mischief awaits. This type of e-mail is sometimes known as the *419 scam*. Reportedly, it violates Section 419 of the Nigerian penal code. (Nigeria is one country where running these confidence games is a major industry.) Never respond to one of these e-mails. Never. Period. The people who run them are experts at exploiting that tiny flicker of hope that, against all reason, the story is true. They can even make large sums of money appear in your bank account for a while. These sums disappear when the bank finds out that no funds are available to cover a transfer along the line. Don't respond. Ever.

Phishing is sending mail that pretends to be from one of your regular business contacts, such as a major bank, eBay, or PayPal. You're asked to update your records, validate your credit card, or confirm a purchase that you obviously didn't make. These messages often appear to be authentic, with corporate logos and valid links to the real company's website — even links to the company's privacy policy or a web page where you can report suspected fraud (always a nice touch). But they all contain an action link that takes you to a fake website — which, again, looks like the real thing. There, you're asked to enter your password, credit-card number, date of birth, mother's maiden name, and other details such as an expiration date — everything that a hard-working identity thief could want. Dealing with these e-mails is tricky. The messages describe situations that *could* be true — unlike that e-mail from the heartbroken spouse of an executed African dictator with $35 million in a frozen bank account who found you through a mutual friend.

The most dangerous button

One button on your computer screen can get you into no end of trouble. It's the Send button in your e-mail program. When you click it, your message is on its way, irretrievable. It's all too easy to click the Send button when you think you've finished your message, particularly if you're replying to a message that ticked you off. E-mail correspondence is different from speaking to someone in person or on the phone. No tone of voice exists to clue you in to the underlying emotions, and e-mail lacks the instant feedback of objections, grunts, and even pauses. Also, e-mails are written documents, easily preserved and searched for. Political scandals, billion-dollar lawsuits, and criminal trials have turned on a surfaced e-mail message.

E-mail may be the most powerful tool ever created for creating misunderstanding. Even if you think that your message is levelheaded and couldn't possibly be taken the wrong way, it may contain typos and grammatical errors that change its meaning or just create an impression of carelessness.

Get into the habit of clicking the Save As Draft button rather than the Send button. Go have a cup of coffee, and give yourself some time to think it over. Then read the e-mail aloud — even to an empty office — before you send it. If you're really upset, skip the e-mail, and make a phone call instead.

One of my favorite *Mary Tyler Moore Show* moments was when Rhoda showed Mary a letter that Rhoda had written, professing undying love for a man she'd just met. When asked for ways to improve the letter, Mary replied, "The important thing is that you don't send it." Sometimes, the best use of mail is to get your thoughts on paper and then just leave them in the Drafts folder.

Spearphishing is an even more insidious practice aimed at breaching security at corporations and government organizations. The attackers take the time to research employees, often through social-networking sites, and craft e-mail exchanges designed to develop trust before suggesting a booby-trapped website to visit or requesting a password. Major companies in the computer-security business have been compromised by such techniques.

If you think that a message from eBay, PayPal, your bank, or some other source you're familiar with isn't authentic, don't click any of its links, handy though that may seem. Instead, type the URL of the business (www.ebay.com, for example) directly in your web browser's address bar. Then navigate to your personal account, and log on to see whether any such requests are pending. If you're still not sure, call the company, using a phone number from a recent bill or bank statement — not from the suspect e-mail. Finally, if you work in an organization that has important secrets to protect, and you develop a new online buddy, watch out for anything unusual in his or her requests.

Communicating Beyond E-Mail

E-mail is far from the only way to communicate using a computer. Some people even think it's passé. With your Mac and an Internet connection, you can take your pick of programs and services for reaching out to others. The following sections cover the most popular ones: iChat and other instant-messaging (IM) systems, FaceTime, Skype (the favorite program for free Internet phone calls), and social-networking sites.

Your Mac offers plenty of ways to communicate: by text, voice and video. The following sections introduce you to examples.

Instant messaging and iChat

You used to see ads in the New York subway for a stenography school that read "if u cn rd ths u cn gt a gd job." Nowadays, the ability to read that ad just means that you use text *instant messaging,* or *IM.* The difference between IM and e-mail is that IM is live. You and the other person are both online at the same time. You type, the other person sees what you type, and he types something back.

Systems like this, and the same abbreviated argot, go back to the dawn of electronic communication, with Morse-code telegraphers chatting with one another over hundreds of miles of wire. The deaf community has been using this type of communication for decades, under the name TDD. The early Internet introduced the system Internet Relay Chat (IRC), which was similar, but no permanently assigned names existed. It took commercial services, such as America Online, to add that important feature. Texting has since been added to cellphones, with the phone number serving as a unique identifier. It's the primary mode of communication for teens and young adults.

Unfortunately, the different commercial services rarely allow intercommunication among their systems. The Apple iChat program comes close to being a universal communicator for instant messaging, and it can do a lot more than "how r u?" text messaging. In iChat, you have these features at your disposal:

   ✔ **Communication with other IM clients:** You can chat with people who use AOL Instant Messenger (AIM) as well as Apple's own MobileMe Mac.com system and Google Talk. iChat also supports Jabber, an open standard for IM. Jabber in turn lets you connect to ICQ and Yahoo! Messenger. You can also chat directly with other OS X users on your local network by using Bonjour.

✔ **Exchanging messages with a mobile phone:** You can use iChat to send and receive text messages to a cellphone if you have an AIM account. The messages are free, and you can use your Facebook login. After you're connected to AIM in iChat, choose File➪Send SMS. Enter the recipient's phone number in the pane that pops up, and you're ready to text.

✔ **Voice and live video communications:** The latter requires you to have a suitable video camera. (iMacs and Apple laptops have one built in, as do current Apple Cinema Displays.) You can invite as many as nine other people for a voice conference or three other people for a videoconference. Video is transmitted via the ITU H.264 standard, which sends high-quality pictures over a limited bandwidth. You can videoconference with people on Windows computers as long as they have AOL Instant Messenger version 5.5 or later. It gets better:

  • *iChat Theater:* Lets you share a slide show or Keynote presentation with friends or business associates. They even see a live image of you as you give your presentation.

  • *iChat Screen Sharing:* Lets you and another person control a single computer desktop, making it easy to collaborate on a project or help someone with a computer problem.

  • *iMessage:* Apple's iMessage service lets users of iOS5 devices — iPads, iPhones, and iPod touches — send instant messages to each other without using your cellular carrier's pricey SMS service. It lets you know when the other party has received and read your message and when he or she is typing a reply, and it includes end-to-end encryption. As of this writing, Apple has not said if this service will be available to Mac users, but I predict it will be.

  • *OS X Server:* Lets businesses set up private, secure iChat systems on their local networks. The internal system can include non-Mac computers.

✔ **Parental controls:** Finally, iChat includes parental controls that let you limit what your kids can do and with whom they can chat.

All you need to set up iChat are the account names and passwords for each chat account you use. If your Mac doesn't have a built-in camera, you can use a FireWire camera or any USB camera that's UVC (Universal Video Class) compliant.

Other IM systems

You can use your Mac to chat on other IM systems, including AIM, Google talk, and Yahoo!. Yahoo! Messenger and MSN Messenger both have OS X clients that you can download for free:

- ✔ **Yahoo! Messenger:** `http://messenger.yahoo.com/mac.php`
- ✔ **Microsoft Messenger for Mac:** `www.microsoft.com/mac/messenger`
- ✔ **Mercury Messenger:** `www.mercury.to` (offers a Java-based MSN client that runs on OS X)

The MSN Messenger client is also included in Microsoft Office.

Certain tricks let you access MSN by using iChat via Jabber servers. They're not for the fainthearted, though. This link can get you started: `www.allforces.com/2005/05/06/ichat-to-msn-through-jabber`.

Still another alternative is Adium, a popular open-source messaging client for OS X that supports AIM, Google, ICQ, Jabber, MSN, and Yahoo!. You can download it for free at `http://trac.adiumx.com`.

Video calls with FaceTime

Apple's FaceTime video calling was introduced with the iPhone 4, allowing users of the iPhone 4 and iPad 2 or later models to see the person they're talking to. Mac users with built-in cameras can use FaceTime as well. FaceTime is included in Lion. To use FaceTime on an older Mac with the Snow Leopard operating system (10.6.6 or later), you first must download the 99-cent FaceTime app from the Mac App Store (⌘⇨App Store).

Internet telephony via Skype

Apple FaceTime and iChat have voice communications built in. Other systems allow voice communications over the Internet (VoIP), which are more like using a telephone. The Skype system from Microsoft (`www.skype.com`) is an example and is free when you talk to other Skype-equipped computers. These computers can be Mac, Windows, and Linux machines, as well as iPhones and other mobile devices. Some new television sets have the Skype service built in. Skype can also transfer files and do video, if you have a camera.

Skype offers a paid service that lets you call telephones all over the world for a small fee. Other paid services include inbound calls from telephones, voice mail, SMS messages to and from cellphones, and video conferences with more than two participants.

Google Voice

Google aims to fulfill all your telephoning needs. You must have at least one phone number: landline or wireless. Google gives you a new phone number that can ring on any or all of your existing lines; you pick up whichever is closest. You can make free phone calls to any other personal computer in North America (Mac, PC, or Linux) and free or cheap calls elsewhere. Video chat requires both parties to have installed a free browser plug-in. Google text-to-speech software can send transcripts of your voice-mail to your e-mail inbox. SMS messages are free. Google Voice apps are available for the iPhone and Android phones. You can specify phone numbers to block. If you have a Gmail account, signup is easy at http://google.com/voice.

Oooo, it's ooVoo

Another new contender in video calling, ooVoo (www.oovoo.com), offers free six-way videoconferencing as well as the usual free computer-to-computer calling and cheap computer-to-phone calls.

Social-networking sites

Social-networking websites — Facebook, Google+, LinkedIn, MySpace, Twitter, and the like — operate over the World Wide Web, and your Safari browser connects you to them just fine. All you need are your passwords. Facebook now lets you use its platform to exchange e-mail with other Facebook users. Apple's iPhoto makes it easy to upload your photos to these sites (see Chapter 12). And see Chapter 14 for ways to make social-networking sites even more fun and useful with your Mac.

Chapter 9

Networking the Mac Way

· ·

· ·

Computers without network connections are like caged animals — they're safe from the dangers of the jungle but never realize their full potential. And Macs are great network prowlers. They can connect to just about anything and prowl the Internet jungle with a sure foot.

Apple uses widely accepted standards such as Ethernet and Wi-Fi for digital communication between computers. Apple leads by integrating multiple networking technologies into its products and by fielding innovative ways to make networking easier to use. One example is Bonjour, a set of software tools that lets your computer find other services (such as printers and other computers) on a local area network without your having to type magic incantations.

In this chapter, I cover the basics of Macintosh networking, including setting up wired and wireless networks. I also cover accessories such as keyboards, mice, and cellphones that network over short distances by using Bluetooth technology. At the end of this chapter, I discuss unique ways of networking and sharing files over your network.

Getting Wired with Ethernet

Important elements of the technology in Macintosh computers originated at the Xerox Palo Alto Research Center (PARC). The most famous example is the graphical user interface, but *Ethernet,* invented at PARC in the mid-1970s, was just as revolutionary. It let computers talk to each other without one being made a master of ceremonies that dictated which computer could talk and when. The key idea in Ethernet was teaching computers "manners" so that they kept their messages short and didn't interrupt another computer when it was talking. And if by chance two computers started talking at the same time, both would silence themselves for a random few microseconds, making it less likely that they would collide a second time.

All recent Macs except the MacBook Air have an Ethernet port (two in the Mac Pro), as do many PCs and quite a few printers and other devices, including Apple TV. All you need to connect two such computers is an Ethernet cable. For the Air, add an Apple USB–Ethernet adapter. The cables are inexpensive, and you can find them in varying lengths at computer and electronics stores, as well as many drugstores and supermarkets. With two devices connected via an Ethernet cable, you can create a local network that lets you transfer files easily.

Many offices have Ethernet jacks in the walls, allowing you to plug in to the corporate network. Check with your friendly IT staff before you do. And while many hotels offer Wi-Fi, some still provide Internet service through Ethernet.

Although connecting two devices with a cable is easy, you most likely want a network that's a little more capable. Your home network can enable two or more computers to share a printer and an Internet connection, for example. To complete that type of setup, you have a bit more work to do to set up an Ethernet network. The following sections walk you through the process.

Configuring Ethernet on your Mac

For the most part, Ethernet just works. If you need to configure its settings, follow these steps:

1. **Select ⇨System Preferences and then click the Network icon.**

   You see the Network System Preferences pane, shown in Figure 9-1 with Ethernet selected.

2. **Select Ethernet in the sidebar.**

   The pane you see tells you your Mac's IPv4 address and the IP address of your router, assuming that your Mac sees it. Write down your router's IP address on a sticky note or blank label, and stick it on your router. You want it handy if you need to configure the router.

3. **(Optional) Click the Advanced button to see the pane shown in Figure 9-2, with a row of buttons labeled TCP/IP, DNS, WINS, Wi-Fi802.1X, Proxies, and Hardware.**

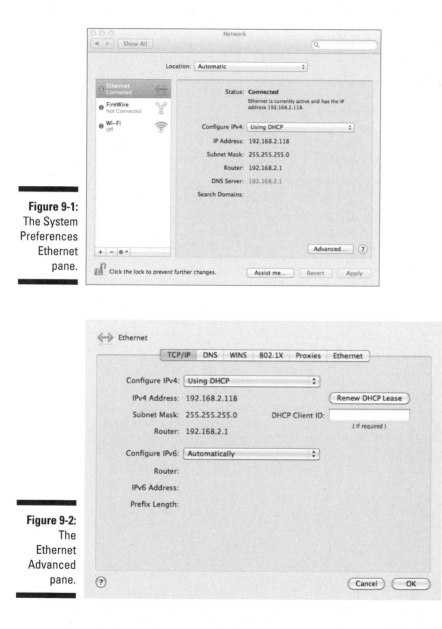

Figure 9-1:
The System
Preferences
Ethernet
pane.

Figure 9-2:
The
Ethernet
Advanced
pane.

If you aren't a networking guru, don't mess with any of these settings unless someone instructs you to do so, such as a tech support person from your Internet service provider (ISP) or office IT department. Because many of these support people have limited Mac training, it's good to know where to find these settings. You may click the Hardware button to see the unique address assigned to your Macintosh's Ethernet. It's a Media Access Control (MAC) address (no relation to a Mac computer). You can also find it in the Hardware section of the About This Mac More Info display on the Apple (🍎) menu. The Hardware Advanced pane also shows the local IP address of your Mac and the IP address of your router. You can see your address in the new, nobody-is-using-it-yet IPv6 addressing scheme. Click Cancel to leave this pane without saving any of the changes I told you not to make.

Understanding routers

If you want to connect more than two computers and hook them all up to the Internet, you need an Ethernet router. This small box has several Ethernet jacks so that you can plug in each computer. You use a special jack to connect the router to your high-speed Internet modem or to another router. Some routers also include a Wi-Fi access point. I get to that topic in the next section.

Your router has a small computer inside that knows how to send the right messages to the right computer attached to it. Most routers have blinking lights in front that clue you in to what's working and active. Routers provide several capabilities, such as firewalls (for increased security) and parental controls. You typically configure a router by using your web browser; its setup screen appears as a website with a special address.

Devices on your Ethernet are automatically assigned IP addresses in one of the special ranges that are reserved for private networks. These addresses never go out on the public Internet, so you and your neighbors can be using the same addresses on your respective home networks without a problem. The numbers are usually assigned automatically. From the outside, your local network is known by the globally unique IP address assigned to it by your Internet service provider. Your computers (you can network more than one) use their internal addresses, and your router converts those addresses to the external address automatically as needed through a process known as Network Address Translation (NAT).

Hooking up your router

You may already have a router as part of your PC installation. If so, you just need to run an Ethernet cable from your Mac to an empty port on your router. If not, and if you want to share your Internet connection with multiple computers, you should purchase a router. Apple makes some nice ones, including Time Capsule, which also includes a large hard drive for over-the-network backup. See Chapter 2 for more information.

The exact procedure for setting up a router can vary for different models, so look over the instructions that come with it and then save them with the other papers that came with your Mac. The installation generally goes like this:

1. **Run an Ethernet cable from your high-speed modem to your router's WAN port.**

2. **Run an Ethernet cable from each computer you want to wire to the network to one of the router's LAN ports.**

   If you have a Wi-Fi router, you don't need to run a cable to a Wi-Fi–equipped computer, though you can if you want.

3. **Hook up power to your router.**

   Typically, you plug the power unit that came with the router into an outlet on the wall or a power strip and then plug the power unit's wire into your router.

Configuring your router

Your router sits on your network like any other computer. Most routers — but not Apple's, which I explain in a bit — put up their own website on your local network that you access with any web browser, such as Safari. You configure the router through this website. Don't confuse this website with the router manufacturer's website, such as www.linksys.com. The one you use to change settings is literally inside your router and is accessible only from computers on your local network.

Your router typically keeps one internal IP address for itself, and you need to know that numeric address to access the router's internal website with your browser. The default address that your router uses is in its manual. In case you lost it, here are the IP addresses most often used by popular manufacturers, though the one used for your model may vary:

- **D-Link:**192.168.0.1
- **Linksys:** 192.168.1.1
- **Netgear:** 192.168.0.1
- **SMC:** 192.168.2.1
- **USRobotics:** 192.168.123.254

With the IP address in hand, you can set up your router as follows:

1. **Open your web browser, and type your router's IP address on the address bar.**

2. **When the router's logon screen appears and asks for a password (and, on many models, a username), enter the information that's requested.**

   If you assigned a password and forgot it, the simplest thing to do is to reset the router. The downside is that you lose any configuration information, such as game ports, that you previously set up. First, you might try one of the common default passwords: `admin`, `password`, `1234`, `12345`, and none (that is, leave the password field blank).

   If all else fails, reset your router. You can often press a small button hidden behind a hole in back of the case. The standard method is to use a toothpick or straightened paper clip. After it resets, your router accepts a default username and password. Again, check your manual. If you don't know your router's default password, try the ones listed in the preceding paragraph or check the booklet that came with the router. If you can't find it, check the manufacturer's website. It helps to know the router's model number, too. Also, this website compiles default usernames and passwords for routers: `www.phenoelit-us.org/dpl/dpl.html`.

3. **After you get past the router's logon screen, you see what looks like a miniature website with many pages you can navigate to change settings.**

   Figure 9-3 shows a typical router configuration page.

   Exactly what you can do varies by model, but common capabilities include these actions:

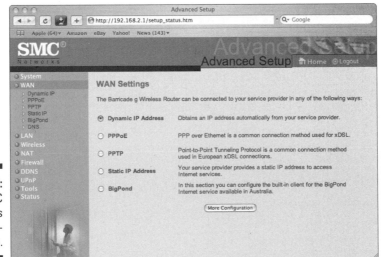

Figure 9-3: An SMC router's configuration screen.

- Set a new username and password.

- Configure how your router connects to your high-speed Internet modem.

- Turn on or off a built-in firewall that helps protect computers on your local network from attacks over the Internet. To do this, you block most *ports*, which are special code numbers that your computer can respond to.

- Allow certain ports to be visible through the firewall — a capability needed for many online games, certain services such as virtual private networks (VPNs).

- Set parental controls, such as limiting Internet use on certain computers to certain hours. (See Chapter 17.)

4. **When you're done, follow the prompts to save your settings, if necessary, and exit your router's internal configuration page.**

Networking Wirelessly

Apple didn't invent Wi-Fi wireless networking, but it was the first company to popularize its use, under the brand name *AirPort.* A geekier name for the same thing is its Institute of Electrical and Electronics Engineers spec number, IEEE 802.11. All new Macs, including all laptops, come with Wi-Fi built in and ready to go.

Ethernet has a geek name, too: IEEE 802.3. As the numbers suggest, Wi-Fi is related to Ethernet. But rather than send short messages over wires, Wi-Fi sends them by way of radio signals. The Wi-Fi protocol is more complicated than Ethernet's because radio signals can fade in and out as laptops move around, and you can move from one access point to another automatically. Also, Ethernet is typically carried by wires that run completely inside your building, but Wi-Fi signals can penetrate your outside walls, which makes security a major issue that the Wi-Fi protocol must handle.

Understanding access points

The heart of a Wi-Fi network is an *access point* that supervises the communications. An access point may be built into your Ethernet router, or it may be a stand-alone unit. Each access point has a limited range of up to about 300 feet, or 100 meters; you can have multiple access points, however, and they can talk to one another. To let Wi-Fi computers within range access the Internet, at least one access point has to connect to your Internet modem, usually with an Ethernet cable.

Another way to share: AirDrop

AirDrop provides another way to share files with another nearby Mac. No special setup is needed; AirDrop automatically discovers other Macs. An AirDrop icon appears in any Finder window's sidebar. Click it, and OS X finds nearby Macs willing and able to share (both must be running AirDrop, so they must be using OS X Lion or later). If they have entries in your Address Book, you see a contact photo as well. Just drag the file onto the recipient's Mac's name or contact photo. AirDrop sets up a direct Wi-Fi connection between the two computers; you don't need a Wi-Fi base station signal or cable connection between the two machines. You can use AirDrop on a bus, train, or airplane (but not during takeoffs and landings, please).

Wi-Fi comes in several flavors, denoted by lowercase letters attached to the geek name: 802.11a, 802.11b, 802.11g, and 802.11n. The 802.11b version was the first one that Apple introduced. It's also the slowest: nominally, 11 Mbps (megabits per second). The 802.11g version came later and can operate at 54 Mbps. The *a* version is as fast as *g* but operates on a different frequency band. The latest version, 802.11n, is as much as five times as fast as *g* and can use both frequency bands. New Macs support all four standards.

The speeds listed for the various versions are maximum speeds. The speed you see depends on many factors, and it's usually no more than half the maximum. A big advantage of the faster speeds is the ability to stream media files between computers, iPads, iPhones, iPods, and to your home entertainment center's Apple TV. If you're connecting to the Internet by using Wi-Fi, you're also limited by the speed of your Internet connection, which — even with high-speed cable or DSL service — is often slower than even 802.11b. Be aware that a Wi-Fi network automatically throttles down to the speed of its slowest member, so if you have an older laptop that only knows how to speak 802.11b, you may want to turn it off or shut down Wi-Fi on it when it's not in use.

Dealing with Wi-Fi security

Another issue Wi-Fi has to deal with is security. Ethernet signals are pretty much confined to the wire, so unless a snoop enters your premises and taps in, your communications stay private. Wi-Fi is radio, however, and can go beyond your walls. A snoop could park on your street and possibly pick up your Wi-Fi signal with a laptop or receive it from miles away with a high-gain directional antenna. (Instructions are available on the Internet for making a good antenna out of a Pringles potato chip can.) So the Wi-Fi folks added an encryption option, which evolved into these two options:

- **WEP (Wired Equivalent Privacy):** The first form of encryption, WEP, was meant to offer the same level of security you enjoy with wired Ethernet. Researchers soon found gaping holes in its design, however, and hackers can easily break it with tools that are widely available on the Internet. Using WEP is like posting a "Keep Out" sign on your property. Honest people respect it; crooks don't.

- **WPA (Wireless Protected Access) and WPA2:** These two newer security standards were added in response to the problems with WEP. The latter, WPA2, has the geek name of IEEE 802.11i. WPA and WPA2 provide protection more like a high chain-link fence. (WPA2 adds barbed wire on top.) But a fence isn't worth much if the gate has a lock that's easy to pick. To take full advantage of WPA and WPA2, you need to set a strong, cryptovariable-grade password or passphrase when you set them up. I tell you how to pick strong passwords in Chapter 10.

If you have to use WEP for some reason, be especially careful to check whether the websites you visit are secure — look for the closed-lock icon — before entering passwords and other personal information. If you need to access corporate or other sensitive sites, ask whether they support a virtual private network (VPN). VPNs use end-to-end encryption, so data intercepted by wireless snoops is meaningless to them.

Setting up your Wi-Fi hardware

Most of the heavy lifting required to set up a Wi-Fi network takes place at the access point or base station. In the sections that follow, you find out how to set up Wi-Fi connections in several ways. I start by explaining the Apple access point and other access points, but these aren't your only options. Depending on your setup, you may want to make your Mac an access point or just network several computers wirelessly. Read on for details.

Configuring Apple's Time Capsule base station

If you already have a Wi-Fi router or access point, you can use it with your Mac. (See the next section in this chapter.) But if you don't have one, want to move up to the faster 802.11n standard, or just want more coverage in your home or office, consider getting the combined Apple Wi-Fi base station and backup disc, Time Capsule. Chapter 2 offers a quick overview of what Time Capsule offers. One cool trick worth noting here is that Time Capsule can stream content — such as music, movies, and slide shows — to an Apple TV in your home entertainment center. The streamed content can come from your Mac or the shared disk. Everything plays together. Welcome to the future.

A RADIUS you can ignore

When you set up an access point (other than AirPort), you may see configuration options for RADIUS or 802.11x. They're generally used by enterprise-scale installations that have computer servers set up to manage user authentication. Wi-Fi access points can be set up to communicate with these Remote Authentication Dial-In User Service (RADIUS) servers to get their cryptographic keys, and so on. It's good stuff but probably not something you need for a home or small office. If you work in a large enterprise that uses RADIUS, the IT staff can clue you in on what to do. If you *are* the IT staff, try reading a different book.

If you don't want the backup drive, Apple sells a similar product without one: AirPort Extreme. It has the same connection ports as Time Capsule, including the USB port, so you can add an external backup drive if you want. To set up your Time Capsule or AirPort Extreme from OS X, you run the AirPort Utility. It's in the Utilities folder that's inside your Applications folder. If you want to access the shared printer and hard drive from your PC, you load on your PC the Bonjour for Windows software that comes with the base station. You need to be running at least Windows XP with Service Pack 2.

Configuring other base stations

Most non-Apple Wi-Fi base stations are built into a router and are configured via web browser, as described in the section "Configuring your router," earlier in this chapter. When you enter the browser's IP address, username, and password, you see the usual router web page (such as the one shown in Figure 9-3, earlier in this chapter) with router configuration options plus additional ones for wireless, which include options for these tasks:

✔ Turn on Wi-Fi so that your hardware is enabled. This is also the place where you can turn off Wi-Fi if the need arises.

✔ Specify which Wi-Fi modes are allowed — your old friends *a, b, g,* and *n.*

✔ Give your network a name, or *service set identifier (SSID).* Avoid using a name that reveals your identity, such as `thereinholds`, and don't use a default name like Linksys because a common SSID simplifies attacks on Wi-Fi security. Some routers offer a unique SSID based on the unit's serial number— that's fine, though boring. Otherwise, be creative.

✔ Decide whether to broadcast that name. Turning off SSID broadcast makes it a little harder for snoops to find you, but it's also harder for you to find your own network.

✔ Decide whether to turn on security, and if you do, decide which mode to use: WEP, WPA, or WPA2. If you know that all the computers and other Wi-Fi devices you're using are relatively new and support WPA2, that's the security mode to use. Otherwise, I suggest WPA, which works with most stuff out there except for some game controllers. WEP is a last resort, to be avoided if possible. See the section "Dealing with Wi-Fi security," earlier in this chapter, for details.

✔ Decide what password to use for wireless security. The password you're asked to enter has nothing to do with your computer's logon password and should be different. WPA and WPA2 are both quite strong encryption schemes, as long as you use a WPA password that's hard to crack. WPA uses its password as a cryptographic key, and that key can be broken if the password is too simple. (I discuss picking strong passwords in Chapter 10.) But the bottom line is to use 16 or more random letters. Write them down, and keep them somewhere safe. Yeah, I know, someone told you never to do that. I don't agree. You can read my reasons in Chapter 10. If you forget your Wi-Fi security password, reset the unit as described in the section "Configuring your router," earlier in this chapter, and create a new password.

Making your Mac a Wi-Fi access point

If you have a Wi-Fi–equipped Mac connected to the Internet by a wired Ethernet connection or even a dialup modem, you can turn that Mac into a Wi-Fi access point and share the connection with other Wi-Fi-equipped Macs and even PCs.

To do this, follow these steps on the computer that has the Internet connection:

1. **Choose ⌘⇨System Preferences or click its Dock icon and then click the Sharing icon.**

2. **Select Internet Sharing in the Services list.**

3. **From the Share Your Connection From pop-up menu, choose the way this computer is connected to the Internet (typically, Ethernet, FireWire, Modem, or Bluetooth).**

4. **In the To Computers Using section, select the Wi-Fi check box.**

5. **Click the Wi-Fi Options button.**

6. **Assign your new network a name.**

7. **Turn on encryption, if you like (feeble WEP is the only option), and enter a password.**

8. **Click the OK button.**

9. **Make sure Wi-Fi is turned on (click the Wi-Fi logo in the Finder menu to check and turn it on if it isn't already).**

10. **Back in the Sharing pane, click the Start button in the Internet Sharing section.**

Your other computers should see your new Wi-Fi network now. When you no longer want your Mac to serve as an access point, go back to the System Preferences Sharing pane and click the Stop button for the Internet Sharing service.

Creating a network with no base station

If you just want to network with a bunch of other Wi-Fi–equipped computers, you don't need no stinkin' base station. Just follow these steps:

1. **Click the Wireless icon in the Finder's menu bar.**

2. **Select Create Network in the list you see.**

3. **Give your network a name.**

4. **Turn on wimpy WEP encryption, if you like.**

    This form is all that Apple offers, so don't use it for sensitive information.

    For some added protection, be sure to use 128-bit mode with a random password that you change frequently. See `http://diceware.com/airport.html`.

    You're on the air.

Windows can do this trick, too, and you can join Windows networks and Windows computers can join Mac networks. These computer-to-computer networks show up in a separate section of the Wireless icon list.

If you're in a public place, like an airport, and see a signal in the Wireless icon list with a name like Free Wi-Fi Access or Open Hot Spot, it's probably someone else using a computer-to-computer network that they made with that name. At best, they're playing with you; at worst, they're up to no good.

Windows users who log in to these sites often receive a free virus sampler for their efforts, and Mac viruses may show up one of these days. So stay away from computer-to-computer networks you don't know about, and definitely don't give out personal information, such as a credit-card number or even a home address; criminals pay for information such as "The Smith family is waiting to board a plane to Europe."

Connecting with Wi-Fi

After you set up your hardware, you're ready to connect to your network. Turn on AirPort (the Apple name for Wi-Fi) by following these steps:

1. Click the Wireless icon at the top of your screen (see Figure 9-4).

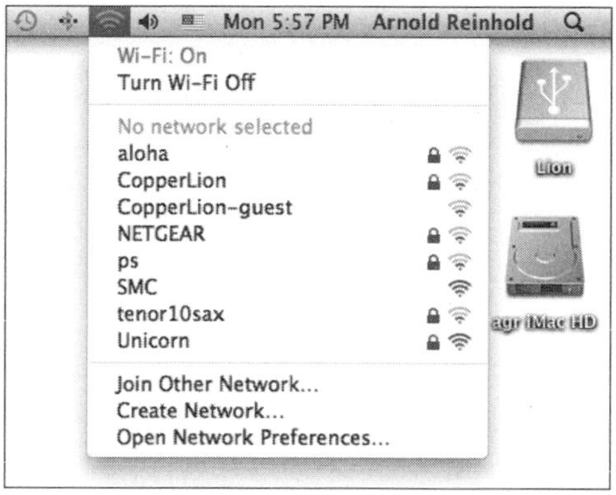

Figure 9-4:
You have lots of Wi-Fi networks to choose among, including two that are open.

```
🕐  ✴·  📶  🔊  ▣  Mon 5:57 PM  Arnold Reinhold  Q

       Wi-Fi: On
       Turn Wi-Fi Off

       No network selected
       aloha                    🔒 📶
       CopperLion               🔒 📶
       CopperLion-guest            📶
       NETGEAR                  🔒 📶
       ps                       🔒 📶
       SMC                         📶
       tenor10sax               🔒 📶
       Unicorn                  🔒 📶

       Join Other Network...
       Create Network...
       Open Network Preferences...
```

2. Click the Wireless icon again, just once.

Be patient. Count to five.

In a couple of seconds, a list of wireless networks that your Mac can hear appears (similar to the list shown in Figure 9-4). Ideally, yours is in the list.

3. Select your network.

4. Enter your password when you're asked to do so (assuming that you set one).

If you're joining a network that doesn't broadcast its name for the world to see, choose Other from the Wireless icon's menu. Then you're prompted for the name of the network (spelling counts); the type of security used; and the password, if any.

Figure 9-5 shows the AirPort pane of the System Preferences Network pane. Be sure to select the Show Wi-Fi Status in Menu Bar check box. The Advanced button shows you the AirPort networks that your Mac considers to be preferred and the order in which it tries to connect to them, while giving you the option to change that information.

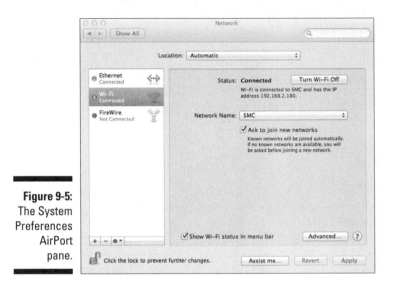

Figure 9-5:
The System
Preferences
AirPort
pane.

Fixing interference problems

The performance you enjoy can also be reduced by interference from other radio signals. The *b* and *g* versions of Wi-Fi operate on a radio band, 2.4 GHz, where unlicensed operation is permitted. This band is shared with other users, including Bluetooth hardware, cordless telephones, microwave ovens, and amateur radio, not to mention your neighbor's Wi-Fi network. The *a* version operates at 5 GHz, also unlicensed, but at a less-cluttered spot on your microwave dial. Wi-Fi can use several channels in each band — the number varies by country — so a fair amount of band sharing is possible.

Somewhere in the back of your computer's manual with all the other legal notices, you should see this notice:

This device complies with Part 15 of the FCC Rules. Operation is subject to the following two conditions: (1) This device may not cause harmful interference, and (2) this device must accept any interference received, including interference that may cause undesired operation.

This legalese applies within the United States, of course, but other countries have similar rules. If you have interference, you're usually on your own.

You can take the following steps to combat interference and other signal problems:

- ✔ **Move your laptop.** Closer to the access point is usually better, but even a small change in position and orientation can help. (One-quarter wavelength at 2.4 GHz is about an inch and a quarter — which can be the difference between a null signal and a hot spot.)

- ✔ **Move the access point.** Put it in a more central location; hang it high on a wall; or move it away from a known source of interference, such as a cordless phone's base station or a microwave oven. Experiment.

- ✔ **Adjust the access point's antenna.** Try small increments. If the access point has two antennas, point them in different directions, at right angles to each other.

- ✔ **Turn off your cordless phone, and unplug the base station.** If that step reduces the interference, move your cordless phone and base station farther from the access point and from your laptop. Then plug the base station into a different outlet. If those steps don't help, replace your cordless phone with a model that operates on a different frequency band (the band is usually marked on the package), or just go back to wired phones. (You probably carry a cellphone, anyway.)

- ✔ **Get a new microwave oven.** You can easily tell whether your microwave oven causes network problems: The problems happen only when it's cooking. If the microwave is used infrequently, you might just live with the interference, but if it's used a lot — say, in a small office at lunchtime — consider buying a newer model. It's cheap, and you can return the new one if it's no better. Also, make sure that the microwave is on a different electrical circuit from your laptop and access points.

- ✔ **Buy a Wi-Fi repeater.** Repeater units plug into a wall outlet and retransmit Wi-Fi signals from your access point for greater coverage. Having a second signal source may reduce interference problems.

- ✔ **If all else fails and you really need to get online, look for a wired Ethernet jack that you can use.** If you don't have a cable, set up a temporary computer-to-computer Wi-Fi network (as I describe earlier in this chapter) on a computer that does have Internet access, and go online via that computer's Internet connection.

Getting Personal with Bluetooth

The mission of the Bluetooth wireless technology differs from Wi-Fi's. Wi-Fi connects the computers and other devices within a home or place of business to create a local area network. Bluetooth has a much shorter range — about 30 feet. It's designed to create a personal network around an individual. The most familiar examples are Bluetooth headsets; a friend calls them *Borg implants,* after the evil *Star Trek* cyborgs. These units fit over your ear and connect wirelessly to Bluetooth-equipped cellphones. They let the wearer talk hands-free.

Bluetooth is also used to connect a keyboard and mouse to your Mac without wires. Nintendo uses Bluetooth in its Wii game controllers. Bluetooth can link your Mac to your iPhone, iPad, and other cellphones, allowing address-book updates to be shared among all devices, in the process known as *synchronizing*. You can use Bluetooth to access the Internet via a cellphone that supports tethering, usually an extra-cost service from your cellular service provider.

Bluetooth was the nickname of a tenth-century Danish king, Harald I, who unified many warring tribes. Like its namesake, Bluetooth networking can help you unify many disparate devices to create your own personal-computing empire. Next-generation Bluetooth will let small devices talk to one another without an intervening personal computer.

Pairing before sharing

Two Bluetooth devices can't talk with each other until they've been formally introduced through a process called *pairing*. You can easily understand why this process is necessary. You don't want your Bluetooth cellphone chitchatting with the cellphone of the person sitting next to you on the bus (unless that person is cute). You may wonder how to pair the devices if they can't talk to each other. The answer is that you have to put one of them in the special state known as *discoverable*. How you do this differs for each device. In some cases, you press a special button or hold down a regular button longer, or you must navigate through a cellphone-menu maze. The details are in each device's manual. This leads me to state the following law:

King Harald's First Law of Bluetooth: *Never throw out the instruction booklet supplied with a Bluetooth device.* In Chapter 4, I suggest that you find a place to keep all the manuals and discs that come with your computer and accessories — one you won't forget about. You can keep cellphone and Bluetooth papers there, too. If you do lose the booklet, check the device manufacturer's website. Most sites have instructions for recent models.

Configuring Bluetooth

You configure Bluetooth on the Mac side by clicking the Bluetooth icon at the top of your Mac's screen. The menu you see includes options to turn Bluetooth on and off, make your Mac discoverable by other Bluetooth

devices, and browse for files on Bluetooth devices. You can also open the
Bluetooth preferences screen, shown in Figure 9-6, which is also available
in System Preferences. Click the File Sharing Setup button to enable sharing
files with other devices over Bluetooth.

Figure 9-6:
The
Bluetooth
preferences
screen.

Networking in Other Ways

Ethernet, Wi-Fi, and Bluetooth are the main ways to network Macs, but the
following other tricks may come in handy:

- **FireWire:** You can connect a FireWire cable between two Macs that have
  FireWire ports, and OS X can use that cable as a network connection.
  FireWire shows up in the System Preferences Network pane's pop-up
  menu, just like Ethernet and AirPort. You simply choose it and configure
  it, if necessary, the same way you would configure Ethernet.

- **FireWire disk mode:** Another way to use FireWire to transfer data
  between two FireWire-equipped Macs is to reboot one of them (not
  both) while holding down the T key. That Mac starts up in what Apple
  calls FireWire disk mode. You see a large FireWire logo dancing around
  your computer's screen. At that point, if you plug the other end of the
  FireWire cable into the Mac you didn't reboot, the first Mac's hard drive
  appears on the second Mac's desktop as just another hard drive. Then
  you can move files to it or transfer files out of it, just like on any external
  hard drive.

✔ **Sneakernet:** The ultimate fallback networking scheme is to use a USB flash drive to transfer data from one computer to another. A flash drive can easily fit in your pocket, and most drives incorporate a loop so that you can attach them to a keychain. Some people hang theirs around their necks on a lanyard. (Osama bin Laden used this method to stay in touch while he was in hiding. A trusted courier would take his e-mails on a thumb drive to an Internet café, send them, and load up any replies to bring back.) Wearing sneakers is optional.

Sharing Files Over Your Network

Regardless of how you establish your network, you probably want to use it to share files with other connected computers.

Sharing files from your Mac

You can tell your Mac to make files available to other computers on your local network or even over the Internet. From an administrator account, follow these steps:

1. **Select \uf8ff⇨System Preferences or click its Dock icon, and click the Sharing icon.**

   You see the Sharing pane, shown in Figure 9-7.

Figure 9-7: The System Preferences Sharing pane.

2. **Select the check boxes next to the sharing modes you want to use.**

   Personal File Sharing allows other Macs to access files on this machine. To let your PC see your Mac files, click the Options button, select the Share Files and Folders Using SMB check box, and specify which accounts on your Mac can use Windows sharing. Normally, only the Public folder is shared, but you can specify other folders to be shared.

You can select more than one sharing mode, but because each has potential security risks, don't select more modes than you plan to use.

Sharing files from your PC

I cover setting up PC file sharing from Windows XP in Chapter 6. (You right-click a folder you want to share, choose Properties, and select the Share This Folder on the Network check box.) File sharing from Windows 7 is controlled from the Share With menu. You select the check boxes next to the modes you want to enable. Alternatively, you can use public folders that are in each library, such as the Public Documents folder in your Documents folder. Find the Network and Sharing Center Control Panel, and click Change Advanced Sharing Settings. Under Public Folder Sharing, select Turn on Sharing so anyone with network access can read and write files in the Public folders. See windows.microsoft.com/en-US/windows7/Share-files-with-someone for more detailed instructions.

Seeing the files you shared

To see shared files from your Mac, follow these steps:

1. **Select Connect to Server from the Finder's Go menu, and click the Browse button.**

   Alternatively, you can click the Network icon in the Sidebar of an open Finder window.

2. **Click the Servers line.**

   You see the Network browser, shown in Figure 9-8.

3. **Click the server you want to access and log on.**

   You need a password for the other machine, if one has been set.

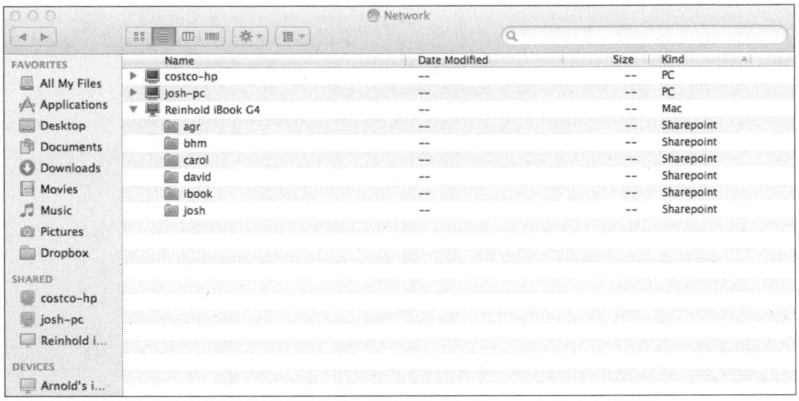

Figure 9-8:
The OS X
Network
browser.

The procedure from a PC running Windows is quite similar. Click the Network Neighborhood icon or choose Start⇨ Network Places (Start⇨My Network Places in Windows XP).

Chapter 10

Staying Secure in a Connected World

*A*s you most likely know, the convenience of hopping on the Internet has its downside: viruses, spyware, identity theft, and more. You're better equipped to avoid these hassles if you have at least a basic understanding of what they are and how to keep them at bay. One reason why you may be switching to a Mac is precisely because you're looking for better security.

In this chapter, Mac security features are in the spotlight. You find out not only what Mac OS X does behind the scenes to keep the gunk away from your computer but also how to take advantage of features and techniques that improve on its already good defenses — namely, strong passwords and file encryption tools.

For tips on avoiding scams and other security issues that commonly arrive via e-mail, flip to Chapter 8.

What Makes a Mac More Secure?

Macs have a reputation for security on the Internet, and for the most part, it's well deserved. Critics say Macs have such a small share of the overall computer market that computer criminals and hacker hobbyists don't consider them worth the time to mount an attack. That may indeed be part of the story, but Mac users aren't complaining about being ignored. Popularity isn't always a good thing.

Mac security, however, owes as much (if not more) to its underlying foundation as it does to the size of its market share. Apple built OS X on top of the Unix operating system, which AT&T developed for its internal use, back when it was the telephone monopoly in the United States. Unix had good security tools that have evolved over the intervening decades, and Apple added more.

Modern operating systems, such as OS X and Microsoft Windows, assign different levels of privilege to different programs. Operating systems are the gatekeepers of a computer, deciding which programs are allowed to run and what they're allowed to do. Intruders have two goals: to run their evil programs on your computer and to get maximum privileges for their programs. After they get that gold pass, the programs can install themselves in the innards of the operating system in ways that are hard to detect. The maximum permission level on many operating systems is the *root* level, and hacker tools that can penetrate to this level are *rootkits*.

Windows XP lets many programs run at a maximum privilege level. If an attacker can subvert one of these programs — and he often can — the hacker is home free. OS X is more careful with the privileges it doles out. You can tell Windows to be more careful, too, but doing so can cause problems for legitimate programs that were designed to operate at a high privilege level. OS X has always restricted application program privileges, so all Mac applications are cool with those restrictions.

Just as in Windows, users can adjust security settings up or down in Mac OS X, but because OS X is shipped with security set at a high level to begin with, and most people never mess with the settings, Mac viruses are hard to spread. Epidemiologists have learned that they don't have to inoculate an entire population with a vaccine to stop an epidemic. As long as a large-enough fraction of the population is immune, the disease stops spreading. It works the same for computers. Having most Macs set at a high security level makes it difficult for any Mac virus to propagate.

Critics of Apple complain that the iPhone and iPad run only third-party software sold through Apple's App Store. This policy has kept malware off iOS devices, however, whereas evil programs are a problem on Android. Now the Mac App Store provides Mac users a way to find safe software that they can use.

Windows 7 security is much improved over that of Windows XP, but some important Windows 7 security features, such as disk encryption and network backup, are available only in higher-priced "professional" versions of the operating system. Also, many malware writers have vast Windows experience and have been able to circumvent many of Microsoft's improvements. By contrast, when a malware writer tries to attack OS X, Apple can devote its full resources to eliminating that threat. Further, OS X Lion includes heavy-duty security improvements, including Find-My-Mac and FileVault full disk encryption, both of which I discuss later in this chapter, along with other security measures that make it harder for hackers to attack a Mac, but are not visible to the user.

Still, as Apple's market share increases, more attack attempts are expected, so don't let down your guard completely just because you bought a Mac. In this chapter, I share simple ways to protect your new machine.

Protecting Yourself with Passwords

Never tell anyone your password. Eat five servings of fruits and vegetables every day. Use a different password for every account. Get 30 minutes of aerobic exercise 4 times a week. Always select passwords with uppercase and lowercase letters, numbers, and special characters. Every time you're with that special someone, be sure to use a — well, you get the idea. We're continually bombarded with good advice — advice that we know we should listen to — but most of us fall short.

As computers and Internet technology have crept into more and more aspects of our daily lives, our use of passwords has exploded. E-mail, instant messaging, online banking, brokerage accounts, automated teller machines, computers, tablets, Internet routers, multiplayer games, social-networking websites — they all ask for passwords. Then we need a bunch more at work and school. The average computer user accesses dozens of different password-protected thingies, and the consequences of forgetting a password or having one fall into the wrong hands range from inconvenience to disaster.

Your Mac isn't an island, and no amount of fiddling with its security settings can protect you if you don't use passwords wisely. But advice that made sense when most people had 1 or 2 passwords to remember becomes impossible to follow when people have 20 or 30 to keep track of. Increasingly, computer-security experts are realizing that the traditional password policy is unrealistic at best and counterproductive at worst. So in the following sections, I present some suggestions for using passwords that you can actually follow and that can make your computer far more secure than the vast majority out there.

Use a common password for unimportant accounts

If someone figures out the password for your newspaper subscriptions and other informational websites that demand registration for no good reason, it's not the end of the world. So you can reasonably use one password for all those accounts.

Use separate, stronger passwords for important work accounts and for personal accounts such as e-mail, social networking, and online banking, where real potential exists for misuse that can cost you money or enable identity theft.

Write down your passwords

Few people can memorize as many passwords as they need for optimal security. It's too easy to forget the passwords that you don't use daily. Instead, they just keep recycling one or two easily remembered passwords. If software at work makes them pick a password with mixed cases and special characters, they add the minimum needed to get past the password police.

You're more likely to pick strong passwords if you know that they're written down someplace so that you run no risk of forgetting them. The trick is keeping the list safe. The classic Post-it note stuck to your monitor isn't what I have in mind. Good choices include the following places:

✔ **Your wallet:** You have other valuable information in there already, such as your credit cards and driver's license. You're careful with it by habit. If you lose it, you quickly notice that it's gone, and you can change the passwords on your computer accounts at the same time you're canceling your charge accounts.

✔ **A clever hiding place at home:** Use your ingenuity. A slip of paper doesn't take up much space. You probably have lots of nooks and crannies. But be sure to pick a location you'll remember. The first place you think of is one you'll likely remember again.

✔ **A safe-deposit box:** Although it's awkward when you need to add new accounts, it can be a good place for your master list. Keep recent changes in your wallet. If you plan ahead, your next of kin will have a much easier time dealing with your estate if someone can acquire a list of your passwords after you're gone. If you want to take some secrets to the grave, use a separate password and leave it off this list.

✔ **A password manager program:** These applications keep all your passwords in an encrypted file. All you need to remember is one master password. Also, most of these programs offer to generate strong random passwords for you when you open new accounts.

Mac OS X has the built-in password manager Keychain. OS X automatically uses Keychain to store the passwords it needs, such as for Wi-Fi, networks, and accessing various websites. You can see the passwords it stores, and add more entries if you want, by opening Keychain Access in the folder that opens when you choose Applications⇨Utilities. You need to enter your login password to see the stored passwords. Figure 10-1 shows the Keychain Access displaying a stored password. To add a new password, click the plus-sign icon (+) in the bottom-left corner of the window.

Quite a few password manager applications (known as *apps*) are available for the Mac, iPhone, iPad, and iPod touch. Some are free or cost 99 cents, and others cost $10 — relatively expensive, as apps go. One problem with this category of application is that you have no easy way to move your data from one application to another. You generally have to type everything again — a real pain if you have lots of passwords. So try the one you selected for a while before you enter all your data.

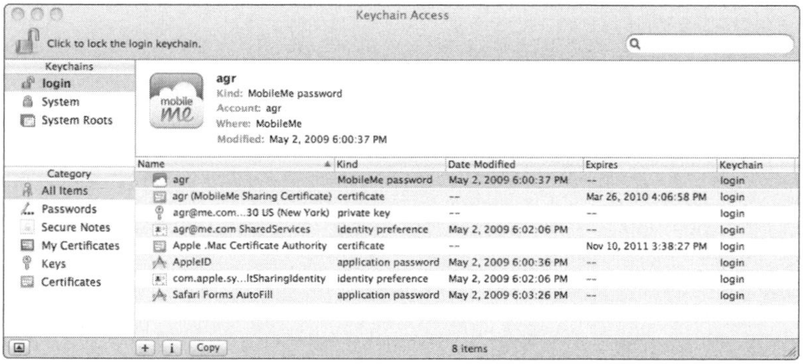

Figure 10-1:
Keychain
Access.

None of the iPhone, iPad, or Mac password managers I've found is open-source, so it's impossible to check how well the encryption and password-generation features are implemented. Some of these apps allow only a numeric code to access your data — and that's not secure enough. I've been using SplashID, which syncs with a Mac or PC if you purchase the more expensive version made for those platforms.

Shareware password managers are available for Mac OS X, including the Java version of Password Safe (`http://passwordsafe.sourceforge.net`) and Password Gorilla (`www.fpx.de/fp/Software/Gorilla`). Both are free and open source; they're compatible with each other and with their Windows and Linux versions.

Change passwords only when you have a good reason

I know — the password police say to change passwords every few months. Some companies configure their software to require periodic changes. I find this advice to be dubious at best for most people. A miscreant who gets hold of your password is likely to use it promptly. Also, people who are forced to change passwords soon learn the minimum change they need to make to get past the password-change program — and attackers know those tricks, too. The time to change passwords is when you think they may be compromised, such as when you have to give someone else a password — never a good thing to do, but it happens — or when a trusted employee quits or is fired. Using a sensitive password at a cybercafé is another occasion for a change.

Assessing risk

Security doesn't exist in a vacuum. You have to consider the risks you face. For computer security, risks fall into two major categories: outside and inside. *Outside risks* refer to things that bad guys can do without entering your premises: sniff your Wi-Fi signal from your parking lot, capture your data as it makes its way through the Internet, or just steal your laptop, for example. *Inside risks* cover things that can be done by guests, family members, fellow employees, and the cleaning people.

By using passwords, you make outside risks generally easier to protect against than inside risks. A determined insider has too many ways to capture your password, ranging from installing keystroke-capture software on your computer to placing a concealed video camera above your desk. (With tiny, inexpensive wireless cameras, this trick is now alarmingly easy to pull off.)

The best practice for large organizations that demand strong internal security is to require *two-factor authentication.* Users demonstrate who they are to the computer by knowing a password or PIN *and* by having in their possession a small device called a *token.* Some tokens plug into the computer; others display a number that changes frequently. The user types the number into the computer along with the password during login. At least one vendor, Cryptocard.com, supports two-factor authentication on Macs.

Picking powerful passwords

Passwords are like medicine: If all you have is a common cold, you may pick up whichever remedy catches your eye on the drugstore shelves. But if you have a serious condition, you want prescription drugs that are tested and known to work. Picking passwords is similar. If you're protecting stuff that doesn't matter all that much, most any password will do. But if your password is guarding information that could do real harm if the wrong people got hold of it — harm to yourself, your family, your business, or your clients — you need a method of picking passwords whose quality is measurable.

You find lots of advice on how to create a password, and much of it is negative. Don't pick a single word in a dictionary. Don't use a password shorter than eight characters. Don't use passwords that people who know you might easily guess, such as the name of your kid, pet, or significant other. The positive advice mostly asks you to do something clever, like think of a famous quote, lyric, or title and then abbreviate it — 2bornot2b, 0saycanuc, or S2Mac4D, for example. The problem is that people who write password-cracking programs know all these tricks and have built them into their programs. Also, those password-cracking programs and dictionaries are widely available on the Internet.

Seeing the amazing power of random

Few silver bullets in life exist, but one is available for picking passwords. If you pick the letters or symbols of your password at random and make it long enough, the odds of someone guessing it become astronomically low.

Most security experts don't push random passwords, out of concern that most users won't accept them. The passwords seem to be ugly and hard to remember. Because it's possible that you've now read several chapters of a computer-advice book, however, I think you're exceptional and may be willing to put in the little bit of effort needed to get the best security you can.

One reason why I take a contrarian view on some standard password maxims is that they encourage less-secure behavior. Asking people to have separate passwords for every account, telling them to never write down passwords, and forcing them to change passwords regularly absolutely guarantees that they'll find ways to circumvent the process. The ways most users do that are all too predictable. I think it's better to write down a random password than to memorize an easy one that won't stop an attacker, anyway.

Another old saw asks people to include a mix of uppercase and lowercase letters, digits, and special characters in their passwords. The well-intentioned idea is to make their passwords more random. But most people simply add a digit or special character to their favorite password, and they typically do that in predictable ways, too. Security expert Bruce Schneier recently found that the most commonly used password on MySpace.com is `password1`.

Scoring a password

One nice thing about random passwords is that you can measure their strength. You can easily assign a point score that says how hard they are to guess. Each additional point means that it's twice as hard to guess the password.

The way you figure the score is quite simple: Each character or symbol in the password scores a certain number of points, and you just add them up. The number of points per character depends on how many possibilities you choose among. If you pick a character at random from the 26 letters *a* to *z,* it receives 4.7 points. If the possibilities include the 26 letters and the 10 digits 0 to 9, you receive 5.1 points per character. Pick at random from any of the 94 possible characters on a standard U.S. computer keyboard — lowercase and uppercase letters, digits, and special characters — and you score 6.5 points per character.

TECHNICAL STUFF

The true meaning of password points

You may be wondering what these points I keep talking about represent — or not, in which case, feel free to skip this sidebar. The points I'm using refer to the concept of entropy, and in the technical literature, the points are bits. *Entropy* measures how random things are; the concept goes back to the 19th century, when scientists were trying to figure out how to make better steam engines. One *bit,* or point, is the amount of randomness introduced by flipping a fair coin. The formula I use to assign points to passwords was discovered by the great physicist Ludwig Boltzmann and is carved on his tombstone.

The thing to note is that the fancy passwords score more — but not that many more — points per character. An 11-character password of single-case letters *a* through *z* has the same strength as an 8-character password made up of all 94 possible keyboard characters: about 52 points. Which password style you choose is mostly a matter of taste. Both styles are equally secure. If you use your password a lot, saving three characters may be worth the trouble. On the other hand, if you travel to other countries and plan to use local computers there to log on to your accounts, you may have trouble. Some of the special characters in your password may not be on the keyboards you find there, and the ones that are present may be in unfamiliar locations on the local keyboards. Also, typing special characters on handheld devices such as the iPhone can be a pain.

Remembering passwords that contain special characters can be easier if you use short nicknames for the special characters. Table 10-1 offers some suggestions.

Table 10-1	Nicknaming Special Characters		
Character	*Name*	*Character*	*Name*
`	Ding	{	Sneer
~	Twiddle	}	Smirk
!	Bang	[	Uh
@	At	]	Duh
#	Hash	|	Pole
$	Bucks	\	Back
%	Ears	:	Eyes
^	Hat	;	Wink
&	And	"	Quote

Character	Name	Character	Name
*	Star	'	My
(	Frown	<	Mouth
)	Smile	>	Nose
_	Under	,	Tear
-	Dash	.	Dot
+	Plus	?	Huh?
=	Equals	/	Slash

Another way to memorize a random password is to make up a story that goes with the letters and symbols. To remember the following password

```
1!30c;tF
```

you might make up a story about hearing 1 bang when you were 30 and seeing a winking tall fighter. I have a Google spreadsheet online (and shown in Figure 10-2) that converts ten random letters to a memorable sentence. `twpxjrufhc`, for example, converts to "Tom's wild peacocks expertly join rude uncles finding happy comfort." The sentence is just to aid memory; you use the ten characters as your password. You'll find a link to the spreadsheet at DitchMyPC.com.

Figure 10-2:
Use this table to turn random letters into a sentence that can help you remember your password. Look up the first letter in column 1, the second in column 2, and so on.

	1	2	3	4	5	6	7	8	9	10
A	Arnold's	amazing	artists	always	arrest	angry	ants	arousing	awful	admiration
B	Bob's	big	brothers	boldly	batter	bossy	boys	bringing	boastful	bliss
C	Charlie's	cuddly	cats	craftily	cover	crazy	crooks	causing	cold	comfort
D	Dona's	deadly	ducks	deftly	drop	dumb	doctors	defying	dumb	delight
E	Ed's	empty	editors	easily	engage	eager	eels	enjoying	easy	energy
F	Frank's	fine	frogs	foolishly	fight	fat	foxes	finding	fast	fame
G	Gloria's	golden	goats	gaily	grab	green	goons	gaining	glorious	growth
H	Hana's	handy	hippos	hopelessly	hold	heavy	horses	helping	happy	health
I	Ivy's	interesting	infants	intensely	inject	incompetent	idiots	insulting	intense	interest
J	Jane's	jolly	judges	joyously	jolts	jealous	jokers	joining	juvenile	joy
K	Ken's	kissable	kittens	kindly	keep	kinky	kings	killing	keen	karma
L	Lucy's	lonely	llamas	laughingly	lash	lowly	librarians	leaving	lurid	love
M	Mary's	merry	mermaids	morosely	mangle	mad	monsters	making	messy	music
N	Nancy's	nice	nuns	noisily	nab	naughty	nerds	noting	neglected	nothingness
O	Olga's	old	owls	often	ogle	oily	orcs	owning	open	obsession
P	Pete's	pink	peacocks	playfully	pester	poor	pigs	packing	proud	power
Q	Quincy's	quiet	quails	quickly	query	quaking	queens	questioning	queer	quality
R	Randy's	red	rodents	regretfully	ruin	rude	robbers	rejecting	redolent	refreshment
S	Sue's	smooth	snails	swiftly	slay	snarky	slugs	seeking	simple	success
T	Tom's	tiny	tigers	timidly	tackle	tired	thugs	testing	tenuous	truth
U	Uri's	urban	umpires	urgently	upset	ugly	uncles	urging	useless	unity
V	Vivian's	vivacious	vampires	vividly	view	vicious	vandals	viewing	velvet	victory
W	Walt's	wild	wolves	willingly	wrestle	wimpy	wardens	wishing	witty	wisdom
X	Xavier's	eXotic	eXecutives	eXpertly	eXpel	eXcited	eXperts	eXtracting	eXtreme	eXcess
Y	Yolanda's	yelping	yankees	yearningly	yank	yellow	youths	yielding	yummy	yogurt
Z	Zed's	zigzagging	zebras	zealously	zone	zany	zombies	zooming	zesty	zeros

Permitting Password Assistant to assist

The phrase *pick at random* is easier said than done. Computers are designed to do the same thing every time you run a program. Most computer programming languages include random-number-generator functions that aren't truly random. Better operating systems, including OS X and Windows, have ways of making things truly random, measuring exactly how long it takes hard-drive arms to move, for example. Unfortunately, many programs on the Internet that claim to make random passwords don't use these tools.

OS X includes its own password generator: Password Assistant. It's designed to help you pick passwords for your Mac OS X accounts, but you can use it for other purposes. Here's one way to do that:

1. **Open Keychain Access (in the Utilities folder, inside the Applications folder).**

2. **Click the plus sign near the bottom to create a new entry.**

   You don't have to save your new password in Keychain, but you can if you want. This is just one way to reach Password Assistant.

3. **Click the key icon next to the Password field.**

   The Password Assistant window appears, as shown in Figure 10-3.

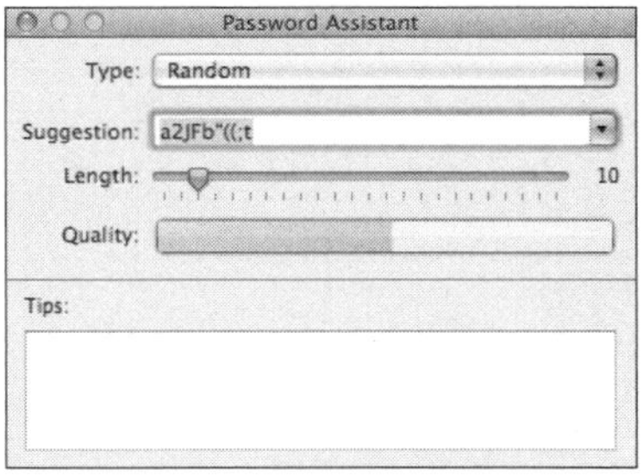

Figure 10-3:
OS X
Password
Assistant.

4. **From the Type pop-up menu, choose Random to create a password.**

   For an explanation of the other options, see the nearby sidebar "Ordering up passwords from Password Assistant."

5. **If you want your password to be a particular length, move the Length slider.**

   See the section "How long does it have to be?", later in this chapter, for details about how password length affects security.

6. **After you select the password you want from the Suggestion field, write it down, save it in Keychain — or both.**

Ordering up passwords from Password Assistant

Password Assistant truly excels when you need a secure random password, but if you've just plain had it with thinking up your own passwords, Assistant offers many more options:

✔ **Memorable** offers passwords made up of two dictionary words separated by a number and a special character, such as `rig25{laden`. They're good for medium-level security with a strength in the 40- to 45-point range. Longer passwords of this type aren't much stronger, so pick one about 12 characters long.

✔ **Letters & Numbers** mixes uppercase and lowercase letters with digits, such as `io5ItCqm8N`. Used that way, the passwords are worth almost 6 points per letter. If you don't want to mess with the Shift key, make all the letters the same case, in which case their worth drops to 5.2 points per letter. This number isn't much of a loss,

but remember to type your single-case version: `io5itcqm8n`. Don't cut and paste from Password Assistant.

✔ **Numbers Only** is handy for picking new personal identification numbers (PINs) for credit cards and so on, but you need a long number for a strong password. Digits are worth 3.3 points each.

✔ **Random** uses all characters on the keyboard and produces passwords that look like `G!0chN6-j2`. Score 6.5 points per character.

✔ **FIPS-181 Compliant** makes up letter-only passwords that are relatively easy to pronounce, such as voofyaidia. The method used is specified in a U.S. government Federal Information Processing Specification — hence, the name. FIPS-181 passwords are worth 4 points per letter.

7. **To save your new password in Keychain, fill out the Keychain Item Name and Account Name fields, and click the Add button; otherwise, click the Cancel button.**

If you use computers a lot, you'll face the need to come up with a new password from time to time, often in situations when you're in a bit of a hurry. If you click the arrow next to the Suggestion field, Password Assistant shows you a list of candidate passwords. Write down a bunch on a slip of paper, and carry the list in your wallet so that you always have a few passwords handy.

Finding other ways to pick random passwords

Be leery of password-picking programs you find while perusing the Internet. Many are poorly written, and it's hard to tell which ones do an acceptable job. The password managers I mention earlier in this chapter are good. Here's a link to a password generator that I wrote (and trust): www. theworld.com/~reinhold/passgen.html.

One way to guarantee that your password is random is to select the letters one at a time by using ordinary, six-sided dice, as follows:

1. **Throw the pair of dice.**

2. **Use the two numbers you roll to pick a character from Table 10-2.**

   Use the die that lands to the left to pick the row, and use the other die to pick the column. (Yes, *die* is the singular of dice.) So rolling 3, 5 adds the letter *q* to your password.

3. **Keep rolling and picking letters or numbers from the table until the password is the length you're looking for.**

   See the next section of this chapter for details.

Table 10-2		Generating Passwords by Rolling Dice			
	1	**2**	**3**	**4**	**5**	**6**
1	a	b	c	d	e	f
2	g	h	i	j	k	l
3	m	n	o	p	q	r
4	s	t	u	v	w	x
5	y	z	0	1	2	3
6	4	5	6	7	8	9

How long does it have to be?

Your password, that is. As with other size questions, this one generates much controversy. Here are some guidelines that I think are reasonable for most users:

- ✔ **Low security** doesn't require much to achieve. An eight-character Password Assistant Memorable password does fine. Alternatively, you can recycle an old, inactive password that you remember well, as long as you haven't used it in a while and it isn't similar to others you use.

- ✔ **Medium security** doesn't stop a determined and skilled attacker, but the attacker will probably go pick on someone else who's an easier mark. I suggest at least 46 points, a 7-character Password Assistant Random password, 10 random letters, or a 12-character FIPS-181 pronounceable password. Breaking it into two words may make it easier to remember. (If you're unsure what the points mean, see the section "Scoring a password," earlier in this chapter.)

✔ **High security** is an open-ended concept, but I suggest at least 56 points, a 9-character Password Assistant Random password, or 11 random letters and numbers.

✔ **Cryptovariable passwords** are for programs that turn your password into an encryption key. Most applications that employ passwords use them as gatekeepers. Know the password, and you're allowed access to the computer or program in question. But some passwords work harder; they're used as the key or cryptovariable in an encryption algorithm. Examples of passwords that need cryptovariable strength include

- WPA and WPA2 Wi-Fi wireless network passwords (see Chapter 9 for more on Wi-Fi security)

- Your OS X master password

- FileVault passwords

- Passwords for encrypted e-mail

- Passwords of other disk-encryption schemes

For cryptovariable applications, people often use passphrases rather than passwords. A *passphrase* is longer than a password and often made up of words selected at random, on the theory that a sequence of words is easier to memorize than a long sequence of letters. See www. diceware.com for suggestions for picking a strong but memorable passphrase by using dice.

Cryptovariable passwords should have at least 65 points. This requirement can be met with a 10-character Password Assistant Random password, 14 random letters, or a 5-word Diceware passphrase.

✔ **Windows passwords:** If you continue to use your Windows computer along with your Mac, know that a longstanding security flaw exists in Windows XP and earlier versions of Windows, having to do with support for the old network standard LAN Manager. You can turn off LAN Manager (and it's a good idea), but you can prevent the problem entirely by using passwords that are at least 15 characters long.

Hardening OS X

Out of the box, OS X offers good security. But you can do several things — besides picking good passwords — to make it even stronger. Read on for details about using FileVault, making encrypted volumes, and using other security tricks and tips.

Locking up your data with FileVault

With FileVault, OS X encrypts your entire hard drive. All the data on the computer is scrambled with the widely accepted AES-128 cipher.

Using FileVault is an excellent idea if you store sensitive data and travel with a laptop, or if many people have physical access to your computer. Microsoft has a similar feature, BitLocker, but it's available only in the more expensive versions of Windows 7.

✔ Because FileVault encrypts your hard drive by using your login password, your account should have a high-security-level password. If you have a password that is fewer than 15 characters, choose a stronger, cryptovariable-level password, as described in the section "How long does it have to be?", earlier in this chapter, and write down that password. Write neatly so you can read it later (I've failed at this).

✔ To change your login password to the stronger one you picked, select ⌘➪System Preferences, click the Users & Groups icon.

To turn on FileVault, follow these steps:

1. **If you are using a laptop, make sure the charger is plugged in and working.**

2. **Select ⌘➪System Preferences and click the Security & Privacy icon.**

3. **Click the FileVault tab at the top, if it isn't already highlighted.**

   You see the FileVault setup window, shown in Figure 10-4.

Figure 10-4:
The FileVault setup window.

4. **Click the lock icon in the lower left and enter your password.**

5. **FileVault will show you a recovery key that looks like this:** UMCH-XD3F-JUPT-VY37-KFGD-6GJN. **Write it down and keep it in a safe and secure place, preferably separate from where you keep your password. You can use the recovery key to unlock your disk if you forget the password.**

6. **Click Continue. FileVault offers to store the recovery key for you. If you agree, you must choose three security questions and provide answers for each. Apple suggests choosing answers you are sure to remember, because no one, "not even Apple," can obtain your recovery key without the exact answers to the questions.**

7. **When you've entered the questions and the answers (I recommend writing those down, too) or chosen not to store your recovery key with Apple, click Continue.**

8. **You are offered to restart your computer or to cancel. This is your last chance to stop the encryption. Click Restart to encrypt your disk.**

   Depending on how much data is on your hard drive, the initial encryption process can take quite a while.

Making an encrypted volume

If you have some data that you want to protect but don't want to go to the bother of encrypting your entire hard drive, you have another option: Create an encrypted disk image. This file looks like a disk volume when you open it. It looks much like the volume typically created when you download an application. It even has the same .dmg extension, but you need a password to open it.

To create an encrypted volume, follow these steps:

1. **Go to the Utilities folder inside your Applications folder and open Disk Utility.**

2. **Choose File⇨New⇨New Blank Image.**

3. **Pick a size for your volume that's large enough for everything you plan to store in it, with room to spare.**

   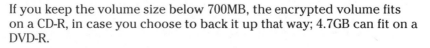

   If you keep the volume size below 700MB, the encrypted volume fits on a CD-R, in case you choose to back it up that way; 4.7GB can fit on a DVD-R.

4. **Give the volume a name, such as** Super Secret War Plans **or** Recipes.

5. **Select AES-128 or AES-256 Encryption.**

6. **Click the Create button.**

Advanced Encryption Standard (AES)

The security features in OS X use an algorithm, the Advanced Encryption Standard (AES), for scrambling data. AES was selected by the U.S. National Institute of Standards and Technology (NIST) in 2001 after a lengthy public competition. The winning design was submitted by two Belgian researchers, Vincent Rijmen and Joan Daemen. AES is a *block cipher:* It takes data in 128-bit chunks and scrambles it into another 128 bits. The exact way it scrambles the data is determined by another block of digital data, called a *key* or *cryptovariable.* AES comes in three flavors, with 128-, 192-, or 256-bit keys. Apple uses the 128-bit version. Although it didn't participate in the original design and selection, the U.S. National Security Agency has stated that the AES cipher can be used to protect classified information; the 128-bit version, which Apple uses, is approved for information at the Secret level. That doesn't mean that you can use Macs to take home classified documents. The NSA has a stringent approval process for devices used to store and transmit such data; you must consider a lot more than the strength of the codes. But it's a strong vote of confidence in AES.

Encrypting hard drives is tricky. You have to encrypt blocks of data separately so that you can write to the disk without re-encrypting the whole drive. This can lead to a number of security issues. Apple uses AES in a U.S. Government-approved mode called AES-XTS, or IEEE-P1619 that deals with such issues.

A stronger version of AES doesn't add security if you're using a password as a key unless the password has a comparable number of bits. Here's what a 192-bit-strength password looks like:

```
erdl ubym 09ie u9fj lbg9 f4dd 7s1t
           zwmi 6iyd0
```

If you're not willing to use such a long password, don't expect more bits in the cipher to add security.

---

7. **When prompted, enter a password.**

   If you click the small key icon, Password Assistant appears and offers suggestions. See the sidebar "Ordering up passwords from Password Assistant," earlier in this chapter, for more on using this feature and for password selection in general.

8. **If you don't want OS X to store the password in Keychain, deselect the Remember Password check box.**

Enhancing your Mac's security

Besides choosing good passwords, you can do several things to make your Mac even more secure.

Setting safer settings

Choose ➪System Preferences, click the Security & Privacy icon, and then click the General tab. You see the window shown in Figure 10-5. You can select several check boxes to enhance your Mac's security, usually at the price of some minor added inconvenience in operation. Here's a rundown of the check boxes and what they mean for your security:

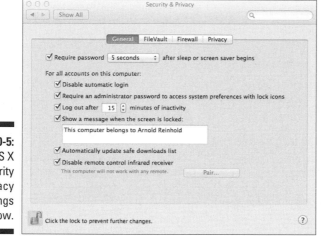

Figure 10-5:
The OS X
Security
& Privacy
settings
window.

✔ **Require Password *X* Minutes After Sleep or Screen Saver Begins:** A common security problem is the unattended machine: You go get a cup of cappuccino, and someone sits down at your computer and does as she pleases. Selecting this check box (and, perhaps, the Log Out After *X* Minutes [or seconds] of Inactivity check box) can help prevent this situation, but you have to type your password *a lot.*

✔ **Disable Automatic Login:** Select this check box if you care about security. If you don't select it, the computer automatically logs in to the primary account without asking for a password whenever you (or anyone else) restarts it.

✔ **Require an Administrator Password to Access System Preferences with Lock Icons:** If many people share your computer (your kids, in particular), and you want to retain strict control, select this check box. Otherwise, don't bother.

✔ **Log out after *X* minutes of inactivity:** I find this option somewhat ineffective. There's always an application asking to save a document before logging out or some other confirmation dialog that blocks the logout. Requiring a password after sleep, the first item on this pane, works better.

✔ **Show a message when the screen is locked:** A very handy feature that lets you choose to display something like "This computer belongs to Sarah Jean. Please call (617) 555 2368 if found" on the login screen. There *are* good people out there.

✔ **Automatically update safe downloads list:** Apple has software that warns you if you are about to download malware. This setting lets your Mac get the latest malware definitions daily. Keep it checked.

✔ **Disable Remote Control Infrared Receiver:** Someone with a remote could have your computer display images that you'd rather not share. If this prospect frightens you, select this check box.

Keeping up to date with Software Update

Computer security is a moving target. Researchers and hackers are continually finding holes in software, and new revisions of software intended to add features can also inadvertently introduce new security bugs. Apple works hard to correct problems and periodically distributes corrections over the Internet. Out of the box, your Mac checks for available updates weekly. To check now, choose ⬛⇨Software Update. You can change how often automatic checking occurs by choosing ⬛⇨System Preferences and clicking the Software Update icon. The Software Update pane is also the place to check which updates have already been installed.

Securing your e-mail

If you use programs such as Pretty Good Privacy (PGP, from `www.pgp.com`), Gnu Privacy Guard (GnuPG from `http://macgpg.sourceforge.net`), or Hushmail.com to encrypt and electronically sign e-mail, you'll be glad to know that Mac versions of these programs are available. Remember to transfer your PGP key rings with the rest of your files.

Watching out for phishing

As a PC user, you undoubtedly encounter *phishing* — getting e-mail messages that look like legitimate requests from upstanding organizations. The message includes a link that opens what seems to be the website of that organization, where you're asked to enter your account number, password, and any other personal info that the hackers think you can be conned into surrendering. If you have any doubt that the message is phony, don't click the link in the message. Go to the organization's website by typing its URL in your browser's address field, and navigate to your account.

Locking it up

Computer security is almost meaningless without physical security. If a sophisticated attacker gets to spend quality time alone with your Mac, all the fancy technology may be of no avail. Laptops are easier to steal than desktop machines, but they're also easier to lock in a desk or safe. All Mac laptops and the Mac mini have a hole in the side that's designed to accept a mechanical locking device, such as the type made by Kensington.

Another cheap thing to do is to record your computer's serial number. Choose About This Mac, and find the serial number listed in the hardware Overview section. You need the serial number to file a police report if your laptop is lost or stolen.

Find My Mac

If you choose System Preferences iCloud, you are given the option to "Allow Find My Mac to use the location of your Mac and allow guest access when the screen is locked." Guest access here only allows a guest to use the Safari web browser. If someone finds your Mac and takes advantage of the guest access, Apple can tell roughly where they are. You then get a message on your iPhone, iPad, or iPod touch that lets you play a sound and send a message to the Mac, lock the Mac, or wipe its hard drive.

Emptying the Trash securely and erasing free space

If you store sensitive data on your computer, particularly on a laptop, get in the habit of choosing Finder⇨Secure Empty Trash whenever you want to empty the Trash. Trash is the Mac equivalent of the Windows *Recycle Bin,* the place where files are moved when you delete them. Otherwise, your data remains in unassigned areas of your hard drive until the operating system needs that space to store something else. With today's large hard drives, that may be never.

The Secure Empty Trash option can take a while if you're deleting large files, and even if you're careful to use it all the time, you should write over all the free space on your hard drive every so often. Apple supplies a tool for doing this, which works as follows:

1. **Open Disk Utility.**

   It's in the Utilities folder, inside the Applications folder.

2. **Select your hard drive and then click the Erase Free Space button.**

3. **Choose one of the three overwrite options.**

   The default option, which overwrites all free disk space with 0s just once, can take an hour or more — longer if your disk is big and relatively empty. The 7-pass method can take overnight, and the 35-pass method for the paranoid can take a couple of days.

Virus protection?

Coming from the Windows world, you may feel naked without a virus-protection program. At the time this book was written, no reported OS X viruses were in circulation. (The buzz phrase for *in circulation* is *in the wild.*) Although Apple has done a good job with OS X security, no one claims that it's perfect, and Apple market share is increasing, making it an ever-more-tempting target for virus writers. Several PC antivirus companies offer programs for OS X. OS X has a feature called File Quarantine that does a safety check on files you download in applications like Safari, Mail, and iChat. The check takes place when you try to open the downloaded file, and OS X warns you to trash the file if it detects malware that it knows about. Also, OS X checks with Apple daily for new forms of malware. Based on the current situation, I think you can hold off buying a Mac antivirus program as long as you check Software Update regularly, keep an eye on at least one independent Mac-information website, and hang on to your PC-user caution about installing strange software.

One exception, of course, is Microsoft products. If you use Windows on your Mac you certainly should use some antivirus program for Windows. Even if you plan to use Windows infrequently, at least install Microsoft's free Microsoft Security Essentials antivirus package. If you run Office 2011 and exchange files with Windows users, be aware that there have been viruses that propagate using the Office macro facility. Although a macro virus is rarely a danger to a Mac, it could be, and in any case you don't want to pass a virus on to a client who runs Windows. It's a good idea to disable Word macros unless you know you need them. Choose Word⇨Preferences⇨Security and check the box Warn before opening a file that contains macros.

TIP

I suggest using the default one-pass method unless you're clearing an older hard drive — one with a capacity of 15GB or less. Current guidelines for the U.S. National Institute of Standards and Technology (NIST Special Publication 800-88) say that modern high-capacity drives "can be effectively cleared by one overwrite." I've also talked to a major data recovery company, and it can't retrieve files that have been overwritten even once. For older drives, use the 7-pass erase; on a smaller, older drive, 7 passes won't take long. If the security provided by overwriting isn't enough, your best option is physical destruction. See the section in Chapter 6 on safely destroying your PC hard drive.

Chapter 11

Connecting with iDevices, iTunes, and iCloud

*1*ntroducing a successful new product is hard enough, but rarely does a company establish a whole new product category. Apple's iPod, iPhone, and iPad have each done just that. Sure, there were music players, web-capable cellphones, and tablet computers before, but Apple defined what these categories mean and opened huge markets for each.

Meet the iDevice Family

If you have one of these iDevices — the iPod, iPhone, or iPad — or are planning to get one, know that your Mac plays well with them and that together, they let you enjoy your digital life the way you want it, whenever you want it, and wherever you want it.

The magical, musical iPod

If you don't own an iPod, iPad, or iPhone, but you still love music, find something to use as a bookmark here while you go to the store and buy one. The iPod is the greatest improvement in recorded music since the introduction of high fidelity in the 1950s, and Apple has incorporated its musical capabilities into the iPhone and iPad. Owning a portable iDevice welds music to your personal space. It becomes something that you always have with you. William

Congreve got it right in *The Mourning Bride,* back in 1697 (reportedly while attending an early Vista planning meeting):

> *Musick has Charms to sooth a savage Breast,*
> *To soften Rocks, or bend a knotted Oak.*
> *I've read, that things inanimate have mov'd,*
> *And, as with living Souls, have been inform'd,*
> *By Magick Numbers and persuasive Sound.*

Yes, an iDevice can do other things, but the ability to add one's favorite music to the unavoidable humdrum of the day — that's life-changing.

The indispensible iPhone

Pundits ridiculed Apple's decision to enter the cellphone market, pointing out that Apple would face insurmountable competition from established giants like Nokia, Microsoft, and BlackBerry maker Research In Motion. Now Apple is the leader in smartphones, although Google's Android operating system is making a strong showing, and Nokia and Microsoft have joined forces to regain a foothold.

The iPhone can do pretty much anything a computer can do, and then some. It can surf the web; play movies, TV programs, music videos, and games; and display your photograph collection. A vast selection of applications (apps) is available to do everything from playing games to assisting surgeons.

The iPhone connects to the Internet in two ways:

- ✔ Via your cellphone carrier's data service
- ✔ Via Wi-Fi at home, at work, or near a hotspot

Dual access makes the iPhone a reliable communicator. Also, when it has a good Wi-Fi signal, the iPhone can even make high-quality video calls to other iPhones, iPad 2s, and Macs via FaceTime.

The addictive iPad

Even with Apple's success with the iPod and iPhone, pundits still dissed its iPad release. Microsoft had been pushing tablet computers for years and never found a market. Even after iPad was announced, some critics panned it as being just an oversized iPhone or iPad touch, way too big to fit in your pocket.

In many ways, the iPad *is* a big iPhone: It runs the same apps and operating system; it connects via Wi-Fi and, optionally, with the cellular network. But the iPad's screen is much larger than the iPhone's, and that difference vastly enhances what you experience when you use it. Controls that take finicky finger fussing on the iPhone and iPod touch work effortlessly on the roomier iPad, making the Internet and apps come alive.

Mac OS X Lion incorporates many of the features that make the iPad so easy to use, such as Multi-Touch gestures, Launchpad, and full-screen applications. I say more about those features in Chapter 15. But more important, OS X Lion and version 5 of the iOS operating system used in the iOS devices play well together. Apple has two tools that keep all these devices working together: iTunes and iCloud. The remainder of this chapter introduces and helps you start using both of these tools.

Getting in Sync with iTunes

If you have an iPhone, iPad, or iPod, you probably already know about iTunes. It's the lone program from the iLife collection that's available for Windows PCs, and it used to be necessary to use an iDevice (and still is needed for older iPods). Many Windows users who don't own iPods use iTunes as their music player. The short story is that iTunes on the Mac is pretty much the same as iTunes in Windows.

iTunes is a program for organizing and playing media — including music, video, and podcasts — on your Mac. If you have an iPod that you used with your PC, you're already familiar with iTunes because it's necessary for syncing your iPod. If not, you'll find iTunes to be a lot like Windows Media Player, only better. It's an easy way to find and enjoy

- Music
- Movies and TV shows
- eBooks via the iBookstore
- Audible.com audio books and podcasts
- Other digital content

When you first open iTunes, you have a few setup tasks to complete. The first task is completing the Setup Assistant, which lets you make iTunes your default music player. If you use iTunes on your PC, be sure to step through "Importing your iTunes collection," later in this chapter. If you're new to iTunes, check out the tips on playing with iTunes, which explain a few basic tasks you need to know to work in the iTunes program.

Setting up iTunes

When you first get your Mac, you need to follow a fairly simple setup process to organize all your music. Follow these steps:

1. **Double-click iTunes, either on the Dock or in Launchpad.**

   The Setup Assistant appears.

2. **Work through the Setup Assistant, which offers to have iTunes handle audio content from the Internet, making it your audio-helper application.**

   Unless you downloaded other audio software, the alternative is to use Apple QuickTime. Stick with iTunes for now.

3. **When iTunes offers to search your home folder for MP3 and AAC music files, click the option that says you agree.**

   If you've transferred a bunch of music files from your PC to your new Mac, this search is an opportunity to organize all those files in iTunes. See the next section, "Importing your iTunes collection," for more details about importing music into iTunes.

   Always double-check that you've backed up all the files. You can easily add them later, if you prefer. See the next section for details.

   When the Setup Assistant is done, iTunes offers to take you to the iTunes Store, which I cover in "Shopping the iTunes Store," later in this chapter.

Importing your iTunes collection

If you already have a collection of music and videos on your PC, copy the files from your PC to the Mac. (See Chapter 6.) Have you done that already? If so, you may need to follow these steps:

1. **On your Mac, open iTunes, and choose File⇨Add to Library.**

2. **Find the folder that contains all the music and video files you copied to your Mac.**

3. **Click the Choose button.**

   iTunes on the Mac adds the PC files to its library, all neatly organized the way you had them. If you have any .wma files, however, you need additional software to play them. You can download inexpensive solutions at Flip4Mac.com and www.easywma.com.

Digital rights management and iTunes

In the past, music sold over the Internet has been protected by *digital rights management (DRM)* technology, which encrypts the music data and allows play only on authorized devices. The iTunes Store now sells music without DRM restrictions. Such files aren't subject to the old five-computer limit, and they can be played on any music player, not just on iPods. TV shows, movies, and software are still subject to DRM restrictions, however. Also, if you bought music from iTunes before 2009, it's likely to be protected by DRM. Apple allows you to remove the DRM encoding for 30 cents per song or 30 percent of an album's price. Remove the DRM by selecting Upgrade to iTunes Plus on the iTunes Store home page.

When you're ready to ditch the PC, I suggest that you disassociate your PC from your iTunes Library. Only authorized computers can play restricted media that you've purchased from the iTunes Store, and Apple limits the number of computers that you can associate with your library. These restrictions don't affect the newer DRM-free music, but do affect videos, you may as well disassociate your old PC while it's still running. For the steps, see the nearby section "Managing authorizations in iTunes."

If your PC is so hosed that you can't recover your iTunes Library, and you don't have a backup, you still have hope. Apple allows you to transfer from your iPod to another computer the music you previously purchased from the iTunes Store. In iTunes, choose File⇨Transfer Purchases from iPod.

Two freeware programs — Ollie's iPod Extractor and Senuti — are also available to copy any songs from your iPod to your Mac without duplicating the ones that are already there. Find them in a Google search, or try your favorite download site.

Managing authorizations in iTunes

The Apple digital rights management scheme lets you play DRM-protected media purchased from the iTunes Store on as many as five computers at any time. If you're planning to keep your PC for a while and you aren't close to the five-computer limit, you can leave the PC authorized.

To authorize your Mac, just try to play one of your purchased songs. iTunes asks for your Apple ID and password. Be sure to enter the ones you used to purchase the song. You have to perform this task for only one purchased song.

When you're ready to get rid of your Windows PC, be sure to deauthorize it first by following these steps:

1. **Open iTunes on your PC.**

2. **Choose Store⇨Deauthorize Computer.**

3. **Select Deauthorize Computer for Apple Account.**

4. **Enter your Apple ID and password.**

5. **Confirm your intentions.**

Apple determines a Windows computer's identity by looking at several factors, including the amount of RAM and the hard drive size, so don't mess with these factors before you deauthorize your PC. (Macs have a hardware serial number, so changes such as replacing the hard drive or adding RAM don't affect things.)

If your PC is so messed up that you can't run iTunes to deauthorize, or if you just forgot to do it before you ditched the PC, your PC stays on the list of machines that count against your five-computer limit. You have an escape valve, however: When you've used all five slots, you can blow them *all* away and reauthorize only the computers you still want by playing a purchased song on each of them. Apple limits you to resetting the authorized computer list only once a year. To reset the list, follow these steps:

1. **Choose View My Account from the iTunes Store menu.**

2. **Enter your password.**

    If you've reached the 5-computer limit and haven't exercised this option in the past 12 months, you should see a Deauthorize All button in the Account Information screen.

3. **Click the Deauthorize All button.**

4. **Play a song on each computer that you want to authorize.**

Playing with iTunes

After you transfer your library to the Mac, it's time to enjoy your music and other media files in their new home. You won't find things much different from iTunes on your PC. If you're new to iTunes, here are a few popular tasks to help you get started:

✔ **To sync your iPod to your iTunes Library:** Just plug the iPod cable into a USB port on the Mac that has the library stored on it. You can sync to only one iTunes Library.

✔ **To create a new playlist:** Click the plus icon (+) at the bottom of the iTunes sidebar.

✔ **To add a tune to your playlist:** Simply drag it from the music list to the playlist's entry in the sidebar.

✔ **To create a mix disc:** Insert a blank writable CD and choose File⇨ Burn Playlist to Disc.

Filling iTunes with Music and More

You can fill your iTunes Library in a few ways. The iTunes Store is the hub for the many types of content that iTunes can play, including music, movies, TV shows, and podcasts. Adding music from a CD to iTunes is easy, too. The following sections explain the most popular options.

Shopping the iTunes Store

When you first start iTunes, it opens the front window of the iTunes Store. If iPod has revolutionized the way we listen to music, the iTunes Store has revolutionized the way music is sold.

Notice that I say *sold,* not *distributed.* Only a fraction of the songs that people store in iTunes (or play on iDevices) has been purchased through the iTunes Store. Much of that music comes from compact discs that people already own and simply copy to iTunes.

It seems that the recording industry didn't think through all the implications when it switched to CDs from the older vinyl LP records — the kind with a wiggly spiral groove that made a needle vibrate to reproduce sound. After computers and the Internet became fast enough, the digital data on CDs was too easy to copy and share.

Apple figured that many people would do the right thing and buy their music, instead of downloading it for free, if the price was right and the process was convenient enough. Users have downloaded more than 15 billion songs from the iTunes Store, and it's the top music retailer in the United States. Amazon. com now sells MP3 music, which is DRM-free as well.

To get to the iTunes Store, open iTunes, and click iTunes Store in the sidebar. You see a screen with ads for various offerings and a list of different types of content that are for sale. The following steps walk you through the store:

1. **Click the Sign In button in the top-right corner.**

2. **If you already have an Apple account (if you used iTunes on your PC, for example), enter your account name and password; otherwise, click the Create New Account button, and have your credit card handy.**

   After you complete the sign-up or sign-in process, you can move to Step 3.

3. **Browse by genre or enter a search term in the search box in the top-right corner of the iTunes window.**

   The iTunes Store has a huge selection of recorded music, but Apple makes it easy to find what you want. Search results appear in the bottom half of the iTunes window, and you can sort by genre, title, artist, album, popularity, price, or running length. Just click the headings in the listing.

   If you double-click a song's entry in the list, you hear a minute-and-a-half selection from the song.

4. **To purchase a song or other item, click the Buy button, and you're asked for your password — if you're not already signed in — or to confirm your decision to buy.**

   The song, album, or other item is automatically downloaded to your Mac and then to your iPod the next time you plug it in.

Apple has tried to make shopping simple at the iTunes Store by having an easy-to-understand price structure, but pressure from content owners has forced Apple to allow greater variation in pricing. In return, Apple has eliminated DRM restrictions on downloaded music — though not on other content, such as movies and TV programs. At the time I write this book, songs cost 69 cents, 99 cents, or $1.29 apiece; TV shows are $1.99; and 30-day movie rentals are $3.99 for current hits and $2.99 for older flicks. Music albums, complete TV seasons, and feature movies can range from $8 to $15 and up. High-definition versions of TV programs and movies are often available for an additional charge.

Another big category in the iTunes Store is apps for the iPhone, iPad, and iPod touch. Many apps are free; others range in price from 99 cents to $10 and more. The App Store has been a runaway success, with more than 425,000 apps and 14 billion downloads.

Copying CDs to iTunes

If you've never used iTunes, you'll want to add some music. If you own music CDs, you can add them to the iTunes Library simply by sliding them into your Mac's CD/DVD slot. iTunes should open automatically, but if it doesn't, launch it in the usual way by double-clicking its icon. iTunes copies the files from the CD to its library after asking for confirmation.

The AAC compression scheme is used by default when iTunes imports CDs. You can change to another format, such as MP3, by following these steps:

1. **Choose iTunes⇨Preferences.**

2. **Click the General icon and then the Import Settings button.**

3. **Choose the import format you prefer.**

   Your choices are AAC, AIFF, Apple Lossless, MP3, and WAV.

   You can change many other options in the iTunes preferences pane, including playback options (such as subtitles and closed captioning) and parental controls.

Adding video to iTunes (and an iPad)

Transferring video is another matter. Video that you download from the iTunes Store isn't a problem, but you can't simply put a movie DVD into your Mac and transfer the movie to view on your iPad. Movie DVDs have copy protection, whereas music CDs generally don't. Some movies come with a "Digital Copy" facility, where you insert the DVD and then enter a code to download the digital version for free. If yours doesn't, you have to do two things to make such a transfer possible:

✔ Extract the movie from the DVD in an unencrypted format.

✔ Convert the file to one of the video formats that the iPad can understand.

Software is available to perform each step. A Google search for *"DVD to iPad"* should turn up several resources. The first step involves getting past the copy protection on the DVD. The movie industry says that doing so is illegal, though some people say you should have the right to view the DVDs you own any way you want.

Video that isn't copy-protected, such as your home movies, must still be converted to an iPad-, iPod-, iPhone- or Apple TV–friendly format. One way to do this is to use iMovie, which is already installed on your Mac. Choose iTunes from the iMovie Share menu and select a resolution appropriate for your iDevice from the choices given. I tell you more about iMovie in Chapter 13.

Sharing your iTunes Library

You share your iTunes Library with other devices on your local network (Wi-Fi or wired Ethernet) by following these steps:

1. **Choose iTunes⇨Preferences.**

2. **In the preferences pane that opens, select the Sharing tab.**

3. **Choose to share your entire library or only selected media types, such as music, movies, TV shows, podcasts, or specific playlists.**

   These settings let you limit what your kids can listen to on their iPods and iPads.

   Parents can further restrict what kids can hear and view by selecting the Parental Control tab in the iTunes preferences pane (see Figure 11-1). The settings in this pane can disable certain types of content and set age-rating restrictions.

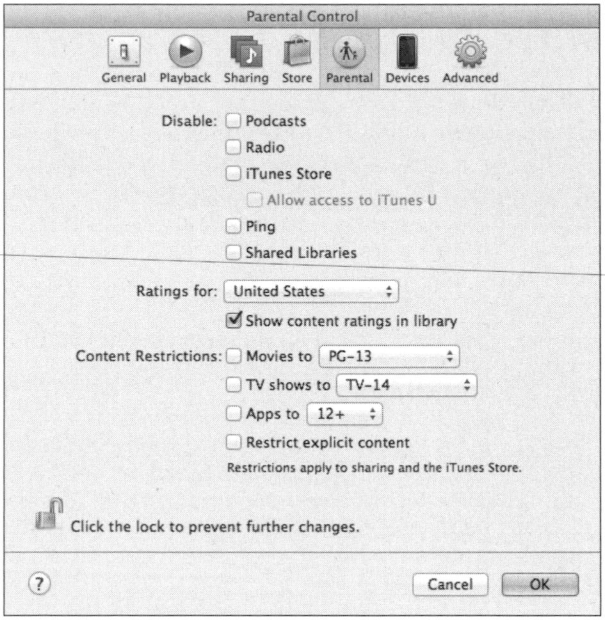

Figure 11-1:
The iTunes Parental Control preferences tab.

Subscribing to podcasts

Podcasts are talks, performances, or pretty much any kind of digital content that someone thinks someone else may be interested in. You can listen to podcasts on your computer, but what makes them special is that you can easily download them to your iPod, iPad, or iPhone. Indeed, the introduction of the iPod made podcasts popular.

iTunes U

Wouldn't it be nice if the top professors at the world's greatest colleges recorded their lectures as podcasts so that you can enjoy the best teaching the world has to offer as you commute to work or burn some calories on the treadmill? Well, they have, and you can. The iTunes Store section iTunes U is chock-full of great talks and courses. Nothing but time and effort are required to benefit from the finest education that universities have to offer. iTunes U doesn't offer degrees, of course, and you miss the classroom camaraderie and beer parties in the dorms, but you don't go into lifelong debt paying tuition bills, either. Courses in iTunes U are absolutely free.

Podcasts can be just audio, or they can be video. You find them in the iTunes Store by clicking the Podcasts link. You find thousands of podcasts on every imaginable topic to choose among, broken into many categories. If you find one that you like, you can have others in the series download to your iDevice automatically as they appear by clicking the Subscribe button. Podcasts awaiting your attention are marked with a blue dot in the Podcasts section of your library. Podcasts that you've listened to lose the blue dot and are automatically removed the next time you sync your device unless you mark them as unread by right-clicking their names.

iCloud for You

iCloud is a collection of Apple online services that are free to Apple customers. (It used to be named MobileMe, .Mac [or "dot-mac"], and iTools before that.) iCloud includes these services:

- ✔ **Photo Stream:** Take a picture on one iDevice, and it's automatically pushed via Wi-Fi to all the others you own. Apple stores up to 1,000 photos online for 30 days. You can move any photos you want to keep to an album or your Camera Roll, and you can share your photo stream with other iCloud users.

- ✔ **Music on the cloud:** When you buy music from the iTunes Store, iCloud lets you use it on any iDevice you own. You can see all the music you purchased from Apple in the past and ask to have those tracks downloaded to your iDevices as well, all for no extra charge.

What about all that music you ripped from CDs that you already own? Apple's got a solution for that as well. It's a little complicated, so take a moment to get up and stretch before continuing.

Okay, better? Here's how it goes. Sign up for iTunes Match at $25 per year by searching for **iTunes Match** at `www.apple.com`. Apple will scan your iDevice and find any music on it that's already in the iTunes Store. (Apple currently has more than 18 million songs in its collection.) Apple keeps track of the stuff that matches in iCloud and lets you play it on any iDevice you own — as well as your Apple TV — whenever you want, assuming that you're connected to the Internet. Matches are played back at 256Kbps iTunes Plus quality, even if you used a lower quality setting when you ripped that CD. You have to upload any tracks that aren't in the iTunes Store, but Apple thinks that most songs you own are already there, so most of your music collection will be available for you to play after the scan is done.

✔ **A me.com electronic mail account for each user** (such as `SteveJobs@me.com`). Mail addressed to your me.com account is automatically sent to your Mac, iPhone, iPad, and/or iPod touch. You can even access your mail on someone else's computer by using a web interface.

✔ **Synchronization and online storage for documents:** If you use the same application on more than one device — say, Keynote on your Mac and iPad — you can keep documents synced between devices through the cloud. iCloud also makes sure that apps you purchased for one iDevice are available for all the others you own. The basic plan offers 5GB of storage space, including your e-mail, documents, and photo albums. The limit doesn't include Photo Stream and music. Apple will happily rent you more space if you need it.

✔ **Contacts and calendars:** iCloud can synchronize all address books and calendars that live on your desktop or laptop or your iPhone or iPod and in Microsoft Outlook, the Windows address book, Google, and Yahoo!.

✔ **Backups:** Data from your iOS devices is automatically backed up to iCloud every day, assuming that a Wi-Fi signal is available. Apple saves time and space by backing up only what has changed since your last backup. iDevice data that iCloud backs up includes purchased music, apps, books, photos, and videos in the Camera Roll; device settings; app data, screen layout, text and MMS messages; and ringtones.

Many services that iCloud provides are also available for free from other Internet services. Google and Yahoo! offer free e-mail with address books and online storage, for example; Dropbox.com hosts up to 5GB of documents for free; and sites such as Flickr.com host your photos for free. iCloud, however, ties everything into a single package that's reliable and easy to use. The time you save by not having to figure out how to use a bunch of free services is worth something, too.

Part IV
More Software, More Choices

In this part . . .

Macs come with a ton of software. I introduce the Apple iLife digital lifestyle suite and discuss other software that comes with your Mac. These programs are simple but powerful and fun to use. They let you buy and listen to music, manage your photo collection, edit your videos, make your own music, and put your creations on the World Wide Web. And, because they come from Apple, all the programs play well together. But if you're a long-time Windows user, there could be an application in Windows that you miss. You have several options for running Windows on your Mac. I discuss them in the last chapter of this part, Chapter 16.

Chapter 12

Picturing iPhoto

*O*nce upon a time, taking photographs involved buying a roll of film, loading it in a camera, shooting 24 or 36 pictures, taking the film out of the camera (remembering to rewind first!), taking the exposed film to a camera store or drugstore, waiting a day or more, picking up the pictures, selecting a few negatives to be copied or enlarged, sticking the rest in a shoebox until the day you have more free time to organize them (which birthday party was that, and who's the guy next to Aunt Harriet?), and then pasting them into a photo album. More serious photographers experienced a long interlude in a dark room with red lights and temperature-controlled trays of smelly chemicals.

Except for those who truly love the film process — and there's a lot to love — digital cameras have taken over photography. Good-quality digital cameras are inexpensive, and top-of-the-line models, which are quite affordable, rival the best 35mm film cameras for image quality. Try to buy a cellphone now that doesn't have a camera. The main camera in the iPhone is a respectable 5 megapixels. You have no more film to buy, and that shoebox is now a hard drive, but you're likely still waiting for the free time you need to organize your photos.

Wouldn't it be helpful to have a program that can suck down photos from any camera as soon as you plug it in, keep shots organized according to when you took them, let you see a large swath of your collection spread out onscreen like a light table, and let you annotate and organize photos into albums and slide shows? Shouldn't the program also display a slide show on your screen or television set, and maybe add music from your iTunes collection? Also, why not allow you to ship those photos off for printing on your color printer or send them to a professional shop — and maybe even a place that will print a bound book of your photos so that you can have paste-free albums?

That's iPhoto in a nutshell. If you've used Google Picasa on your PC, you're familiar with the concept. But with iPhoto, you have nothing to download: It's all waiting for you in the Applications folder. (If you love Picasa, you'll be glad to know that it has a version for the Mac. I discuss it later in this chapter.)

Getting Started with iPhoto

If you own a digital camera, you most likely can use it with iPhoto. iPhoto supports most brands and models. iPhoto knows about almost every digital camera out there. Just shoot a few pictures and plug your camera into the appropriate USB or FireWire port. Many Mac models also have a slot to read SD Cards; see Chapter 2 for which ones do. SD Cards are used on many camera models to store images, so you can transfer your photos that way as well.

When iPhoto first starts, it asks whether you want it to take over every time you plug in your camera. You could go to your camera manufacturer's web page to download its software, but why bother? Just say Yes.

You likely have many valuable images stored on your PC. You can move your collection from your PC to your Mac through iPhoto by importing photos. iPhoto adds your photos to its database and creates thumbnail versions for fast display. In the following sections, you find out what image files you can work with in iPhoto, and see the tips and how-tos you need to know before importing your image collection.

Checking out supported file types

iPhoto can read a wide variety of file types, including those listed in Table 12-1.

Table 12-1	Image File Types That iPhoto Supports	
BMP	*FlashPix*	*GIF*
JPEG/JFIF	Photoshop	PICT
PNG	RAW	TIFF

RAW is the native format for high-end digital cameras. iPhoto supports dozens of camera models' RAW image files; visit `http://support.apple.com/kb/HT3825` for the current list. If you create movies with your still camera, iPhoto supports several movie formats, too.

iPhoto lets you export files in their original form or converted to JPEG, TIFF, or PNG format.

Setting up a successful import

iPhoto can store up to 250,000 photos — about 250 shoeboxes' worth. iPhoto has its own idea about how to store photos in its library, however. If you already have a large collection of digital photos, all organized in folders, you may want them kept that way. You can order iPhoto to do just that, as follows:

1. **Choose iPhoto⇨Preferences.**
2. **Click the Advanced button.**
3. **Deselect the Copy Files to iPhoto Library Folder When Adding to Library check box.**
4. **Close the preferences pane.**

Now whenever you import photos, iPhoto leaves them organized the way you had them in the folders you set up, rather than using the normal method of filing the photos by date. If you edit one of those photos within iPhoto, however, it saves the edited version in its library, leaving the original where it was.

Importing your photos

To import your photos into iPhoto, follow these steps:

1. **Copy your PC photos to the Pictures folder on your Mac.**
2. **Open iPhoto, and choose File⇨Import to Library.**
3. **Find the folder or folders with the photos you want to import, and select them.**
4. **Click the Import button.**

You can also just open iPhoto and drag the folder with your pictures to the iPhoto window. iPhoto makes a new event for each OS X folder you import., but if that folder has subfolders containing pictures, the subfolder events will be at the same level as the parent folder, so any hierarchical organization may be lost.

You may want to experiment with bringing folders into iPhoto one at a time to find the way of organizing the photos in iPhoto that works best for you.

After you move all your photos from your PC into iPhoto, you should back up your OS X Pictures folder. If you enabled Time Machine, it does the backup for you. If not, or if you like the added security of having a backup in a separate place, copy your Pictures folder to a DVD-R, thumb drive, or external hard drive. For extra credit, find a safe place to store the backup that isn't in your home — maybe your office, a safe-deposit box, or even a friend's house.

(A friend's house burned down recently, and he lost much of his photo collection.) I cover various ways to back up data in Chapter 6. Having all your photos organized and safely backed up off-site is a great feeling.

Organizing the iPhoto Way

iPhoto has its own way of storing and organizing photos. You can choose to look at them in several ways, all listed on the left side of the iPhoto window:

- ✔ **Events:** iPhoto groups all photos you take in a single day into an *event* that you can name. As you slide your mouse pointer across an event's cover image (Apple calls it a *key photo*), you see all photos in the event — an effect that Apple calls *skimming*. (Make any photo in an event its key photo by right-clicking it.) You can move individual photos from one event to another simply by clicking and dragging. To merge two events, drag one event into the other. To split an event, open it by double-clicking, select the photo that you want to begin the second half of the split, and choose Events⇨Split Events. You can also select individual photos for the split by holding down the Command key (⌘) while clicking photos.

- ✔ **Photos:** You see all your photos as though they were laid out on a light box and can scroll through your entire library.

- ✔ **Faces and Places:** Apple has built face recognition into iPhoto and can organize your photos by who's in them and where they were taken. For more on Faces and Places, see "Finding faces," later in this chapter.

- ✔ **Albums:** An *album* is a named set of photos. A photo can be in more than one album. The photo is stored only once, however, so having photos in more than one album doesn't waste space. Albums work a lot like playlists in iTunes. To create a new album, choose File⇨New Album, or click the plus icon (+) in the bottom-left corner of the iPhoto window. You add photos to an album by selecting and dragging them from the main display.

- ✔ **Smart Albums:** A Smart Album contains photos based on search criteria you select. It works a lot like Spotlight. To make a Smart Album, choose File⇨New⇨Smart Album. Select your criteria (such as date in the range of 12/24/2010 to 12/26/2010) in the dialog that appears, and click OK.

- ✔ **Folders:** Folders in iPhoto are a way to add organization to your collection. You create a new folder by choosing File⇨New⇨Folder. Folders can contain albums and other folders; they can also contain slide shows, books, calendars, and other iPhoto projects. Again, you can drag things into and out of a folder, and move them around as you want. Items can be in only one folder, however.

Viewing and sorting your photos

The main iPhoto display area, shown in Figure 12-1, shows small versions of your photos arranged on a dark background, much like a slide sorter from the film era. How small? The slider on the bottom-left border of the iPhoto window lets you adjust the thumbnail size to suit your needs.

Figure 12-1: The main iPhoto display in Photo mode.

iPhoto offers several ways to see just what you want:

- Select Photos in the sidebar, and all your photos are displayed.
- Click a folder or an album, and just those photos are shown.
- Choose View⇨Sort Photos and then select one of the following options:
  - **By Event:** This option is the default view.
  - **By Date:** The date is stored with the file when you import your photo. If your camera included a date in the photo file, iPhoto uses that date.
  - **By Keyword:** You can add keyword tags to a photo by pressing ⌘+I. iPhoto comes with a simple set of keywords, but you can invent your own by choosing Windows⇨Manage My Keywords.
  - **By Title:** A photo's title is the name or number given to it by your camera, or its filename if you've imported it, but you can change the name by selecting View ⇨ Titles and clicking on the title you want to change.

- **By Rating:** The By Rating sort doesn't refer to how professional-looking iPhoto thinks your photos are. You assign your own rating to photos, from one to five stars. It's worth remembering the keyboard shortcuts. Select the photo or photos you want to rate, and press ⌘+1 for one star, ⌘+2 for two stars — up to ⌘+5 for five stars. Pressing ⌘+0 means no rating. If you forget, choose Photos⇨My Rating. The submenu that appears has all the options and reminders for the shortcuts.

- **Manual:** Move photos around by dragging them. This option is ideal for slide shows.

You can also select the Ascending or Descending sort order.

Finding faces

iPhoto can help you organize your photos by the faces they contain and where you were when you took them. This section explains how these features work.

First, lower your expectations. Apple face-recognition technology is far from perfect, but it's a big help if you have lots of photos of people. The technology has two parts: finding faces in images and assigning names to the individual faces. iPhoto is better at the first part than the second — you get a lot of wrong recognition matches, some weirdly inappropriate — but iPhoto makes it quite easy to correct wrong matches. And yes, it can handle more than one face in an image.

To get started, follow these steps:

1. **Click the info button at the bottom of the screen.**

2. **Click a photo in your iPhoto library that has a good face shot of a person you want iPhoto to keep track of.**

   iPhoto will find full faces in the photo, but sometimes doesn't notice profiles.

3. **Type the name of the person in the label.**

   iPhoto tries to find a matching name in your Mac's address book.

4. **If iPhoto finds the right name, click it; otherwise, just finish typing the name you want to use for the person and then click that name when you're done.**

5. **Click the small arrow (>) next to the person's name.**

   iPhoto tells you whether it found other photos that it thinks may contain the same person's face.

6. **Click Confirm Additional Faces at the bottom of the iPhoto window.**

   iPhoto shows you just the face in each photo that it thinks is the same person, with the words *click to confirm* below.

7. **Confirm or correct the names that iPhoto has matched with the faces.**

   To confirm, click each correct face once. The person's name appears below the face in green.

   To tell iPhoto that it messed up, double-click a face; the name changes to red with the word *not* in front. If you're not sure of an image, just leave it unclicked.

8. **Review the photos you categorized, and if you got one wrong, click the face to change from green to red or from red to green.**

9. **When you have all the photos and faces squared away, click Done.**

   iPhoto may show you another batch of faces. Later batches tend to include more erroneous matches but also many good calls. In a few minutes, you'll have all photos of that person tagged.

After you tag faces, you can click Faces in the sidebar to see a tile for each person you named. Double-click a tile to see all pictures in which you tagged someone.

Finding where in the world that picture was taken

Fancier digital cameras, including the ones in newer iPhones and iPads have a global positioning satellite (GPS) receiver and add location information to each image — a process known as *geotagging*. The geotag contains geographic coordinates, longitude, and latitude, but iPhoto knows how to read these geotags and translate the position into intelligible information, such as Boston or Paris. It even knows about popular spots where lots of pictures are taken, such as the *USS Constitution* or the Eiffel Tower.

To check out your photos' geotags, follow these steps:

1. **Click Places on the left side of the iPhoto window.**

   You see a Google map of the world, with pins showing the locations where you took the geotagged photos in your library.

2. **Double-click near the pins to zoom in further — all the way down to street level.**

If your camera lacks GPS, or if you have old photos that aren't geotagged, you can add locations to individual photos or events because the shots made in a single day are often in the same locale. Follow these steps:

1. **Click a photo or an event to select it and then click the small *i* button in the bottom-right corner.**

   You see a map with space to Assign a Place.

2. **Click there and enter a city name, or type an address and ask Google to look it up.**

You can also name places that you use often, such as your home or a favorite campground. Then you can use that name as a shortcut when geotagging your photos. In iPhoto, choose Window➪Manage My Places and then click one of the addresses to edit its name.

Editing Your iPhotos

Even the best photographers appreciate the ability to adjust digital photos after checking how those photos turned out. Although iPhoto isn't the most powerful photo editor, it comes with many tools for fine-tuning your photos.

When you select a photo in the main display and click Edit at the bottom of the window, iPhoto presents several editing icons, as shown in Figure 12-2. Unlike higher-end editing programs, iPhoto doesn't give you a bewildering array of tools and options; it gets right to the point.

Figure 12-2: Editing options in iPhoto.

You have these options on the Quick Fixes tab:

- ✔ **Rotate** turns photos in 90-degree increments. The default setting is clockwise. You can make counterclockwise the default by choosing iPhoto⇨Preferences or by pressing the Option key while clicking a photo.

- ✔ **Enhance** applies filters that Apple thinks will generally do the right thing. (They usually do.)

- ✔ **Fix Red-Eye** asks you to simply click the center of each eye in a portrait. iPhoto does the rest. This option may not work on photos of cats or dogs, however, as they tend to reflect a different color.

- ✔ **Straighten** lets you correct for a small tilt in your camera relative to the screen — up to plus or minus 10 degrees. A temporary grid overlays your photo to help you make the adjustment.

- ✔ **Crop** selects the area of the photo you want to see, using a gray overlay that you can move or adjust to size.

- ✔ **Retouch** gets rid of scratches and dust marks. Just rub over them with the cursor.

Two more tabs give you more control of your improvements. Go wild here:

- ✔ **Effects** displays buttons that lighten, darken, and adjust the overall warmth of your photo, as well a matrix of image special-effect treatments, such as Black & White, Antique, Sepia, Matte, Vignette, Edge Blur, Fade Color, Boost Color, and None. Pick the one you like.

- ✔ **Adjust** shows a pane with sliders that control individual attributes such as exposure, contrast, saturation, definition, highlights, shadows, sharpness, noise, temperature, and tint.

No matter what you do to a photo, you can always get back to an earlier version by selecting Edit⇨Undo or clicking the Revert to Original button at the bottom of the edit pane.

Sharing Photos in Slide Shows and Prints

What do you do with all those photos? Why, show them to someone else, of course. iPhoto excels in having tools that let you share your images (including slide shows) and make prints.

The simplest way to share photos is online, either on photo-sharing sites or by e-mail:

- ✔ **Photo-sharing sites and communities:** You can upload selected photos to your Facebook or Flickr account, letting the world see your photos or protecting them with a password.

- ✔ **E-mail:** Highlight the photos that you want to share with friends by e-mail; then choose Share⇨Email or click the Share button at the bottom of the window. iPhoto asks you to select which photo size to send.

If you want a fancier way to share your photos, try slide shows, prints, or photo books. The following sections explain these options in more detail.

Spicing up photos with a slide show

At its simplest level, creating a slide show involves selecting a bunch of pictures and putting them in order to tell a story. In iPhoto, that's just the beginning. Here's how to create a slide show:

1. **In iPhoto, select and arrange your photos in the main display, perhaps using an existing album.**

2. **Choose File⇨New⇨Slideshow, or click the Create icon at the bottom of the window.**

   An icon for your new slide show appears in the sidebar (you can rename that icon), and Slideshow view appears in the main display.

3. **Rearrange the thumbnails of the images that appear at the top, if you like.**

   At the bottom are icons that allow you to add excitement to your show. You can choose among a variety of *transitions* (ways to change from one slide to the next).

4. **If you want to add background music to your show (from your iTunes Library, GarageBand, or the sample selections supplied with iPhoto), click the Music icon in the bottom-right corner of the window.**

5. **When you're done, click Export at the bottom of the window, or choose an export option from the Share menu.**

   You can display your show onscreen, burn it to DVD, watch it on your Apple TV, or use it in other ways such as podcasts or online presentations.

Printing photos with iPhoto

Although slide shows and e-mail are handy, many people still appreciate photos that they can hold in their hand. Until everyone carries a video iPod, an iPhone, or an iPad, paper prints still have a role. iPhoto offers the following print-creation options:

✔ You can print photos on your color printer by choosing File➪Print.

✔ You can order professional prints for a fee over the Internet by choosing File➪Order.

✔ You can use iPhoto tools to make custom greeting cards, post cards, calendars, and album books from your photos. Drag photos one at a time, or ask iPhoto to "flow" a bunch of photos into the template you select; then click the Create icon at the bottom of the iPhoto window (refer to Figure 12-2) to get started.

Moving Up to Aperture

Apple sells a more advanced photo-management software package named Aperture (see Figure 12-3) that's aimed at professional photographers. It has more support for RAW images and can work with a much bigger photo library. It has additional image-editing capabilities and can also integrate with Adobe Photoshop. Aperture has tools that help you manage projects and work with several versions of the same photo at a time. A handy image loupe magnifies a small area of the photo as you slide it over the screen.

Figure 12-3: The Apple Aperture photo software with loupe tool.

If you're serious about photography and have invested big bucks in camera iron and glass, the $200 Aperture price tag shouldn't be an obstacle to moving up.

The Picasa alternative

The Google Picasa photo-management tool has long been popular on PCs. (There are rumors that Google may rebrand it Google Photo.) Perhaps you've been using it for your photos. The good news is that Google now has a version of Picasa for the Mac, and you can download it for free at `http://picasa.google.com/mac`. Like its PC cousin, Picasa for the Mac leaves your photos where it finds them — unlike iPhoto, which prefers to move all your images to its library. When you first launch Picasa on your Mac, it goes through your photos on your Mac's hard drive, even those in your iPhoto library. Then you can look through all your images by date and folder. You can also make simple image edits, fix red-eye, make photo collages, and upload images to the online Google Picasa Web Albums. (A Google plug-in lets you do this from iPhoto as well.) Google is extra-careful with your iPhoto library, not making any changes but asking instead whether you want to store edited iPhoto images separately.

The only bad news is that Google doesn't provide a way to move your Picasa collection from the PC to the Mac. Sure, you can move all your photos, and Picasa will preserve their folders. But other organizational changes you may have made on the PC side (such as making albums) aren't transferred.

Chapter 13

Producing Movies and Music on Your Mac

In This Chapter

▶ Editing your own movies with iMovie

▶ Burning DVDs with iDVD

▶ Making music and picking up an instrument with GarageBand

So far, I've covered the basics: surfing, sending and receiving e-mail, listening to music, and organizing and viewing digital snapshots. But your Mac's built-in iLife software lets you do more-exotic things: editing and publishing movies, creating your own music and podcasts, and even learning to play an instrument. The Apple iMovie and GarageBand programs let anyone try his or her hand at these activities. What you do with these tools depends on you. I can only help you get started.

Producing Your Own Epic with iMovie

Great movies aren't created in a studio or on location: They're created in the editing room. The pioneering Russian filmmaker Lev Kuleshov proved the point by splicing a shot of a famous Russian actor between shots of a plate of soup, a girl at play, and an old woman in a coffin. It appeared that he was looking at each one. Audiences who were shown the short admired the different emotions that the actor displayed as he viewed each scene, but Kuleshov had used the same shot of the actor in each setting. The juxtaposition or montage created the strong emotion in the minds of the viewers.

For most of the 20th century, films were edited by cutting strips of film apart with a blade, arranging them artfully, and splicing them together to form the master image. Many specialized machines were invented to help in the cutting room. But no filmmaker in the first eight decades of motion pictures imagined the powerful editing capabilities that are supplied with your Macintosh for free in the form of iMovie. Professional filmmakers now use even more capable software products. Apple makes one of the best, Final

Cut, which I talk about later. But if you've never edited film, the limitations of iMovie won't hold you back for some time. As Walter Murch, who won three Oscars for editing and sound mixing, put it:

> *Film editing is now something almost everyone can do at a simple level and enjoy it, but to take it to a higher level requires the same dedication and persistence that any art form does.*

By the way, Murch was honored with a fourth Oscar nomination for *Cold Mountain,* which he edited by using Apple's Final Cut Pro on a Macintosh G4 — a wimpy machine compared with the Macs now on sale.

Importing video from your camera

First things first: Make sure that you have enough hard drive space. Movies use lots of bits. Fifteen minutes of conventional video can occupy 3.2GB to 10GB of space — the highest numbers apply if you're shooting in high definition (HD). Remember that you need space for all the raw footage you plan to edit, not just for the final product. I suggest buying an external hard drive with at least a terabyte of storage for any large film-editing project you undertake. If your Mac has a FireWire port, buy a drive that includes a FireWire interface, because FireWire offers better video performance than USB 2.0. A Thunderbolt hard drive (which I cover in Chapters 2 and 3) would be even better.

If you have digital-camcorder footage that you want to edit, follow these steps to import it into iMovie and begin editing:

1. **Connect your video camera to your Mac with the camera's cable, and put the camera in the proper mode (typically, PC Connect).**

   You should see the iMovie Import window, and a list of clips. If not, choose File⇨Import from Camera. Video from an iPhone should load automatically when you sync it in iPhoto.

2. **Select the clips you want to import in Manual mode or select Automatic in the Import window to import them all.**

3. **When you're ready, click Import All or Import Checked.**

   FireWire camcorders show additional controls that let you rewind and fast-forward to the segments you want to download.

4. **Select the disk where you want the data to be stored, and choose whether to add the video to an existing event or start a new one.**

iMovie automatically divides your video into separate clips by looking at the time codes recorded on the tape. Stills from the beginning of each clip, and roughly every 4 seconds thereafter, appear in the Clips pane in the bottom of the iMovie window, shown in Figure 13-1. You adjust the interval between stills with the slider in the bottom-right corner. As you move the mouse pointer over each clip, you see it play, and iMovie stores video clips in a common library by event, as iPhoto does. You see a list of events stored in your library in the bottom-left corner.

Importing video from your PC

If you have video that you transferred from your PC, you can incorporate it into your iMovie project by choosing File➪Import. iMovie, which can accept any format that QuickTime understands, can work with high-definition video sources, including HDTV in 720p and 1080i formats.

One thing that vanilla QuickTime can't understand is Microsoft Windows Media (.wmv) files. Plug-ins from flip4mac.com can usually solve this problem.

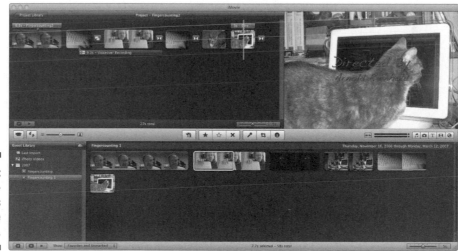

Figure 13-1:
The begin-
ning stages
of an iMovie
project.

Finding other sources for video

You can use the following other sources to insert video into your iMovie:

- **Built-in camera:** Want to try out iMovie but don't own a digital camcorder? If you have a recent Apple laptop or iMac, or purchased a recent Apple Cinema display for your mini or Mac Pro, you already have a built-in iSight camera, which you can use as an input source for iMovie. Just click the Camera icon on the central toolbar. iMovie shows you sitting in front of your keyboard with a button that lets you start and stop recording from iSight. Lights, camera, *action!*

- **Your late-model iPhone, iPad, and iPod touch all have cameras that are capable of video recording.**

- **A webcam:** Most FireWire webcams and some newer USB webcams work with iMovie. So can many additional USB webcams if you use drivers from the macam project (`http://webcam-osx.sourceforge.net`). Cameras that comply with the UVC standard should work without any special drivers. See `www.mac-compatible-web-cam.com` for a list of compliant cameras.

- **iPhoto:** You can add still photographs to your iMovie project and animate them by using the Ken Burns effect (see the nearby sidebar "Ken Burns and his effect"). If your camera takes videos, iMovie imports them automatically from iPhoto.

- **Internet video:** A vast amount of video is available on the World Wide Web. Anything that you download in a QuickTime-compatible format, you can import into iMovie. But be careful of copyright issues. (When I first typed the preceding sentence, the fifth word read *copyfight.* That typo pretty much sums up what you want to avoid.)

Editing video in iMovie

Editing is where the fun begins. The following steps walk you through the basic process of using iMovie:

1. **Edit each clip to show just what you want to include in your movie.**

   Click a clip, and an adjustable yellow box appears, showing the segment you selected.

2. **Drag the clip to the project pane in the top-left corner, placing clips in the order you like.**

   You can use different segments from the same cut. If you just click a clip, iMovie selects a four-second segment. To play a selected clip, press the spacebar.

3. **Add sound, photos, titles, scene transitions, and animated maps by clicking the icons to the right of the central toolbar.**

   Click an icon to see the options, and drag each one you want to your project window, placing them where you want them — even between clips.

   Sound sources include iTunes, two sets of prerecorded effects, and your Mac's microphone. To record narration, click the microphone icon.

4. **Continue editing your movie until the clips and effects are arranged the way you want.**

   You can rearrange elements of your movie by dragging. Click an element to edit it and press Delete to remove it from the movie.

5. **(Optional) Choose File⇨Versions to save a *checkpoint* (the current version of your movie) so you can go back to it if your later edits mangle what you've done up to this point.**

   If you just want to save your project, know that iMovie saves your project as you work on it.

6. **When your movie is ready, choose an option from the Share menu to transfer it to iTunes, an iPod, the web, and more.**

   One sharing option, DVDs, uses a separate iLife application that I talk about in "Burning Movies with iDVD," later in this chapter.

If your hand was a bit shaky when you took that once-in-a-lifetime shot, iMovie may be able to fix your precious video. Select one or more clips, and choose File⇨Analyze for Stabilization. (You're also given this option when you import video from a camera, and iMovie will then mark footage that is too shaky to stabilize, but the process can take quite a while, so you may prefer to import first and then stabilize only the clips you want to use.)

Working with themes and precision editing

Like other iLife programs, iMovie comes with Apple-designed themes. Drag a bunch of clips to the project window. Rearrange them the way you like and pick a theme by choosing File⇨Project Theme and clicking the theme you want. iMovie fills it in with your clips. You won't win any awards for editing, but after just a few minutes of work, you have a serviceable movie, complete with title and credits, that lets you share a special vacation or birthday party with family members and friends.

At the other extreme, iMovie gives you fine-grain control of each clip transition. Choose Window⇨Precision Editor (⌘-/), and iMovie replaces the bottom clip window with a screen that lets you get each transition just right — even carrying the audio from the first clip into the next one.

Ken Burns and his effect

The documentary films of Ken Burns have brought to life, for millions of viewers, whole eras of American history, including the building of the Brooklyn Bridge, the rises of jazz and baseball, and the development of radio. For his most acclaimed series, *The Civil War,* Burns faced an opportunity and a problem. The Civil War was fought after the invention of photography, and archives were filled with black-and-white images, some by excellent early photographers such as Mathew Brady. These archives presented an opportunity to tell the story of this horrific war visually, but Burns's problem was how to keep from boring an audience that was used to seeing movie footage of war. He solved the problem by panning the camera across the still images and slowly zooming in or out to create a sense of motion. *The Civil War* won numerous awards, including two Emmys, for its ability to not just convey the facts of history, but also examine its emotional impact.

Apple has incorporated into its iLife suite the technique that Ken Burns made such masterful use of. It's even called the *Ken Burns effect.* It operates by default in iPhoto slide shows and even in the OS X screen saver, but you can customize the effect by selecting starting and ending versions of the image. The same feature is available in iMovie (select a clip, and press the C key), allowing you to incorporate iPhoto stills into your cinematic projects as dynamic images.

Moving up to Final Cut

You can accomplish a lot with iMovie, but it has its limits. When you're ready for the training wheels to come off, Apple has excellent industrial-strength solutions waiting for you at the Mac App Store, at consumer-strength prices.

The top-of-the-line Apple video-editing program is Final Cut Pro X. Not many computer programs win Emmys, but an earlier version of Final Cut Pro has. The software has been used to edit more than three dozen feature-length films, including *The Social Network,* which earned Angus Wall and Kirk Baxter an Academy Award for Best Editing. Final Cut Pro X has new features that make editing easier by keeping related things together when you move them around. It supports most high-definition formats. Two related video programs are also available from Apple:

- ✔ **Motion:** This animation package creates nifty motion graphics in real time.
- ✔ **Compressor:** This audio and video compression application automates encoding and format conversions.

Figure 13-2 shows the rich interface of Final Cut Pro X. For more on iMovie and the subject of the next section, iDVD, see *iLife '11 For Dummies* by Tony Bove.

Figure 13-2:
Final Cut
Pro X.

Photo courtesy of Apple, Inc.

Burning Movies with iDVD

When your epic is ready, pull down the iMovie Share menu to find all the things you can do with it, including

- ✔ Placing it in iCloud so that you can view it on your iPod, iPad, iPhone, or Apple TV. (Chapter 11 introduces iCloud.)

- ✔ Uploading it to YouTube.

- ✔ Exporting it in QuickTime or another format that Apple Final Cut accepts.

- ✔ Burning it to a DVD, which you do by using iDVD, the topic of this section.

Apple iDVD is something of a one-trick pony: It transfers content to DVD-R so that it can be shown on ordinary DVD players. The content includes stuff you created with other iLife applications (your iMovie films and iPhoto slide shows) and other video content you may have on your hard drive.

You need a Mac that can burn DVDs. The MacBook Air doesn't have an optical drive, but Apple offers an optional external USB DVD burner.

If you want only to back up your media or other files to a DVD, you don't need to use iDVD. The OS X Finder lets you do that. Just don't try to play your backup DVD on your home entertainment center.

Most of what iDVD does is kind of boring: converts stuff to the right video formats and puts the bits in the places on the DVD where consumer players expect them. But Apple can add pizzazz in one place: themes for the main DVD menu. Here's how it works:

1. **On the right side of the main screen of iDVD, click an Apple-created theme that you like.**

   Figure 13-3 shows a general theme selected. The images in the drop zones and the revolving text can be customized, say, to highlight scenes from a family trip.

2. **Drag movies and photos from the Finder or any iLife application to designated image areas within the themes.**

   iDVD can even animate the images so that your menu is even more inviting.

   If you want a scene-selection menu, you can ask iDVD to add one before burning based on your iMovie chapter divisions.

3. **Choose File➪Burn DVD.**

If you need to create a DVD quickly, use the OneStep DVD function, which burns the entire contents of the tape in an attached mini-DV camcorder. To use it in iDVD, choose File➪OneStep DVD.

Figure 13-3:
The iDVD theme selection screen.

Composing with GarageBand

There's an old joke about someone asking a New Yorker how to get to Carnegie Hall. "Practice six hours every day" is the reply. Making music has traditionally required both talent and manual skills that take years to master. People who don't start young and keep working at their instruments are consigned to taking guitar or piano lessons in adult-education classes, where they may progress to the point of being able to plunk out a few tunes at a party.

Computers have leveled the playing field somewhat. Programs such as Apple GarageBand, shown in Figure 13-4, come with prerecorded loops that you can transform and combine to create the sound you want. You can add your own tracks by connecting a keyboard or another instrument that has a MIDI or USB interface, or just use the onscreen keyboard. If your performance isn't quite up to snuff, you can try again or edit out the imperfections. You can also add tracks that were performed live and recorded with a microphone.

Apple offers add-ins to GarageBand in the form of $99 Jam Packs, which include

 ✔ Remix Tools Jam Pack
 ✔ Rhythm Section Jam Pack
 ✔ Symphony Orchestra Jam Pack
 ✔ Voices
 ✔ World Music Jam Pack

Figure 13-4:
Garage-
Band lays
down
tracks.

You can export your composition to iTunes or use it as part of the soundtrack for your slide show or iMovie. The latter uses may be among the most valuable aspects of GarageBand.

If you plan to distribute your iLife compositions beyond your circle of family and friends, you can't just dub in selections from your favorite group's album, even if you purchased it fair and square from the iTunes Store. What you bought entitles you only to listen to the copyrighted music — not to incorporate into your own work. Original music and sound effects that you create in GarageBand, even those that use prerecorded Apple loops, are yours to use as you see fit.

For an in-depth look at recording music with GarageBand, check out *iLife '11 For Dummies,* by Tony Bove.

Podcasting with GarageBand

If you want to try your hand at podcasting (creating audio or video essays that are distributed over the 'net and often played on iPods), GarageBand has the tools you need.

You can use the built-in microphone in your Mac. GarageBand can enhance the sound and reduce background noise. If you use a musical soundtrack, GarageBand can automatically "duck" the soundtrack under your voice when you're speaking. Add sound effects and other cute noises, if you like, by clicking the loop icon near the bottom-right corner of the GarageBand window; GarageBand comes with over 400 of these effects. You can also have a video track with a title screen and other photos you may want to add.

Because programs such as GarageBand make podcasting easy, everyone can do it, and it seems that everyone *is* doing it. If you want your podcasts to stand out, follow these tips:

- ✔ Pick topics you know about.
- ✔ Take the time to develop an outline or a script.
- ✔ Pick one point, and make it well.
- ✔ Keep it short.
- ✔ Lose the "umm"s and "uh"s and "like"s.

Learning to play an instrument with GarageBand

If you always wanted to play guitar or piano, or if you already play but want tips from outstanding musicians, GarageBand can help. The program comes with introductory lessons for each instrument. Click Learn to Play on the left side of the GarageBand window to try them out. You can download eight more free lessons for each instrument by clicking Lesson Store. But that's not all: The Lesson Store also sells artist lessons featuring popular performers, including Sara Bareilles and Sting. Each artist lesson teaches you to play a simple version of one of that artist's hits. All lessons are highly interactive, making clever use of GarageBand's power to help you practice. You can even record your practice sessions in GarageBand and save the tracks you like. If you record, GarageBand will mark where you went astray so that you know what to work on.

Moving up from GarageBand

Just as in iPhoto and iMovie, Apple has better music-creation tools ready whenever you are: Logic and Logic Pro. One classic rite of passage for new musical groups was coming up with the thousands of dollars needed to rent a sound studio for a few hours so that they could cut a demo tape. Modern groups have found that for a lot less money, they can build sound studios in their basements to keep up with the pros. A Mac is often at the heart of this process. You need additional equipment, including good microphones, preamps, and a multiple-input audio interface with a USB or, preferably, a FireWire interface (if your Mac has a FireWire port). Sites such as www. tweakheadz.com have lots of resources to help you get started.

If you're serious about home recording and want a guide to help you learn professional techniques, check out *Home Recording for Musicians For Dummies*, 4th Edition, by Jeff Strong.

Chapter 14

Building Your Space on the Web

*P*sychologist Abraham Maslow suggests that we have a hierarchy of needs. After our physical requirements for survival and safety are met, and we have satisfactory personal relationships (friends, marriage, children), we seek to establish our presence in the larger world, a process that Maslow calls *self-actualization*. In the past, it might have meant running for political office, joining a performing group, or writing a self-help book. Now, more and more people seek recognition as individuals and find ways to make an impact on the world by creating a personal space on the Internet.

In this chapter, you find out a few popular ways to create your space on the web:

  ✔ **Building a website:** Your Mac comes with excellent tools for expressing your thoughts, feelings, and ideas — iPhoto, iMovie, GarageBand — that I've talked about in the preceding three chapters. The final element of the iLife suite, iWeb (which I describe in this chapter), lets you pull together all that creative content and let others view it by way of the World Wide Web. You also discover how to get your own domain name and find a few tips for building a successful site.

  ✔ **Finding web storage and sharing space:** Find personal space for storing files, hosting your site, and sharing.

  ✔ **Social networking:** If you haven't already, check out sites such as Facebook, Twitter, and LinkedIn.

Creating a Website

When you're setting up your own presence on the web, building your own site offers the most creative possibilities but is also the most technical. To make web-page creation accessible to those without the technical knowledge, Apple iWeb brings the iLife predefined-template concept to the process of building personal web pages. The program comes supplied with 21 themes. Each theme has coordinated templates for the welcome page, narratives, photos, movies, blogs, and podcasts (see Figure 14-1). You can modify or customize the templates, if you want. iWeb relieves you of coding and other internal web-page tasks, and its automated tools simplify blogging.

In the sections that follow, you find details about working with iWeb, as well as tips for building a successful site and getting your own domain name.

Starting your first iWeb site

If iWeb isn't on your Dock, you can find it in your Applications folder or via LaunchPad.

Figure 14-1:
An iWeb template.

When you launch iWeb, you're asked to choose a theme for your website. Here's what you need to know about themes as you get started:

✔ **Your theme options enable you to set a look and feel for your site.** The Apple web designers have supplied more than 20 themes, with looks that range from highly elegant and professional to frivolous and whimsical.

✔ **The themes help you coordinate pages for different types of site content.** Each theme includes matching page designs for a welcome screen, biographical information, photos, albums, movies, blogs, podcasts, and a blank theme page that you can easily customize for whatever inspires you.

✔ **You can switch themes easily.** Pick a theme to get started. Because all pages follow a similar organizational style, you aren't locked into your initial theme choice after you start building your page. For the most part, you can change themes at will.

Each theme-page template except the blank one is filled with placeholder pictures and text so that you can see what the result will look like. The body text consists of a Latin passage by the ancient Roman orator Cicero, in which he explains that no one deliberately seeks out grief. (He wrote the passage centuries before Windows was created.) You can customize the placeholders as follows:

✔ **Replacing text:** Double-click any bit of text to select it and then just type what you want, or cut and paste it from another document.

✔ **Deleting placeholders:** To get rid of an element you don't want, select the element and press Delete.

✔ **Replacing placeholders with photos:** On the right side of your screen, you see the Media Browser — an area with headings labeled Audio, Photos, Movies, and Widgets. Click Photos, and you see photos and albums from your iPhoto library. Select a photo and drag it to one of the placeholder images, and your photo appears instead.

If you have lots of photos, you may find it more convenient to search in iPhoto itself and then drag the selected photo from iPhoto to the iWeb placeholder image. All iLife programs cooperate nicely.

You can continue to replace photos until you find the one that best suits your purpose.

✔ **Moving and resizing images:** You can also click and drag images to move them, and you can resize an image by clicking it and then dragging the control boxes that surround it. If you move something by mistake, just choose Edit⇨Undo or press ⌘+Z.

✔ **Adding new elements to a page:** You can add elements to any page, such as text boxes, shapes, images, and movies. For text boxes and shapes, click the appropriate icon at the bottom of the iWeb window. To add photos and other media, drag them from the Media Browser.

✔ **Putting a widget on a page:** Another type of element that you find in the Media Browser is a *widget,* which is a block of programming code in Hypertext Markup Language (HTML) and JavaScript, the computer language that describes web pages. Widgets perform specialized functions, such as displaying Google Maps or YouTube videos. You can even display paid advertising by using the Google AdSense program. By *paid,* I mean that you're paid when people click the ads. See the sidebar "Google AdSense," later in this chapter, for more information.

The individual pages of your site have a navigation bar at the top that lets visitors move from one page to another. Clicking that bar while you're in iWeb to select a different page to edit is tempting, but it doesn't work. You have to use the navigation pane on the left side of the iWeb window to access different pages in the site you're editing.

Saving your pages is no different from saving them in any other Mac or Windows app: Choose File➪Save. If you forget, like all apps, iWeb asks whether you want to save your changes when you quit the program.

Publishing your site

Just because you've built a site in iWeb doesn't mean that it's online for all to see. When you're ready to share your creation, you have to publish it to the web.

Before you share your site with others, take a look to make sure that all placeholders have been replaced with your content. Also, be sure to give your site a name. To get ready to publish your site, follow these steps:

1. **Click the top icon in the navigation bar on the left side of the iWeb window.**

2. **In the Site Publishing Settings pane that appears, name your site, provide a contact e-mail address, and (optionally) make your site private by requiring guests to enter a password you select.**

3. **(Optional) Select the Facebook check box at the bottom of the pane to tell iWeb to notify your Facebook profile automatically whenever you change your site.**

4. **In the Publishing settings pane, select the web-hosting service where you want to publish your site.**

   The iWeb application will upload your site by using File Transfer Protocol (FTP).

   Your hosting service should provide you the server address, username, password, directory path, and protocol you must use with FTP.

5. **To close this pane, click some other element on the navigation bar.**

6. **After you enter all the information, click Publish at the bottom of the iWeb screen.**

   Apple nags you to ensure that you have the rights to all content you're putting online. Publishing can take a few minutes, so don't close iWeb until you receive confirmation that your site has been published. The confirmation box tells you the web address of your site, which you should write down somewhere, and gives you the option of announcing your site by sending e-mail or visiting the site immediately.

If you find mistakes (everyone does) or want to add or change information, don't worry. Open the site again in iWeb, make your changes, and click Publish again.

The Internet can be a dangerous place for young people. Before you let your kids set up their own web pages or join social-networking sites, take a close look at the section in Chapter 17 that talks about Macs for kids. In particular, make sure that they don't include too much personal information. I suggest that you not share the FTP password with your kids. That way, you can review any web content before your kids share it with the entire world forever.

Moving up from iWeb

iWeb is narrowly focused on personal web pages. You may be able to adapt its templates to a simple business, but that's about it. Apple doesn't offer a high-end program for web-page design. If you're looking for a program that's more robust than iWeb, I suggest looking into the following options:

- ✔ Adobe Dreamweaver is the tool professionals use most often. For help creating a site with Dreamweaver, check out *Dreamweaver CS5 For Dummies* or *Web Sites Do-It-Yourself For Dummies,* 2nd Edition, both by Janine Warner.

- ✔ Several other website editors are sold for the Mac. Two popular ones are BBEdit (www.barebones.com) and Sandvox (www.karelia.com/sandvox).

- ✔ The SeaMonkey web-application suite (www.seamonkey-project.org) includes a free website editor.

Making websites that work

With tools such as iWeb, creating a web page is easy. Making one that accomplishes your goals is another matter. Here are some tips for making your website effective:

✔ **Make sure that you're providing information that someone else cares about.** You don't need a large audience, but you must address the needs of your niche. Content counts.

✔ **Say what you most need to say on the first page a visitor sees.** Keep it simple. You have, at most, ten seconds to persuade visitors to delve deeper into your site. Be sure to include any keywords that you want Google to index in the initial paragraphs.

✔ **Pick an easy-to-remember web address.** Pick one that's in the .com top-level domain, if you can. No, the names aren't all taken. If a name you like isn't taken, register it immediately. One-year registrations are cheap. Mark the renewal date a month ahead on your iCal calendar so that you don't forget to renew. Some domain-name registrars, such as GoDaddy. com, renew you automatically, but you must keep your credit-card information up to date. After you settle on a name, don't change it. Links to your site are priceless.

✔ **On the garish World Wide Web, restraint stands out.** Use color and graphics to enhance your messages. Avoid clichés such as animated .gif files and (especially) Under Construction signs. If one of your pages isn't ready, don't link to it until it is.

✔ **Put up what you have now and improve it later.** The visitors you missed today won't be back tomorrow.

✔ **Test your site by using different browsers.** Include Internet Explorer in Windows (a good use for your old PC) and Mozilla Firefox on Mac and Windows. Test your site on a dialup connection, too.

✔ **Ask someone who doesn't know your site to find it and check it out while you watch.** Keep your mouth shut during the evaluation — it isn't easy — and take notes or, better, videotape the session. You want to understand how a new visitor experiences and navigates your site so that you can make any changes needed to improve the user experience, as well as make sure that your visitors do whatever you're hoping they'll do on your site.

✔ **Keep your site current.** Inspect it at least one a month. Out-of-date information destroys the credibility of your entire site. Regularly purge references to "upcoming" events that have already happened and to dead external links. Don't include high-maintenance items such as events if you aren't prepared to keep them updated. Less is more.

✔ **Make your website accessible** to people with vision problems and other disabilities. You'll find lots of suggestions at the W3C Web Accessibility Initiative (www.w3.org/WAI).

✔ **Give visitors a compelling reason to return to your site.** That reason depends on the goals of your site, but it must have a clear benefit for visitors, not just for you.

Google AdSense

If you sign up for the Google AdSense program and place the AdSense widget on your site, Google automatically puts ads on your page. You can choose among several ad formats, ranging from the discreet to the garish. Google selects ads to show to your visitors based on the content of the site and on information that Google and its partners have accumulated about your visitors. Yes, all your web activity is being tracked, and if you use AdSense, you're helping with the tracking. You won't get rich with AdSense unless you have a spectacularly popular site. Google pays you each month, but only after your earnings exceed $100. The folk singer Linda Lavin once complained, "You can make hundreds of dollars as a folk singer." That limit on expectations applies to websites that use AdSense, even ones that receive hundreds of hits a day.

Getting your own domain name

Having your own domain name makes you a first-class citizen on the Internet. Web addresses have several parts strung together by periods, like this:

```
www.dummies.com
```

You decode a web address from right to left, as follows:

- **Top-level domain (TLD):** The rightmost part of a name (com, in the preceding example).

- **Organization or website name:** Located to the left of the TLD (dummies). Two-letter TLDs are reserved for countries, such as us, fr, or uk. Three-letter TLDs denote a type of use. The most widely known is .com, typically used for commercial sites. Many browsers, including Safari, insert .com into the web address if no TLD is specified, so this TLD is particularly desirable.

- **Particular service within the organization:** The part to the left of the organization name (www).

The www, which stands for World Wide Web, is common in web addresses, but large organizations often further subdivide their web addresses by site or department.

The last two hunks of a host name are known as the *domain.* dummies.com, for example, is a *domain name.* (In some countries, an extra hunk identifies broad categories, as in bbc.co.uk, in which co has a meaning similar to .com.)

Domain names are assigned by various registrars. The price ranges from $8 to $35 per year, and you usually have to pay the first year's fees up front. I've had good experiences with GoDaddy.com. For a list of organizations that can register a domain name for you, see `www.icann.org/registrars/accredited-list.html`.

Internet service providers often charge substantial additional fees for setting up and supporting new domains. But registrars such as GoDaddy often offer a free service that sends people who enter your domain name in their browsers to the more clunky address that your Internet provider chooses. Visitors to `http://ditchmypc.co`, for example, are automatically redirected to `http://web.me.com/agr/Site/Welcome.html`.

The folks in charge of the Internet naming system, ICANN, have started selling top-level domain names to organizations that can afford the $185,000 price. So we'll soon be seeing websites with a single name, such as `apple` or `sony` or `cocacola`, or maybe `store.apple`.

Hosting Your Website

When your website is ready for the world to see, you need a place to store it online where others can see it via a service called web hosting. Apple used to provide such a service as part of its MobileMe package, which is being replaced by iCloud. As this book goes to press, web-hosting service isn't among the services available from iCloud, but hundreds of companies provide this service for a fee. Many are oriented toward large business users, and some specialize in small customers, but all of them typically require more technical knowledge than beginners have, and their customer service is spotty. I expect that new vendors will emerge to fill the need for Mac-friendly web hosting, but for now, here are some web-hosting options that are currently available:

- ✔ Many domain registrars, such as GoDaddy.com, offer website hosting.

- ✔ Your Internet service provider may offer website hosting. Comcast Internet service (`comcast.net`), for example, includes access and storage through its Personal Web Pages and Online Storage features.

- ✔ Services like Tumblr (`www.tumblr.com`), Squarespace (`www.squarespace.com`), and Drupal Gardens (`www.drupalgardens.com`) include web-page-creation tools and site hosting.

Social Networking from Your Mac

You don't need your own website to establish a personal presence on the Internet. Several sites designed to give people a place to do their thing have become wildly popular, including the following:

- Facebook (www.facebook.com) was originally intended for college students, but it's increasingly used by people in older and younger age brackets.

- LinkedIn (www.linkedin.com) focuses on your work life, and helps you find and network with people who can help your career.

- MySpace (www.myspace.com) is a bit more freeform, offering sites that cover everything from dating to business to music distribution and the promotion of TV shows and movies.

- Ping, Apple's social network for music lovers, is available through iTunes at www.apple.com/itunes/ping.

- Twitter (www.twitter.com) lets you send short text messages, or *tweets,* from your computer or cellphone so that your friends and others can read them.

If you already have an account on one of these social-networking sites, you don't have to do anything when you switch to a Mac; just log in to the site with your Safari browser, and do what you usually do there. You need your site passwords, however. If you forget them, the sites generally will mail a new password to the e-mail address they have on file for you. So test your passwords to make sure that they work (and write them down) before you abandon your old e-mail account. See Chapter 10 for tips on password management.

The Mac App Store offers a wide variety of social-networking resources specifically for your Mac, as well as apps for your iPhone, iPod touch, and iPad. You can also find OS X support groups for Mac users on many social-networking sites. Try searching for **"macintosh computers"** on Facebook.

Should you friend your teenager?

Facebook and other social-networking sites allow a member's full content to be viewed solely only by other members who have mutually agreed to be friends on the site. That arrangement raises the question of whether parents should insist that their kids make them friends (*friend them,* in the argot) on these sites. Parents need to supervise younger kids' Internet activities, but the case can be made to allow older teens some privacy online. They'll be on their own in a few years anyway, and giving them the opportunity to experiment and even make mistakes online while you're still active in their lives can be a good learning experience for them. It's a tough judgment call that you have to make. Still, a review of the online guidelines for young people that I present in Chapter 17 is always in order.

Chapter 15

Enjoying Other OS X Goodies

Mac OS X is filled with programs and features that make time spent in front of your computer more productive, more interesting, and more fun. In this chapter, I introduce some of my favorites.

Finding Windows Fast with Mission Control

The more useful computers become, the more cluttered the screen gets. At any given time, you may be working with half a dozen applications simultaneously, each with multiple windows open. Mission Control, shown in Figure 15-1, provides the following shortcuts to help you find the window you're looking for:

✔ **Press F3 or swipe up with three fingers.** All open windows shrink and arrange themselves on your screen in neat little piles by application. (The icon on the key suggests the separated windows.). You see an overview of everything, including your Desktop, Dashboard, and any Spaces you've set up at the top. (I tell you about Dashboard and Spaces later in this chapter.) Click the window you want, and it moves to the front. Or put your cursor over a pile and spread four fingers on the trackpad, and that pile expands. Press F3 again or swipe down, and your screen returns to its previous mess.

✔ **Press Control+F3.** It works like pressing F3 but rearranges only the windows of the application you're working in. Or click and hold any application's icon in the Dock to see a list of its open windows.

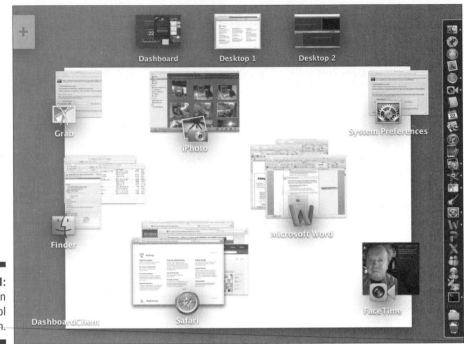

✔ **Press ⌘+F3 or spread with four fingers.** This action makes all windows disappear so that you can see your Desktop. (The windows don't completely go away; you can see their edges along the border of your screen. Clicking one of those window edges moves you out of Exposé with that window in front.)

✔ **Press F4 or swipe right.** This action opens the Dashboard.

Apple sometimes moves these keys around, depending on the keyboard you have. Also, you can pick different keys to perform these functions and make the corner of your screen a hotspot for the same actions. Follow these steps to check on your key assignments and to make changes:

1. **Choose ⊛⇨System Preferences.**

2. **Select Mission Control.**

   You see a pane similar to the one shown in Figure 15-2.

3. **Select the keys for which you want to perform an action.**

4. **Click the Hot Corners button if you want to use an onscreen corner to initiate an action.**

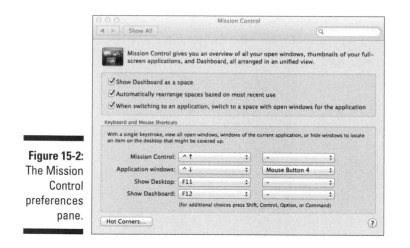

Figure 15-2:
The Mission
Control
preferences
pane.

Padding Around with Applications

With OS X Lion, Apple has brought many of the innovations it devised for the iPhone and iPad back to the Mac. In this section, I describe some of the iPad-inspired tricks you can enjoy on your Mac.

Getting apps going with Launchpad

Pinch with four fingers on the trackpad or click the Launchpad button in the Dock (it looks like a rocket ship). You see a full screen of icons for the applications you have installed on your Mac, much like those shown in Figure 15-3. From the Launchpad screen, you can do the following:

✔ **Click any icon to launch that app.** Click white space, press Esc or pinch with four fingers to leave Launchpad.

✔ **Move around the icons, if you want.**

✔ **Scan pages of apps.** If you have more than one page of Launchpad apps, move between them with two finger swipes or presses of the arrow keys. Some apps are organized in folders.

✔ **Create new folders** by dragging an app icon onto another.

✔ **Delete an app from your Mac.** Click its icon until it starts shaking; then click the black X that appears. If you delete an app that you purchased from the Mac App Store, you can download it again at no charge.

If you own an iPhone, iPad, or iPod touch, all this will seem familiar because those devices have the same feature.

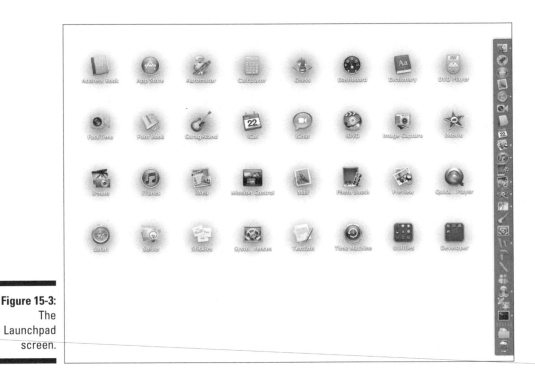

Figure 15-3:
The
Launchpad
screen.

Skipping the clutter with full screen apps

Some of us do better working on one thing at a time. If you find having lots of windows open saps your focus, like listening to the TV and radio while having a conversation on the phone, Apple has a nice surprise for you. When you're using an application, try the following trick:

1. **In the top-right corner of the window that you're working on, click the icon that shows a pair of arrows pointing away from each other.**

   The window fills your entire screen.

2. **To see the application's menu, move your cursor to one of the top corners of your screen.**

   The menu appears, and you see a symbol with arrows pointing together that gets you out of full-screen mode. (The aptly named Escape key performs the same trick.)

3. **If you have several windows open, move from one to another in full-screen mode with a three-finger swipe on your trackpad or the top of your Magic Mouse.**

   Not all apps support full-screen mode yet, however.

Getting back where you started with Resume

When you quit an application, OS X remembers what windows were open and where you were in each application, and restores them when you relaunch the application. This feature can be handy when you shut down to carry your laptop somewhere and then want to continue your work where you left off. On the other hand, if you were doing something that you'd rather not share, this feature could be embarrassing. You can turn it off by choosing System Preferences⇨General. Just clear the check box labeled Restore Windows When Quitting and Reopening Apps.

Saving your work automatically with AutoSave and Versions

Another bit of good advice that's often ignored is saving your work frequently. OS X Lion saves documents that you're working on automatically and lets you go back in time to see different versions of the file.

If the application you are using supports AutoSave, when you click the name of the document in the document window's title bar, you see a small disclosure triangle next to the name. Click the triangle and you see several options:

- **Lock:** Prevents any further changes. (If you try to make a change, you're asked to unlock.)
- **Duplicate:** Saves a copy with your changes up to this point.
- **Revert to Last Opened:** Returns the document to the state it was in when you started this editing session.
- **Browse All Versions:** Displays a screen modeled after Time Machine, listing your current version and all past versions, so you can select the one you want.

Organizing Work Areas with Spaces

I'm one of those people who always have several projects going on at one time. My fantasy is to have a studio where I can have a table or workbench for each project so that I can walk up to it whenever I want and pick up where I left off. Apple hasn't offered me a studio, but OS X provides the next-best thing — a bunch of virtual work tables named Spaces. You can have as many as 16 of them. You can assign specific applications to specific spaces or make an application available to all spaces. You create a Spaces desktop as follows:

1. **Open Mission Control.**

2. **Move your cursor to the top-right corner of your screen (or the top left if your dock is on the right, as in Figure 15-1).**

3. **Click the plus sign that appears.**

4. **Click the new blank desktop box appears at the top of the Mission Control screen.**

    A blank desktop appears.

5. **To get started, just move to your new Spaces Desktop and open the application you want to use there.**

After you set up a new space, you can switch between Spaces in Mission Control or by making three-finger swipes to either side. Holding down the Control key and pressing the left or right arrow keys also works.

Searching for Files with Spotlight

After you use computers for a while, sooner or later you'll have trouble finding a file, even though you *know* that it's on your computer somewhere. The Spotlight search tool helps you find that file by typing words that the file likely contains and other characteristics, such as its name, the date you created it, and which kind of file it is. Searching through gigabytes of hard drive space can take time, even on a fast computer, so Spotlight keeps an index of every word you use in documents, e-mail messages, and other areas. It does this in the background, so you hardly notice, but these indexes make searching very fast.

A Spotlight icon is located on the menu bar in the top-right corner of your screen. Click it to open a search box. You see search boxes in each Finder window, too. You can also press ⌘+F when the Finder is open.

Customizing searches

You can tell Spotlight what your search preferences are and how you want to see results. To do so, choose ⇨System Preferences and click the Spotlight icon. You see a pane similar to the one shown in Figure 15-4. Deselect the items that you don't want to search. You can drag individual lines up and down to reorder the way items appear in a search.

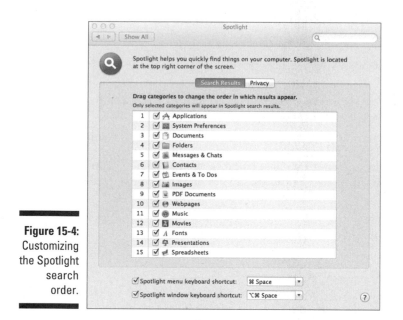

Figure 15-4:
Customizing
the Spotlight
search
order.

You may have information on your Mac that you'd prefer not be found in a search, of course. Click the Privacy tab in the Spotlight preferences pane, and drag into the window those files and folders that you don't want to be searched. Spotlight doesn't return matches from those files and folders.

Spotlight normally tries to match all the words you type in its search box. If you want to search for dogs *or* cats, type **dogs | cats**. If you want to search for pets but not dogs, type **pets -dogs**.

Searching with Smart Folders

Wouldn't it be convenient to find all files associated with the Zorchcastle Project without having to do a search every time? Spotlight offers a tool that lets you do this: Smart Folders. Here's how the tool works:

1. **Create a folder by choosing Finder➪New Smart Folder.**

   If your project isn't named Zorchcastle, you're out of luck: Smart Folders works only with Zorchcastle. (Just kidding.)

2. **In the Smart Folder's search area, enter the words or other criteria you want.**

   You add more criteria by clicking the little plus-sign icon (+) in the top-right corner.

3. **To keep your handy new Smart Folder around, click the Save button (also in the top-right corner) and give the folder a name.**

   Keep the Smart Folder around, and it will always show the files that match the criteria you set, including new files you saved after you set up the Smart Folder. The Smart Folder stays wherever you put it, such as on the Desktop or in your Documents folder. You can find it the same way that you find any other folder.

   Figure 15-5 shows a Smart Folder looking for files created in the past month whose names start with the letters *Chap*.

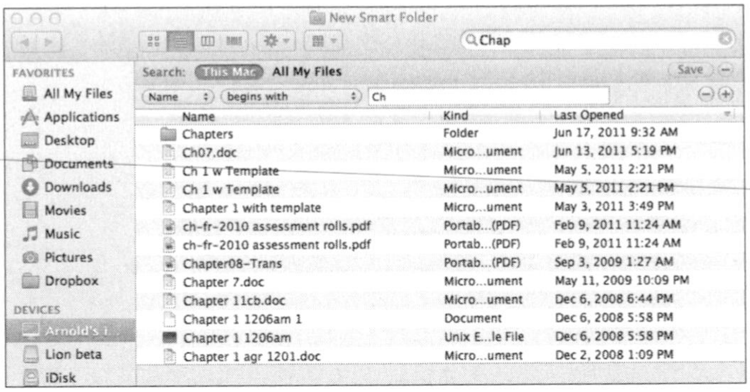

Figure 15-5:
A Smart
Folder.

Adding Handy Widgets to the Dashboard

Dashboard provides an easy way to see and use *widgets,* which are mini-applications that grab specific information from the Internet or help with narrow but useful tasks. Figure 15-6 shows a typical Dashboard arrangement, including a calendar, Wikipedia search widget, weather program, clock, translator, and more. You can move widgets around, add new ones, and drop stale ones. You're in charge. Some widgets are silly, some are fun, and some are indispensable after you're used to having them around.

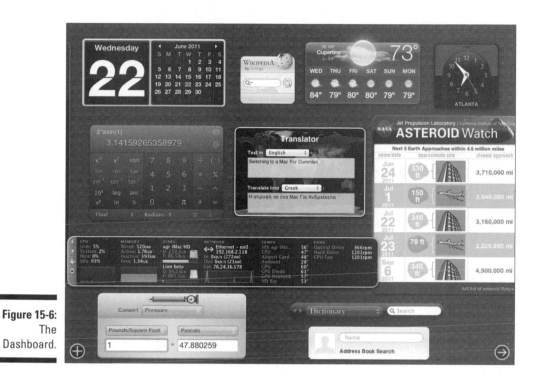

Figure 15-6:
The
Dashboard.

To work with widgets, you just need to know a few tips:

- ✔ **To make your widgets appear:** Press F4 on an Apple keyboard (F12 on a third-party keyboard) or the key with a meter icon on it, or swipe to the right with three fingers. The screen fills with colorful widgets on a Lego background.

- ✔ **To add more widgets:** Click the plus sign (+) in the bottom-left corner. A scrolling list appears at the bottom of your screen. Click the icons for the widgets you want to add.

- ✔ **To delete widgets:** Click the plus sign to do this task, too. When you do, all current widgets show up with an X in their top-left corner. Click the X, and they're gone.

- ✔ **To adjust settings:** Many widgets have a lowercase *i* in their bottom-right corners. Click the *i,* and the widget flips over to show you which settings you can adjust to customize it.

Apple includes a collection of widgets with OS X, but many more are available from www.apple.com/downloads/dashboard. Many are freeware, and some ask for a fee. Many work only when your computer is connected to the Internet.

You can have multiple instances of a widget running simultaneously with different customizations, such as a clock with different time zones or weather reports from different locales. Some of the widgets supplied with OS X are described in this list:

- **Address Book:** Gain easy access to your contact list.

- **Calendar:** What day is the 23rd of next month?

- **Dictionary and thesaurus:** Don't guess — look it up.

- **Flight tracker:** Where's that flight now? When will it arrive?

- **Language translator:** Translate a sentence or two between Chinese, Dutch, English, French, German, Greek, Italian, Korean, Russian, and Spanish.

- **Movies:** Find what's playing where, see previews, and buy tickets from Fandango.

- **Phone book:** Let your mouse do the walking.

- **Ski report:** Packed ice or fresh powder?

- **Stickies:** These items don't fall off your monitor.

- **Stocks:** Watch your favorite securities and funds fluctuate.

- **Tile game:** Check out this classic.

- **Unit converter:** Sure, it can convert from metric to English, but it also knows currency exchange rates.

- **Weather:** Look up the temperature highs and lows and a six-day forecast.

- **World time:** Is it too early to call Tokyo?

You even have a Widget widget to help you manage all your widgets. To see the widgets available and add some to your Dashboard, press F4 to open Dashboard and then click the plus sign (+) in the bottom-left corner of your screen.

Download more

You can find many more widgets to play with. Here are some examples, all of which are freeware:

- **Countdown Dashboard:** Make a countdown timer to any event you choose: graduation, vacation, dental appointment, or book deadline, for example.

✔ **Corporate Ipsum:** Generate nonsense text whenever you need it, such as "interactively orchestrate superior portals without team-driven platforms, collaboratively actualize plug-and-play outsourcing and maintainable applications, distinctively simplify front-end platforms before backward-compatible relationships."

✔ **Fans:** Your Mac has cooling fans inside that spin at different rates depending on how hard your CPU is working. Seriously. The first time my normally quiet MacBook started to sound like an airplane taking off was a tad alarming. The Fans widget shows animated fans spinning to match the current speed of your real fans.

✔ **I Love Lamp:** You've seen or heard of the infamous lava lamp from the 1960s? Get it at www.islayer.com/apps/ilovelamp/.

✔ **iStat Pro:** Display the status of the CPU, memory, hard drives, internal and external IP address, bandwidth, battery, uptime, and fans.

✔ **Kennedy Space Center Video:** Watch what's happening at everyone's favorite spaceport. You have more than a dozen webcams to choose among.

✔ **Mirror:** See yourself onscreen and touch up your hair. (This widget uses your iSight camera.)

✔ **Starry Night:** See the planets and constellations as they appear right now at any location on Earth.

✔ **Sudoku:** Get your rivals at work hooked on this wildly popular numbers game. Sudoku and career success are ensured.

Thousands more widgets are available, and more keep popping up.

Roll your own

You can select a portion of a web page and create a widget that shows the latest version of just that piece — a feature that Apple calls *WebClips*. Follow these steps:

1. **Open Safari and go to the website you want to widgetize.**

2. **Choose File⇨Open in Dashboard or click the Dashboard icon in the Dock.**

3. **Select the section of the page you want to capture.**

Apple even provides the Dashcode program to help you build your own widget. The possibilities are endless. You could, for example, make a widget to track your favorite blog. Dashcode comes with Apple's Xcode software development environment, which I describe in Chapter 19.

Saving Time with Automator and AppleScript

Every now and then, you face a task that's highly repetitious. A bunch of photos have to be sized to fit a catalog, or some illustrations have to be numbered a certain way to work with a publishing system, for example. Apple provides a couple of techniques for completing the task.

If you're comfortable with computer programming, OS X comes with a scripting language named AppleScript. Most OS X applications can be invoked from AppleScript programs, so you can use the applications as tools in your program — say, to extract an address from Address Book or rotate an image with Preview. You can find all the details in *AppleScript For Dummies,* 2nd Edition, by Tom Trinko.

Most of us aren't eager to write programs every time a tedious chore presents itself, so Apple has a simple way to automate your life — named, interestingly, Automator (see Figure 15-7). OS X includes a library with hundreds of Automator actions you can choose among. You can even ask Automator to watch what you're doing as you work through the routine once and record your actions. Then you can play back or edit your actions.

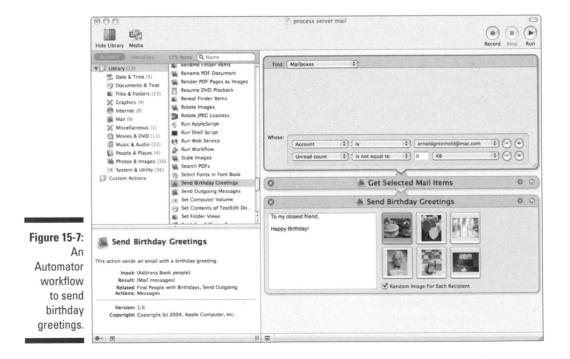

Figure 15-7:
An
Automator
workflow
to send
birthday
greetings.

Apple has a nice tutorial on using Automator at `www.macosxautomation.com/automator/`.

Chapter 16

Oops, It's a PC: Running Windows on Your Mac

Since the beginning of the rivalry between Apple and Microsoft, one continual point of contention was the underlying hardware. Microsoft designed its products to run on the Intel *x*86 microprocessor series. Apple used Motorola 680x0 "micros," later switching to the PowerPC, jointly developed with Motorola and IBM. Apple ran ads showing Army tanks guarding a G3 Mac, briefly subject to U.S. arms export regulation, while stating that Windows PCs were harmless.

The Earth moved on June 6, 2005. Pigs flew. All flights to Hades were canceled because the runway had frozen over. On that day, Apple CEO Steve Jobs announced that Apple would begin using microprocessors from Intel in all its new products.

Jobs concluded that Intel had a better plan for developing the kind of microprocessors Apple needed and did the unthinkable. The transition went surprisingly smoothly. All Macs sold now not only have Intel microprocessors inside, but also closely adhere to industry standards for PC design. They are truly PCs. If you take a fancy to the elegant Apple hardware but have eyes for only Windows 7, you can get the Mac you like and just run Windows 7 on it. You do have to buy a Windows 7 license separately — an added expense — but otherwise, you have just another Windows machine.

The real win for Mac owners is having the ability to run, quite easily, both Mac OS X and Windows applications on the same Mac. The tricky part is choosing which of several methods to use. You have three main candidates. Here's a quick rundown (I explain each one in more detail in this chapter):

✔ **Dual booting:** You pick your poison when you boot up your computer: OS X or Windows. Dual-booting capability is built into OS X, but again, you need to obtain a Windows license. Apple named this technology *Boot Camp.*

✔ **Virtualization:** Run both operating systems at the same time and switch between them effortlessly. OS X and Windows play nicely together. Two vendors now offer this solution: Parallels.com and VMware.com. Also, a free, open-source solution, VirtualBox, is available at `www.virtualbox.org`.

✔ **API translation:** Run Windows applications on your Mac without installing Windows. This method doesn't work for all applications yet, but if you need to run only a few applications or games that are on the "okay" list, you save money and aggravation by not buying and installing Windows. See "CodeWeavers: Wine on a Mac," later in this chapter.

Pulling the Rabbit Out of the Hat

Magic starts with understanding the obvious. How can you run both OS X and Windows? Well, if you bought a Mac and still have your old PC, it's easy: Just turn them both on. You have the situation shown in Figure 16-1. I labeled one computer a Mac and one a Dell, but the second one can be any Windows PC. Indeed, as I just mentioned, because your new Mac is a PC, the computer on the right can be another Mac.

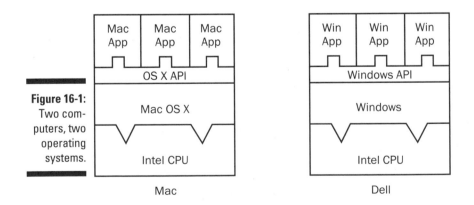

Figure 16-1: Two computers, two operating systems.

If you don't care about spending money, you can buy two Macs, leave OS X on one, and replace OS X with Windows on the other. You'd be in the situation shown in Figure 16-2, which isn't too different from Figure 16-1.

Why can't I run OS X on a Dell?

You may be wondering, "If Macs are just like any other PCs, why can't I run OS X on a Dell or an HP or any other Windows box that doesn't come from Apple?" It's a good question, and it has two answers.

First, some components in the Windows PC probably require drivers that aren't available for OS X. Windows drivers don't work in OS X. Apple makes drivers only for the components it uses in making Macs. This reason prevents cross-use only to a point. You find overlap in components, and some people are skilled enough to create the necessary drivers (at least for the more popular configurations of Windows PCs) and make them available. If you want an unsupported, likely unreliable, possibly illegal installation, I won't say which Google search to try.

The other reason is that Apple doesn't want you to run OS X on a Windows box — at least

for now. Apple makes money selling the complete package: hardware and software, and avoids the cost and risk that supporting other vendors' hardware poses to its reputation. At the moment, it isn't ready to license OS X for other computers — it may never be — and it certainly doesn't want people to pirate OS X. So Apple has built tests into OS X that can detect a non-Apple PC. Exactly how closely guarded a secret is it? The company has even applied for patents on certain techniques for concealing the methods it uses.

One benefit of having OS X run only on Apple hardware is that Apple doesn't require registration for each new OS X installation. Microsoft, by contrast, requires such registration in its Windows Genuine Advantage program, and changes in a PC's configuration can trigger a request to reregister.

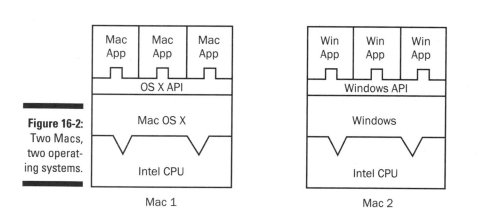

Figure 16-2:
Two Macs, two operating systems.

When you install an operating system on a computer, it's stored on your hard drive. Well, you can have two (or more) hard drives and install a different operating system on each one. Then you can tell your Mac (and your PC) which hard drive you want to *boot* (start up) from.

You don't even need two physical drives. You can split or *partition* your hard drive into two (or more) sections, called *volumes*. From then on, the computer considers each volume to be a separate hard drive, and you can install different operating systems on each volume, with only one physical hard drive. This situation is depicted in Figure 16-3.

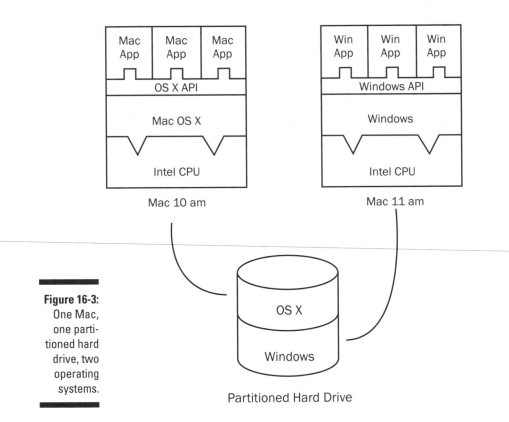

Figure 16-3:
One Mac, one partitioned hard drive, two operating systems.

At 10 a.m., you boot your Mac in OS X to check your mail and search the web for information you need for a presentation you're working on. At 11 a.m., you reboot into Windows to run some corporate applications that require Internet Explorer. At 11:30, you reboot into OS X to finish that presentation in Keynote. It's a tad tedious, but it all works.

Getting Started with Boot Camp

Boot Camp is included with Mac OS X 10.7 (Lion) and the earlier 10.6 (Snow Leopard) and 10.5 (Leopard). To use it, you need these two items:

- ✔ An Intel Mac with at least 20GB of free hard drive space
- ✔ A bona fide installation disc for Microsoft Windows XP (Service Pack 2 or later, Home or Professional), Windows Vista, or Windows 7 — the full version, not a Windows upgrade

To get started installing Windows with Boot Camp, follow these steps:

1. **Make sure that your Mac is fully backed up.**

   If you use Time Machine, verify the time of last backup by clicking its icon in the Finder menu bar (which looks like an analog clock face). Then disconnect the Time Machine hard drive. Boot Camp repartitions your internal hard drive, and though it's supposed to do this in a way that keeps existing files intact, things can go wrong. See Chapter 5 for more on backing up.

2. **Launch the Boot Camp Setup Assistant (in your Utilities folder).**

3. **Click the Print Installation & Setup Guide button.**

   You'll want printed instructions when you're in the middle of installation and your computer isn't usable.

4. **Follow the guide's instructions.**

   They vary by Mac model, so there's no point in repeating them here.

5. **When asked, indicate how big you want to make the Windows partition.**

   The answer, of course, depends on how much space you need and how much space is available on your Mac's internal hard drive. I suggest 40GB as a minimum. The Windows installer may complain that your hard drive isn't formatted properly. Let it reformat the hard drive it sees — your new partition — as NTFS.

   For more information on installing Windows, see `www.apple.com/support/bootcamp`.

After you install Windows by using Boot Camp, you select which operating system you want — Windows or OS X — by holding down the Option key (the Alt key, if you're using a Windows keyboard) while starting up. If you don't hold down the Option key, you get OS X unless you change the default by choosing ⬛⇨System Preferences⇨Startup Disk. I'd include a screen shot of Boot Camp in action, but you already know what Windows looks like.

Virtualize Me

Dual booting can grow old fast if you need to switch several times a day. Wouldn't it be wonderful if you could run both operating systems at the same time and switch between them as easily as you switch between applications in OS X? The technology that makes such a switch possible, *virtualization,* has been around since the 1960s, but it has taken off in the past few years and become a hot topic in computing.

With virtualization, an extra layer called a *hypervisor* is inserted between the operating system and the computer. Operating systems include supervisor software, so the term *hypervisor* was invented to connote something with even more authority than a supervisor. The hypervisor's role is to divide the CPU's attention among two or more virtual machines, each with its own operating system. This concept is shown schematically in Figure 16-4. Each virtual machine looks to its operating system as though it had a complete, unvarnished CPU all to itself. The hypervisor ensures that each virtual machine gets a fair share of the real CPU's resources and decides which operating system gets to appear in which window on the real computer's display and where to direct mouse and keyboard actions.

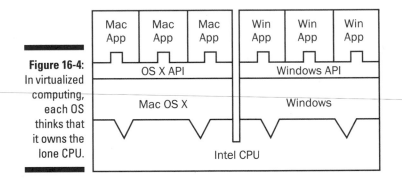

Figure 16-4:
In virtualized computing, each OS thinks that it owns the lone CPU.

In the following sections, you find out about the pros and cons of virtualization, as well as about programs you can use to add this hypervisor to your system. The three virtualization solutions for OS X are Parallels from Parallels.com; VMware Fusion from VMware.com, which is owned by EMC Corp; and the open-source VirtualBox project. I explain all three products in more detail later in this section.

The pros and cons of virtualization

Virtualization is the most convenient solution to running Windows on a Mac. Both operating systems run at the same time, and you can switch back and forth quickly, with no rebooting. Virtualization also supports a wide variety of operating systems. You want MS-DOS, Linux, or OS/2 on your Mac? No problem.

Virtualization has these disadvantages:

✔ It's the most expensive solution for running Windows on a Mac if you buy a commercial virtualization package and obtain a Windows license.

✔ The hypervisor layer causes a small performance penalty, though special hardware in the Intel processors used in Macs — known as Intel Virtualization Technology (VT-x) — speeds virtualization.

✔ You have to deal with two different operating systems.

✔ It discourages you from making the leap to OS X because the more familiar Windows programs are always easily available.

✔ Peripheral support may be less than ideal.

Parallels

Parallels was the first company to sell virtualization for OS X. Its product, Parallels Desktop, runs on any Intel Mac, though Parallels recommends having 15GB of free hard drive space. It supports a wide range of guest operating systems, 32- and 64-bit, including the ones in this list:

✔ Most versions of Microsoft Windows, starting with 3.1 and including 98, Me, various Servers, XP, Vista, and Windows 7

✔ Many popular Linux distributions, including CentOS, Debian, Fedora Core, Mandriva, Red Hat, SUSE, Ubuntu, and Xandrox

✔ FreeBSD 7 and 8

✔ The legendary IBM OS/2 Warp 4.5 and eComStation

✔ Solaris 9 and 10

✔ MS-DOS 6.22

Parallels has a Parallels Transporter feature that migrates your existing PC to the Mac, which greatly simplifies the process of getting on the Mac. It can also use a Boot Camp partition if you've created one.

Perhaps the sweetest feature of Parallels Desktop is Coherence, which lets you run Windows applications from the Mac Desktop as though they were Mac applications. You don't even have to look at Windows. You can even drag and drop files between the two operating systems. Windows apps show up on the OS X Dock with a *W* symbol that indicates their Windows origin.

Parallels offers a separate tool, Compressor, that the company claims reduces the size of a virtual machine stored on your hard drive by 50 percent or more, saving disk space and improving performance. Parallels also offers an app for the iPad and iPhone that lets you control your virtual machine remotely.

Parallels has support for USB 2.0, Windows 3D, and DirectX 9. You can even use the built-in camera on your Mac. See `http://kb.parallels.com/en/5028`.

VMware Fusion

VMware largely started the *x*86 virtualization business in 1998. The company is a leading supplier of virtualization products, such as its VMware Workstation, in the Windows and Linux enterprise markets. Its virtualization product for the Mac, VMware Fusion, is based on the same proven technology. So even though VMware entered the OS X market a little later than Parallels, it brings along considerable depth of experience, supporting more than 60 guest operating systems. Virtual machines created with other VMware products can run on the Mac; similarly, virtual machines created with VMware Fusion on the Mac can run on other systems. VMware has a Virtual Appliance Marketplace where you can find hundreds of preconfigured virtual solutions to try on your Mac.

One neat feature allows you to take a snapshot of your VMware virtual machine when you have it set up the way you like it. Then you can roll back to that configuration with a single click whenever you want. You can copy and paste text between Windows and Mac applications, and drag and drop files from one to the other. VMware also offers full USB 2.0 support and runs some games that depend on DirectX 9.0. VMware has similar installation requirements to Parallels Desktop and can also use an existing Boot Camp partition.

Choosing between Parallels and VMware is tough. They're both good products, and because both offer free trial versions, you can check out both products. If you work in an organization that uses other VMware products, that fact may tip the decision in favor of VMware.

VirtualBox

VirtualBox is a free, open-source virtualization product that's designed for business and home use. It supports a wide variety of guest operating systems. You can download it from `www.virtualbox.org`. Like most free software, it can be more difficult to use than a commercial product and only limited support is available if you run into problems, mostly in the form of online forums with other users.

Because virtualization takes place at the deepest level of your computer if something goes wrong it can bring everything to a halt. If you have limited experience working with open-source software, I would suggest picking one of the two commercial virtualization solutions — they're worth the modest expense.

Imitation: The Sincerest Form of Flattery

One problem exists with the dual-booting and virtualization approaches: You need a copy of Windows. That's an added expense, and it means that you have one more operating system to maintain and update. You probably just want to run some Windows-only applications. Suppose that you could sneak them onto your Mac without having to install the whole Windows boat. You can do that, too — sort of. I say "sort of" because the technique works with only certain Windows applications, though the list is growing.

Why running Windows applications will (or won't) work

Windows programs run on the same Intel microprocessors as newer Macs. So why can't you just insert a Windows program disc in your Mac and start it up? The reason is that all applications have to talk to the operating system to receive basic services, called *application program interfaces,* or APIs, such as opening files or being notified whenever the user clicks a mouse button. Unfortunately, the APIs that Mac OS X provides are set up quite differently from the ones Windows provides. They speak different languages, in effect.

The Wine project (www.winehq.org) started in 1993 with the aim of running Windows programs on Intel-based Linux computers by building a layer of software that would sit on top of Linux and provide the APIs that a Windows program would expect. This approach is illustrated in Figure 16-5. It's had limited success because there are hundreds of APIs, some imperfectly documented, and many change with each new release of Windows.

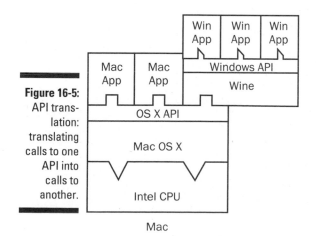

Figure 16-5:
API translation: translating calls to one API into calls to another.

CodeWeavers: Wine on a Mac

Mac OS X shares a Unix heritage with Linux. So when Apple announced that it was switching to Intel microprocessors, it created the possibility of running Wine on Macs. The idea was so attractive that a company called CodeWeavers.com decided to make a business of creating the OS X version of Wine. The company offers three products:

- CrossOver Mac is for Windows applications, except games. It currently supports Microsoft Office 2007, 2003, XP, 2000, and 97 in Word, Excel, PowerPoint, and Outlook. (However, Access is supported only in Office 2000.) You also find support for Microsoft Project and Visio and for Intuit's Quicken.

- CrossOver Games is for selected Windows games, including most of the popular Steam repertoire, such as *Half Life 2* and *World of Warcraft*. See `http://store.steampowered.com/browse/mac`.

- CrossOver Pro includes both the applications and games products and additional support.

These solutions cost a lot less than a Windows license, but CodeWeavers freely admits they work fully with only a few Windows programs. The list is expanding, and you can influence CodeWeavers' priorities in getting applications to work. See `www.codeweavers.com/compatibility`. Because CodeWeavers offers a free trial period, you have little to lose — except some time — and a lot to gain by downloading the trial versions and checking out your favorite PC apps and games.

Security issues

Having Windows at your disposal on your Mac is neat, but remember that it's still Windows. You should follow all security and antivirus guidelines recommended for Windows on a PC, including downloading Microsoft Security Essentials, enabling Windows Update, and installing up-to-date antivirus software. As a former Windows user, you know the drill.

Be wise: Retrieve your mail and do your web surfing in OS X, and restrict Internet access on the Windows side to situations in which it's needed, such as accessing sites that you already know about and trust and that require Internet Explorer or ActiveX. You should also pick a password for Windows that's different from the one you use on the Mac. See Chapter 10 for password suggestions.

One advantage of running Windows on a Mac is that you can keep important files on the Mac side, using shared folders. Then, if your Windows machine becomes infected by nasty malware, you can simply delete the Windows virtual disk and restore a copy that you saved when you were sure it was in a clean state, or simply reinstall Windows from the original disc. Virus hunters use virtualization for this very reason.

Part V
Specialty Switching Scenarios

The 5th Wave   By Rich Tennant

"Don't be silly - of course my passwords are safe.
I keep them written on my window, but then I
pull the shade if anyone walks in the room."

In this part . . .

We're all different, and the problems and opportunities we encounter when we switch computer systems depends on our situation and needs. In this part, I deal with topics that may not interest everyone who switches. The first chapter of this part covers kids, seniors, and people with disabilities. Then I discuss using Macs in business settings, the heartland of Windows dominance. The last chapter in this part dives a bit deeper into OS X and introduces the Unix layer underneath all the graphical glitz. Folks who are switching from computer operating systems other than Windows XP, Vista, or Windows 7 might want to check out the Bonus Chapter on this book's website at `www.dummies.com/go/switchingtoamacfd`. In particular, users of older Mac operating systems can find upgrading to OS X challenging.

Chapter 17

Switching with the Whole Family in Mind

*B*uying a computer for home use involves a special set of challenges. In a work environment, personal computing may just mean that each employee has his own machine. But in a family setting, *personal* means much more. Computers become part of us, woven into our daily routine and even into our psyches. The choices we make about which computers we give our children and how we set them up can affect their development. For an elderly person or someone with a disability, having the right computer can improve quality of life.

In this chapter, you find out about features and software on your Mac that help kids, parents, and the whole family enjoy a home computer that much more. I also discuss situations in which an iPad may be more suitable.

Macs for Kids

Kids take to computers like raccoons to suburbia. It may not be the environment that nature intended, but kids quickly become comfortable — perhaps too comfortable — in front of a screen.

Check out these positive factors about computers for kids. Computers do the following:

- Provide an outlet for artistic expression and creativity
- Offer information about every topic imaginable (much of it true)
- Let kids chat with friends and be at home at the same time without running up minutes on their cellphone accounts
- Offer opportunities for personal contact with new people and cultures
- Help develop and improve reading, writing, and language skills
- Support kids with special needs and their parents

You find some big negative aspects as well:

- Videogames can be unbelievably addictive, especially for boys.
- Time spent in front of a computer is time not spent doing chores or homework, or engaging in ordinary play.
- Our kids are getting fat from lack of physical activity. TV is the main culprit, but computers are catching up.
- Kids generally can't resist the temptation to download music and videos without paying for them.
- It's too tempting for kids to copy material from the web and pass it off as original schoolwork.
- Like suburbia must seem to raccoons, the Internet is littered with "garbage cans."

Establishing parental control

If you're switching your kids to a Mac, you have a unique opportunity to regain some control of their computer use. You have to act fast, though. Your kids probably know more about computers than you do, so you should set things up correctly from the beginning. I go over the steps in more detail here than for other topics because establishing control of your kids' computer use is vital and because I know how harried and time-constrained most parents are.

The first thing you must do is make yourself the administrator for your kids' Mac. *You* should be the one to work through the start-up sequence described in Chapter 4 and become the first user of the computer. If you're adding your kids' accounts to the Mac you use, you have in effect already done this.

Next, set up a separate account for each child who will use the computer. If you have more than one child and are giving each one her own Mac (what good parents you are!), you should still give each kid an account on each machine. That way, if one child borrows an older sibling's Mac, she still has the restrictions you impose.

Computers and young children

I'm not convinced that young kids (fourth-graders or younger) need to have computer access. Young kids need to relate to the real world and, especially, to other people. They do that by playing with toys, kids, and adults. Computers are mostly a distraction from the task of being children. Perhaps you can make an argument that computers are less-passive babysitters than television. But neither is particularly desirable, and kids' computer use should be supervised anyway. The iPad is even more seductive for young children because of its simplicity. Many cool educational apps and experiments introducing those apps on iPads in elementary school have shown very promising results, but these devices can be just as addictive as computers.

Think long and hard before introducing your kids to computers, and make careful choices about how much time they're allowed to use them, as well as what kinds of programs and websites they're exposed to.

Setting up accounts is easy. Follow these steps:

1. **Choose System Preferences, and click the Users & Groups icon (the one with a silhouette of two heads).**

   The pane shown in Figure 17-1 appears.

2. **Click the plus sign in the bottom-left corner to add a new account.**

   You may have to click the lock icon first and enter your password.

3. **When you see a pane that asks for the name and password of the new account, as shown in Figure 17-2, fill in the name and password you want your child to have.**

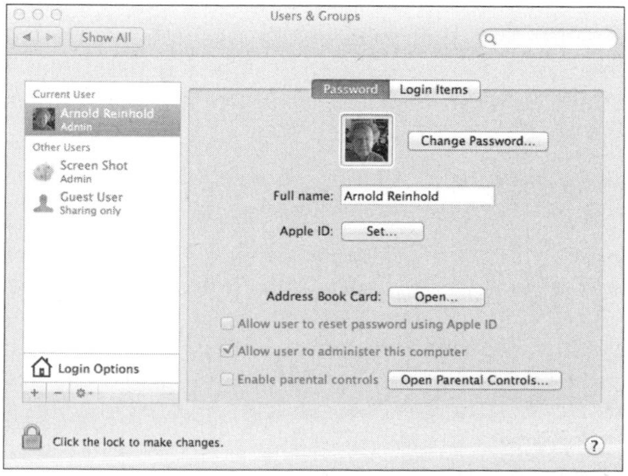

Figure 17-1: The Users & Groups system preferences pane.

Figure 17-2:
The New
Account
pane.

Here are some tips for choosing names and passwords specifically for kids:

- Because the account name and short name are used in OS X for many purposes and may show up during Internet use, *do not include your kids' last names on the account.* Sarah or Sarah Jean should do fine.

- In Chapter 10, I emphasize the security value of using random passwords. If anything, security is more important for kids on the Internet. You can ask OS X to suggest a short (eight to ten characters), random password of letters and numbers by clicking the key icon next to the Password field.

- An alternative for very young kids is to combine a name and number from two different parts of their lives, such as a character from a favorite story and their room number in school.

- Tape your child's password to his bed until the child memorizes it. It doesn't take long.

- While you're at it, help your child make up a separate password for all the junk Internet sites that require registration. Some sites reportedly collect passwords and offer them for sale for nefarious purposes.

4. **Because this account is for a child, choose Managed with Parental Controls from the New Account pop-up menu.**

   Other account options include Standard and Administrator. Don't give your kids administrative privileges. They'll pester you from time to time, though, to enter your password so that they can do something that requires these privileges, such as installing downloaded software. Trust me: You want to know about these events. Ask questions about how the software will be used, and ask to visit the website from which it came. Don't be afraid to veto the installation.

5. Click the Create User button.

When you're done, you see the Users & Groups system preferences pane again, this time with the new account highlighted (see Figure 17-3).

Figure 17-3:
Sarah Jean's account is ready for parental controls.

[Figure shows Users & Groups preferences pane with Current User: Arnold Reinhold (Admin); Other Users: Screen Shot (Admin), Sarah Jean (Managed), Guest User (Sharing only). Reset Password button, Full name: Sarah Jean, Apple ID: Set... Allow user to reset password using Apple ID, Allow user to administer this computer, Enable parental controls checked with Open Parental Controls... button. Login Options. Click the lock to prevent further changes.]

6. Select the account you just created, if it's not already selected.

7. Check the Enable Parental Controls check box.

8. Click the Open Parental Controls button.

The Parental Controls System pane appears, as shown in Figure 17-4. You see tabs for several panes:

- Apps
- Web
- People
- Time Limits
- Other

Each pane has settings that let you sculpt your child's computer and Internet use.

9. Using the information in the sections that follow, set up the controls for your child's account.

By logging on as the administrator under your own account, you can return to the Parental Controls settings to adjust them, if necessary. Just choose ⌘⇨System Preferences.

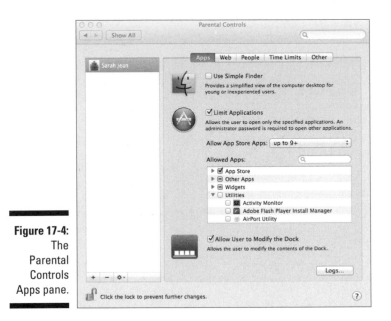

Figure 17-4:
The
Parental
Controls
Apps pane.

The Apps pane

The first item in the Parental Controls Apps pane (refer to Figure 17-4) lets you require Simple Finder for this account. Simple Finder replaces the usual OS X Desktop with a screen that contains big, square buttons. Each button launches an application from the list of those you permit. Many applications provide reduced menus when Simple Finder is in use. Simple Finder removes much of the complexity of the OS X interface and makes the computer more of an appliance.

Below that check box is an area where you can limit the applications this user can launch to only those that you specify. Simply deselect those you don't want to allow access to. At the bottom of the pane is a check box that lets you give this user the ability to modify the Dock. Some young kids mess with the Dock and then pester you to find the stuff they dragged off it (just to watch it go poof). Deselect this check box if this behavior becomes a problem.

The Web pane

The Web pane, depicted in Figure 17-5, offers several options that limit what Internet content your kids can see. The mutually exclusive options offered are:

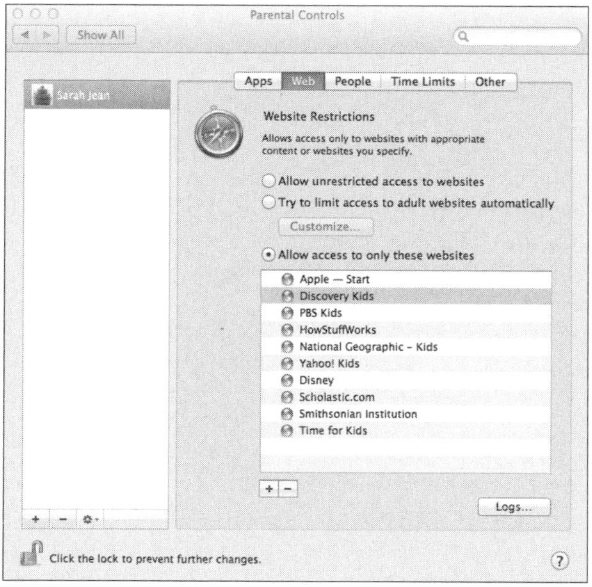

Figure 17-5:
The
Parental
Controls
Web pane.

> ✔ **Allow Unrestricted Access to Websites:** Select this radio button only for older kids. You can still check the logs to see where they're going.
>
> ✔ **Try to Limit Access to Adult Websites Automatically:** This option uses filters that attempt to determine what is and isn't kid-appropriate. The filters aren't foolproof, occasionally letting bad stuff in and at the same time limiting access to sites that are harmless. Also, filters often block sites that provide sound information on health, sex, and what's happening to kids' bodies as they mature.
>
> If you select this radio button, the Customize button becomes enabled. Click it, and you see a pane with two text areas. In the top one, you specify sites that are always allowed — perhaps a site with health information for kids that you've already reviewed. The bottom one lists sites that are never allowed — a trickier proposition, because so many exist.
>
> ✔ **Allow Access to Only These Websites:** This option may be the sanest one for the younger set. Apple starts you off with a list of recommended sites for kids. You can surf sites first and add ones that you deem appropriate. You can even add Safari bookmarks and folders to this list.

The Logs button at the bottom of this pane lets you specify information you want to collect about your child's computer use, such as websites visited, websites blocked, applications used, and iChat activity.

The People pane

As I mention in Chapter 8, your Mac is an excellent communication tool. Your kids will figure out that much faster than you do. The People pane, shown in Figure 17-6, lets you decide to whom they can talk to by way of e-mail or instant messaging (IM). Note that the controls in this pane apply only to Apple Mail and iChat. If your kids can download another mail or IM program, such as AIM or Skype, all bets are off. Some mail programs, such as Yahoo! Mail and Gmail, require only a web browser. So if you want your whitelist restrictions enforced, you must limit the programs your children can download and also block access to e-mail sites.

Figure 17-6:
The
Parental
Controls
People
pane.

This pane also lets you specify an e-mail address — yours, presumably — where notifications are sent when your kid attempts to exchange mail with someone who isn't on the whitelist. Click the Logs button to select which of your kid's activities you wish to track and over what time period (for example, the last week).

OS X keeps track of what your kids are up to online. You can see the logs by periodically visiting the People pane.

You can choose to see logged activity for websites your child visited, websites he attempted to visit but to which access was blocked, applications he used, and iChat conversations he engaged in.

The Time Limits pane

I love this feature. Other programs for limiting kids' use are often too complex for mere parents to understand, much less set up and explain to their kids. This one is easy. The Time Limits pane (see Figure 17-7) gives you two types of control: limiting the amount of time a child can use the computer each day and blocking any use after bedtime. You find two sets of controls for each limit: one for weekdays and the other for weekends. It's simple, and it works.

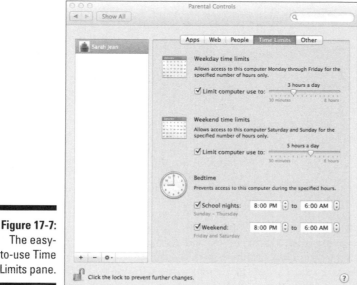

Figure 17-7:
The easy-to-use Time Limits pane.

The Other pane

The Other pane, shown in Figure 17-8, gives you several more options to restrict what your kids can do on the Mac:

- ✔ **Hide Profanity in Dictionary:** This option limits access to inappropriate content in dictionaries, thesauruses and Wikipedia. At some stage in your child's development, however, it may be better for her to find out what words mean from a dictionary than on the street.

- ✔ **Limit Printer Administration:** This option may be a good idea for very young kids, but if you don't select it, kids who are a little older may learn enough to help you with *your* printer problems.

- ✔ **Limit CD and DVD Burning:** Keep this box checked until you set clear guidelines on what your kids can and can't share with friends.

- ✔ **Disable Changing the Password:** Knowing your kid's password makes it easier to check what's on his computer.

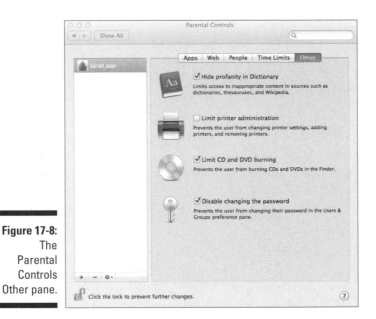

Setting limits

Having all these tools at your disposal is great, but setting limits can be hard. It's always easier to start with more restricted access and then add time and privileges as the child matures and demonstrates responsibility. For very young children, not having computer access may be the easiest starting point.

Discuss reasonable computer limits with other parents in your circle. A group consensus can be easier to enforce. Also, pay attention to your own computer use. Kids learn by example.

Keeping kids safe online

Incidents in which kids get hurt and that have any connection to the Internet always get great play in the press. Incidents in which kids get hurt on the street or at the playground are less newsworthy. Still, your kids need to develop online smarts about online conduct. Avoid heavy-handed lectures and threats of draconian punishment, though. You want your child to feel safe coming to you if she encounters anything that feels creepy.

Here are basic guidelines that you should review periodically with your kids:

- ✓ **Keep your personal information private.** Consider your last name, address, and phone number to be private information that's not to be shared with people you meet online. Be careful if the online person asks a lot of questions about you, such as where you go to school or what your parents do for a living.

- ✓ **Protect your password by keeping it to yourself.** No one should ever need it.

- ✓ **Be aware that people often aren't who they say they are.** Sometimes, people on the Internet pretend to be quite different from who they truly are. A child may pretend to be an adult, or an adult may pretend to be a kid. Someone may pretend to be a teacher or doctor or police officer when they aren't. A boy can even pretend to be a girl, or vice versa.

- ✓ **Ask your parents or guardian before meeting someone in person.** Never agree to see someone in person whom you first met online without asking your parents first.

- ✓ **Remember that people can find out a lot about your family on the Internet.** If someone you don't know says that he's a friend of your family and asks you to go with him, don't go just because he seems to know a lot about you and your parents.

- ✓ **Let your parents or a trusted adult be your confidant.** If someone is making you feel uncomfortable or scaring you, tell your parents. Especially be sure to tell your parents if the person asks you not to. Don't close the chat window or turn off the computer.

Accessing social-networking sites

Social-networking websites, such as Facebook.com and Twitter.com, have integrated themselves into the social lives of teenagers and may older people. Facebook, originally aimed at high school and college students, has almost 700 million active users. (It had 16 million when I wrote the first edition of this book and 200 million by the second edition.) Facebook encourages its members to build profiles with personal information, including descriptions and photographs of recent activities. Members designate other members as "friends" who then gain additional access to their page. Facebook has privacy options that members can select which limit information nonfriends can see and what will be revealed about them in a search. Members use the site to send messages to other users.

Facebook requires members to be at least 13 years old and sets privacy restrictions on minors, but kids and adults can always lie about their age.

If I give my kids a Mac, won't they be unprepared for a Windows world?

I've heard this objection more than once. For now, the working world is dominated by Windows. Many colleges require entering students to have a Windows laptop — though others prefer Macs. One answer, of course, is that Macs can run Windows (see Chapter 16). So if your child takes his MacBook to school, he can use whatever software is required. But you have a better response. For years, Microsoft has followed Apple's lead in introducing new interfaces and features. Several reviewers have remarked on the similarities between Windows 7 and OS X. So giving your kids a Mac may be the *best* way to prepare them for the Windows of the future.

Young people start using these social-networking sites at about the same time they stop listening to what their parents say. Still, it's worth having a conversation with your teen about short-term and long-term privacy concerns. Remind your kids that potential employers and colleges also look at candidate profiles on these sites, and talk to them about the dangers of meeting in person people whom they know only online. At some point, they won't bring you along, but you can still implore them to at least bring along a friend for the first meeting.

Also see Chapter 14 for more information on whether parents should "friend" their kids.

Downloading music and video

Another aspect of kid culture on the Internet — downloading music without paying for it — continues to generate controversy. The recording industry blames the practice for a slowdown in sales. Other people question this position, pointing to the high prices of CDs and a lack of compelling new music as the cause.

The Recording Industry Association of America (RIAA) and the Motion Picture Association of America have managed to shut down free file-sharing sites such as Napster and Grokster early, through legal action. But other peer-to-peer systems such as BitTorrent.com, which have no central indexing service — and which are used for other purposes — have proved to be more difficult to stop. So the RIAA has started taking legal action against individual downloaders and their parents. Although some people have fought these suits, most are forced to accept expensive settlement terms.

Whatever you think of the RIAA and MPAA's tactics and its justification, much can be said for staying out of its gun sights. Most people agree that performers deserve to be compensated for their work. Giving your kid an iPod or iPhone and a computer without giving him the means to pay for songs and videos is asking for trouble. You might give him a monthly allowance at the iTunes Store, perhaps based on chores or schoolwork. Go to the iTunes Store and click the iTunes Gifts link in the Quick Links section.

Finding software for kids

Kids have lots to do with just the iLife suite supplied with all Macs. You can buy or download many other titles for free, but adult supervision is required whenever software is downloaded from the Internet. The Mac Apps Store ranks applications by suitable age range, and you can limit download age levels for App Store purchases via settings in the Parental Controls Apps pane, described earlier in this chapter. Many major websites have special sections for kids. Also, a Google search for *kid-safe websites* turns up several guides to this type of site. But no substitute exists for checking out new sites yourself before letting your kids visit.

Apples for Seniors

The extraterrestrials who monitor our television signals must be certain that no one over 40 buys Apple products, because no one older ever shows up in its TV commercials. The truth is that people over 40 are *more* likely to buy Macs. One reason may be that older consumers seek quality over price. They remember how difficult it was to use computers, and they know who made it easy.

A still-older generation, composed of the parents of the 40s and 50s set, in many cases has never used computers. Personal computers offer many ways to improve the lives of these seniors, and Apple products such as Macs and iPads are ideal choices for them. Although some seniors start riding motorcycles and take up scuba diving, most have a harder time picking up new skills.

And the easy to use Screen Sharing feature in iChat makes it much easier to provide support when questions do arise.

Exploring the Mac benefits for seniors

Seniors can benefit by using a Mac or iPad in these areas:

   ✓ **E-mail and instant messaging:** These features are great ways to stay in touch with friends and family members, particularly grandchildren who are away at school.

- **FaceTime and iChat:** Video calling can enable seniors to be part of family events, even if they can no longer travel easily.

- **Voice over IP (VoIP) services:** These calls can help keep phone bills down, especially for relatives in the "old country."

- **Social networking:** Sites such as Facebook aren't just for college students anymore. Seniors are finding them to be helpful places to connect with old friends and make new ones by posting photos of grandchildren, vacation trips, and other mementos.

- **Health-maintenance and medical-condition sites:** Online support groups exist for almost every medical condition imaginable.

- **Internet shopping:** Seniors who have limited mobility can be empowered by shopping on their own.

- **Disability sites:** Apple's focus on clean user interfaces can make it easier for seniors with disabilities to use. I talk more about Macs and people with disabilities in the next section of this chapter.

Simple Finder, which I mention earlier in this chapter as a way to make Macs easier for young children to operate, can perform the same function for seniors who may be unfamiliar with computers. To give your elder family member a complete guide to using a Mac and its software, written with the needs of a computing beginner in mind, check out *Macs For Seniors For Dummies,* by Mark L. Chambers. For more on the iPad, see *iPad For Seniors For Dummies,* 2nd Edition, by Nancy C. Muir.

Determining which model to buy

If you're buying a computer for your parents, consider that you may end up being their main source of technical support. Buying them a device that's easier to set up, easier to show them how to use, and less likely to require help with problems such as viruses and malware will save you time and money in the long run.

More important, giving your folks a computer that's easy to use and less trouble-prone makes them more likely to use it and derive benefit from it.

For seniors who travel regularly, a basic MacBook is an inexpensive, do-everything companion. By seeking hotel accommodations that include Wi-Fi Internet access, seniors can stay in touch anywhere in the world. Using their digital camera and iSight, iPhoto, and iWeb, they can share their travel experiences with family members and friends almost as these events happen.

A good alternative is the Wi-Fi equipped iPad 2 or later. It's even lighter and has two built-in cameras for using FaceTime and seeing the surroundings. The ultrasimple iPad is ideal for seniors who have never used a computer and have limited interest in picking up new skills. For seniors who have some computer experience or who are more ambitious, the Mac offers more possibilities. A useful way to preserve family history, for example, is to digitize old family photos by using a scanner or commercial service and then asking your parents to annotate them in iPhoto. If typing is a problem, you can put the photos in a slide show and have your parents record their comments in GarageBand as they step through the photos.

For those who mostly stay at home, the iMac is hard to beat. It's a single unit, so no wires will become accidentally disconnected, resulting in panicked service calls to you. The low-end model has everything seniors need.

If seniors enjoy sharing photos of their grandkids, an iPhone or iPod touch is another useful gift, allowing them to always carry a whole library of photos with them. With Apple's iCloud service, photos and other files are easily shared among Macs, iPads, iPhones, and iPod touches.

Macs for Specific Needs

OS X provides an array of accessibility features that enable people to use the Mac in ways that are different from — or more comfortable than — the standard setup of reading onscreen at the default sizes and using the keyboard and mouse to give computer commands. You control most of these features from the Universal Access pane in System Preferences.

The lone exception is VoiceOver, the Apple screen reader, which has its own setup utility in the Utilities folder. But that utility can also be easily accessed from the Universal Access Seeing pane, shown in Figure 17-9.

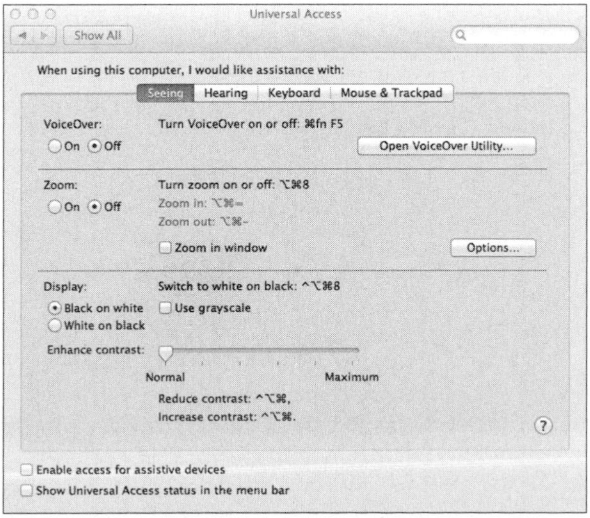

Figure 17-9:
The Universal Access Seeing pane.

The following sections introduce the available options and describe how they work.

Setting up the screen when you have limited vision

When you click the Universal Access icon, you see the Seeing pane (refer to Figure 17-9), where you can control features that aid people with vision difficulties.

Here's a quick introduction to the available features:

- **VoiceOver:** This pane turns VoiceOver on or off and can send you to the VoiceOver setup utility. I explain VoiceOver in more detail in the next section.

- **Zoom:** When you enable the handy Zoom feature, you can magnify the screen by pressing ⌘+Option+=. Pressing ⌘+Option+– (⌘+Option+hyphen) reverses the magnification. There's also a check box that constrains the zooming to the active window.

- **Display:** In this section, you can change the screen from black on white to white on black, if that helps. Move the slider to adjust the contrast, if you like. This option also inverts colors, so also check the Use Grayscale box to make images less garish.

- **Enable Access for Assistive Devices:** Selecting this check box enables your Mac to work with a variety of assistive technologies and software packages designed to help users with special computer-use needs. For more information, see www.apple.com/accessibility/.

Macs vs. iPads for special needs

Which device — an iPad or a Mac — is most appropriate for a person with special needs depends on what those needs are. An iMac's big screen is ideal for someone with limited vision who can read very large print. A MacBook Pro's multiple USB ports allow many assistive-technology devices to be connected. The simplicity of the iPad is compelling for many others. Some people do better with a keyboard than a touchscreen, whereas the reverse is true for others. A Mac's grater processing power may do a better job with voice-to-text programs like Dragon Dictate. Talk with an occupational therapist or other assistive-technology professional as well as other users and caregivers with similar needs before deciding.

Listening rather than reading

The Apple VoiceOver screen reader, located in the Utility folder, is designed to make using a Mac easier by speaking the contents of the screen. Although that idea may seem to be a simple and obvious one, for someone who's trying to use a computer this way, a poorly designed screen reader is almost useless. A user wants the screen reader to speak the text of interest at the moment and as little else as possible. The user also wants to be able to speed the reading as much as possible without losing intelligibility. Otherwise, work becomes painfully slow.

Therefore, it isn't surprising that VoiceOver comes with a plethora of customizable options. It offers several voices, including Alex, a voice that's engineered to work well when its speed is increased.

You find ten options in the sidebar, each with many more options:

- ✔ **General** lets you control portable preferences.

- ✔ **Verbosity** (see Figure 17-10) controls how much VoiceOver says in various situations, such as when it encounters a misspelled word. A user may want a different behavior when she's reading a memo she received versus when she's proofreading her own writing.

- ✔ **Speech** lets you choose among some two dozen virtual speakers and adjust their settings. Most of these speakers are more fun than productive. Voices with real names, such as Alex or Kathy, tend to be more suited for serious use than those with nicknames, such as Bubbles. (You can find exceptions, though. Princess isn't bad, but Albert is.) The Pronunciation tab lets you customize how special characters, initialisms, abbreviations, and other elements are spoken.

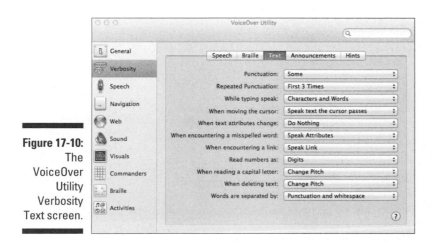

Figure 17-10: The VoiceOver Utility Verbosity Text screen.

- **Navigation** determines what VoiceOver does as you move around the screen and change focus.

- **Web** controls how you hear the content of web pages — from beginning to end (DOM order) or with common elements grouped for faster scanning.

- **Sound** controls sound output.

- **Visuals** controls how VoiceOver elements, such as its cursor, are shown onscreen.

- **Commanders** lets you assign special functions to the numeric-keypad keys, as well as set keyboard and navigation shortcuts.

- **Braille** has settings for Braille input and output for people with visual disabilities.

- **Activities** lets you customize VoiceOver for specific tasks. The settings you want when working in a word processor, for example, may be different from those you'd use while surfing the web.

Adjusting settings in the Hearing pane

Compared with the Seeing pane, the Hearing pane is pretty simple. A personal computer is controlled primarily by visual cues, anyway. In this pane, you can tell OS X to flash the screen when it issues an alert — a handy feature for those of us with full hearing. You also find a button that opens the Sound System Preferences pane, where you can combine both audio channels into one and adjust the volume of your Mac's audio. Generally, you can also do that by using your keyboard. On newer Apple keyboards, F12 makes the sound louder, F11 makes it softer, and F10 turns it off and on. Also F5 turns VoiceOver on and off.

Changing how the keyboard works

The Keyboard pane, shown in Figure 17-11, offers settings that can make using a keyboard easier:

- If you have difficulty completing complex key presses (such as the ⌘+Option+= combination for Zoom, mentioned earlier in this chapter), try turning on Sticky Keys. The Sticky Keys option, which is controlled from this pane, lets you press the keys one at a time to effect the combination you want. For the Zoom example, you'd first press ⌘, and then Option, and then the equal sign (=). You can also control what feedback OS X gives you when you do this.

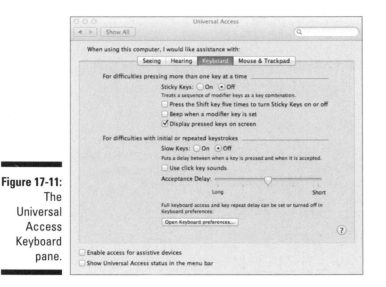

✔ Another problem that some people have is unsteady hands; they may accidentally press a needed key more than once. Another option in this pane, Slow Keys, lets you set a delay between key presses to reduce this problem.

✔ Note that you can find additional settings related to the keyboard in the Keyboard pane of System Preferences.

Speaking of keyboards, several specialized keyboards are available to assist with various problems, ranging from repetitive stress injuries to inability to use one hand. As long as a specialized keyboard uses a USB interface, the keyboard should work on a Mac.

Mousing the way you like

Some people have a hard time using a computer mouse or trackpad. If the default mouse or trackpad setup doesn't work well for you or someone in your household, give the following options in the Universal Access Mouse & Trackpad pane, a try:

✔ **Turn on Mouse Keys:** For people who have trouble using a mouse, Apple provides an alternative: moving the cursor around the screen by using the numeric keypad. After Mouse Keys is turned on, pressing any digit other than 5 or 0 moves the cursor a short distance in the direction of that key (relative to 5). The 5 key acts like a mouse click. The 0 key acts like press and hold — say, if you want to drag a file to a folder. When you have the file where you want to drop it, press 5 to release the hold.

Mouse Keys work best with a keyboard that has a separate numeric keypad. If you have a laptop or standard-size keyboard and want to make extensive use of this feature, consider adding the Apple Keyboard with Numeric Keypad or an external USB numeric keypad.

Mouse Keys is a feature worth knowing about if your mouse or touchpad is ever unusable and you're in a rush to finish something.

✔ **Increase the mouse cursor's size:** Another feature that's located in the Universal Access Mouse & Trackpad pane and that's valuable for all users lets you make the mouse cursor arrow bigger. Particularly when your monitor has high-resolution display settings, you can easily lose that sucker in the Desktop clutter.

If mice don't work for you, options other than Mouse Keys are available for Macs:

✔ **Trackballs:** Have a smooth, round ball on top that you roll in various directions to control the cursor.

✔ **Touchpads:** Allow you to control the cursor by sliding your finger on a sensitive surface. Apple laptops have touchpads built in, the top of the Magic Mouse also functions as a touchpad, and you can buy Apple's Magic Trackpad to use with your desktop setup. (See Chapter 2.)

✔ **Graphics tablets:** Have a flat surface with a position-sensing pen. If you use one, you can take advantage of Apple Ink technology, which can turn handwriting into text that you can use in any application.

Again, you should buy one of these devices with a USB interface. More than one pointing device can be attached and active at the same time. Even if you like using a mouse, having an alternative way to enter text can reduce problems with repetitive stress.

If you use your mouse a lot and feel pain from repetitive stress, one suggestion that I've found useful is to move the mouse and mouse pad to the other side of the keyboard so that you use it with your nondominant hand — the left hand, in my case. It takes a little getting used to, but if you're starting to feel fatigued in your dominant hand, it's worth a try.

Chapter 18

Switching Your Business to Macs

. . . .

. . . .

Microsoft owns the enterprise desktop. Owns it. Most of Apple's growing market share comes from home and educational users. Many large companies still have strict Windows-only policies. Lots of business software is available only for Windows. So why even think about using Macs? Why did we kill a bunch of trees to bring you a chapter pushing Macs for businesses?

In this chapter, you find out how Macs can produce a good return on investment for a business, as well as services and products that help small and midsize businesses stay nimble and competitive, with Macs working for them behind the scenes.

Why Use Macs in Your Business?

The cop-out answer is that Macs now run Windows, too, as I explain in Chapter 16. That does at least answer the concern about Windows-only software you might need for your business. But by itself, that isn't much of a reason. Buying a Mac that may cost a few hundred dollars more than a PC and then paying Microsoft a license fee doesn't make business sense if all you're getting is a pretty computer that runs Windows. Sure, iMacs look spiffy in front offices, and MacBook Airs turn heads at meetings, but that won't convince the bean counters.

Total cost of ownership

One justification for businesses switching to Macs is *total cost of ownership*. Macs may cost a bit more up front, but savings can be achieved down the road. Here's why:

- Training costs are lower because Macs are easier to use.
- Support costs are lower because Macs have fewer software problems, and users can often fix their own problems.
- Macs seem to have a longer service life than Windows machines, so they don't need to be replaced as often.

The total cost of ownership argument has some merit. One organization I work with pays more than $1,000 per year in support expenses for each Windows PC it owns. Cutting that expense down would go right to the bottom line.

But the counterargument usually given is that the organization has already made large investments in a Windows-oriented support organization. Firewalls and antivirus and intrusion detectors are already in place. In the short run, adding Macs may increase the cost because any additional support costs are a new expense. Who has time to worry about the long run?

Increased productivity

You can easily count the initial purchase price of computers you buy. Support costs are more difficult to calculate, but a well-run organization has a handle on those as well. The impact of your choice of computer platform on individual worker productivity is much harder to measure. Most organizations don't have expense-tracking codes for "I'm purging viruses," "The network is down," "I can't get the printer to work," or "I'm waiting for tech support to call back." Pesky problems like that don't just eat up time; they also sap energy, enthusiasm, and morale.

You get what you pay for

To succeed in the intense competition of a global economy, everything a business does has to stand out from the crowd. Mediocre tools ultimately lead to mediocre work. Your salesperson's PowerPoint presentation will look like every other salesperson's PowerPoint presentation. The huckster with a Mac and a Keynote show will stand out.

Although it's hard to gauge productivity, it's not so hard to measure the effect of improvements. Suppose that working with a Mac increases productivity just 5 percent. (I think it's more.) Sum up the annual pay of each worker who uses a computer. Add fringe benefits and direct overhead — stuff like the cost of office space and administrative support. Now multiply that number by 0.05. That's how much using Windows costs you each year.

Tighter integration with iDevices

Our electronic lives are migrating from our desks to our laps and now to our pockets and purses. Some of us feel naked without a live Internet connection at hand. The Apple iPhone, iPad, and iPod touch — which I call iDevices — have created an integrated mobile computing future where we have with us all the tools that we rely on, wherever we go. Businesses have taken note. The iPhone is challenging the BlackBerry, even in the enterprise. The iPad is gaining acceptance in business even faster than the iPhone. The iPad's even replacing satchels filled with paper maps and handbooks in commercial aircraft cockpits; it's lighter, easer to read, and automatically kept up to date.

Technology revolutions create business opportunity. Your customers are now online when they're on the go. Ask yourself what that means for your business. Will it enable your customers to find you more easily? Will knowing your store is nearby encourage them to drop in? If you offer free Wi-Fi on your premises, will customers linger longer and buy more?

Apple is leading the way in mobile computing and is working hard to make Macs part of that by bringing iDevice features to the Mac and by using its iCloud service to link Macs and iDevices. And Apple's development tools for iDevices, which I describe in the next chapter, run only on the Mac. Working with Mac and Apple gives you a head start over competitors that are still on Windows.

The only constant in business is change

The best reason to switch to Macs is because computer technology is changing, and changing the world along with it. Apple, not Microsoft, is leading the charge. Microsoft is too busy making money off the way things were. Stay hitched to Microsoft, and you'll always be safely in the middle of the pack — except that the middle of the pack is where businesses wither and die.

What are some of these changes? Here's a partial list:

- **Electronic commerce:** The Internet now drives economic growth and levels the playing field between large and small companies. People who buy online shop online, and word of web drives sales. First impressions of early customers are aggregated by Twitter tweets and Facebook likes and then spread worldwide. Lapses in quality are magnified. You have to get it right the first time.

✔ **Web 2.0:** The World Wide Web is now a two-way medium. Consumers are spending more of their time viewing content produced by other consumers. A clever YouTube spoof can undo a multimillion-dollar marketing campaign. Speed is of the essence. It can't wait 'til the Monday morning staff meeting.

✔ **Globalization:** Your next competitor could emerge from a country you never heard of. So could your next technology supplier. And so could your next market.

✔ **Open-source business software:** The open-source model has been quite successful in the development of BSD Unix, Linux, and Gnu, and groups trying to create nonproprietary software systems are getting into the game. These groups are using open standards and open-source code to create software that meets basic business needs. The wide adoption of XML as a standard for data interchange has spawned many efforts to create nonproprietary data exchange formats for specific business needs, such as `hr-xml.org` in human resources. As these efforts mature, they provide viable, platform-independent alternatives to expensive software packages. Mac OS X and Linux share a Unix heritage and generally work well together. A great deal of Linux software has been ported to Macs, so tools can be used on both platforms.

✔ **Software as a Service (SaaS):** The other new approach to business software is for vendors to host the software on their own servers and sell the services over the Internet on a subscription basis — typically, a per-user, per-month fee. This solution reduces the need for in-house hardware and support personnel, and allows employees to access the service from remote locations. SaaS systems are accessed by way of standard web browsers, reducing the importance of being on one operating system versus another.

✔ **Virtualization:** The relationship between computers and operating systems is no longer monogamous. One operating system can span several processor cores, and one processor can support several operating systems at one time. The impetus for standardizing on the operating system you've always used makes less business sense. Pick the best tool for the job. You can find an introduction to virtualization in Chapter 16.

✔ **Computer crime:** In the good old days, malware (such as computer viruses and worms) was created by hobbyist hackers who were interested in the intellectual challenge. Now such activities are a big, if illicit, business and a significant distraction for legitimate businesses. Direct costs occur in terms of data theft and denial of service and in the indirect costs of cleanup, damage remediation, and reporting. Finally, there's the hard-to-measure loss of customer trust and its impact on sales. The malware-free Apple track record has saved its users expense and can instill confidence in customers. OS X Lion features enhanced security, and the App Store provides safe delivery of software.

✔ **Internet content delivery:** Widespread high-speed Internet access has led to the Internet's becoming a primary means of information content delivery. Traditional media are feeling the heat. College students with the right concept, like the students who created YouTube and Facebook, can become billionaires almost overnight.

✔ **Lean and mean organizations:** To stay competitive in a tight economy, businesses are streamlining, outsourcing grunt work, flattening organization charts, and increasing the span of control and the number of workers per manager. The emphasis is on lean-and-mean organizations in which each employee has the ability to recognize opportunities and to respond to challenges, and is held accountable for performance. These workers need the best tools available.

If you're feeling some of these changes in your business, stop thinking of computers as a cost center, like lights and lavatories. Realize that when computers are used properly, they're competitive weapons. Realize that many of the most creative employees prefer Macs, and respecting their choice attracts them to and retains them for your firm. Realize that the quality of the tools you give your workers affects your products and services in ways that are hard to measure but are inescapable.

Macs in Small Businesses

The case for Macs is easiest to make in a small business. You're unlikely to have a staff of information technology professionals wedded to doing things "the Microsoft way." To run a small business and grow it into a bigger business, you must have a can-do attitude. Two of the most important software tools for small businesses, Microsoft Office and QuickBooks (from Quicken.com), already run on Macs, although the Mac version of QuickBooks has fewer features than the Windows version. FileMaker Pro, from Apple, is highly regarded as a database that can be easily customized by nonprogrammers. It's a cross-platform solution between Mac and Windows, with shared access using your in-house network. You can also find many specialized programs for Macs, such as AutoCAD computer-aided design and cash-register operation.

SaaS applications such as ConstantContact.com and Salesforce.com are a natural fit for small businesses because they allow you to have world-class applications at affordable prices without the need to hire IT support staff. (For details on SaaS, refer to "The only constant in business is change," earlier in this chapter.) Also, choosing Macs makes a statement to prospective staff and customers that you are forward thinking and open to new ideas.

Macs in Midsize Businesses

Midsize businesses need an edge to survive against increasingly large corporate giants. Small businesses find niches too insignificant to attract the giants' attention. But when a midsize firm finds a good market, a large company is soon sniffing around. The midsize firm had better be more nimble and creative and in closer touch with its customers' needs.

The World Wide Web makes reaching customers easier for midsize firms. Internet advertising, such as Google AdWords, targets customers who have already shown interest in your product categories. The networks of self-published writers known as the blogosphere can make or break your product. Having selected employees write blogs about your industry can be more effective than advertising in traditional ways, such as in trade magazines. OS X has tools that make blogging easy. Video iChat and Facebook coordinate responses from different groups in different locales quickly, simply, and without expensive travel.

Macs for the Enterprise

Steve Jobs thinks that the PC era is coming to an end, and many analysts agree with him. He sees a future of mobile devices, such as the iPhone and iPad, always connected to the Internet, and storing data in and obtaining services from the great computing cloud. This vision (if it's true, and that's only a matter of degree) could affect every business on the planet. Can any large organization afford to wait on the sidelines?

I'm under no illusion that this book will persuade any large company to toss all its Windows boxes and switch everyone to Macs. I'd be happy if the book lowered the barriers to using Macs in a few organizations. The IT staff in some companies still promulgate strict Windows-only rules. The common exception is the graphics department, which produces print and other media for outside consumption. My only suggestion is to give Macs a try in other places. Equipping a small department or field office with Macs is a low-risk experiment. The computers can be converted to Windows, if need be. What do you have to lose?

For more on Mac applications in businesses, visit the Apple business site, www.apple.com/business/mac. Also try www.macenterprise.org, a community of IT professionals sharing information and solutions to support Macs in an enterprise.

Chapter 19

Desktop to Dashcode: OS X Advanced

. . . .

In This Chapter

▶ Taking a look at the file-system structure

▶ Introducing the Unix inside

▶ Demystifying text files

▶ Developing software on a Mac

. . . .

*A*pple OS X is a complex piece of software. It draws on rich heritages, including earlier versions of Mac OS; Unix, particularly the Berkeley System Distribution (BSD); NeXTSTEP, developed by a company Steve Jobs founded when he left Apple; and the Mach kernel project at Carnegie Mellon University. In this chapter, I dive into some of the OS X inner workings. Feel free to skip this chapter if you aren't interested in these details.

Peeking at the File System Structure

One of the most visible influences of Unix on OS X is the way the file system is organized. A top-level directory or folder contains these folders:

▶ **Applications:** Holds the entire iLife suite and applications that come with OS X. Applications you install, such as Microsoft Office, normally go here. It also contains the Utilities folder, where you find programs such as Disk Utility.

▶ **Library:** Contains other "under the hood" files that are needed systemwide. A Library folder also exists within the System folder, and one Library folder is available for each user, albeit hidden by default.

✔ **System:** Contains OS X itself. Nothing you would want to work with directly dwells in this folder.

✔ **Users:** Holds each user's home folder and the Shared folder. You can see other users' folders, but you can't look at files within them without permission unless you're an administrative user. Everyone with an account on your Mac can see the Shared folder.

You can add files and folders at the top level, but doing that generally isn't a good idea unless you have a good reason. Normally, you add files only to the Applications folder (as part of installing software), to the top level Library folder (for example fonts, sounds, and AppleScripts that you want all users to be able to access), or to your user folder.

Exploring your user folder

Each user folder also has a standard set of subfolders. Some longtime computer users become quite irritated by all this structure when they first encounter it, but Windows has a similar structure. Swallow hard; it's worth getting used to.

The standard folders in a new user directory are described in this list:

✔ **Desktop:** This folder holds all files on your Desktop. Having them in a folder like any other is handy. If your Desktop gets too cluttered for you to find things easily, you can see its contents in a Finder window instead, and use the folder-sorting tools to arrange the files and folders on the Desktop by name, date, size, and other criteria. The Desktop folder is also handy when you're making manual backups because you can simply copy all Desktop content to an external hard drive, thumb drive, or optical disc.

✔ **Documents:** Apple intends for you to put all your documents in this folder. You don't have to, of course, but doing it the Apple way prevents hassles. You can, and should, add subfolders to whatever depth you want within the Documents folder. This is the place to go wild and make yourself at home.

If you have all your files neatly organized on your old computer, copy them all to the Documents folder. Then move pictures, movies, and music to the appropriate folders listed in the following bullets.

✔ **Library:** Programs store data that's unique for each user, such as preferences and caches. You normally don't add files here yourself, with the possible exception of fonts or some plug-ins. (This folder isn't the place to store your e-books.) OS X Lion hides this folder by default; holding down the Option key when accessing the Finder's Go menu makes the folder visible.

- ✔ **Movies:** Store your iMovie projects here.

- ✔ **Music:** Stash the iTunes Library here.

- ✔ **Pictures:** Store your iPhoto shoebox here.

- ✔ **Public:** In addition to the system-wide Shared folder, each user has this special folder with permissions set so that any user on the Mac can access the folder. Within this folder is a folder named Drop Box, in which other users can place files and folders but can't look inside. Only the user (and a computer administrator, of course) can see what's in the Drop Box folder.

- ✔ **Sites:** This folder contains web page files you created for OS X Web Sharing to publish on the Internet — or on your organization's intranet.

OS X provides an All My Files option at the top of each Finder window's Sidebar. Select this option to browse through every file you created without regard to what folder its in.

Understanding file permission basics

Permissions determine who can do what with a file. Traditionally, you find three levels of permission in a Unix system:

- ✔ **Owner:** Each file in OS X is owned by someone (such as a user with an account) or something (such as the system).

- ✔ **Group:** A file is also assigned to one group. Groups consist of one or more users. A user can belong to more than one group, and groups can include other groups.

- ✔ **Other (sometimes called world or Everyone):** *Other* refers to anyone who has authorized access to the computer.

Also in the Unix tradition, you can do these three things with a file:

- ✔ Read it (r).
- ✔ Write to it (w).
- ✔ Execute it (x).

The execute permission takes a bit of explaining. For program files, including scripts, it means that you can run the program. For directories, it means that you can see which files are inside the directory. It doesn't mean that you can open those files; you just see their names. The letters next to each action are abbreviations that are sometimes shown in directory listings.

With this structure, you have nine possibilities. Each level of ownership can have any combination of read, write, and execute access to a file so long as owner has privileges at least as high as group and group at least as high as world.

This approach to organizing permissions may seem complex, but it isn't complex enough for some situations. A file can be assigned to only one group. What if you want different groups to have different permissions? I hope that your personal life isn't this convoluted, but in large organizations, it easily can be.

A more complex set of permissions in OS X is named Access Control List (ACL). Each file and directory can have an ACL, which is an ordered list of rules. Each rule says that so-and-so can do such-and-such. OS X ships with ACLs turned off, fortunately. The tools you use to administer them are included in OS X Server.

If you right-click a file and choose Get Info from the shortcut menu (or just press ⌘+I), you see the Info window shown in Figure 19-1. It's somewhat analogous to the Properties window in Windows.

Figure 19-1:
The Info
window
for a file. I
clicked the
Sharing &
Permissions
disclosure
triangle
to show
details.

Permission information is toward the bottom. You may have to click the tiny disclosure triangles to view all the details.

Because permissions are so important to the underlying system software, OS X keeps track of what permissions are supposed to be set for system files and applications installed with the Apple installer. The OS X Disk Utility (located in the Utilities folder) has a Repair Permissions option for resetting the permissions back to their pristine values. You should run Repair Permissions every couple of months or as a first step if your system is behaving weirdly.

Commanding Unix

When I say that OS X is built on top of Unix, you might imagine that I mean the way a house is built on top of a foundation: A door or hatch is at the ground level, and if you open it, you walk down a creaky set of stairs to a place that's damp and kind of dark, with pipes and wires going every which way. It's good to know about if you blow a fuse or if the heat isn't working, but it's no place to hang out.

Uh-uh. That's not what I'm talking about. What I mean is more like a city built on top of another city. Tap a magic mirror, and you're transported to an underground metropolis. The people dress funny and speak a different dialect, but the place has lots of interesting places to visit and things to do.

You find a brief introduction to Unix in the sections that follow. You can find more online at www.freebsd.org or pick up a copy of *UNIX For Dummies,* 5th Edition, by John R. Levine and Margaret Levine Young.

The magic mirror is Terminal

The magic application that takes you from the outer world of OS X to the inner world of Unix is appropriately hidden and unpretentious. It's called Terminal, and it's in the Utilities folder inside the Applications folder. Double-click the Terminal icon, and you see a window such as the one shown in Figure 19-2. The window is labeled with your short username and then bash – 80x24.

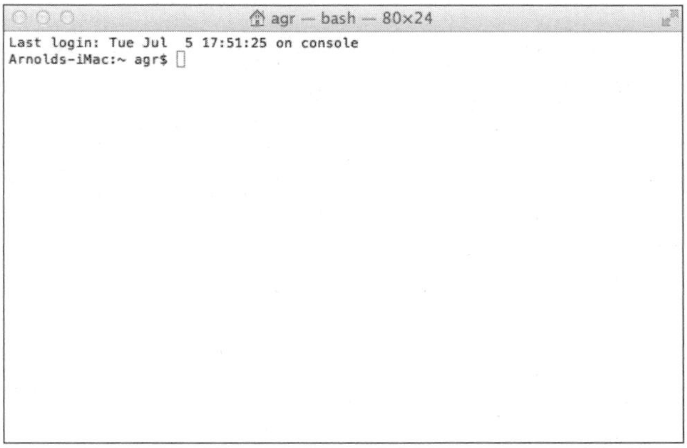

```
○ ○ ○              ⌂ agr — bash — 80×24
Last login: Tue Jul  5 17:51:25 on console
Arnolds-iMac:~ agr$ ▯
```

Figure 19-2:
The
Terminal
window.

Here's a rundown of what you see in the Terminal window:

- ✔ The last number indicates that the window holds 24 lines, each one 80 monospaced characters long.

- ✔ Drag the bottom-right corner of the window, and you can make it bigger or smaller, but the 80-character initial width has a long history: It's the number of characters in an IBM punch card. (Remember "Do not fold, staple, or mutilate?")

- ✔ The word *bash* in the window label isn't requesting an aggressive act. It's the name of the Unix program attending you — something that the Unix world calls a *shell*. It's much like the Windows command interpreter, cmd.exe.

- ✔ The $ character in the Terminal window is the bash prompt. (Windows uses a right-facing arrow > for its prompt.) Type anything at the prompt and press Return, and the shell program — bash by default in OS X — tries to carry out your wishes.

- ✔ bash stands for *Bourne-again shell*. It's an open-source remake by the Gnu project of an earlier shell (sh) written by Stephen Bourne when he was at Bell Labs. sh and other popular Unix shells (such as csh, zsh, ksh, and tcsh) are available as well, in case you grew up with one of them and prefer it.

bash is more powerful than the Windows cmd.exe, but Microsoft has a Windows PowerShell that's somewhat comparable. (My technical editor says, "Yeah, comparable in the way that a Geo compares to a Maserati.")

Bash ain't Windows

You find several differences as well as similarities between the Windows command line and Unix. Many of these differences go back to the early days of DOS and were deliberately introduced to ward off legal problems with AT&T, the developer of Unix:

- ✔ **Pathnames:** A *pathname* specifies where a file is located, starting at the top-level or root directory. Windows separates names with a backslash (\), and Unix, like the Internet, uses an ordinary forward slash (/). Versions of Mac OS 9 and earlier used a colon (:).

- ✔ **Hidden files:** Filenames that start with a period (.) are normally hidden and are often used to store the settings for various programs. Type **ls –a** to see them.

- ✔ **Home directory:** Unix uses the tilde character (~) as an abbreviation for the home directory. You sometimes see this syntax on the Internet as well. One URL for my home page, for example, is `http://theworld.com/~reinhold` (`www.arnoldreinhold.com` redirects you there.)

- ✔ **Switches:** Like Windows commands, Unix commands have switches that follow the command name to modify its action. In Windows, switches are indicated by a forward slash. In Unix, switches are usually indicated by a hyphen (–).

- ✔ **More about commands:** Windows uses `help`. Unix uses `man`, which stands for *manual*. In Unix, type this line:

```
man command-name
```

OS X comes with thousands of `man` pages, mostly inherited from BSD Unix. Unix aficionados love `man` pages because they don't waste verbiage on cute analogies and historical asides, and they tend to be authoritative. Beginners often find them maddeningly terse. Use the `apropos` command to search `man` pages.

Working in the Terminal window

As in Windows, you can use an asterisk (*) as a wildcard in a filename in most commands. Also like Windows, `bash` can complete a partially typed command or filename, if it can figure it out, when you press Tab.

You can copy text from the Terminal window, but you can't cut or insert text. If you can paste text into the Terminal window, it's appended to whatever you've already typed after the prompt.

If you drag an OS X file or folder icon to the Terminal window, the pathname of the file or folder is inserted where you're typing.

Introducing Unix commands

Unix has many commands, but I discuss just a few important ones in this section: some that work with directories, some that work with files, and a few miscellaneous but commonly used commands.

Folders are called *directories* in Unix. Commands that refer to filenames, as most do, assume that you're talking about files in the working directory. When you open the Terminal window, the working directory is set to your home directory, abbreviated as ~. You see the current working directory and your username to the left of its prompt. Table 19-1 lists common directory-related commands.

Table 19-1	Unix Directory Commands
Command	*What You Do with It*
ls	List the names of the files in the working directory. For more complete information, use ls -alF (see Figure 19-3).
cd *directoryname*	Change the working directory to the one you named.
cd ..	Move up one directory level.
cd	Return to your home directory.
pwd	Display the pathname of the current directory.
mkdir *newdirecto-ryname*	Make a new directory.
rmdir *directory-name*	Remove (delete) an empty directory.

As in Windows, you can redirect the output of a command to a text file, so if you want a record of the files in a folder, follow these steps:

1. **Type cd, followed by a space.**

2. **Drag the folder's icon to the Terminal window.**

   Its pathname should appear after the cd command.

3. **Press Return.**

4. **Type** ls > mydirectorylist.txt **and press Return.**

A file named mydirectorylist.txt appears in the folder you chose. You can open the file in TextEdit to see a list of the files in that directory.

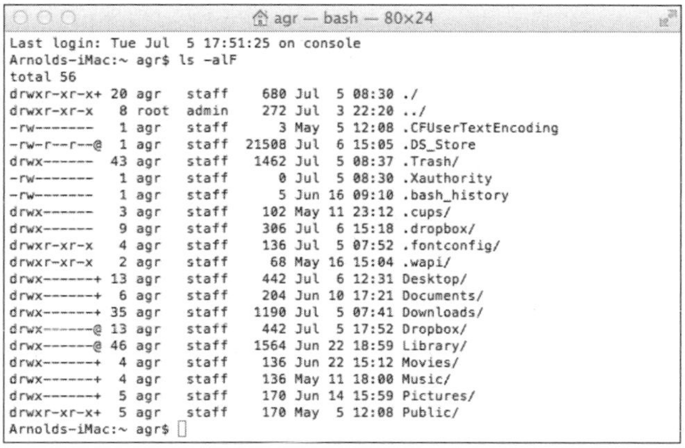

Figure 19-3:
Listing files with the Unix ls –alF command. Characters on the left are file permissions.

```
000                    ☆ agr — bash — 80×24
Last login: Tue Jul  5 17:51:25 on console
Arnolds-iMac:~ agr$ ls -alF
total 56
drwxr-xr-x+ 20 agr    staff     680 Jul  5 08:30 ./
drwxr-xr-x   8 root   admin     272 Jul  3 22:20 ../
-rw-------   1 agr    staff       3 May  5 12:08 .CFUserTextEncoding
-rw-r--r--@  1 agr    staff   21508 Jul  6 15:05 .DS_Store
drwx------  43 agr    staff    1462 Jul  5 08:37 .Trash/
-rw-------   1 agr    staff       0 Jul  5 08:30 .Xauthority
-rw-------   1 agr    staff       5 Jun 16 09:10 .bash_history
drwx------   3 agr    staff     102 May 11 23:12 .cups/
drwx------   9 agr    staff     306 Jul  6 15:18 .dropbox/
drwxr-xr-x   4 agr    staff     136 Jul  5 07:52 .fontconfig/
drwxr-xr-x   2 agr    staff      68 May 16 15:04 .wapi/
drwx------+ 13 agr    staff     442 Jul  6 12:31 Desktop/
drwx------+  6 agr    staff     204 Jun 10 17:21 Documents/
drwx------+ 35 agr    staff    1190 Jul  5 07:41 Downloads/
drwx------@ 13 agr    staff     442 Jul  5 17:52 Dropbox/
drwx------@ 46 agr    staff    1564 Jun 22 18:59 Library/
drwx------+  4 agr    staff     136 Jun 22 15:12 Movies/
drwx------+  4 agr    staff     136 May 11 18:00 Music/
drwx------+  5 agr    staff     170 Jun 14 15:59 Pictures/
drwxr-xr-x+  5 agr    staff     170 May  5 12:08 Public/
Arnolds-iMac:~ agr$ ▯
```

Table 19-2 lists that are commands commonly used for working with files in the Terminal window, and Table 19-3 explains other handy commands that anyone getting started in Terminal will likely want to know.

Table 19-2	Working with Files
Command	*What You Do with It*
cp *filename1 filename2*	Copy a file.
chmod	Change permissions for access to a file. Study the man page before using this one.
diff	Compare two files line by line (assumes text).
more *filename*	Display a text file one page at a time. Press the spacebar to see the next page; press Q to quit. The man command works through more.
mv *filename1 filename2*	Move a file or change its name.
rm *filename*	Remove (delete) a file.

When you're working in Terminal, you don't have a Trash area to which deleted files are moved, pending their ultimate disposal. Delete something, and it's gone. In general, Unix has no Undo function.

Table 19-3	Miscellaneous Commands
Command	*What You Do with It*
Control+C	Terminate most operations.
date	Display the current date and time.
echo	Repeat whatever appears after the command (after expansion).
help	Display a partial list of bash commands.
history	Display the last commands you typed. You can redo a command by typing an exclamation point (!) followed immediately (no space) by the number of that command in the history list. To repeat the last command, type !!. To repeat the last filename, type !*.
pico	Use a simple Unix text editor. Hold down the Control key (^) to give it commands.
ps	Display a list of running processes.
sudo	Carry out commands for which the account you're using lacks authority. You're asked for an administrator's password.

Text files

Plain-text files seem like the simplest, least complicated form of computer data, but Windows PCs, Unix computers, and Macs format these files differently. For the most part, if you use standard word processing applications, you needn't worry about these differences, but if you're mucking around with the innards of OS X or moving text files back and forth between operating systems, it helps to be aware of the issues.

Unix text files terminate lines with an ASCII LF (line-feed) character (decimal value 10). Windows uses the pair of characters CR (carriage return) and LF (decimal values 13 and 10, respectively). Mac OS 9 and earlier used just CR (decimal value 13). Carriage return and line feed go back to the days of mechanical teletype machines, which had a printing element that went back and forth on a carriage across a roll of paper. Moving the paper up one line was a separate operation from returning the carriage to the left edge of the page.

OS X would rather forget about text files altogether. By default, TextEdit can read any of them, but it doesn't save in text format, preferring the RTF format. (You can tell TextEdit to use text format by choosing Format⇨Make Plain Text.) Some third-party Mac text editors use the OS 9 convention, ending lines in CR, though they often give you a choice. The Unix commands in OS X speak Unix, however, and expect LF unless you specify otherwise with a switch.

Developing Software on a Mac

Many years ago, my parents asked what I wanted for my 16th birthday. "A computer," I replied. They asked what that was; few people had heard of them back then. Then they asked what one cost. "Five hundred thousand dollars," I replied. It was a bad joke on my part (the first of many, you may be thinking). The smallest computer IBM made would occupy most of our apartment, and back then, half a million dollars was a lot of money. We all had a good laugh, and I ended up with a shortwave radio receiver.

The reason why I wanted a computer was to run programs I'd write. That's what one did with a computer for the first couple of decades. It was lots of fun. The iMac I'm writing this book on is a million times faster than the computer I lusted after as a 15-year-old. That's not hyperbole; it's probably closer to ten million times faster.

But the iMac is harder to program. Sure, much better programming languages (too many of them) are available, and compilers do their thing in seconds for all except the biggest programs, but everything is so-o-o much more complicated.

Introducing Xcode

Apple hasn't figured out how to make programming a Mac anywhere near as easy as using one. No one has. But Apple is trying its best, and supplies a complete programming environment, called Xcode, for your Mac. Xcode is a free download from developer.apple.com and supports a variety of compiled programming languages: Objective-C, C, C++, Java, and AppleScript. Objective-C is the native language for OS X, but the others can be used as well. Apple also supports scripting languages, including Perl, Python, and Ruby on Rails. Xcode is built on top of many standard Gnu–Unix tools, including the GCC compiler and GDB debugger. All the standard Unix tools are there in their native forms as well.

Xcode also has many Apple-specific tools, such as Interface Builder. The Xcode package includes most Apple developer documentation. You even find a Research Assistant to help you find application program interface (API) details and the other arcane stuff you need to write programs these days.

Dashing to the Dashboard with Dashcode

Apple provides a much simpler environment than Xcode for creating Dashboard widgets. It's *Dashcode,* and it includes templates that let you quickly create an RSS feed, a podcast or photocast viewer, a countdown timer, or a gauge. A blank widget template is also available if you want to be more creative. You can find out more at `http://developer.apple.com/tools/dashcode`.

When you're ready to release your spiffy widget, Dashcode collects all the little bits of stuff that must be present and packages them for distribution as a professional-looking widget. Apple distributes selected widgets in the Mac App Store.

Programming the iPhone and iPad

More than 425,000 applications have been developed for the Apple iPhone, iPad, and iPod touch — the iOS devices. The App Store distributes these applications on a 70–30 basis: The developer keeps 70 percent of the sale price, and Apple keeps 30 percent. Many people have made a nice income from developing iOS device applications; Apple has paid more than $2.5 billion to developers. If you have some programming skills and a novel idea for an app, the following steps help you gather the basics for programming apps:

1. **Make sure that your app doesn't already exist by searching the App Store and Google.**

2. **Register as an Apple developer at `http://developer.apple.com/`.**

   (It's free, but you agree to the Apple terms and conditions, which include a nondisclosure agreement.)

3. **Download the iOS Software Developer's Kit (SDK), available only for OS X.**

   You can test your application on an iPhone or iPad simulator included in the SDK, but to test it on a live phone and release it to the store, you have to pay a fee that covers issuing you a digital signature that you use to sign your code. Apple doesn't want anonymous software on iOS devices.

For help getting started with the actual programming, check out *iPhone Application Development For Dummies,* 3rd Edition, by Neal Goldstein.

Part VI
The Part of Tens

The 5th Wave   By Rich Tennant

"He saw your MacBook and wants to know if he can check out the new Mac OS X features."

In this part . . .

The tense tenor of tens tosses tenacious tendrils, testing our tentative tenets. This tract's top text tackles ten terrific OS X troubleshooting tricks. Text two tenders ten techniques to tame Terra's terrifying trials. Text three portends thy PC's termination, tendering ten tenuous though tenable extensions to the thing's tenure.

Chapter 20

Ten Terrific Troubleshooting Tips

Macs have a deserved reputation for reliability, but they're not perfect. Computer software is extremely complex, and stuff happens. In this chapter, I present suggestions for dealing with problems that can arise and tips for preventing problems in the first place.

Take Care of First Things First

Take two aspirin and call me in the morning. Every field has its basic nostrums. Here are the basic remedies every Mac user should know:

- ✔ **Back it up.** It's the first rule of computing. The Apple Time Machine automates the process if you attach a second hard drive and turn on Time Machine (see Chapter 5). In addition, I recommend making a periodic manual backup of your most important files, such as completed projects, to DVD-R, a flash drive, an online service, or an additional external hard drive.

- ✔ **Reboot.** Choose ⌘⇨Restart. See the section "Reboot a Hung Mac," later in this chapter, for more details.

- ✔ **Avoid finger panic.** It's easy to forget how many fingers you have resting on your trackpad or Magic Mouse. When that happens, it seems like windows are flying about as though they're possessed. Consider turning off some finger gestures you never use anyway by choosing ⌘⇨System Preferences⇨Trackpad (or Mouse).

- **Check the hard drive.** Run Disk Utility in the Utilities folder. Select your hard drive. Click the Repair Permissions button. Then click the Verify Disk button. If Verify Disk reports a problem, you can boot from the RecoveryHD partition that is preinstalled on your Mac hard drive by holding down the Option key when you reboot. Running Disk Utility from that system gives you the option to repair your disk. Do it.

  If you can't find your installation disc, do a safe boot: Shut down your Mac. Press the power button. Right after the startup "boing," hold down Shift. After the safe boot is complete, restart your Mac. Safe booting repairs your file system as it starts up.

- **Fix the preference file.** If an application is acting up, the file where it keeps your preference settings (the .plist file) may be messed up. One way to deal with this problem is to change preference settings and close the application. For Finder problems, also change the System Preferences Appearance settings.

  Another approach is to close the troublesome application, open the Library folder in your home directory by choosing Go⇨Go to Folder and type ~/**Library** in the text box that appears, and then open the Preferences folder. Find the .plist file for the troublesome application and change its name by tacking .old or something similar to the end of the filename. Then restart the application, which now opens showing its default preferences.

- **Zap PRAM.** Every Mac stores basic info it needs in a small, separate memory area known as *parameter RAM,* or *PRAM.* To reset it, hold down the P and R keys while you reboot.

- **Replace the system battery.** If you have a new Mac, you won't run into system-battery problems for years. Its small battery keeps the clock and PRAM working when power is off; it's not the one that powers your laptop. But if you have an older Mac that's behaving weirdly (a common symptom is the wrong date at startup), the small battery on the motherboard that keeps the clock and PRAM working may have run down. These batteries are easy to replace on the Mac Pro, but it requires a service call on other Macs.

  Replacing the battery is also a common solution to problems with wireless devices. If you use a wireless keyboard and mouse, and they don't seem to be working, replace their batteries.

- **Figure out whether it's the hardware.** If your Mac is crashing frequently, it may have a hardware problem. For starters, disconnect all peripherals and see whether you still have problems. If they go away, reconnect devices one at a time to try to isolate the evildoer. If the problems don't go away, run the diagnostic disc that came with your Mac. It typically offers you a fast and more thorough mode. Try fast mode first. Then do the slow test overnight. If the diagnostic program reports an error, write down exactly what it says, with all the error numbers, and take that info along with the sick computer to your service tech, or have it ready when you call AppleCare.

Watch the Spinning Beach Ball

Macs rarely crash, but applications sometimes hang. *Hanging* means that the application is no longer responding to input from the keyboard or mouse or "unexpectedly quits." A common indication is a spinning beach-ball cursor that doesn't go away. The spinning beach ball is normal from time to time when an application is busy. It's the equivalent of the hourglass cursor in Windows. You can tell that a specific application is responsible if the spinning beach ball shows up only when the cursor is over one of that application's windows.

Show a little patience. The application may be waiting on an Internet resource or reorganizing its sock drawer. Go have a cup of coffee. Safari in particular sometimes takes a while. If the beach ball is still spinning when you get back, I recommend handling the problem as follows:

1. **Try pressing ⌘+Tab to cycle to other applications you may have open, and save your work.**

2. **Close these applications, using the Quit command (press ⌘+Q).**

3. **If the Quit command doesn't work, you can try a more drastic measure by following these steps:**

    a. *Choose *🍎*▷Force Quit or press ⌘+Option+Esc.*

    This step opens a small window showing all applications that are active. If one of yours is hung, OS X probably notices and marks it as not responding in the Force Quit window.

    b. *Select the hung application in the window and click the Force Quit button.*

    If the Finder is hung, pressing ⌘+Option+Esc may offer you the option to relaunch it. Otherwise, you must reboot.

Reboot a Hung Mac

If the preceding steps don't work, your Mac may be hung. You can shut it down, but you'll lose any unsaved work. Hold down the power button while you slowly count off 10 seconds (one one-thousand, two one-thousand, three one-thousand, …). That's not to calm you down. A little processor in your Mac called the System Management Controller looks for the extended push and shuts down the main computer.

If that doesn't work, unplug the computer from its power source, and wait 15 seconds. If it's an older laptop with a removable battery, remove the battery and put it back again after 15 seconds. This method won't work with new Mac laptops, however, because they don't have a removable battery. For these Macs, you can reset the System Management Controller by following these steps:

1. **Shut down the laptop by holding down the power button for 10 seconds.**

2. **Make sure that the laptop's power adapter is plugged into the laptop and a working wall outlet or power strip.**

3. **Find the Shift, Control, and Option keys on the left side of your keyboard (the ones on the right side won't work for this).**

4. **At the same time, hold down all three keys with your left hand and press the power button with your right.**

5. **Now release all the keys and buttons, and wait for your Mac to power down.**

6. **Press the power button to restart your laptop.**

   A restart after a forced shutdown may take a little longer than usual because your Mac knows that it wasn't turned off normally and is checking things out.

For more on the System Management Controller and symptoms that suggest restarting it, see Apple Knowledge Base article HT3964 at `http://support.apple.com/kb/ht3964`.

If your Mac keeps hanging while it's booting up, and you've tried everything else, lift it about half an inch and drop it on a hard surface right after you reboot it. The resulting jar is often enough to get a stuck hard drive spinning again. If this tip works, take the hint: Your hard drive is dying. Back up your files *now,* and take your Mac in for service.

Reconnect to the Internet

Your browser whines that you aren't connected to the Internet. Mail complains that it can't find the server. Debugging Internet connectivity problems can be frustrating. Many steps are involved in getting you online, and any of them can be the problem.

Safari offers you a Network Diagnostics button in the dialog that appears when Safari can't connect. Click it. You see a list of the steps needed to connect, with colored lights that turn green if Safari passed a step successfully and red if it didn't.

If the Network Diagnostics feature doesn't help you resolve your problem, the following list offers other testing advice:

- **Test for service.** Before you spend too much time tracking down possible problems, try these simple tests. If you have another computer or mobile device that connects via your home network, see if it has Internet service. (If your mobile device also can connect via your cell phone data plan, go to its settings screen and see if Wi-Fi is working on your network.) If you're connected by a telephone line (dialup or DSL), ensure that you have a dial tone on your landline telephone. If you use a cable modem, ensure that you have TV reception. If not, the problem isn't in your computer equipment. Call your phone company or cable company.

- **Cycle the power.** Shut down your computer, and turn off power to every device, including your modem and router. Count to 30. Then power up the devices one at a time, starting with the modem, followed by the router and access point and then the computer. Often just cycling power to the router and modem does the trick.

- **Check the blinking lights.** If you have a modem and router or a Wi-Fi/AirPort access point, check that their lights are on and appear to be normal.

- **Can you hear me now?** If you're using Wi-Fi/AirPort, determine whether you have a strong-enough signal — at least two solid arcs on the Signal Strength icon on the menu bar. If not, click the icon to turn it off and back on. Move your laptop. Moving closer to the router or access point is usually better, but any move can help. See Chapter 9 for more tips on getting a signal and solving interference problems.

- **Follow the wires.** Check to make sure that your router is connected to your cable, DSL, or satellite modem. They, in turn, should be connected to a cable TV outlet, phone jack, or satellite receiver, as appropriate. If you're using a wired Ethernet connection, check the cable to your computer as well. Gently disconnect and reconnect them at each end. You have to press a little tab to remove the cable, just like on a telephone cable. You should hear a little click when the cable snaps into place as you reconnect it. If you're using DSL, your phone company may have supplied you with filters to put between your other phones and the wall jack. Make sure they are installed on all phones and that you did *not* install one between your modem and the wall jack.

✔ **Check network settings.** Choose System Preferences, and click the Networks icon. Make sure that its settings match the instructions your Internet service provider (ISP) gave you. Also, check your router's settings. See Chapters 8 and 9.

Handle Printing Problems

Most long-term Mac users have gotten calls from friends that go something like this: "I know you suggested I buy a Mac, but the salesman said the ZorchPC is just as good, and he saved me $300 on a package. I got it set up all by myself, but the printer doesn't work. Could you come over and help me?" Apple's Bonjour technology has made connecting a printer much simpler, even in the Windows world. But sometimes, you click the Print button and nothing happens. The following steps can help you resolve your problem:

1. **Click the Print & Scan icon in System Preferences.**

2. **Make sure that your printer is listed in the window that appears.**

   Your printer manufacturer and model number should be listed in the window. If not, make sure that the printer has power, and check the connection cables.

3. **Look at the printer's lights and display for any error messages, such as one saying that it's out of paper or ink. Add the requested paper or ink and then press its Resume or OK button.**

4. **Turn off the printer, wait until it shuts down completely, and then turn it back on. Wait until the printer says it's ready.**

5. **Ensure that all cables are connected.**

   Refer to the "Follow the wires" item in the preceding section.

6. **Download the latest drivers from your printer manufacturer's website.**

   Avoid using drivers on the disc that came with the printer. They're often out of date.

If you've done all these things and still don't have a solution to your printing problem, check the printer manual for other suggestions and the service number to call.

Reset Passwords

Okay, everybody forgets a password sooner or later. That's why I advise most users to write down passwords and keep them in a safe place. See Chapter 10. Here's how to handle forgotten passwords:

- **If a user on your Mac forgot his password:** Reset it to a new password by clicking the Users & Groups icon in System Preferences. You must click the Lock icon and then enter your administrator password. If the person forgot the user's keychain password, use Keychain Access, located in the Utilities folder.

- **If you forgot your administrator password:** To reset it, reboot using the RecoverHD reinstalled on your computer, and hold down the Option key while you reboot. Select Disk Utility and choose File⇨Reset Password.

Eject CDs, DVDs, and Flash Drives

Most Macs come with *slot-loading* optical drives: You insert a CD or DVD into the wide, thin slot on your Mac where it just fits. (Never insert a miniature CD or DVD into that slot.) If you're having trouble ejecting a CD or DVD, here are some tips:

- The Eject button is on the keyboard, in the top-right corner, and is marked ⏏.

- You can also right-click the disc's icon in the Finder and choose Eject from the menu that appears, or click the Eject icon next to the disc's name in a Finder-window sidebar.

- OS X won't eject a disc if a program thinks that it's using the disc. If your disc doesn't eject when you click the Eject button, close the application that was last using it (or close all applications, if you're not sure which one is using it).

- If all else fails, restart the computer while holding down the mouse or eject button. That should eject the disc.

Flash drives and other removable hard drives have to be "ejected" as well. There's no mechanical response; you still have to unplug them yourself. But ejecting tells OS X to finish what it was doing and leave the file system on the removable device in a proper state. Right-click the drive icon, and choose Eject from the shortcut menu. Wait for the icon to disappear from the Desktop and then wait a few seconds more before unplugging the drive.

If you removed a flash drive prematurely, the file system may be damaged. Even if the drive isn't readable on your Mac (try a reboot first), it may be readable on another computer, including your old PC. If you're able to read it, back it up by copying its contents to the hard drive of the machine that could read it. You can reformat a flash drive on your Mac by using Disk Utility. Select the FAT file system format. You lose all data on the drive.

Track Down Weird Noises

If your normally quiet new Mac starts making loud noises that sound a bit like a jetliner revving for takeoff, don't be alarmed. The Intel processors in your Mac use more power when they're thinking hard, as when they're rendering movies or 3D images. They can sense their own temperature and call for the fans in your Mac to blast some air to cool things down. Sometimes, an application crashes in a way that keeps the processors and the fans at full tilt. A reboot usually quiets things. The Dashboard widget iStat Pro from `www.islayer.com` reports on system temperatures and fan speeds.

Prevent Running Out of Disk Space

If you find that your Mac's hard drive is filling up for no reason, you can try several fixes. For starters, empty the Trash. The command is in the Finder menu.

Next, check for extraordinarily large files to delete or back up to a removable drive or disc, as follows:

1. **In the Finder, open a new Finder window (press ⌘+N).**

2. **Open your home directory (normally, the House icon in the sidebar).**

3. **Choose Finder➪View➪As List.**

4. **Choose Finder➪View➪Show View Options and select the Calculate All Sizes check box.**

   When this check box is selected, OS X makes the added effort to show you how big each folder is — not just each file. The calculation typically takes a few minutes.

5. **Look to see whether any of your folders seems unreasonably large, and if so, look for unnecessary stuff to delete or move elsewhere.**

   Do the same procedure on subfolders as needed.

Another possible cause of disappearing disk space is overgrown log files. Unix can generate lots of logs as applications do their thing. OS X runs special maintenance programs periodically to clean them out. They run in the wee hours of the morning, so be sure to leave your Mac on overnight sometimes. A reboot can often help. You can also use shareware programs that clean out the logs. Yasu (from `jimmitchell.org/yasu`) and Onyx (from `www.titanium.free.fr`) are two popular utilities that do this.

A final possibility is defragmenting the hard drive. OS X tries to keep individual files from fragmenting, but the disk structure as a whole can suffer from having too many small, unused patches. Apple recommends against defragmentation for most users, as long as they aren't doing disk-intensive work (such as video editing) and the hard drive isn't close to being full.

Your hard drive may be filling up because you have lots of files you want to keep, of course. In that case, consider getting a large external hard drive and using it to store your media files (video, photos, and music take up a lot of space. . . .especially video), as well as any large files and folders that you use infrequently. You generally should keep free at least 20 percent of the space on your main drive.

Keep Your Mac Safe and in Tiptop Shape

Taking care of a Mac is mostly common sense. For the most part, no special tricks are required. You just need to pay attention to the software, the hardware, and your habits every so often.

To maintain the software, keep these points in mind:

- Keep software up to date. OS X checks Software Update once a week unless you change its settings. I suggest leaving them as they are.

- Dig out Disk Utility from the Utilities folder every few weeks, and run Repair Permissions. If security is a concern, run Erase Free Space as well. Do this overnight because it can take a while.

- Be judicious in the software you download and install. Although malware hasn't been a big problem on Macs, there's always a first time.

The biggest risk in installing every software gizmo that catches your eye is that some products are poorly written and can make OS X less stable. If possible, use Apple's App Store. Programs there are checked by Apple.

✔ When your Internet connection is working properly, take a look at your router and modem — the box that connects your network to the telephone line, TV cable, or satellite dish. Notice what the blinking lights look like when everything is okay so that you can recognize the difference when everything isn't okay.

Following these tips can help you keep the hardware in good working order:

✔ The MagSafe connector is designed to keep an Apple laptop from falling if someone trips on its power cord. But avoid balancing yours precariously on top of books, papers, and other work-surface litter. Remember that MagSafe protects only the power cord. Someone tripping on an Ethernet, USB, FireWire, or audio cable can still send your laptop flying. Also avoid making sharp bends in the power cord, particularly where it meets the MagSafe connector, to prevent eventual failure.

✔ Don't use cleaners that contain alcohol, ammonia, or other strong solvents on your computer. Also, don't spray any liquids directly on your computer. Apple suggests using a soft cloth dipped in a little plain water for cleaning display screens. If that's not sufficient, Klear Screen from `www.klearscreen.com` is recommended.

✔ Your Mac is designed to run in an ordinary home or office environment. Avoid running it in excessively hot locales or places where it's exposed to direct sunlight. If you put your laptop on a soft or cluttered surface, make sure that the fan exhaust (which is at the hinge) isn't blocked.

✔ Keep an eagle eye on your laptop in public places. Be especially vigilant while you're going through airport security.

Last but not least, the following tips can keep you computing comfortably day in and day out:

✔ If you spend much time at your computer, you owe it to yourself to take ergonomic precautions. Repetitive-motion injuries are best avoided altogether. Comfortable seating that puts your keyboard and mouse or trackpad at a level where your forearms are at right angles to your body tops the list. Apple has extensive suggestions at `www.apple.com/about/ergonomics`.

✔ Finally, you weren't put on this planet to be a computer peripheral. Practice the push-away exercise several times a day. Place both hands at the edge of your desk, and slowly push your body away from the keyboard. Then get up and walk outside for a while.

Find Help

I mention some common problems in the preceding sections and suggest how to fix them. But I can't foresee everything that can happen. You can turn to several other places when problems arise that the preceding tips don't fix.

Google

I always check the Internet first. Usually, someone else has come up with an answer to the same problem, and Google (www.google.com) can find it if you come up with the right search request.

Be sure to include the term *OS X* or *Mac* in your search; otherwise, the answer gets lost in PC replies. Google seems to know that *OS X* is a single search term, even though a space is in it. But don't be too specific at first. You may have a MacBook, but the person who solved your problem may have seen the same problem on an iMac. Try searching different ways, such as once with the word *printer* and once with your printer's make and model.

Also, try your search at Google Groups. Click the More link at the top of the Google home page.

The online Mac community

The fabled loyalty of Mac users is reflected in a strong online community of Mac websites. Some are dedicated to rumors of new products; others strive to keep up with the latest problems and their fixes. Here are a few to check out:

- **MacInTouch.com:** Is one of the most comprehensive sites, with a strong focus on reviews and issues with new products and freshly released software

- **Mac OS X Hints (http://hints.macworld.com):** Is filled with tips on solving problems and improving performance

- **Macnn.com and MacRumors.com:** Lets you read the latest Mac stories, along with user discussions

- **LowEndMac.com:** Has resources you can use with an older Mac

Apple

It may seem surprising that I don't list Apple first in help resources. But Google and the online communities can be checked in seconds and often pop up relevant links to the Apple website. Because so many problems are quickly resolved this way, it's worth trying Google and online communities before calling AppleCare or visiting your local Apple Store's Genius Bar.

But Apple is the ultimate resource. New Macs typically come with 90-day free telephone support. You can extend this period by purchasing AppleCare, which generally is a good idea if this is your first Mac. See Chapter 3 for more on the Apple service options.

User groups and consultants

Numerous Apple user groups are scattered about the planet. Apple will try to find one near you if you visit www.apple.com/usergroups. Getting to know the folks in your local user group can be valuable when you're stuck and in a hurry. Having a Mac-knowledgeable friend to call can make all the difference. Your local user group can also recommend good Mac consultants in your area and give you some idea about what fees to expect. You'll meet some nice people, too.

Chapter 21

Ten Ways Your Mac Can Help the Planet

*Y*ou can use your Mac to get your work done, stay in touch, and just have fun, but you can also employ it in ways that help the environment and humanity. In this chapter, I describe ten of them, plus two more.

Saving Energy with Energy Saver

The Energy Saver control panel, shown in Figure 21-1, lets you adjust settings that can reduce your Mac's energy consumption. To see it, choose ➡System Preferences➪Energy Saver.

If you have an Apple laptop, you have a choice of settings: one for operating on battery power and one for when you're connected to the power adapter. The default settings are based on the assumption that you want to use less power when you're operating on battery power so as to extend battery life. But there's no reason to waste energy when you're on the power adapter. To select the energy-saving setting while you're using your power adapter, follow these steps:

1. **Choose ➡System Preferences➪Energy Saver.**

2. **If you're using a laptop, click the Power Adapter tab.**

3. **Adjust the settings for Computer Sleep and Display Sleep to half the values shown.**

   While you're at it, make the same changes under the Battery option.

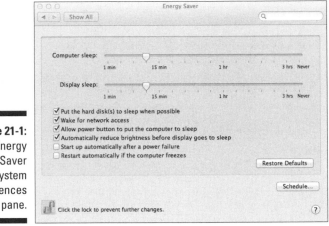

Figure 21-1:
The Energy
Saver
System
Preferences
pane.

If you find the system is going to sleep too often, you can click the Restore Defaults button in the Energy Saver pane to get back to the factory settings.

If you've set your security options to require a password after the computer goes to sleep, you may find a shortened sleep setting really annoying. Choose ➪System Preferences ➪Security& Privacy and in the General tab change the Require Password After Sleep or Screen Saver Begins Setting from immediately to, say, 1 minute. That gives you time to wake up your Mac when the screen goes dark while you're thinking without having to retype the long password I suggest (in Chapter 10) that you use for good security.

Organizing Your Accessories for Power Savings

Ever notice any of those tiny power adapters you have plugged in around your home or office? They power or charge the increasing number of electronic gadgets you have: computers, printers, modems, routers, cellphones, and videogame controllers, for example.

Whenever an adapter is connected to an electrical outlet, it consumes a little power even when the device that it powers is turned off or disconnected. If all your adapters are plugged in all the time, that power adds up to significant energy use. Unplugging the adapters when they aren't in use is one way to save energy, but it can be a bit tedious. An alternative is to plug into their own power strip all the chargers that can be turned off at night so that you can turn them all off together.

If you want to make this process a bit more automatic, consider getting a Coleman Cable Smart Strip. This unit looks like an ordinary power strip, with color-coded outlets, one of which is a control outlet where you plug in a device (such as your computer) that you turn on and off. The strip senses when this happens and turns six other outlets on and off automatically, in sync with the control device. If you plug accessories (such as displays and USB hubs) into the strip, and they're off when your computer is off, you save standby power. The strip also has three outlets that are always on for devices that need to stay on, such as a router that other people use. A Google or Amazon search should find several vendors of these strips.

Running on Alternative Power

Generating your own power — running off the electrical grid — by means of renewable power is the ultimate form of energy saving. Taking your entire home or business off-grid is one way to do this, but it's beyond the scope of this book. (Check out *Solar Power Your Home For Dummies,* 2nd Edition, by Rik DeGunther, if this topic appeals to you.)

If you want an off-grid Mac, a laptop is your best bet because it consumes less power and comes with a battery so that you can work when the sun is behind a cloud or at night. All you need is a solar battery charger. Several chargers of this type are on the market, but many don't fit the MagSafe power connector on your Mac laptop. Two products that offer this vital link are

 ✔ Solar Cell Apple Juicz (www.quickertek.com)

 ✔ Voltaic Solar Laptop Charger (www.voltaicsystems.com)

Neither is cheap, but if you need to be online from someplace sunny with no commercial electric power or you just want to make a green statement, this type of charger may be for you.

A final option is to see whether your electric utility lets you choose your energy supplier. If so, sign up for one that generates electricity from an alternative source, such as wind, hydro, or solar.

Monitoring Power Use

Your computing setup consists of more than just your Mac. You also may have a printer, a display, an external hard drive, a scanner, a camcorder, a router, an HDTV, and other devices. If you're keeping your PC, it and its peripherals will be plugged in as well. But how much energy does each one use?

Measuring the power and energy consumption of peripherals and other electronic gadgets that run off wall outlets is easy with the Kill A Watt EZ electricity usage monitor from P3 International (www.p3international.com). This compact meter, which costs about $50, plugs into a standard outlet or a power strip. You plug the unit to be tested into the outlet on the front of the Kill A Watt. An LED display shows you the power and energy use since the last time you reset the meter. The Kill A Watt can also display instantaneous power, voltage, current, and power-factor levels. (The *power factor* measures how close a load comes to an ideal resistor; low power factors mean energy is being wasted.) You can check other appliances in your home that plug into a 120-volt outlet, such as refrigerators and lamps. After you know how much energy your equipment uses, you can identify the best ways to reduce energy consumption, whether it's turning off peripherals or installing compact fluorescent bulbs in your desk lamp.

iChat: The Green Way to Visit

Transportation fuel use — for automobiles and airplanes — is a major source of carbon dioxide, a gas that traps heat in the atmosphere and contributes to global warming. Cutting down on travel can reduce your carbon *footprint* — the amount of carbon dioxide you produce as a result of your activities. It can also save you money.

Short-notice airfares have long been the bane of small business. If you live in Boston, want to visit Aunt Ellie in LA, and can plan your trip two weeks in advance, you can often easily find a nonstop round-trip flight online for less than $300. But if you need to go tomorrow to solve a customer's problem or make that last-minute presentation to win a sale, you spend close to $1,000.

Using the Apple iChat to hold a videoconference, rather than catch that last-minute flight, can save you enough to cover the cost of your Mac. The FaceTime camera built into your iMac or laptop is all you need. Plug-in cameras are available for Mac minis and Pros and are built into Apple Cinema displays. You can even video-conference with Windows users who are using AOL Instant Messenger for Windows.

You always see yourself as well as the other people on the call. If you have visual materials to make your case, iChat Theater lets you share an iPhoto slide show or a Keynote presentation while letting your audience see you as you talk them through it.

If you're working on a proposal or report with a remote colleague who also has a Mac, you can edit the same document or search the web together with iChat screen sharing, which lets one chatter control the other chatter's Desktop.

For more on iChat, see Chapter 8.

Automating Your Home

Years ago, home automation meant buying X10 lamp modules from Radio Shack and putting a controller on the night table so that you could dim the lights from your bed. Home automation now means that you control every electrical device in your home, fine-tune your heating and air conditioning, and even patch in alternative forms of energy. You can also add video surveillance and intrusion-detection systems, with security images shipped off-site where an intruder can't get at them. You can control all these tasks remotely and securely over the Internet.

The Indigo software package from www.perceptiveautomation.com lets your Mac control both X10 and the newer Insteon family of home automation controls.

If you're using your Mac as a home controller, be sure to select Energy Saver in System Preferences, click Options, and check the Restart Automatically after a Power Failure box.

Living the Paperless Portable Life

Okay, this is a pet fantasy of mine, but did you ever think about how much of our living situation is devoted to storing and managing papers? Imagine scanning every piece of paper that matters to you and storing it all on an external hard drive (such as Time Capsule, covered in Chapter 5). Legal documents that you need in their original forms can be stored in a rented safe-deposit box, along with jewelry and small mementos. If you have books and bigger tchotchkes that you can't part with, rent a small storage room or a corner of a friend's basement. Imagine getting everything you need down to a laptop and portable hard drive. You're free! You can go anywhere at any time.

Even if you aren't ready to go this far, you can still cut your use of paper. You're probably already using texting and e-mail to stay in touch with friends. Here are a few other suggestions:

- **Use online bill-paying systems.** Your bank or broker probably offers such a service.
- **Ask to get bills and statements via e-mail rather than on paper.** Many banks, utilities, and other vendors offer this service.
- **If you're in school, ask your instructors whether they accept essays and other submissions in electronic form.** Many teachers require electronic submissions these days.
- **Turn off your printer and see how long you can get by without it.** You save on ink and toner cartridges as well. (Don't forget to recycle your old ones; many stationery stores take them back for credit.)

Curing Cancer

Your Mac is one powerful computer. How powerful? One Mac sent back in time to the 1940s or '50s could alter the balance of power in the world. Yet yours spends most of its time patiently waiting for commands. Can I find you a web page? Can I? Can I maybe read you your e-mail? Pretty please?

Rather than consign your Mac to total boredom, you can give it interesting work to do — work that helps cure cancer and other diseases. Living cells assemble proteins by linking different amino acids in a sequence specified by the cell's DNA. As the protein is completed, it folds itself up into a 3D shape that determines how it functions in the cell. These days, biologists can determine a protein's sequence from the DNA, but figuring out how it folds up takes extremely demanding calculations. The Stanford University Folding@ home project uses the idle cycles on your Mac to help carry out these computations. Visit `http://folding.stanford.edu`, and download the OS X client. You have lots of options to choose among, but start with the screensaver version, which makes only moderate demands on your computer and quickly gets out of the way when you want to get your work done. After the Folding@home screen saver has run long enough to produce some results, it displays the molecules it's working on so that you can see what's being accomplished.

Helping with Exploration of the Universe

Those probes launched into space take lots of pictures — more than professional astronomers have time to look at in detail. Amateur scientists are helping catalog those images and look for unusual phenomena. You can help; you don't need a backyard telescope, and the pros will even train you. Two such projects are

- **Galaxy Zoo** (`http://galaxyzoo.org`), which seeks help classifying the millions of galaxies photographed by the Hubble Space Telescope and looking for supernovas in those galaxies.
- **Moon Zoo** (`http://moonzoo.org`), where you'll be looking for different types of craters on the Moon in more than 2 million images taken by NASA's Lunar Reconnaissance Orbiter.

You'll find many more interesting opportunities to help space scientists at `www.zooniverse.org`.

Retiring Old Electronics Responsibly

Computers wear out. Macs last longer than PCs on average, but even they die or become obsolete eventually. Disposing of them improperly can add to landfill pollution. Worse, in many cases, old computers are shipped to Third World countries, where they're stripped of valuable parts in unsafe conditions, often by children. The section in Chapter 22 on recycling equipment safely explains better ways to get rid of old equipment.

Fighting Malware

Malware used to be just a nuisance, slowing your computer and maybe trashing files you forgot to back up, but it's becoming more serious. The U.S. Defense Department has concluded that cyber attacks can be an act of war. Keep the peace by keeping your Mac software up to date. There's a good chance that your old Windows PC has already been taken over by some criminal gang. For extra credit, keep that PC turned off when you're not using it. The bad guys can't use it when it's off.

Switching a Friend to a Mac

The Mac's environmentally friendly design and long service life makes it ideal for environmentally conscious users. Apple competes against other computer companies that are battling to see which can produce the cheapest Windows computer. These perpetual price wars lead to corner cutting and products that need frequent replacement.

The one thing that has kept Apple alive through difficult years is the loyalty of its customers. If you like having a commercial alternative to Microsoft and Windows, consider helping a friend make the switch. If you found this book to be helpful, so may your friend.

Chapter 22

Ten Creative Uses for Your Old PC

As you wean yourself off Windows, you may wonder what to do with your old PC. One big no-no is throwing it away. Your PC contains toxic compounds that will contaminate soil and water or emit poisonous gases if it's incinerated. Here are ten other suggestions, some more creative than others.

Before you send away your computer, be sure to clear its hard drive of all sensitive files. Dragging items to the Recycle Bin and then emptying it doesn't erase your data. See Chapter 6 for instructions for better ways to delete data.

Sell It on Craigslist

If your PC is of fairly recent vintage, it may have some resale value. I suggest listing it on your local Craigslist website (www.craigslist.org). It's free to use and less complicated than eBay.com. Because Craigslist enables you to create a local listing, you can ask the buyer to pick up the PC, thereby avoiding shipping hassles. You can get an idea of what your computer is worth by checking what's now on sale — but don't assume that the listed asking price is what people are getting.

Load Ubuntu Linux on It

I love OS X, but Linux — the free, open-source operating system — is also becoming an important alternative to Windows. You can download and burn a CD to load your PC with the friendly version of Linux, Ubuntu (www. ubuntu.com).

By the way, this is the only way that I recommend giving your old PC box to your kids. I'd rather see them have a Mac, but setting up and using Linux has real educational value — and fewer games are available for it than for the other platforms. Get the kids a copy of *Linux For Dummies,* by Richard Blum, and let them figure it out.

Give It to Charity

Donating your computer to a worthwhile organization is an admirable thing to do, and you may even get a tax deduction. Most charitable organizations aren't interested in computer donations from individuals, however; they're inundated with them. Your best bet is to contact organizations you know. Never just drop your computer off as a donation because you may be costing your would-be recipient money to dispose if it responsibly. An offer to help set up the PC may be appreciated. Don't take offense if the response is no.

A posting in the free section of Craigslist often works; you can specify a preference for charities, but a donation to an individual often can be a good deed. In any case, be sure to include all the software discs and documentation that came with the PC, if you still have them.

Use It as a Pedestal

Years ago, my employer sold all its computers to a leasing company and leased them back on a seven-year note. The equipment was obsolete after three years, so we kept the racks the computers were mounted in (which is where the leasing company's inventory tags were affixed) and used them as printer stands. The bean counters from the leasing company dutifully came around every six months and were satisfied to see that the stuff that secured their loans (and our printers) was still there. A PC makes a great plant stand, but be sure to install the antitipping hardware that probably came with it.

Also, two PCs of the same height, with a wide board across them, create a nice work surface for young kids.

Have Your Kids Take It Apart

These days, kids don't get much opportunity to see how things are put together. Place the computer on an old bedsheet, give the kids a screwdriver set, and see how far they can go in taking apart the computer. Hard drives are a bit tricky to open — you usually find one or two screws below the "you'll void the warranty" labels — but they're full of fascinating parts, including some powerful magnets.

Adult supervision is required. Some parts have sharp edges. Those magnets are strong enough to pinch if two snap together. This activity isn't one that kids younger than 5 should be anywhere near because small parts are a choking hazard. And *never* try to take apart a video monitor or any computer that includes a CRT display: It has high voltages inside, and its CRT tubes can implode violently. See "Recycle It Safely," at the end of this chapter, for disposal tips.

Enjoy It as Art

If you've never looked closely at a computer's circuit board, you're missing a cultural experience. Those *objets d'art* are marvels of design, filled with colorful electronic components, including numerous integrated circuits in mysterious black slabs, covered with thousands of tiny copper traces that carry all the signals. I think circuit boards are worthy of hanging on your wall. Some craftspeople even use them as raw material for jewelry. Others have gone so far as to make furniture out of them.

Use It for Target Practice

I'm not seriously suggesting this one. It can be dangerous and may be contrary to laws in some locations. But years ago, when I had a gig at a local company that made spreadsheet software, someone brought in a 386 PC filled with .30 caliber bullet holes. Everyone appreciated the gesture.

Disconnect from the Internet

One way to continue to use a Windows machine safely is to disconnect it from the Internet. Unplug its Ethernet cable, and remove any wireless networking card. If the machine has built-in wireless capability, such as Intel Centrino, change the password on your wireless network hub, and don't give the PC the new password. For extra credit, turn off wireless networking (in the Network Connections section of Control Panel) or remove the wireless card, because the PC can still connect through a neighbor's open hub. When you need to move files between the PC and your Mac, use a USB flash drive.

Keep It for Old Media

If you have a PC old enough to have 5¼-inch floppy-disk drives, wrap it in one of those big plastic bags you get from the dry cleaner, and store it in the basement. Sooner or later, the world will no longer be able to read those old disks, and you'll be a hero for saving your machine. Or not. (And if some of the dire predictions for cyberwar come true, old machines may be the only computers that still work.)

Recycle It Safely

Keep computers and displays out of the town dump. Did you know that an old CRT monitor can contain 4 pounds of lead, not to mention the cadmium, mercury, bromated fire retardants, and other noxious stuff in the computer itself? Also, many computer recycling operations send computers and displays to developing countries, where they're dismantled under hazardous conditions — often by children — and worthless parts are simply dumped somewhere.

Here are a couple of tips to help you safely recycle an old and unwanted computer:

✔ In the United States, the Apple Recycling Program accepts your old computer and monitor — regardless of manufacturer — when you buy a new Mac. It also takes back old Macs, cellphones, and iPods, even if you don't buy anything. Finally, it takes old computers that still have value and gives you an Apple gift card for the estimated value. Visit www. apple.com/recycling for more details.

✔ Find an e-Stewards recycler at www.e-stewards.org. The e-Stewards recyclers ensure that your PC is properly disposed of: It will never end up in a landfill, it will never be incinerated, it will never be shipped out of the country for "processing" by unprotected children in developing nations, and it won't get sent to a federal prison for "processing" by inmates.

Appendix

Mac Speak versus Windows Speak: A Translation Glossary

~ : The tilde character, used in Mac OS X and other Unix operating systems; an abbreviation for "the home directory of." Sometimes called *twiddle.*

.Net: Also known as "dot net," the Microsoft software framework for web services. See also *Mono,* a compatible system that runs on other platforms, including Mac OS X.

.ps: A PostScript file.

.sit file: A StuffIt-compressed Mac file. (A version for Windows exists, too.)

10BaseT, 100BaseT, 1000BaseT: Ethernet signaling standards at 10, 100, and 1,000 megabits per second. The last is also called Gigabit Ethernet.

16-bit, 32-bit, 64-bit: When referring to a program or operating system, the maximum size of program addresses used. More bits allow more memory to be addressed; the amount doubles for each added bit.

68K: Motorola 68000 series microprocessors, used in the original Macintosh; superseded by the PowerPC and then the Intel Core line.

accessibility: The ability of software and hardware to be used by people with disabilities.

ACID: A set of criteria for database systems intended to ensure that all transactions are handled properly — completed either completely or not at all — even if a system failure occurs during processing. The letters stand for *atomicity, consistency, isolation,* and *durability.*

Acid2 test: A series of documents used to test browser compliance with industry standards. The Apple Safari browser passes.

Acrobat Reader: A free program from Adobe.com used to read PDF files. The OS X Preview feature performs many of the same functions.

ADA: The Americans with Disability Act, a U.S. law requiring reasonable accommodations for workers and customers with disabilities. Also, Ada, a computer programming language developed under the auspices of the U.S. Department of Defense.

adware: Software that's provided for free but displays advertising.

AES: Advanced Encryption Standard, a strong encryption cipher developed in Belgium and adopted by the U.S. government. See Chapter 10.

AIFF: Audio Interchange File Format, an Apple-developed format for sound files. It's lossless but tends to be large compared with compressed formats such as MP3. It's the same idea as Microsoft's WAV format.

AIM: AOL Instant Messenger, an instant-messaging (IM) system supported by AOL and iChat.

AirPort: The Apple brand name for Wi-Fi wireless networking; also called IEEE 802.11.

alias: A small file that points to another file.

Android: An open-source operating system for non-Apple smartphones, sponsored by Google.

Apache: A popular program, supplied with Mac OS X, for serving web pages over the Internet. Visit www.apache.org.

Aperture: The high-end Apple program for still photographers; not included in Mac OS X.

API: Application programming interface, a set of services that one program (such as an operating system) provides to another.

app: Short for *application,* as in Apple's marketing slogan "There's an app for that." This slogan is not to be confused with the day-care-center slogan "There's a nap for that."

App Store: An online store that sells apps, typically at low prices or for free. The App Store was first popularized for use with the iPhone, but a version, the Mac App Store, is built into OS X Lion and provides Mac OS X apps.

Apple I and II: The original Apple computers, based on an 8-bit microprocessor (the 6502).

Apple key: A key with the Apple logo (🍎) and the command symbol (⌘), also called the *Command key* or *fan key*. Newer keyboards have only ⌘ on the key, but the name persists.

Apple lossless: An audio file format that features lossless compression and that can be played on iPods, iPhones, and iPads.

Apple remote control: A small infrared remote that can command Macs, Apple TV units, and most iPod models.

Apple store: Apple retail outlets, including a website (`http://store.apple.com`) and bricks-and-mortar (or, more often, glass-and-silicone) stores that you can walk into. They're located in many major cities and shopping centers.

AppleScript: A programming language that allows repetitive tasks on a Mac to be automated. Many Mac apps can respond to AppleScript commands and are said to be AppleScriptable.

AppleShare: The Apple file-sharing technology for local networks.

applet: A small program in the Java language that can be automatically downloaded and executed by your browser.

AppleTalk: An older Apple networking technology that has been largely replaced by industry-standard technologies such as AirPort, Ethernet, and TCP/IP.

ARM: A type of microprocessor used in many cellphones and all Apple iOS devices, known for getting a lot done with very little battery power. One of its earliest uses was in the Apple Newton PDA.

ASCII: American Standard Code for Information Interchange, a way of encoding characters in 8-bit bytes that's widely used in modern computers, though increasingly being replaced by Unicode and UTF-8.

ATA: Advanced Technology Attachment, a widely used standard for connecting hard drives and optical drives to computers. A newer version called SATA, or serial ATA, is used in Macs.

Automator: A facility in Mac OS X that simplifies the creation of workflow scripts to perform repetitive tasks.

bash: Bourne-again shell, a Unix shell (see also *shell*) developed by the GNU project and used in Mac OS X. See Chapter 19.

baud: A measure of modem speed that means one symbol per second. Bits per second is more commonly used these days. You earn a high geek point if you understand the distinction.

BinHex: An older Mac format for sending binary data encoded as an ASCII text file.

BIOS: Basic Input/Output System, firmware in a PC that determines what happens when you turn on power. Intel Macs and some newer PCs use EFI instead.

bit: The basic unit of information, with only two possibilities, represented by 0 and 1 or on and off.

BitLocker: A disk encryption scheme in the Pro versions of Windows 7. See *FileVault* and Chapter 10 for the Mac equivalent, which comes with all current versions of Mac OS X.

BitTorrent: A popular system for sharing files on the Internet, capable of handling very large files.

blacklist: A list of e-mail or chat addresses you don't want to hear from. See also *whitelist*.

Blender: A powerful, open-source 3-D modeling and animation system available for the Mac. Blender is free, but a donation is suggested.

Blue Box: An early code name for what became the Classic environment in Mac OS X for PowerPC. Other code names from the same era include *Red Box* and *Yellow Box.*

Bluetooth: A wireless networking standard for short-range uses such as connecting computers, wireless keyboards and mice, and cellphones.

Blu-ray: An optical disc the same size as a DVD but capable of storing ten times as much data; used for high-definition movies.

BMP: A graphics file format used in Windows.

BNC: A coaxial connector type used in high-end video equipment.

Bonjour: An Apple-sponsored technology (originally named *Rendezvous*) to allow devices such as printers to announce their presence over local computer networks.

boot from CD or DVD: To start your computer from a compact disc or DVD. Hold down the C key on a Mac while restarting.

bootstrap: Short for *pulling yourself up by your bootstraps* and usually shortened to just *boot*. The term refers to the complex process by which computers start up when power is first applied.

broadband: A high-speed transmission technology used with cable modems that allows multiple streams of information on a single coaxial cable.

browser: A program that finds and displays information on the World Wide web. Macs come with the Safari browser.

BSD: Berkeley System Distribution, a variant of the Unix operating system developed at the University of California, Berkeley. A variant, FreeBSD, is the basis for Mac OS X.

byte: A block of information — usually 8 bits.

cable modem: A small box that connects your computer or router to the cable TV system.

Carbon: A set of application program interfaces provided by Apple to make it easier to convert older Mac programs to Mac OS X. See also *Cocoa*.

CD-R, CD-R/W: A compact disc that can be written on by a computer — for example, a Mac. CD-Rs can be written only once; CD-R/Ws can be erased and rewritten multiple times. CDs store about 700MB of data; DVDs store more.

CD-ROM: Compact Disc Read-Only Memory, used in a compact disc that contains data that can't be modified.

CERT: Computer Emergency Readiness Team, a U.S. group that responds to viruses and other computer and Internet attacks.

Claris: A no-longer-used brand name for Apple software.

Classic: A feature of Mac OS X that allowed older Mac OS 9 programs to run. Classic isn't supported on Intel Macs or in Mac OS X releases after Tiger (10.4).

client: A computer that uses the services of another computer; also, someone who helps pay the bills.

cloud: The combined forces of all the computer servers out there in the Internet. Supposedly, the cloud is the next hot thing in computing, allowing us to store all our data on distant servers and access it on small mobile devices. The cloud has to solve many security problems before I trust it with my digital life, however. See also *iCloud.*

Cocoa: A set of application program interfaces provided by Apple for building native Mac OS X applications.

codec: Short for *compressor/decompressor,* a piece of software necessary to compress a media file or to process a compressed media file.

Command key: The keyboard key with the ⌘ symbol on it, located on either side of the spacebar on Apple keyboards.

Component video: An analog video-signal standard in which picture information for different colors is carried on three separate wires (usually red, green, and blue).

composite video: An analog video-signal standard in which all picture information is carried on a single wire (usually yellow).

console: A text stream in which Unix-based operating systems send out messages about their operations. One console is running in Mac OS X, but you must launch the Console utility to see its output.

cookie: A small blob of data that websites try to store on your hard drive so that they can be reminded of certain information the next time you visit. You can turn cookies off in the Safari Preferences Security tab.

Core 2 duo: Intel *x*86 microprocessors featuring two processors on a chip; still used in some Macs.

creator code: Metadata in the Apple file system that indicates which application should open the file. See also *file type.*

CRM: Customer relationship management software, which helps sales and marketing organizations track leads and customers.

cron file: A file in a Unix-based operating system that lists actions to be taken at specific times in the future.

cryptovariable: Another name for a cryptographic key.

Darwin: The Unix operating system underlying Mac OS X.

Dashboard: A feature of Mac OS X that pops up small, useful programs named *widgets* whenever you press F4. Widgets can be downloaded from Apple.com.

data remanence: The often-recoverable traces of information left behind when you think you've deleted your files. Secure Empty Trash reduces the problem, as does the Disk Utility command Erase Free Space.

dialup: A form of Internet connection in which you dial a phone number that connects you to an ISP. Its speed is limited to about 56 kilobits per second.

Diceware: A technique for generating strong passwords and passphrases by using ordinary dice. Visit `www.Diceware.com`.

Direct3D: One of two popular ways for programs (particularly 3D games) to communicate with graphics cards. Microsoft uses this one. Apple uses the other, called OpenGL.

directory: Another name for a folder, a named collection of files and other directories.

disclosure triangle: A small triangle icon that increases (or decreases) the information you see when you click it.

disk encryption: A method of securing data that scrambles an entire disk rather than individual files or folders. Apple's version is FileVault. See Chapter 10.

distro: Short for *distribution*. Several groups (including Red Hat, Debian, and Ubuntu) assemble and release open-source operating systems based on the Linux kernel. Each group's version is a distro.

DMCA: Digital Millennium Copyright Act, a U.S. law that restricts the circumvention of digital copy protections, such as DRM.

.doc: The extension used by files saved in versions of Microsoft Word before Word 2007. Later versions, including Word 2011, use `.docx`, an XML-based format.

Dock: In Mac OS X, a place where the icons of frequently used applications and folders can be kept. Running applications are also shown. By default, the Dock is at the bottom of the screen. The Dock is roughly the equivalent of the Windows taskbar and tray.

dongle: A small device that plugs into a computer and contains special codes that allow a purchased program to run. Dongles restrict users of expensive software to using only the number of copies they purchased.

DRAM: Dynamic random-access memory, a type of high-speed main memory used in computers. It must have its contents refreshed regularly, but it uses the fewest transistors per bit of any type of solid-state memory. See also *SDRAM.*

DRM: Digital rights management, technologies designed to limit the copies you can make of media you own. Apple uses a form of DRM named FairPlay in some of the media sold at the iTunes Store.

DSL: Digital subscriber line, a form of high-speed Internet access brought to you by your phone company.

DVD: Digital Versatile Disc or Digital Video Disc. This plastic disc, with the same dimensions as a CD (120mm diameter), can store an entire movie in pre-HD resolution. Recordable DVD-Rs and rewriteable DVD-R/W discs are available.

DVI: Digital visual interface, a digital video interface standard used in several Mac models and many PCs.

ECC: Error-correcting code; used on hard drives and sometimes in RAM to catch and fix errors.

EFI: Extensible Firmware Interface, a technology used by Intel Macs to start the computer. It replaces the BIOS in PCs.

EmPower: A connector for supplying low-voltage, direct-current power to airplane seats for use in powering laptops and other devices; defined by the ARINC 628 specification. An earlier version, now named EmPower Classic, used an automobile cigarette–lighter connector.

emulation: One computer pretending to be another with a different instruction set by running a program that knows what to do with each instruction of the foreign computer.

encrypt: To scramble data in a way that's difficult or impossible to undo without knowledge of a secret key.

encrypting file system: See *disk encryption, FileVault*.

entropy: A measure of randomness; the logarithm of the number of possible states a system can be in. When base-2 logs are used, entropy is measured in *bits*.

Ethernet: A method of providing fast computer-to-computer communication over a wire. Ethernet doesn't require one special computer to be in charge, thereby supporting peer-to-peer communication.

Exchange: A Microsoft software product, Exchange Server, that provides e-mail messaging, calendaring, and contact directories in many enterprises. Mac OS X Lion plays well with Exchange.

ExpressCard: An obsolete standard for small plug-in expansion cards. The 17-inch MacBook Pro still has an ExpressCard/34 slot. ExpressCard replaces the PCMCIA PC Card standard and is being replaced by USB and *Thunderbolt*.

F connector: A video coaxial connector with a threaded sleeve, widely used in consumer electronics.

FaceTime: An Apple video-telephone application, first introduced in the iPhone 4 but now available for the iPad 2 and Mac OS X.

FairPlay: The Apple digital rights management system.

fan key: A keyboard key with the ⌘ symbol on it, also called the *Command key*.

FAT: File allocation table, a file system used in older PCs. Macs can read and write devices, such as flash drives, formatted in the FAT format.

file extension: A string of letters added to a filename after a dot to indicate the program that can open that file. Mac OS X also stores a file type that serves a similar purpose.

file path: The sequence of folders or directories leading from the root directory or home directory to the file, such as ~/Documents/Projects/Wiley/S2M4D/Glossary.doc.

file permissions: Codes associated with each file that indicate who can read, modify, or execute the file.

file type: Metadata in the Apple file system that indicates what type of data the file contains. See also *file extension.*

FileMaker Pro: A database management program for Mac OS X and Windows that's sold by the Apple subsidiary FileMaker, Inc.

FileVault: A Mac OS X service that encrypts a user's hard drive.

Final Cut: The high-end, moviemaking Apple software.

finger panic: The confusion that results from not being aware of how many fingers you're using to stroke your trackpad or Magic Mouse.

Fink: A group dedicated to porting Unix and Linux applications to the Mac. Visit www.finkproject.org.

Firefox: An alternative browser that's popular on Macs and PCs.

FireWire: A high-speed data bus for connecting computers, hard drives, video cameras, and other devices; also called i.Link and IEEE 1394. See also *Thunderbolt.*

firmware: Computer programs associated with a computer or another device stored in read-only or flash memory and not normally changed. This ware falls between hard and soft.

Flash: A proprietary format for multimedia data on the World Wide Web. Developed by Macromedia and now owned by Adobe. Flash isn't supplied with Mac OS X Lion; you must install it if you want it. See *HTML5.*

flash drive: A thumb-size device that plugs into a USB port and looks like a hard drive on the Desktop. It uses flash memory — hence, the name. See also *sneakernet*.

flash memory: A solid-state memory technology that retains data even when it isn't connected to electrical power but can be rewritten. This type of memory is used in solid-state drives, flash drives, iPods, iPhones, iPads, and digital cameras.

folder: See *directory.*

FOSS: Free open-source software.

FreeBSD: An open-source distribution of the BSD UNIX operating system. Mac OS X is built on FreeBSD. Other BSD distros exist, such as OpenBSD and NetBSD.

friend: Someone with whom you exchange more private information on social-networking sites. The term is also a verb, meaning to offer and receive permission for such exchanges, as in "I just friended Sam on Facebook."

FTP: File Transfer Protocol, a 40-year-old Internet technology for moving data files. Anonymous FTP sites let you get data with anonymous as the username and your e-mail address as the password. I like the Fetch FTP client for Mac OS X; visit www.fetchsoftworks.com.

GIF: Graphics Interchange Format, an image-file format developed by CompuServe that's popular on the web. It has limited color capability but can display simple animations.

Gigabit Ethernet: Ethernet operating at a billion bits per second; also called 1000BaseT.

gigabyte: One billion bytes, or sometimes 2^{30} bytes or 1,073,741,824 bytes. Some people call the latter number a *gibibyte* to prevent confusion.

GIMP: An open-source image-editing program that's available for Macs. It runs in X11.

Gnu: Not Unix, a project started by Richard Stallman to develop an open-source version of Unix. Gnu developed much of the utility software shipped with Linux, and many Gnu utilities are in Mac OS X. See Chapter 19.

GPG: Gnu Privacy Guard, a free open-source encryption program compatible with PGP. It's available for the Mac, along with a GPGMail plug-in for Apple Mail. See gpgmail.org.

GPL: Gnu Public License, a commonly used legal agreement attached to open-source software that requires an improved version to carry the same license, a concept also known as *copyleft*. See www.gnu.org/licenses/gpl.html.

GUI: Graphical user interface, a way for humans to interact with a computer by manipulating objects and icons on a display screen with a pointing device such as a mouse.

H.264: A video data compression standard used for iTunes Store video and in much Mac software, including iChat and iMovie.

hard drive: The main, permanent data store in most computers. It uses rotating magnetic disks and a read/write head on a movable arm. See also *SSD*.

hash: A cryptographic tool that mushes data into a small block in a nonreversible way. The hash serves as a signature for the file. It's quite difficult to make two files with the same hash. Some common hash algorithms are MD5, SHA-1, SHA-256, and SHA-512. A new generation of hash functions is being developed in a competition hosted by NIST.

HD DVD: A defunct higher-capacity replacement for DVDs. Blu-ray won.

HDMI: High-Definition Multimedia Interface, a standard for high-definition TV cable connectors that includes digital video, similar to DVI and digital audio. HDMI includes provisions for digital rights management.

HDTV: High-definition television, which every couch potato craves.

HFS+: The file system used in Mac OS X.

hibernate: An operating-system feature that suspends operation in a way that can survive a power outage. See also *sleep.*

home directory: The folder that contains all data associated with your user account, abbreviated ~ at the command line.

HTML5: The latest version of the Hypertext Markup Language standard. HTML is the way World Wide Web pages are written, consisting of a mixture of text and tags. HTML5, which is not yet complete, adds tags for video and other media, allowing it to match the capabilities of Adobe Flash.

HyperCard: A programming environment on early Macs that anticipated many hypermedia features of the World Wide Web. HyperCard is a predecessor of AppleScript.

hypertext: A system of writing and displaying text that enables text to be linked in multiple ways, be available at several levels of detail, and contain links to related documents.

ICANN: Internet Corporation for Numbers and Names, a controversial not-for-profit corporation that administers Internet addresses.

iChat: The Apple instant-messaging, voice communication, and videoconferencing software included in Mac OS X. See also *FaceTime.*

iCloud: Apple's data storage, media streaming, and synchronization service included in Mac OS X and iOS. Partially replaces the defunct MobileMe. See also *cloud.*

ICQ: An early instant-messaging service, once owned by AOL and since purchased by Digital Sky Technologies, a Russian company. Users are identified by numbers.

IEC standards (power cord, button icons): International Electrotechnical Commission, a standards organization dealing with electrical and electronic technologies.

IEEE: Institute of Electrical and Electronics Engineers, a professional organization that also sets standards.

IEEE 1394: The FireWire standard, also named i.Link by Sony.

IEEE 802.11: The family of wireless networking standards known as Wi-Fi or by the Apple brand name AirPort. See Chapter 9.

IETF: Internet Engineering Task Force, a group that sets standards for the Internet.

iLife: A family of media-editing and production software included with each Mac: iTunes, iPhoto, iMovie, iDVD, GarageBand, and iWeb. See Part IV.

IM: Instant messaging, an electronic text communication system in which both parties of a conversation are at their computers at the same time and send messages back and forth.

IMAP: Internet Message Access Protocol, one of the two popular ways in which e-mail is handled on the Internet. When you use IMAP, e-mail can be kept on a server and accessed over the 'Net. The other method is POP.

infrared: A form of invisible light in the electromagnetic spectrum with wavelengths just longer than red and shorter than 1mm.

Intel: The company that invented microprocessors; has long made the microprocessors for most Windows PCs and now makes them for Macs.

internationalization: The process of adapting computer software to work in different languages and cultures.

Internet: All the computers in the world talking to one another.

iOS: The operating system Apple uses in its iPod touch, iPhone, and iPad family; also used for Apple TV.

iPad: Apple's tablet. The iPad was the first tablet computer to gain wide market acceptance.

iPhone: Apple's wildly successful version of the smartphone, a pocket computer that does almost everything and also makes phone calls.

iPod: The Apple line of portable music and video players.

IRC: Internet Relay Chat, an early form of instant messaging that's still used on the Internet.

ISA bus: A type of plug-in card used in early PCs and since replaced by PCI.

iSight: The Apple line of video cameras, now built into Macs that come with a display.

ISP: Internet service provider. An ISP takes your money and connects you to the Internet.

iWork: The Apple office-productivity suite that includes Pages (word processing), Numbers (spreadsheet), and Keynote (presentation) software.

Java: A computer programming language, developed by Sun Microsystems, that's widely used in commercial data processing. The term is not to be confused with *JavaScript,* a different language that's designed to be embedded in web pages to add functionality. JavaScript is included in the Safari browser. Mac OS X Lion will offer to install Java if it thinks that you need it.

journaling file system: A file system that keeps track of recent changes separately. In the event of a system crash, the journaled changes can be used to reconstruct a damaged file system, significantly improving overall data reliability. This system is used in Mac OS X.

JPEG: Joint Photographic Experts Group, a body that developed a widely used standard format for photographs (.jpg).

kernel: The innermost part of an operating system, consisting of the stuff that talks to all the hardware. Mac OS X uses the Mach kernel.

kernel panic: An unrecoverable failure in an operating system's inner workings. In Mac OS X, a kernel panic is often a sign of underlying hardware problems. Reboot and back up your computer — now.

key: As used in cryptography, a block of information needed to encode or decode a message.

keyboard shortcut: Using the keyboard to initiate a command without selecting an item from a menu. Often requires pressing a special key, such as ⌘, and then a letter or number.

Keynote: The Apple presentation software that one-ups the ubiquitous Microsoft PowerPoint.

kilo: The standard prefix meaning 1,000. In computing, it sometimes means 1,024, which is 2^{10}. Another prefix for the latter number is *kibi*.

KVM switch: A box that lets you use a single keyboard, video display, and mouse to operate more than one computer.

LaunchPad: An OS X facility that displays all applications as a full-screen array of icons.

LDAP: Lightweight Directory Access Protocol, a system for finding people and resources on computer networks.

Leopard: The Apple code name for Mac OS X 10.5. See also ***Snow Leopard.***

Light Peak: Another name for ***Thunderbolt.***

line in: An analog audio signal amplified to a certain nominal level for connection to other audio equipment.

Linux: An open-source computer operating system inspired by Unix. See also ***Gnu***.

Lion: The Apple code name for Mac OS X 10.7.

Lisa: A short-lived Apple computer that was a predecessor of the Macintosh.

LocalTalk: An early Apple wiring standard for networking that used telephone wires. It has since been replaced by Ethernet and Wi-Fi.

location: In Apple networking, a way to group settings so that they can be easily changed when moving to a different locale, such as from home to work.

lock icon: A small image of a padlock that's shown in web browsers to indicate whether the current connection is securely encrypted (in which case the lock is closed) or isn't securely encrypted (in which case the lock is open). It's worth checking the lock icon before entering personal information in a web form. Also used in System Preferences when an administrator's password is needed to make changes and in the Finder to show that a file is locked.

lossless: A data compression mode that allows all original data to be recovered. Higher compression levels for music and video discard some data and are lossy.

Mac OS X: An operating system developed by Apple, using technology from NeXT, BSD UNIX, Mach, and earlier versions of the Mac OS. Mac OS X is available only for Apple Macintosh computers.

Mach: An operating-system kernel developed at Carnegie Mellon University and used as the basis of Mac OS X's Darwin kernel.

macintouch.com: A popular Macintosh support website.

MacPaint: A classic drawing program included with the earliest Macs.

MacWrite: The earliest Apple word processor for the Mac.

MagSafe: The power connector used on Mac Intel laptops. The connector is held in place by a strong magnet and is designed to pop off safely if someone trips on the cord.

malware: A computer program that's up to no good, such as viruses, worms, and spyware.

McIntosh: A type of edible apple that's popular in New England; also, a brand of audio equipment. McIntosh is not to be confused with *Macintosh*, an Apple, Inc. brand name, or *Mackintosh*, a type of foul-weather coat.

mega: The standard prefix meaning one million. In computing, it sometimes means 1,048,576, which is 2^{20}. Another prefix for the latter number is *mebi*.

metadata: Information about data, such as when it was made, what it means, and where it comes from.

MIDI: Musical Instrument Digital Interface, a way to communicate music as named notes rather than as digitized sounds. It's used to connect digital instruments to computers.

MIME: Multipurpose Internet Mail Extension, a standard that allows Internet e-mail to carry information in a variety of formats other than plain ASCII text.

Mini DisplayPort: A video-out connector used on many Mac models. This port is a smaller version of the VESA DisplayPort that supports the encryption of video signals to protect HD movies from piracy. Thunderbolt ports can accept a Mini DisplayPort cable.

Mini-DVI: A smaller version of the DVI connector, used in older Mac models.

Mission Control: A unified way to display and navigate among all the open applications and windows in Mac OS X. To access it, press F3.

MobileMe: A discontinued Apple service for file sharing, e-mail, personal web pages, and more, partially replaced by iCloud.

modem: Short for *modulator/demodulator,* a device used to send digital signals over analog circuits, such as a phone line or television cable.

Mono: An open-source effort to develop web service tools, compatible with Microsoft .Net, that can run on non–Windows platforms, such as Mac OS X. Visit www.mono-project.com.

MP3: A popular compressed audio format. The acronym stands for *MPEG-1, Audio Layer 3.*

MPEG: Motion Picture Experts Group, a body that sets standards for video compression.

.mpkg: A file format used to distribute Mac OS X software.

MSN.com: Microsoft Network, a portal to the Microsoft collection of Internet services.

Newton: A short-lived Apple product that created the personal-digital-assistant market and ultimately led to the iPad.

NextStep: An operating system, developed by NeXT, that Apple evolved into Mac OS X.

NTFS: NT File System, the file system used in Windows NT, Windows XP, Windows Vista, and Windows 7. Macs can read, but not write, NTFS disks.

NTSC: A standard for standard-definition television signals used in North America, Japan, and parts of South America. See also **PAL video.**

NuBus: An obsolete standard for plug-in cards used on ancient Macs.

object code: The output of a compiler, a version of a program in machine language that the computer can execute.

Objective C: A variant of the C programming language that's widely used in Mac OS X and its programs. It takes a different approach to object orientation from C++.

octet: A fancy name for an 8-bit data field. See *byte.*

Office Open XML: A controversial standard for electronic documents developed by Microsoft and based on its Office suite's internal format; also called *OOXML.* This standard competes with OpenDocument.

Ogg: A nonproprietary multimedia file format. See www.xiph.org/ogg.

open source: An approach to software development in which the original, human-generated instructions and comments are publicly available. Visit www.opensource.org for the official definition.

open-source license: One of several copyright licenses under which open-source software and documentation are distributed. They typically allow wide use but require the same copyright notice to be included in redistributed versions. See www.opensource.org/licenses.

OpenDocument: A nonproprietary file format for electronic documents; also called ODF and the OASIS Open Document Format for Office Applications. This standard competes with Office Open XML.

OpenGL: A nonproprietary way for programs (especially 3D games) to talk to graphics cards. Mac OS X supports OpenGL. This standard competes with Microsoft DirectX.

OpenOffice.org: An open-source suite of productivity applications (word processing and spreadsheet, for example) that runs in Mac OS X.

optical digital audio: A replacement for analog sound wiring in home electronics that uses fiber optics rather than shielded copper wire. Now there's no more annoying hum loop.

OS 9: Short for Mac OS 9, an earlier Mac operating system. Still-earlier system numbers included 4, 5, 6, 7, and 8.

Outlook: The Microsoft e-mail client for Windows.

package: The Apple way of distributing applications for Mac OS X that combines numerous files and folders associated with a program in what looks like a single file. A package is sometimes called a *bundle.*

PAL video: A standard-definition broadcast video signal standard used in Europe and much of the world.

pane: A simple window in a graphical computer interface.

Panther: Code name for Mac OS X 10.3.

parallel port: A printer interface once common on PCs but never used on Macs; also known as a Centronics port or IEEE 1284 port. Adapters for USB are available if you need to use an old printer.

Parallels: A virtualization package that lets Windows and other operating systems, such as Linux, run at the same time as Mac OS X. See Chapter 16.

partition: To divide a hard drive into two, or more, smaller disk volumes. This procedure is sometimes done with a hacksaw or an ax, but Disk Utility is the preferred method.

passphrase: A longer form of a password, made up of several words. See also *Diceware*.

password: A string of characters that you type into your computer to let it know for sure that the person typing is you. See Chapter 10.

PCIe: Peripheral Component Interconnect Express, a third-generation interface standard for computer expansion cards, used in the Mac Pro. This standard replaces PCI and PCI-X.

PDF: Portable Document Format, an Adobe standard for digital documents that can be read on most computers with a free Adobe reader program. Mac OS X uses PDF as its document format, and the included Preview application can read .pdf files.

perpendicular recording: A method of increasing the amount of information that can be stored on a hard drive.

PGP: Pretty Good Privacy, a popular public-key encryption package that's available for the Mac, Windows, and Linux. See also *GPG.*

phishing: The nefarious use of e-mail and websites that appear to be legitimate to collect personal information such as passwords and bank-account numbers. *Spearphishing* consists of more elaborate ruses aimed at a specific person or company. See Chapter 10.

phone plug: A type of audio connector that consists of a long, cylindrical sleeve with one or two insulated contacts at the tip. It comes in ¼-inch, 3.5mm, and 2½mm diameters. This type of plug is not to be confused with the cube-shaped RJ-series telephone plugs.

phono plug: See *RCA plug.*

PhotoBooth: A small but fun application that comes with Mac OS X and takes pictures with the iSight camera. PhotoBooth operates much like the old four-for-a-dollar photo booths in amusement parks and arcades.

Photoshop: The powerful Adobe image-editing software. Photoshop Elements, a much lower-cost, less-sophisticated version, is also available.

PHP: A scripting programming language often used with database programs such as MySQL to create web applications.

PICT: A graphics file format used on older Macs.

PKI: Public-key infrastructure, a way to distribute keys in public-key cryptography.

PlaysForSure: A DRM-protected music format promoted by Microsoft but not supported on its Zune player.

plug-in: A piece of software that can be easily incorporated into an application to increase functionality.

PNG: Portable Network Graphics, a nonproprietary format for storing and displaying images.

POP: Post Office Protocol, the most common way in which e-mail is handled on the Internet. See also *IMAP.*

pop-under: A window that's added behind the window in use so that it appears only when that window is closed or moved; sometimes known as a *leave-behind.*

pop-up: An additional window that appears when you're accessing a website. It's sometimes used to add functionality to a web page but more often for advertising.

pop-up menu: A menu that appears when you click a button or icon that displays a double arrowhead; similar to a Windows drop-down menu.

POSIX: Portable Operating System Interface for Unix, a standard application program interface (API) promoted by the U.S. government to enable programs to be ported easily to different operating systems. Mac OS X supports POSIX.

PostScript: A page description language developed by Adobe.

PowerBook: An earlier brand of Apple laptop.

PowerPC: A microprocessor architecture developed by a consortium of Motorola, IBM, and Apple; and used in Macs after the Motorola 68,000 family until the switch to Intel microprocessors.

PPP: Point-to-Point Protocol, a protocol that connects two computers and is most often used in dialup Internet access. PPP is also called *PPPoE* (PPP over Ethernet).

PRAM: Parameter RAM, a small block of storage used to save information needed during startup. Resetting PRAM is a common Mac nostrum. See Chapter 20.

Pre 2: A smartphone based on HP's webOS, developed by Palm. It competes with the iPhone.

preferences: Application settings in the Mac OS.

propeller key: Another name for the *Command key* (⌘).

protocol: An agreed-on way that computers use to talk to one another.

PS2: A second-generation IBM PC. The electrical connections that it used for hooking up a mouse and keyboard are still used on some PC models. Macs use USB instead.

public-key cryptography: A method of sending secret messages and electronically signing documents that uses two keys: one that can freely be made public and a second that's kept secret by the person who receives the coded message or signs the document.

quad core: Four separate CPUs in one chip.

Quartz: The Apple name for the display-rendering technology in Mac OS X.

QuickTime: The Apple format for multimedia content, which competes with Windows Media and RealMedia.

RAID: Redundant Array of Inexpensive Disks, a way to build large, reliable storage systems from PC-grade disk drives.

RAM: Random-access memory, the main fast memory in a computer.

RAW file: Image data from a digital camera in its original form, with no compression or other processing that can lose information. iPhoto has some support for RAW images; Aperture has much more.

RCA plug: A push-on coaxial connector invented in the 1930s by the Radio Corporation of America to allow phonographs to be played through table radios; also called *phono plug* and *jack*.

reality-distortion field: A humorous reference to Steve Jobs's ability to sell ideas convincingly.

reboot: A shutdown and restart. See also **bootstrap.**

Red Box: A code name for a long-rumored project that was supposed to allow Windows applications to run in Mac OS X, somewhat like Wine. Other code names from the same era include **Blue Box** and **Yellow Box.**

regular expression: A Unix term (also called *regexp)* for a cryptic but powerful way to specify search criteria as a string of characters. The term was popularized by the Unix program grep.

RGB video: A way of transmitting video signals as three separate analog channels for red, green, and blue.

RJ-45: A cube-shaped electrical connector used on twisted-pair Ethernet cables. RJ-45 is not to be confused with the similar, but smaller, RJ-11 connector used on telephones.

root: The top-level directory in a file structure and the highest level of access privilege in a Unix system.

rootkit: A type of malware designed to bury itself inside your operating system in a way that is hard to detect or remove.

Rosetta: The Apple method for running older PowerPC programs on Intel processors. Rosetta is not supported in Lion.

router: A box that helps direct information packets among connected computers to create a network.

RS-232: A standard for serial ports used on older PCs. It's mostly been replaced by USB.

RSA: Rivest, Shamir, and Adleman, an algorithm for public-key cryptography based on the difficulty of factoring numbers.

RSS: A set of standards for delivering web content that's updated regularly. Users subscribe to different feeds that are aggregated and displayed by software in their computers.

RTF: Rich Text Format, an older Microsoft word processing format used by TextEdit and other Mac OS X programs.

RTFM: A suggestion that people read the manual before asking for assistance.

rumors community: A group of websites that speculate about Apple Computer, Inc., and its products, and sometimes publish what they claim to be inside information.

SATA: Serial ATA, a high-performance connection standard for mass storage devices, such as hard drives. SATA is used in many new computers, including Macs.

SCSI: Small Computer System Interface, a connection standard for mass storage devices and high-speed peripherals used in older Macs.

SDRAM: Synchronous dynamic random-access memory, a variant of DRAM that offers higher performance by tying its operation to the CPU's clock pulses. Think of the galley scene in *Ben-Hur*, in which all the slaves pull their oars to the beat of a drum.

serial port: A computer connection that sends data sequentially, bit by bit, over a communication line. See also *parallel port, RS-232.*

shareware: Software programs that are freely distributed over the Internet, with the expectation that people who decide to use them will voluntarily pay a fee to the authors.

shell: An operating-system program that listens to text commands typed by the user. The Windows command-line interpreter is a shell. Mac OS X uses the bash shell by default, though others (such as the Korn shell) are available. Before GUIs, the shell was the outermost, visible part of an operating system; the innermost part was (and is) the kernel. See also *Terminal.*

shut down: To turn off the computer.

sleep: The temporary suspension of the operation of a computer, usually to save energy — particularly, battery power on a laptop.

smartphone: A cellphone that performs many tasks besides making phone calls, typically including access to e-mail and the web.

SMTP: Simple Mail Transfer Program, the basis for electronic mail on the Internet.

snd file: An early Mac audio format.

sneakernet: The system of transferring information between computers by having someone carry the data on removable media — originally, floppy disks, but now flash drives and CD/DVD optical discs.

Snow Leopard: The code name for Mac OS X 10.6.

social engineering: Breaching computer security by tricking authorized users into granting access ("I'm from tech support and I need your password to catch some nasty hackers").

socket: A software port that one program uses to connect to another program running on a different computer.

Software Update: The Apple facility for distributing revisions to Mac OS X and its application programs. It automatically notifies users when new stuff is available — by default, once a week.

Spaces: A feature in Mac OS X that supports multiple workspaces for a single user.

spam: Unsolicited commercial e-mail, the equivalent of junk mail.

Spotlight: The Mac OS X search technology.

spring-loaded: An icon that pops open or takes some other action when the cursor hovers over it.

spyware: Software that covertly gathers personal information about a user, such as web-surfing habits, without the user's consent and conveys it to a third party.

SSD: Solid-state drive, an alternative to hard drives that uses memory chips rather than rotating magnetic disks. SSD is faster and lighter but more expensive.

SSH: Stands for *secure shell*; a program and a set of standards for establishing a secure connection between two computers. It relies on public-key cryptography. Mac OS X has SSH support.

SSL/TLS: Secure Socket Layer/Transport Layer Security, two names used to describe the most commonly used method for securing Internet connections.

startup disk: The disk drive containing the operating system that will be used to start the computer the next time it's turned on or rebooted. The startup disk is set in System Preferences.

StuffIt Expander: A free program that unpacks several compressed file formats, including `.sit`.

sudo: A Unix command that prefixes other commands, causing them to execute with superuser privileges. It requires an admin password in Mac OS X.

SVG: Scaleable Vector Graphics, a standard for two-dimensional drawings.

S-Video: An analog video signal standard that has separate wires for color and brightness. See also *composite video.*

SYLK: Symbolic Link, an older Microsoft spreadsheet file format that's still used at times to exchange data with other programs.

tar file: An archive format used in Unix systems.

taskbar: A Windows feature, located along the bottom of the screen, that's somewhat similar to the Mac OS X Dock.

TCP/IP: Transmission Control Protocol/Internet Protocol, the way computers communicate on the Internet.

telnet: A program that lets you log on to other computers on the network.

tera: The standard prefix for one trillion.

Terminal: A program in Mac OS X that gives you access to the underlying Unix operating system by using a command-line interface.

text file: A computer file that contains only characters, usually encoded in ASCII or Unicode. This type of file uses the `.txt` extension.

thumb drive: A finger-size device containing flash memory that plugs into a USB port and looks like a hard drive on the Desktop; also called *flash drive* or *keychain drive.*

Thunderbolt: A new, super-fast data connection method developed by Intel and Apple that includes MiniDisplayPort and PCIe capabilities.

Tiger: Code name for Mac OS X 10.4.

Time Machine: The Apple automated backup system for Mac OS X Leopard.

trusted platform chip: A tamper-resistant microprocessor chip on Macs and newer PCs that's designed to hold cryptographic keys and certificates. (The rub is, trusted by whom?)

Unicode: A computer character code that attempts to include all written languages in use in the world.

Unix: A computer operating system developed in the 1960s at AT&T Bell Labs. Mac OS X is based on Unix.

USB: Universal Serial Bus, a means for connecting peripheral devices to computers, used in Macs and PCs. USB 2.0 is considerably faster than, but backward-compatible with, USB 1.

V.92: An ITU standard for dialup modems operating at speeds up to 56 Kbps. Used in the Apple Modem.

VGA connector: A widely used analog video cable connector with a D-shell and 15 pins in three rows. Apple sells VGA adapter cables for most Macs.

virtual memory: A technique that allows an operating system to assign more random-access memory than the computer physically has by writing to disk storage any sections of memory that haven't been used recently.

virtualization: A way of splitting the resources of a computer among more than one operating system so that each one thinks it has a separate computer all to itself.

virus: A program that attaches itself to another program or document and then transmits copies of itself to infect other computers.

Vista: A version of the Microsoft Windows operating system that followed Windows XP and has been replaced by Windows 7.

VNC: Virtual Network Computing, a standard for the remote control of a computer desktop from another computer; used in Apple Remote Desktop.

watermark: A collection of bits hidden in a media file that allow digital rights management software to detect copyrighted works.

WAV: A Windows audio file format.

web: Short for World Wide Web, the hypertext system used to display information on the Internet.

WEP: Wired equivalent privacy, a broken encryption scheme for Wi-Fi. See *WPA.*

whitelist: To specify addresses from whom you welcome messages. The opposite of *blacklist.*

widget: A small program run on the Dashboard layer of Mac OS X.

Wi-Fi: The brand name applied to devices that meet interoperability criteria for wireless networking based on the IEEE 802.11 standards. Apple uses the brand name AirPort.

Windows CE: A Microsoft operating system for small devices, such as PDAs and smartphones.

Windows Genuine Advantage: The Microsoft program that discourages people from using unlicensed copies of Windows and is considered too heavy-handed by some people.

Windows Media Player: A Microsoft program and file format for handling multimedia content, usually with the .wmp extension.

Windows Phone 7: The catchy name for Microsoft's new smartphone operating system, adopted by Nokia and others.

Windows XP: The version of the Microsoft Windows operating system that shipped with most PCs from October 2001 until Windows Vista was introduced and, because of public outcry, with many PCs for about a year afterward.

wireless access point: A base station in a wireless network.

WMP: See *Windows Media Player.*

worm: A self-replicating computer program, usually malicious. A worm differs from a *virus,* which attaches itself to another program.

WPA, WPA2: Wireless protected access, encryption for Wi-Fi that's quite strong if you use a long-enough passphrase. See Chapter 9.

WWAN: Wireless wide-area network, a way for mobile computers to connect to the Internet by using the cellular telephone network.

X11: A windowing standard developed at the Massachusetts Institute of Technology that's used in Linux and Unix systems, X11 is included in Mac OS X, allowing your Mac to run programs created for those systems.

XLR connector: An industrial-strength audio connector, typically with three pins.

yarrow: A high-grade, random-number generator used in Mac OS X. High-grade random numbers are essential for computer security programs.

Yellow Box: An early code name for what became the Cocoa environment in Mac OS X. Other code names from the same era include *Blue Box* and *Red Box.*

zero configuration: See *Bonjour.*

zero-day exploit: A computer security attack that exploits an unknown vulnerability in software.

Zip archive: A file that's a collection of other files compressed with the Zip algorithm. Look for Compress in the Finder's File menu.

Zip drive: An obsolete computer mass storage system that used removable cartridges and could store 100MB or more on each cartridge.

Zune: Once the Microsoft personal music player that competed with the Apple iPod, now the music software in Windows Phone 7.

Index